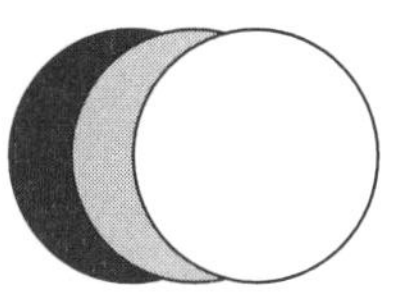

An introduction to family therapy

An introduction to family therapy

Systemic theory and practice

Second edition

Rudi Dallos and **Ros Draper**

Open University Press

Open University Press
McGraw-Hill Education
McGraw-Hill House
Shoppenhangers Road
Maidenhead
Berkshire
England
SL6 2QL

email: enquiries@openup.co.uk
world wide web: www.openup.co.uk

and Two Penn Plaza, New York, NY 10121-2289, USA

First published 2005

A catalogue record of this book is available from the British Library

ISBN–10 0 335 21604 8 (pb) 0 335 21605 6 (hb)
ISBN–13 978 0335 21604 8 (pb) 978 0335 21605 5 (hb)

Library of Congress Cataloging-in-Publication Data
CIP data applied for

Typeset by RefineCatch Limited, Bungay, Suffolk
Printed in the UK by Bell & Bain Ltd, Glasgow

Contents

4 Ideas that keep knocking on the door: emotions, attachments and systems 125

5 Systemic formulation 151

6 Current practice development 2000–2005: conversations across the boundaries of models 172

7 Research and evaluation 198

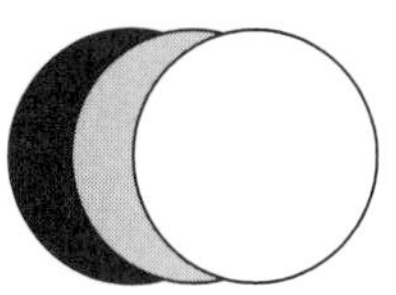

List of figures

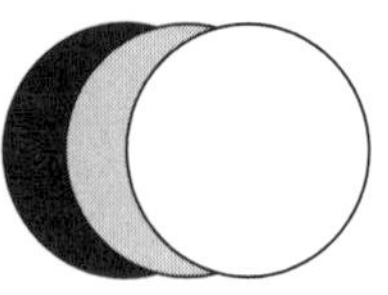

Notes on the authors

Rudi Dallos is a psychologist who has been involved in systemic family therapy for over 20 years. He was previously with the Open University where he had written various texts on family life and relationships. He is currently Programme Director and Reader in Clinical Psychology on the Plymouth University doctoral training course in clinical psychology. He is also consultant clinical psychologist specializing in therapeutic work with adolescents and their families in Somerset. He teaches on several family therapy training courses and is extensively involved in research and supervision. He has written several previous books utilizing both his research and clinical experiences, including: *Working Systemically with Families, Researching Psychotherapy and Counselling, Formulation in Clinical Psychology and Counselling, Family Belief Systems, Couples, Sex and Power* and *Interacting Stories.*

Ros Draper is a therapist and teacher who has made major contributions to the development of family therapy in Britain over the last 30 years. As Senior Clinical Lecturer at the Tavistock Clinic, London, and the Institute of Family Therapy, London, she has worked in both adult and child psychiatric settings. In 1988 Ros co-founded the influential Systemic Thinking and Practice Book Series and her title *Teaching Family Therapy* (1993) remains a key text in the field. More recently Ros has developed ways of working systemically in primary care, educational settings and eating disorder services. Ros chairs the Institute of Family Therapy and Birkbeck College, University of London, course in a Systemic Approach to Management and Consultation, and has a private practice in Hampshire where she works with individuals, couples, families and organizations.

Preface

We are delighted that in writing the second edition we have realized our aim with the first edition of this text, which was to create, from a British perspective, a resource book for ourselves, our colleagues, experienced and new practitioners in the field of systemic family therapy and practice as we approached the end of the second millennium. In the second edition we hope to enable readers to keep up to date.

There is already a rich oral and literary tradition in systemic and family therapy so this book is part story, part chronicle: story, because we describe a series of events and intend to interest and even amuse the reader with our personal descriptions of the complex field of systemic and family therapy, a fascinating variety of ideas and practice which has emerged in the last 55 years. To the extent that these pages reflect our perspectives, we can defer to modernist, postmodernist and constructionist views and, with tongue in cheek, say this book is fictitious. Equally, we claim that this book is our attempt to chronicle and record the people, ideas, practices and socio-political cultural contexts that have contributed to the field in the second half of the twentieth century and beginning of the twenty-first century. We want this second edition of the book to celebrate 55 years of development in the field and provide a useful guide for readers on all five continents that is both coherent and resourceful. Our wish is that this book, above all, be a user-friendly account that preserves important knowledge and memories of events and facts in a fascinating and developing field of inquiry and practice and is a reference book for readers.

The organization of the book reflects our attempt to offer readers a story, a chronicle and a reference book. In the first edition we divided the 55 plus years of history into a first phase, second phase and third phase and can thus locate and track people, ideas and practices as they evolve out of modernism, through postmodernism and constructivism to constructionism. We also wanted to acknowledge the overlap of people and ideas and the way in which contributions to the field from certain individuals vary in all three phases.

The first phase covers the 1950s to the mid-1970s with some references to the intellectual climate of the 1940s which permitted the pioneering work of the following two decades to develop. This phase of systemic and family therapy is comfortably modernist.

The second phase covers the mid-1970s to the mid-1980s. The early part of the phase is characterized by the development of many different models, some of which we describe, and as postmodernism begins to influence the field we describe the emergence of second-order cybernetics and the links in systemic and family therapy theory and practice with constructivism.

The third phase covers the period from the mid-1980s to 2000 and looks at the shift from constructivism to social constructionism as the main theoretical framework for the field. Since the first edition of this book we suggest that there has been a fourth phase characterized by a greater interconnection between different family therapy models and models of psychotherapy. In addition, there has been an extension of 'systemic thinking' seen in the application of systemic ideas to various contexts, such as institutions and organizations.

We offer this schema because we are sympathetic to the amount of painkillers trainees need to take in order to assuage the migraines they develop as they attempt to follow overviews of family therapy schools – structural, strategic, solution-focused, Milan, post-Milan, narrative, postmodern, feminist, postfeminist and so on! We hope to show there are important practical, ethical, moral and political issues attached to the differences emerging in what we call the first, second and third phases of development in the field. Once we recognize these more clearly we can also start to integrate them. As Bateson (1972) suggested, recognition of difference is the key to understanding. Likewise, we agree with George Kelly (1955) that awareness of difference places ideas at contrasting ends of a continuum – this he called a construct. But this does not necessarily imply rejecting either position, rather that an idea only makes sense in contrast to another idea. In our proposed three phases we suggest that there are core themes or constructs along which the approaches lie. For example, the approaches differ in terms of whether difficulties are seen to result predominantly from family dynamics as opposed to societal factors, whether there is an assumption of 'normality' as opposed to an emphasis on diversity or whether family members are seen as self-determined as opposed to constrained by their experiences.

As trainers we know the richness of the field can often be perplexing to both novices and experienced practitioners and teachers alike, so we have included with each of the three phases a series of skill guides congruent with the application of ideas and practices we describe in each phase of development in the field. We have also attempted to contextualize each developmental phase by our descriptions of the cultural landscape out of which ideas grew. Finally, in an attempt to distinguish the chronology from the lenses we, as authors, use, we have a section in each chapter called Commentary, where we offer the reader our more personal reflections.

With each phase there is a story to tell so we have attempted a more factual summary early in Chapters 1, 2 and 3. To help make sense of each highly productive phase in the development of systemic and family therapy, we have also included a useful list at the end of these chapters chronicling key people, texts and events of each phase. Recognizing our bias in the choice of texts, we want to repeat that this book can only be our view of the landscape that is systemic and family therapy, but we have tried to offset the effects of our prejudices by pointing the reader to many recognized seminal texts and reference books with which we cannot compete.

Wishing to write a text from the British perspective, we became clearer about the particular contribution of British therapists to this field over the last 55 years. While few distinct 'models' of family therapy have emerged from Britain, a veritable host of creative applications and adaptations of the core systemic ideas and practices have emerged to influence health and welfare services in Britain as well as abroad. The second edition therefore includes additional chapters reflecting more up-to-date examples of such creative adaptations that are practical demonstrations of the usefulness of systemic theory and practice and the commitment of practitioners to innovative multidisciplinary practice in health and welfare professions.

We offer this book much in the way that as therapists we offer our clients ideas, trusting some will fit and be useful or, if not, will at least serve to clarify the questions you have to ask about this field. If you find this book to be like a guidebook we will be well pleased. Clearly, in many ways, the whole book consists of the authors' reflections; while we do not dispute this, we also hope that this book offers a useful and usable description of the landscape and territory known as systemic and family therapy, that will give readers confidence as they pursue their own enquiries in this field. We are convinced that key players and contributors to the field of systemic and family therapy also contribute in a major way to the understanding of, and wider debates about, psychotherapy. Just as human beings we cannot *not* communicate, so as systemic practitioners we cannot *not* pay attention to the various levels of context included in the drama of the psychotherapeutic encounter between clients and therapists. We are therefore uniquely placed in the community of psychotherapists to contribute to discussion about both the micro and macro aspects of therapeutic processes.

Foreword

It is with real pleasure that I write this Foreword to the second edition of Rudi Dallos and Ros Draper's book, *An Introduction to Family Therapy*. I wrote the Foreword to the first edition, so I trust I am well placed to observe the changes made to the second edition – the expansions, illuminations, amendments and the introduction of new material. The second edition is more than an update. It is an extensive rewriting of what was already an impressive and relevant text, designed for those relatively new to systemic thinking and its applications. This revision has moved the book into a different position, of one that meets the needs of introductory level *and* intermediate level learning and practice. This is no mean feat. It is to the authors' credit that they have managed this transition without losing sight of the needs of both groups, elegantly weaving the introduction of theory, with worked examples, with specific applications in different contexts.

One of the strengths of the first edition was the inclusion of three chapters devoted to tracing the history and integration of systemic ideas and practices, grouped into three broad developmental phases. These chapters have been retained and extensively updated and reworked in the light of a growing rapprochement within the broader systemic field. These chapters provide a clear and helpful introduction to a complex arena, such that more recent innovations in thinking and practice can be clearly grounded in their ancestral origins. Thus will we build a field of scholar-practitioners.

The chapter on emotions, attachments and systems has been retained and elaborated in the light of further research and Rudi Dallos's work on attachment narrative therapy. Its inclusion in the first edition has been vindicated as both a serious attempt to put emotion back into systems thinking and practice, and as a herald of a growing and widening interest in the potential for integration between these two major systems of thought.

The chapter on research will be welcomed by students of systemic thinking. As a research tutor myself, I recognize the struggle between helping students to develop research competence in how they evaluate and use research to inform their practice, versus teaching people how to do it! This chapter addresses the former need while gently helping the reader manage the transition to the latter, by providing a number of worked research examples that show how clinical skills transfer readily into the research arena. The emphasis throughout the chapter is on practice-based evidence, going to the heart of our wish to provide ethically accountable services.

Two new chapters grace this second edition, one on systemic formulation and one on integrative practices. Clinical psychology can make a contribution to the systemic field in how it uses the practice of formulation as one way of promoting the link between theory and practice. Systemic formulation in my experience is the area of practice that most troubles students as they grapple with explanation, prediction and links to practice. Those new to systemic thinking and practice will find this chapter very helpful in finding their way about a number of interrelated and competing ideas, and corralling those ideas to help make sense of complexity in people's lives.

The chapter on conversations across the boundaries of models highlights three areas of work – addictions services, forensic services, and working with post-divorce processes and disputes. They have been chosen because they illustrate the value of clarity in how we bring together different models of psychotherapy under a systemic umbrella, and how such integration furthers practice developments in fields that have less of a tradition of psychotherapeutic working.

Systemic practice has clearly reached into new and diverse areas of practice in the UK. One of the strengths of this book lies in its attention to the needs of UK-based practitioners, across statutory and voluntary services. With the publication of the NICE Guidelines in the UK, we see a growing recognition among policy makers and service managers of the importance of thinking about working with families and kin, and with partners, with inter-professional networks, and across agency boundaries. This book invites curiosity and excitement about systemic practice and supports those practitioners who wish to extend the boundaries of their thinking and practice.

Reading this book has been refreshing and informative. It reminds me of why engagement with systemic thinking has been such a passionate commitment in my life, and offers me a view of how two long admired colleagues think about and use systemic ideas in their day-to-day work. Both Rudi Dallos and Ros Draper are teachers and learners. As teachers, they are generous in their insights and helpful hints; as learners, their restless curiosity keeps us on our toes, just in case we might have thought it time to relax with our own professional development. I wonder if there will be a third edition. I do hope so. I cannot think of two better-placed people to help newcomers to this field find a welcome.

Arlene Vetere
March 2005

Acknowledgements

I would like to thank Hannah Cooper and Jenni Harvey at Open University Press/McGraw-Hill for their ability to inject energy and enthusiasm into the work required to prepare a second edition of this book. I want to thank Harry Procter for his inspiration which initially led me into this field, for his wisdom and sense of fun, and for his continued validation and enthusiasm about this and my other projects. My sincere thanks also to Arlene Vetere who has been a continual source of inspiration and enthusiasm about my work and ideas and from whom I have learnt more than I can remember.

Of course I also want to thank Ros Draper for her perceptiveness, energy and enthusiasm throughout this project. I also want to thank, but am not sure whom, for the telepathic way that Ros and I seem to be able to work.

Finally, thanks to all the families that have provided much of the material for the book and who let me enter into their hopes, dreams and fears. In particular, thanks to some good friends and colleagues, especially Annie Lang and Andy Treacher for their support and ability to sort my undisciplined ideas. Finally, thanks to my family, especially the kids, Tim, Alex and Jas, for always reminding me that, whether I want to or not, I need to hold a 'not knowing' position with them.

Rudi Dallos

Dedication and acknowledgements

This book is dedicated to my daughter, Sarah, whose love, generosity, aliveness and forgiveness have taught me so much about family relationships.

I will not try to acknowledge and thank everyone who deserves a mention here, rather those who come to mind as I write, trusting that anyone who feels ignored or overlooked will be forgiving.

My gratitude goes to my teachers, including Margaret Robinson, John Byng-Hall and Lynn Hoffman, who have each in their way profoundly influenced my thinking and practice, and shared generously of their wisdom; and also to David Campbell and many other colleagues (you know who you are) with whom ideas have been developed and honed over the years.

To the families, individuals and couples who have shared their struggles and stories with me I owe an enormous debt, and to the students who have asked me questions and challenged my answers, I am most grateful for the many opportunities you provided for thinking out loud and developing ideas in simple words that make sense to you.

I do not deserve the loyalty and help I get from my secretaries and friends Sue Palfrey and Tracy Woodward, but I hope they know their patience and efficiency is appreciated: without it the manuscript would never have made it to the publishers.

Thank you to Rudi Dallos, my co-author, for patience and the opportunity to collaborate.

Finally, my thanks are due to Open University Press, Hannah Cooper and the team at McGraw-Hill for their professionalism, support and hard work in bringing the book into being. Thank you all.

Ros Draper

Introduction

Family life in the West on the one hand has typically been seen as private, as a 'haven' – yet at the same time there have been repeated attempts to explore, intervene in, direct, discipline and educate families. There have been attempts to correct the morals of the so-called 'feckless' or 'irresponsible' families, to see single-parent families as 'welfare scroungers' and so on. Aside from such overt attempts at shaping family life and conduct, there is a proliferation of more covert and insidious influences, such as images in magazines, television and films about what is desirable and acceptable – from interior decor to children's education and sexual practices.

These images and stereotypes have spread further to embrace not just families but also the activities of professionals in the business of bringing about change in families. Systemic and family therapy, like other therapies, has changed and developed to acknowledge that a consideration of people's understandings and how these are related to the culture in which they live is vital. There is a growing overlap between the various models developed since the 1950s, the psychological frameworks that professionals employ, and 'ordinary' people's knowledge. Most people these days have powerful ideas and expectations about what therapy will be like as well as their own explanations about what is wrong and what should change.

In this introductory chapter we will consider some voices from people who have experienced systemic and family therapy and from the therapists who have worked with them. How do people experience this process called systemic and family therapy? Is it really experienced as helpful? Do they feel that something has been done to them? How does it change their relationships with each other? Is there some kind of magical experience that means severe problems can change and disappear?

Experiences of systemic and family therapy

A family's view

What follows is an interview with the Taylor family at the end of the last of five one-hour family therapy sessions which suggests some answers to the questions above. Present were Mr and Mrs Taylor and their daughter Barbara (aged 17). The parents had separated prior to Barbara developing a severe eating disorder (anorexia). She had been an in-patient in an eating disorder unit and had taken part in family therapy towards the end of her stay in the unit.

Interviewer: What were your expectations of what this [family therapy] would be like?

Mrs Taylor: . . . We thought it would be pretty stilted for a start and wooden and difficult to talk, and horrible long silences while everyone was staring at their feet and hoping that someone would say something and a wish not to expose the personal things, sort of . . .

Mr Taylor: Being analysed I think . . .

Mrs Taylor: Yes, wanting to curl up and hide everything rather than wanting to properly talk about it, that's my view before we came.

Mr Taylor: Mine was we don't need this. But we've got to go because we have been asked. I've softened about that since because we've got on well.

Interviewer: What about you Barbara?

Barbara: I thought it was a really bad idea. I thought it was going to be awful, I just wasn't going to say anything at all. Being put on the spot and made to say things that you didn't really want to . . .

Interviewer: How has the therapy been different to your expectations?

Mrs Taylor: I thought it was much easier to talk. I was much more relaxed, I was quite surprised and impressed about how easy it was to talk. We all talked, particularly Harry [Mr Taylor], he doesn't like talking. I've been impressed how my family, we've all talked together, talked about things much easier than at home, possibly because you're the adjudicator and perhaps triggered off questions that would have been difficult to get round to in a sensible way in a more intense claustrophobic atmosphere at home when we are getting wound up about talking about things.

Interviewer: Barbara?

Barbara: [laughing] I don't know, Mum sort of said it all. Yes, its been a lot easier here I think.
Interviewer: [to Mr Taylor] How's it been different to what your expectations were?
Mr Taylor: I didn't feel that you were analysing us. It just felt like a discussion which felt like a relief I suppose . . .

The extract suggests that the Taylor family held a variety of powerful expectations regarding what the experience family therapy was going to be like. Some of these seem to resonate with general conceptions of therapy based on the popular views of psychoanalytic therapies, for example that the experience would be emotionally painful and embarrassing.

The family go on to discuss what they found particularly helpful and unhelpful during the course of their therapy:

Interviewer: If you were to put your finger on it what would you say would be the most useful part of what you experienced? And the other side of it, what was the least useful?
Mrs Taylor: I thought what was most useful was hearing Barbara talking about things . . . to hear what was going on in her head . . . can't think of anything that was not useful . . .
Barbara: Yeah, getting my point of view across rather than getting into an argument.
Mrs Taylor: I thought these cameras and the two-way mirror would be a bit off-putting but in fact it hasn't bothered me at all . . .
Interviewer: Could you focus on anything that strikes you as a turning-point or a critical moment in the sessions?
Mrs Taylor: Yeah I can, when Barbara first put her point of view . . .
Mr Taylor: She criticized us [laughter].
Mrs Taylor: Yeah and it's the first time I got an insight into what she was thinking, and it was a big surprise because she was talking in front of you . . .
Barbara: What was I saying? I can't remember.
Mr Taylor: You were saying that I was making you nervous, talking about you eating, not eating enough . . .
Mrs Taylor: A particular example of how . . .
Mr Taylor: That's right I'd done something . . .
Mrs Taylor: Focusing on something we had a go at her about.
Interviewer: It was about not having milk in her cereal?
Barbara: It was because you [Mr Taylor] had only full-fat milk and I watered it down and you said something like . . .

Mr Taylor:	A sarcastic comment . . .
Barbara:	Yeah . . .
Mrs Taylor:	And I'd given you an evil look . . .
Interviewer:	Do you have a main memory [of the sessions] Barbara?
Barbara:	I suppose it was that as well because I was thinking about that a lot and I wasn't going to say anything but perhaps it made me angry in some ways . . . it felt good, I said what I meant . . .
Mrs Taylor:	We had to listen to you and take you seriously.
Barbara:	Yeah I thought you would say I was being stupid or something . . .
Mr Taylor:	It's pretty rare that you criticize us.
Mrs Taylor:	No it's not, you do me . . .
Barbara:	Yeah, I do it quite a lot.
Mrs Taylor:	More and more . . . [laughter]

For the Taylor family the initial prospect of family therapy was clearly quite threatening and anxiety provoking.

Two therapists' views

For therapists too the experience of working with a family embraces a variety of expectations and feelings ranging from apprehension to excitement, competence and impotence at the prospect of being able to assist with what at times appear to be insurmountable mountains of distress. The following is one therapist's description of his experience of family therapy:

> The first meeting with a family is often tinged with a sense of apprehension similar in some ways to other important personal meetings. In some ways it reminds me of the dual feelings of anticipation and apprehension of going to a party or meeting a new group of students, where I will meet strangers who I may in time become close to, or even good friends with. Your thoughts turn over questions, will we get on? will we be able to connect? will I be competent? My feelings also tend to alternate between a pressure that I should be an 'expert' and need to take charge, to make things happen, and alternatively an attempt to reassure myself that it is not my role to do that, things don't work that way.
>
> I still feel an enduring enthusiasm and excitement about meeting families and a sense of privilege of being allowed into their personal world. Even after 16 years of working with families I find myself being surprised at the diversity, complexity and

uniqueness of the ways they live their lives. I think of families through a metaphor of a snowflake – every snowflake has some structures and elements in common in terms of its physical properties but each also has a unique structure. Working with families I am looking for the patterns that they share but also for the creativity and uniqueness.

Perhaps one of the overriding impressions I have about family therapy is that I anticipate that early on I may feel engulfed, confused, overwhelmed and sometimes even despairing that I can help to ease the anger, frustration, pain and suffering they are typically in. However, I now have an expectation that eventually a sense of connection and empathy emerges when I start to gain an insight into how family members see things; their beliefs, understandings, hopes and dreams. From this I then start to be able to understand why they are acting as they are – how these beliefs shape their dynamics and patterns. I can then start to see their actions in a more positive and sympathetic light. I think families start to pick this up and together, between us, a sense of optimism starts to take over. Usually this also includes an ability . . . to start to joke and tease each other, . . . to play with different ways of looking at things. I think it's rare that from this point of connection . . . things don't usually develop positively. When this starts to happen for me it's one of the most positive and worthwhile experiences I can have.

Another therapist's view of her experience of family therapy goes like this:

These days the anticipation and apprehension of a first meeting with a family includes curiosity about how the impressions I have formed from the referral process will fit or not with the experience of meeting family members in the flesh. It never ceases to amaze me how different people can be from my imaginings. There is a tension in first meetings which for me is focused on whether or not we can find a way to talk that seems useful to the family. Can I interest them in the way I am talking and thinking about what they are so generously willing to share with a stranger? Conveying respect and appreciation of the courage it takes to come and talk with a stranger about troubling personal issues is important.

For a therapeutic relationship to develop there has, in my view, to be some shared meanings and beliefs about the distresses leading people to seek therapy, and creating these shared ideas is the risky and exciting part of therapy. Can I offer ideas to family members in a way that makes sense or creates a space in which family members can risk exploring new ideas and thinking out

> loud with one another? I see my job as finding ways that work for family members to speak what may have become unspeakable and to somehow convey that it is safe enough to go together into uncharted and unsafe territory. The territory is uncharted for all of us and does produce butterflies in the stomach. The satisfaction and excitement of working with families comes from the moments when family members realize it is possible for things to change and convey feelings more empowered and less daunted by the work this will take. I hear this less often in words and more often in changes in body language and the emotional atmosphere becoming lighter with less seriousness. In trying to sum up what I believe I hope for as the essence of a therapeutic encounter, I would see it as a meeting from which new connections and meanings emerge for both therapist and family members and all of whom are left at the end with a sense of 'something potentially good having happened'.

In these accounts from families and therapists we can hear both their internal voices – their personal beliefs and views of themselves and the world – and also the common or shared voices of the culture in which they live. We might even argue that it is impossible to separate these: that the personal and the public are invariably intertwined. To be a person, a part of a relationship, a member of a family, involves being bound by a wide variety of meanings shared by our cultures. In particular, we all have some ideas about what it is to be emotionally 'healthy', what it is to have 'good' relationships, what is a 'functional' as opposed to a 'dysfunctional' family. These values tend to be represented in a variety of images in advertising, books, films and in our everyday conversations. Even though we may not agree with some of the common values, or even hold that these are relative and pernicious, we will still be influenced by them in setting out the territory of our thinking – our contrasts or points of opposition for which these common values provide an anchor.

What is the 'family'?

As this book is about families and relationships, it is necessary to offer an overview or map of what the term 'family' may be seen to include. There have been great upheavals and changes in what is meant by the family and family life. In many Western countries, for example in the UK, over 40% of new marriages end in divorce. Many people choose not to marry and there are increasing variations, such as single-parent families and homosexual families. Also, there is greater diversity in people's expectations such that men no longer are expected to be the sole or main breadwinners and there are expectations about greater sharing of domestic roles, such as childcare. Arguably some of these changes are less extensive than might be assumed – for example women, even if they work outside of the home, still tend to take on the bulk of domestic duties as well (Muncie *et al.* 1997). It is easy to assume that in some ways the family is in 'crisis', and this is also seen as a fundamental threat to the stability of society. However, it is cautionary to note, for example, that due predominantly to death at childbirth, stepfamilies were as common historically as might be indicated in the many negative images of 'wicked stepparents' in folklore. So though there have been changes, the voices of concern can be seen not just as responding to these changes, but also as attempting to institute or encourage a particular form of family life and values (Robinson 1993). Arguably some of these traditional values, stressing domestic duties, passivity and duties to be responsible for providing care of children and ageing relatives, have not been in the best interests of women (Perelberg and Miller 1990; Muncie *et al.* 1997).

What we take to be 'the family' and 'family life' is influenced by the ideologies and discourses inherent in the society in which we live at a particular historical point. An analysis at the level of society and culture suggests that 'family life' is shaped by dominant ideologies or discourses about what family life *should* be like. We can see families as reproducing themselves, both literally and ideologically. For example, though the roles of men and women in families and other living arrangements have changed significantly in the last thirty years, by and large women still take most of the responsibility for childcare, men are expected to be the main breadwinners and most of us (in Western cultures) live for the majority of our lives in an arrangement not too dissimilar from a nuclear family. Above all, for many of us the image of the nuclear family still governs our behaviours, expectations and feelings. We may be 'for' or 'against' the nuclear family, but either way it has, until recently at least, set the agenda of our thinking, feeling and choices.

Yet, within Western (and other) societies there is clearly a diversity of ways that people choose to live together. Some of these choices are variations on the nuclear family model, others are quite deliberate and explicit attempts to reject it, such as communal and some single-parent relationships. If we accept that many people make such choices the question remains of how people go about constructing their own varieties of 'family life'. How do they decide how 'normal', as opposed to how 'deviant', they will be? To take a conventional example, a heterosexual couple need to decide when or whether to marry, whether to have children and if so how many, how to divide up the family tasks such as childcare, when a child should leave home, whether they should divorce, whether they should marry again, how they should relate to any stepchildren they might have and so on.

Above all, these decisions suggest the possibility that families do not simply absorb ideologies and discourses but translate them within their own 'family culture' and the traditions and current dynamics in their own families. Between society and the individual is a set of shared premises, explanations and expectations – in short, a family's own belief system. Metaphorically this can be represented as a deck of cards offering a range of options from which particular choices can be made. These options are derived mainly from personal experiences, family traditions and societal discourses. Continuing the metaphor, each family has its own unique set of 'cards' which serves to constrain their perceived options and consequently the choices they make; family members make choices, but not simply in circumstances of their own choosing.

Our 'windows' or accounts from families and therapists can be seen to capture two aspects of family life which at first sight might appear contradictory: on the one hand people do appear to make autonomous decisions about their lives; on the other hand family life can be seen to be characterized by repetitive, predictable patterns of actions. Families are inevitably faced with various tasks – difficulties and problems which they have to find ways of managing. These tasks alter as they proceed through their developmental cycle.

The family life cycle

To capture this notion of a changing, evolving process, the concept of the 'family life cycle' (Haley 1973; Duvall 1977; Carter and McGoldrick 1980) was developed in order to chart some of the major changes or transitions that family life presents, such as the birth of children, children leaving home and bereavements. (The family life cycle will be described further in Chapters 1 and 2.) It is argued that families need to continually adapt and adjust to deal with these tasks, but particularly at these critical transitional points. Each family is seen as developing ways of dealing with the tasks facing them – *attempted solutions*. In turn the choices they make, their attempted solutions, are shaped by the *beliefs* they hold as individuals, as a family and in common with wider society. The recursive combination of tasks, attempted solutions, outcomes and beliefs constitutes the family *system*.

It is possible to see a family evolving and changing as it proceeds through its life cycle as needing to develop and negotiate its way through three distinct but interconnected areas:

1 *the social, cultural and spiritual* – what is perceived as acceptable and desirable in any given society, including traditions, local customs, rituals, mores, legal framework, organization of work and the economy of a group.

2 *the familial* – how people in families jointly negotiate decisions; this is based partly on the internalizations of the cultural discourses and partly on their joint evolution of a set of shared beliefs.
3 *the personal* – each family member has a more or less unique set of personal beliefs. For the parents this may emanate from the accumulated experience prior to forming a family; for all members the personal beliefs also develop as a result of contacts outside the family.

Each family or grouping can be seen as creating, usually from an initial coupling of two people who may become parents of children and later grandparents, a unique interpersonal system. This becomes a family – a system of meanings and actions encapsulating a version of family life which develops from the amalgamation of its members' negotiations and choices based upon their personal and shared beliefs and histories. Though this process is creative, involves a variety of complex issues and is widely thought of as unique, there are some fundamental themes common to any social grouping.

In the main, *external* relationships are the connection to the 'outside' world. A key aspect of this is the development of a family identity. Members develop a set of perspectives, beliefs about themselves as a 'family' and what kind of a family they are: close/distant, argumentative/harmonious, formal/informal, traditional/modern and so on. Families also need to establish ways of interacting with a variety of other systems, such as schools, workplaces, local community, neighbours, friends, in-laws and extended family. Families vary in the beliefs they have about boundaries: some believe that a rigid separation is required, stressing family privacy and self-determination; others believe in a looser, more permeable boundary, with easy access, an 'open house'.

Family identities are not simply constructed by families but in some cases rigid definitions may be imposed, as in ethnic minority families or those containing members who have a 'disability', such as mental health problems or learning disabilities.

As well as functioning in relation to the external or outside world, a family defines itself by various *internal* relationships:

1 *power, intimacy and boundaries* – while family life is complex and varied, these three key issues continuously surface and require families to develop a set of beliefs enabling rules and procedures to be formed (Minuchin 1974; Haley 1976a; Dallos and Procter 1984). The issue of power requires the development of beliefs about responsibilities, decision-making, duties, obligations and commitments. The issue of boundaries includes beliefs about personal space and privacy – the boundaries of the self vs shared activity in the family. The issue of intimacy embraces a complex array of psychological emotional tasks and needs that have to be met, such as affection, sympathy, support, sexual intimacy and so on.

2 *rules and tasks* – in order to function, a family or any other social grouping has to establish some 'ground rules' and to develop some organization so that the basic physical and material necessities are met.
3 *gender* – cutting across these dimensions of family life there is the central issue of gender roles and expectations. The development of gender-specific roles, division of labour, identity, patterning of activity and so on, will be affected by how the issue of gender is negotiated.

These areas of family life – the internal 'private' world and the interface with the wider community – will in turn be influenced by dominant ideologies and discourses. For example, the division of responsibilities within a family is guided by prevailing discourses about appropriate gender roles so that, until recently at least, boys grew up believing that their role in families would be as providers and major decision-makers; and girls that they would be mothers and run the domestic arrangements.

More broadly, families are also expected to undertake certain duties, such as the 'appropriate' socialization of children. Similarly, the recurring public 'panics' about the family being in crisis and moral decline, falling apart, not shouldering its responsibilities and so on, are likely to be absorbed by family members and further regulate a family's internal activities and external relations. Each family develops a set of beliefs governing the boundary between its private, internal world and that of a public, external one. Some families, for example, appear to hold to the beliefs that whatever happens under their roof is essentially private and should be free from outside interference, while others expect, and even invite, outsiders to help manage their affairs or are keen to interact with other families and the local community.

Allowing the family a voice

The beginnings of family therapy, like many histories, took place not in a linear way but in spirals. As an example, we have started this chapter with some voices of families and therapists, their experiences of family therapy. In one sense this helps to 'capture the moment' in hopefully offering a sense of where systemic and family therapy is now and where it may be heading. Families, however we attempt to define them, are made up of people intimately involved with each other. Each member of a family has their own personal stories of their joint journey together and the web of stories, their intersection and weaving together constitute family life.

Many therapists currently emphasize that it is essential that we respect and allow families to voice their stories. To offer analyses, generalization and statistical descriptions without offering the family a voice simply imposes our beliefs as therapists in a disrespectful way. We will have much more to say about all this throughout the book. It is salutary to note, however, that despite many critiques of early family therapy approaches early writings were widely illustrated by rich transcripts of conversations with families. The founder of the structural school of family therapy, for example, starts his seminal book with this conversation:

Minuchin: What is the problem? So who wants to start?
Mr Smith: I think it's my problem. I'm the one that has the problem . . .
Minuchin: Don't be so sure. Never be so sure.
Mr Smith: Well . . . I'm the one that was in hospital and everything.
Minuchin: Yeah, that doesn't, still, tell me it is your problem. Okay, go ahead. What is your problem?
Mr Smith: Just nervous, upset all the time . . . seem to be never relaxed . . . I get uptight, and I asked them to put me in the hospital . . .

(Minuchin 1974: 1)

You may have various thoughts about this short extract: perhaps Minuchin seems somewhat patronizing? Maybe he seems to be too challenging to the family's preferred story? Is he being too charismatic and leaping in before even having collected the barest clinical history? Whatever we may think, however, his work here is open to scrutiny. It offers us a chance to make up our own minds about what is going on, what meanings are being explored, what Minuchin is up to.

Many years ago when we first encountered systemic and family therapy, this visibility and presentation of verbatim material was a breath of fresh air compared to stuffy statistically driven papers, or, slightly better, dead case study accounts from the therapists of their version of what had occurred in therapy. So even the early writings can still feel refreshing and vibrant.

There has also been much change afoot in family therapy. Families' voices have moved centre stage such that some therapists regard therapy as essentially the process of conversing, of telling and making stories. Minuchin would not have described his approach as mainly this. We do not want to fudge changes and evolutionary steps in family therapy's history but neither do we want to miss the opportunity to point out that some of the exciting new territories that have been discovered, and are now on the edge of the map, also resemble some of the impressive earlier ones.

The organizing framework of this book

We propose the use of a four-phase framework which can help to clarify both the differences and the connections between various models and perspectives. Specifically, we suggest that the distinction drawn between first- and second-order cybernetics can be misleading, particularly in that it fails to draw attention to the important and radically different propositions contained within social constructionism and constructivism. Social constructionist ideas emphasize processes whereby choice in families is constructed and constrained by inequalities of power and culturally shared discourses. This contrasts sharply with constructivist views which emphasize individual uniqueness, freedom and autonomy. We suggest that recognition and articulation of these differences can be a step towards developing ways of integrating perspectives as opposed to unnecessary abandonment of useful ideas from the four phases of systemic thinking.

Our organizing framework of first, second, third and fourth phases provides a structure that offers the reader both advantages and disadvantages. On the positive side it helps in organizing and simplifying complex subjects and issues, making them more manageable and comprehensible. Thinking is very much concerned with organizing our experiences into conceptualizations and narratives of various sorts. On the negative side the organization may distract us from and make invisible the complexities and potential contradictions in our knowledge and experience. It is useful to consider Korzybski's (1942) famous phrase, 'the map is not the territory'. Our organization is more or less helpful but not reality itself. Arguably we may never be able to objectively establish that there is a 'real' reality out there.

Early family therapy approaches (the first phase in this book, from the mid-1950s to the mid-1970s) are located in what has been called 'modernity' – the dominant twentieth-century view that the processes of science would enable us to form accurate theoretical, predictive models of the world. Included in this was the view that psychology could and should be science based, on the collection of objective evidence through rigorous observation and experimentation. In effect this represented the methods applied in the natural sciences, and which had appeared so successful in delivering a variety of technological benefits. In family therapy examples of this perspective were early attempts to systematically explore and classify families according to a number of variables and types in order, for example, to establish what characteristic dynamics caused schizophrenia, anorexia or depression in one or more family members (Wynne *et al.* 1958; Kantor and Lehr 1975; Doane 1978; Wynne 1988).

Similarly attempts were made to establish what kinds of treatments were most suited to dealing with different types of disorders (Gurman and Kniskern 1978). Though research outcome and evaluation has not been a strong feature of the development of family therapy many of the assumptions of a scientific–modernist approach were evident in the early studies of the family. For example, that organizational features of a family, such as an ineffective parental 'executive' subsystem (inability of the parents to work together to control the children), could be objectively identified and steps taken to remedy this.

As research and therapy progressed, however, it became increasingly evident that such objective descriptions of families were problematic, not least because different observers tended to perceive a family in different ways. It also became apparent that contrasting ways of working with families could produce equally impressive positive changes. Eventually this led to a shift in family therapy and more broadly in psychology and the social sciences to a postmodern (Papp 1980; Keeney 1983; Hoffman 1993) or constructivist view of the world (the second phase in this book). Briefly this questions the possibility of an objective view of the world and suggests instead that our perceptions of reality are invariably diverse and contested. We can argue that there is a 'real' reality out there but we can only know it through our personal lenses. Consequently this has led to a distinction being made in systemic and family therapy between approaches based on first-order cybernetics and those based on second-order cybernetics, which mirrors the shifts in beliefs from a modern to a postmodern epistemology.

Specifically this represents the move from initially applying an objective, positivist framework to families which believed that through observation and analysis we could come to accurately and reliably map their dynamics. It became increasingly evident that when different therapists and researchers viewed a family their perceptions were frequently quite different. Furthermore, often their interpretations contrasted starkly with the family's own perceptions. This led to what has come to be called second-order cybernetics, namely the view that reality invariably involves a construction, occurs in relationships and is based on feedback. There is not one accurate view of reality but invariably differing perceptions and constructions. These might be called different hypotheses about reality.

The strong version of this view is embodied in Maturana's (1978) concept of structural determinism, which states that the organization of our brain largely determines what we are capable of seeing. We do not simply perceive reality out there but actively construct it. Tom Andersen (1990: 39) offers an elegant metaphor:

> The brain is constantly in action and influences from the sense organs only modify an already ongoing process in the brain. It has been compared with a room crowded with talking people. If a person from outside opens the door and speaks, the speaking is

analogous to the influence of the sense organs. The ongoing activity in the room is changed only to a small extent by the talking from the door.

It is our contention that it is helpful to identify a third phase of development in systemic and family therapy. This emerges from social constructionist theory which suggests that language is a critical ingredient in family life and dynamics. The constructions of reality that family members form can be seen as both unique and diverse in detail but are also constructed from the material, the 'building blocks' that are shared in any given culture or society. Language can be seen to contain these materials, a shared currency of meanings. To take a simple example, until recently gendered language – for example, chairman, housewife, the use of Mrs or Miss to denote marital status – was largely accepted without question as a convention. Racial examples can be seen in the unquestioned use of terms like 'primitive societies' in contrast to Western 'civilized' societies. In clinical areas there was the unquestioned use of terms like neurotic, hysterical, mad or even the apparently benign term 'mental health', which contain assumptions about the nature of distressing experiences, such as these being like an illness, due to personal weakness and lack of will. A social constructionist analysis, however, reveals these to be powerful constructions which become established as natural, self-evident truths and which unquestioningly come to shape our thinking, expectations, gender roles – in short, help to construct family life. Most importantly, it is suggested that such concepts help to maintain a variety of inequalities of power, such as women's subjugation by men, oppression of ethnic minorities and of those experiencing forms of mental distress.

This book, like any other textbook, is a punctuation in time, and therefore at this point in what we have called the third phase (from the mid-1980s to 2000), and in the more recent integrations (which we can think of as a fourth phase), there are more questions emerging about the relationship between systemic and family therapy and other psychotherapies, and specifically whether the differences between the intrapsychic and interpersonal need to be so rigidly held. Perhaps as we enter into the third millennium it is an appropriate moment to talk both about similarities and differences in a field of psychotherapy that is undoubtedly different and distinctive due to the skills and conceptual frameworks required to usefully converse with more than one person at a time.

At the end of Chapters 1–5 we have included a selection of skill guides. The selection reflects our views of what we find useful in our current practice as systemic and family therapists and teachers, as well as skills that seem to us to be enduringly relevant in the field. We hope the skill guides will provide a starting point for new practitioners in the field and do not believe the lists are in any way exhaustive. The skills we have included, however, are representative of the field and will be taught in most systemic and family therapy training courses.

For the sake of coherence we introduce each skill guide by describing the background to the skill, offer some ideas about relevance and usefulness and then describe an exercise that will help the practitioner become familiar with and integrate the skill into his/her repertoire. In order to be able to develop skills for systemic practice, all skills need, in our view, to be experienced by practitioners being, for example, the subject of their own personal genogram or family sculpt or of an inquiry about their family relationship based on circular questioning. Therefore, the skill guides we list are for use both in training therapists and therapy with clients. Trainees and therapists alike will be able to make relevant adaptations so that each skill most appropriately fits the context in which it is being used. We do not, in this book, describe many possible adaptations but offer references for further reading as required.

Chapter 4 focuses on the emotional and attachment aspects of family relationships and though central to family therapy, these have produced less in the way of specific techniques. We offer case studies and a skill guide based around the use of a family genogram to facilitate a mapping of emotions and traditions of attachments, which we have found a helpful approach.

In Chapter 5 we offer ideas about a systemic perspective (accompanied by case examples) of the increasingly important topic of formulation.

Chapter 6 focuses on contemporary practice and attempts to illustrate the application of systemic thinking in a variety of contexts in addition to work with families. It uses the concept of formulation to illustrate how systemic thinking is applied to various problems and situations, again with case studies.

In Chapter 7 there is an overview of the research base supporting the effectiveness of family therapy alongside descriptions of important and hopefully stimulating examples of different research paradigms that have been employed in family therapy research.

Rather than Chapter 8 being an endpoint, we see it as yet another punctuation and, in it, offer some of our thoughts about where the field is now and where it could go. We take license to do some crystal-ball gazing.

At the end of the book we provide some further resources for teachers and trainees. There are topic-specific reading lists (not exhaustive), and guides to such things as first and last sessions in therapy, which we have called formats for exploration, as they are our adaptation of core systemic ideas to our practice and therapy, not specific skills associated with a particular model and concept. We have compiled a glossary of terms used throughout the book. The two articles in the postscript are historical markers (2005) that we offer both as gifts to readers and as relevant punctuations in time for this second edition.

Key texts offering a historical overview of systemic and family therapy

Bowen, M. (1975) Family therapy after twenty years, in S. Arieti, D.X. Freedman and J.E. Dyrnd (eds) *American Handbook of Psychiatry V: Treatment*. New York: Basic Books.

Ferber, A., Mendelsohn, M. and Napier, A. (eds) (1972) *The Book of Family Therapy*. New York: Science House.

Goldenberg, I. and Goldenberg, H. (1980) *Family Therapy An Overview*. Pacific Grove, CA: Brooks/Cole.

Guerin, P.J. Jr (ed.) (1976) *Family Therapy: Theory and Practice*. New York: Gardner Press.

Gurman, A.S. and Knistern, D.P. (eds) (1981) *Handbook of Family Therapy Vol I*. New York: Brunner/Mazel.

Gurman, A.S. and Knistern, D.P. (eds) (1991) *Handbook of Family Therapy Vol II*. New York: Brunner/Mazel.

Hoffman, L. (1981) *Foundations of Family Therapy*. New York: Basic Books.

Hoffman, L. (1993) *Exchanging Voices*. London: H. Karnac.

Howells, J.G. (1975) *Principles of Family Psychiatry*. New York: Brunner/Mazel.

Keeney, B.P. (1983) *Aesthetics of Change*. New York: Guilford Press.

L'Abate, L. (ed.) (1985) *The Handbook of Family Psychology and Therapy*. Homewood, IL: Dorsey Press.

Simon, R. (1992) *One on One: Interviews with the Shapers of Family Therapy*. New York: Guilford Press.

Sprenkle, D.H., Piercy, F. and Wetchler, J. (eds) (1986) *Family Therapy Sourcebook*. New York: Guilford Press.

Walsch, W.M. and McGraw, J.A. (1995) *Essentials of Family Therapy*. Denver, CO: Love Publishing.

Wolman, B.B. and Stricker, G. (eds) (1983) *Handbook of Family and Marital Therapy*. New York: Plenum.

1 The first phase – 1950s to mid-1970s

Cultural landscape

Appropriately for a psychotherapy based on the idea that the whole is greater than the sum of its parts, there were a range of developments in psychology, communications, psychotherapy and elsewhere which prompted the development of systemic theory and therapy, and no one person or event can be credited as its author. Some of these developments were as follows:

- Dissatisfactions with the effectiveness of psychoanalytic and other individual therapies, especially in relation to severe clinical problems such as schizophrenia.
- The emergence of general systems theory as a model and its application to research on human interaction.
- Research into the role of communication in the development and maintenance of severe intractable clinical problems such as schizophrenia.
- The evolving practice of child and marital guidance which brought parts of families together and started to shift the exclusive emphasis from individual treatments.
- The development of group psychotherapies which revealed the powerful therapeutic impact of bringing people together to communicate about their difficulties.
- Indications that psychoanalytic approaches could even lead to an escalation of the problems. Jackson (1957), for example, described how working in a psychoanalytic way with a woman on her own resulted in the deterioration and eventual suicide of her husband, leaving the woman in a considerably more distressed state than at the start of therapy.

- The focus in intrapsychic work on historical factors deeply embedded in the psyche tended to ignore the possible contribution of factors such as the current circumstances, especially interpersonal problems and conflicts that might have had a contributory effect.
- Recognition of resistance, where psychoanalytic approaches had noted that patients were frequently 'resistant' to change. This was seen in terms of the depth of their anxieties and subsequent defensive mechanisms excluding the possibility that change for a person involves changes in their relationships and the roles that others play in their lives.
- Considerations of cost-effectiveness – perhaps one of the most straightforward critiques was that intrapsychic approaches tended to be very long-term, time-consuming and therefore expensive. In the context of limited public funding of healthcare this tended to preclude treatment of large numbers of people.

Influential people and ideas

Seeds of systemic and family therapy

Early systemic ideas appear to have developed and evolved along two pathways. The start of systems theory and cybernetics – a term coined by Norbert Weiner (1961) from the Greek word for steersman – dates back to the Macy conferences in New York in the 1940s, which were attended by scientists, engineers, mathematicians and social scientists with a strong interest in communication and control. The interests were partly driven by military applications in the Second World War and centred on the development of guidance systems for targeting missiles and rockets. A key notion was the principle of *feedback* – how information could loop back into a system in order to enable control in the form of adjustments to be made. A system was seen as able to maintain its stability through a process of self-regulation by using information about past performance, and specifically how this deviated from the desired or optimal setting to make corrections. This not only offered some important practical applications but was also an important philosophical leap in explanations of causation. Rather than seeing events in *linear* sequences, cybernetics proposed that causation was a continuous *circular* process taking place over time. This offered a dynamic rather than static model of the world.

These early ideas developed along two related but different pathways. The first path was a mechanistic one in which cybernetic ideas were employed to design various forms of mechanical control systems. A simple example is a central heating system, a more complex one a rocket guidance system. In its emphasis on the interpersonal nature of problems, first-order cybernetics presented a profound and significant challenge to the existing psychiatric orthodoxy. This challenge held sympathies with the emerging anti-psychiatry movement in the 1960s which voiced extensive critiques of the oppressive nature of the practices of confinement, medication and isolation of those suffering mental distress. In sympathy with anti-psychiatry, it was argued that organic illness models of problems were essentially misguided. A view of problems as interpersonal suggests, for example, that medication should be at most a temporary measure. The systemic view of problems was liberating not only for members of families who were displaying the problems but also for the therapist, as the practice of family therapy promised to offer support and relief for other members. However, this revolution was not without its critics, and there was considerable reluctance to abandon some practices, especially the use of medication for 'serious mental health' problems.

The second path or strand of development was in the application of systems theory concepts to biological systems. Walter Cannon (1932) had earlier suggested the concept of dynamic equilibrium to explain how the body is capable of maintaining steady states despite external changes. For example, despite large changes in external temperature, we are capable of maintaining body temperature very close to 98.6°F (37°C). Similarly, the body is able to maintain an optimal level of blood sugar, light into the eyes, arousal of the central nervous system, balance of various hormones and so on. However, though biological systems can be described in similar ways to mechanical systems, it is important to note some differences and confusions about these that have plagued early systems theory thinking in family therapy. In fact it is possible that the elegantly simple mechanical metaphor used in early discussion, such as a central heating system, subsequently caused an oversimplistic view of families:

1 Biological systems, unlike mechanical ones, are not artificial but are designed through processes of natural selection. Hence they have evolved within and in response to the demands of the external environment in which they are located.
2 Biological systems are fantastically complex, and we have at best an approximate idea of how they work. It is only possible to develop approximate explanations which have the status of inferences, not absolute knowledge.
3 Biological systems have the capacity to evolve and change. This can be in the short term in that systems can make adaptations, for example we can acclimatize to colder or warmer climates. In the long term, through natural selection, more fundamental adaptations may be made.

Key people, places and events (bird's-eye view)

Early family theorists, researchers and therapists focused in the 1950s on the study of schizophrenia in the context of family relationships. The intellectual soil out of which this work grew can be traced to the Josiah Macy Foundation conferences in the 1940s, at which leading scientists, engineers, mathematicians and social scientists of the time explored issues of communication and control.

Ludwig von Bertalanffy, a biologist, proposed a general systems theory as an attempt to develop a coherent theoretical model which would have relevance to all living systems. He believed that the whole is greater than the sum of its parts, and that in order to understand how an organism works we must study the transactional processes occurring between the components of the system and notice emerging patterns and the organized relationships between the parts. **Norbert Wiener**, a mathematician, coined the term *cybernetics* and was especially interested in information processing and the part feedback mechanisms play in controlling and regulating both simple and complex systems. For Wiener, cybernetics represented the science of communication and control in humans as well as in machines.

William Buckley, a social scientist, proposed that human relationships could be seen as analogous to a 'system' in that groups of families could be viewed as a set or a network of components (people) which were interrelated over time in a more or less stable way.

Another influential author was **Korzybski**, who in 1942 published *Science and Sanity: An Introduction to Non-Aristotelian Systems and General Semantics*. His now famous phrase, 'the map is not the territory', was used by **Gregory Bateson** as he developed ideas of the importance of both content and process in human communication.

Bateson, an English-born anthropologist and ethnologist, recognized the application of these mathematical, engineering and biological concepts to the social and behavioural sciences and introduced the notion that a family could be viewed as a cybernetic system, particularly since by assuming social systems, like physical and mechanical systems, were rule-governed, both the uniformity and variability of human behaviour could be accounted for. Although the family was only one of many different types of natural system that interested Bateson, he is credited with providing the intellectual foundation for the field because of his ideas and studies of patterns and communication.

In 1952 **Jay Haley** and **John Weakland** joined Bateson to study (with a Rockefeller Foundation grant) patterns and paradoxes in human and animal communication. In 1954 **Don Jackson** joined their research team and (with a Macy Foundation grant) they studied schizophrenic communication patterns and in 1956 published the seminal text 'Towards a theory of schizophrenia' (Bateson *et al.* 1956). He was also the first to formally and elegantly articulate the model of families as operating in an analogous way to homeostatic biological systems in his paper 'The question of family homeostasis' (Jackson 1957).

In the late 1950s other now well-known family therapy pioneers were studying schizophrenia. **Carl Whitaker** in Tennessee was developing with colleagues a psychotherapy of chronic schizophrenic patients. **Lyman Wynne** and colleagues were developing ideas about pseudo-mutuality in the family relationships of schizophrenics. **Murray Bowen** in Washington proposed an approach to schizophrenic families based on the idea of emotional divorce between members. **Theodore Lidz** in Baltimore was looking at 'marital schism' and schizophrenia. **Ronald Laing** in England was proposing that schizophrenic family members were the most sane members of a family system. **Ivan Boszormenyi-Nagy** in Philadelphia (newly emigrated from Hungary) was also researching into schizophrenia.

In Massachussetts, New York and London respectively, **John Bell, Nathan Ackerman** and **John Bowlby** were working with families who had problems other than a schizophrenic family member.

The end of the decade saw Don Jackson found the Mental Research Institute (MRI) in Palo Alto (1959). Nathan Ackerman created the Family Institute in New York in 1960 (renamed the Ackerman Institute after his death in 1970).

By the end of the 1960s **Virginia Satir** at MRI was recognized as a pioneer in the field with her 'unshakable conviction about people's potential for growth and the respectful role helpers needed to assume in the process of change' (Simon 1992).

Salvador Minuchin *et al.* had published *Families of the Slums* (1967), and Minuchin became director of the Philadelphia Child Guidance Clinic. Jay Haley worked there with him from 1967. The Brief Therapy Project was begun in 1967 at MRI, and Don Jackson died suddenly in 1968.

In Europe, **Robin Skynner** was creating the Institute of Family Therapy in London and a systems group was developed in the Department of Children and Parents at the Tavistock Clinic, London. In 1969 **Sue Walrond Skinner** founded the Family Institute in Cardiff. **Mara Selvini Palazzoli** had begun with colleagues in Italy to look beyond psychoanalysis for a model to work with anorexic and schizophrenic patients and their families. **Helm Stierlin** in Germany was looking at 'the family as the patient'.

This phase saw, in the early 1970s, distinct schools of family therapy emerge: *structural* (Salvador Minuchin); *strategic* (Jay Haley and **Cloe Madanes**); *communication and validation* (Virginia Satir); *existential* (Carl Whitaker); *family of origin* (**James Framo** and Murray Bowen) and more – all of which supported the interventionist role of the therapist.

4 Biological systems have a developmental process and history and the environment impacts on the basic design or phenotype to influence the development of the system.
5 In mechanical systems the patterns displayed are determined by the designer; in biological systems we do not determine the patterns but merely observe them. This observation in itself is an active process and different observers may see different patterns, for example at different levels of the biological system – its behaviour, overall macroscopic structure, microscopic structure, chemical and electrical activity and so on.

It is possible to list further differences but these point to some important issues, perhaps one of the most fundamental being that mechanical systems are fully determined and predictable, whereas with biological systems we can only develop hypotheses or inferences. Put simply, human and biological systems are infinitely complex.

The seeds for the evolution of systemic and family therapy probably germinated simultaneously but at first relatively independently in a number of different settings. Significantly, though, the emergence of family therapy, its guiding theories and practice, was rooted in research. The failure of psychoanalytic and other psychological treatments for serious conditions, such as schizophrenia, led to funding for research into its causation. In turn this research suggested that communication played a strong role in its aetiology and this led to explorations in therapy with families to provide further research data (Lidz *et al.* 1957; Wynne *et al.* 1958; Haley 1962; Bateson 1972). Initially the process of family therapy was in itself seen as a form of research and as providing a rich vein of new and significantly different types of interactional evidence.

There is a story that the development of the first attempts at family therapy resulted from a misunderstanding. John Bell, one of the unsung pioneers of family therapy, is said to have overheard a casual remark while visiting the Tavistock Clinic in London in 1951 that John Bowlby (1969), a prominent psychoanalyst and researcher into childhood emotional attachment, was experimenting with group therapy with entire families. Bell assumed from this that Bowlby was undertaking therapy with families regularly and when he returned to the USA this idea inspired him to develop methods for working therapeutically on a regular basis with entire families. In fact Bowlby only occasionally held a family conference as an adjunct to individual therapy with the 'problem child'.

Bell started his 'family therapy' in the early 1950s but, possibly because he was relatively unambitious and modest, did not publish a description of his work until 10 years later (Bell 1961). This story also indicates the central position that an exploration of communication came to occupy in family therapy. It also suggests, though this has been less emphasized, that even misunderstandings can have creative effects.

Systemic thinking – from intrapsychic to interpersonal

One of the most enduring contributions of systemic thinking has been to offer a view of problems and 'pathology' as fundamentally interpersonal as opposed to individual. Systems theory offered a compassionate view of individual experience but also a reductionist and possibly mechanistic one. Regarding symptoms as interpersonal helped to liberate individuals from the oppressive and pathologizing frameworks that had predominated. Particularly for children and other disempowered family members, it offered a lifeline from the double abuse of being oppressed by the family dynamics and simultaneously being stigmatized for the consequences experienced.

More broadly, the view of individual experience shared with other theories, such as symbolic interactionism, emphasized the centrality of relationships, communication and interaction for the development of identity and experience. Furthermore, it suggested that identity, personality, the self is malleable; individual experience was continually being shaped. People are not prisoners of their pasts, as psychodynamic and to some extent behavioural theories had implied. Systemic thinking suggests that as family dynamics change, so individual identity and experience can change alongside it.

Certainly early theorists were not blind to the importance of individual experiences of family members, but nevertheless such individual experience took a back seat in theory and clinical formulations. Each family member's identity and experience appeared to be determined by their part in the pattern and as a consequence this led to some confusion around the question of individual autonomy and responsibility.

The spotlight of problem explanation moved from the narrow beam that had focused on the individual to a broader one that illuminated the rest of the cast. Eventually it became clear that this spotlight needed to be widened further to consider *who* was holding the spotlight and *where* and *why* the play was being staged. This shift was a profound one and shook the psychiatric establishment to its roots, as well as much of psychology and other person-centred sciences. Problems and 'pathology' which had hitherto been regarded as individual phenomena came to be viewed as resulting from interpersonal processes.

Early formulations promoted the idea of *functionalism,* which had also gained ground in behavioural theories of pathology. This rested on the idea that problems could only arise and survive if they offered some form of gain for members of the family. Work with children provided some of the clearest illustrations and applications of a systemic model.

It was suggested, for example, that a child's problems might have developed from her response to her parents' escalating quarrels, for example by her becoming upset or ill. Eventually these actions would *function* to distract the parents from their own conflicts to show concern over the child. If this process continued for some time the family might come to, in a sense, 'need' the child to be ill or deviant in order to continue to distract or *detour* the conflicts between the parents (see conflict detouring, page 28). Such an analysis came to play a central part in early systemic and family therapy and became increasingly sophisticated as it was realized that the analysis needed to include *all* of the family members, so, for example, a functional analysis might also suggest that the child's symptoms would eventually confer some power and privileges on the child.

Systems theory – biological analogy

Using a biological analogy, systems theory proposes that various activities of the body are composed of interconnected but distinct systems of components that operate together in an integrated and coordinated way to maintain stability (von Bertalanffy 1968; Bateson 1972). This coordination is achieved through communication between the components or parts of the system. To take a simple example, the regulation of body temperature involves an interaction between the sweat glands and perspiration, physical activity, breathing rate and control mechanisms in the brain. These components act together (much like a thermostat) to maintain the temperature of the body within tolerable and 'safe' limits.

Very simply, a system is any unit structured on feedback (Bateson 1972). More fully, a system is seen as existing when we can identify an entity made up of a set of interacting parts which communicate with and influence each other. The parts are connected so that each part influences and is influenced by each other part. In turn these continually interacting parts are connected together such that they display identifiable coherent patterns. These overall patterns are not simply reducible to the sum of the actions of the individual's parts – a system is more than simply the sum of its composite parts. It is the observed pattern that connects the parts in a coherent and meaningful way.

Aspects of mechanical models were also applied to families, with Jackson (1965a) suggesting that a family was similar to a central heating system in that it operated on the basis of a set of rules, with deviations from these rules being resisted. For example, there might be a pattern of interaction which featured an escalating conflict between mother and daughter during which the father would withdraw in exasperation. Eventually the mother would turn to him in anger, accusing him of not helping or caring. Following some hostile exchanges between them, the mother would turn to accuse her daughter of upsetting the whole family.

The family members would not be aware of this pattern of behaviours acting as a rule, but in effect their repetitive and predictable pattern of interaction would suggest that some such rules were in place. This led to the idea that such groupings of components constituted a system.

Emergent properties of a system

Central to systemic theory was the idea that a system has characteristics that are *emergent*. When two or more people interact they are involved in a creative process – a joint construction of actions and meanings. It is not possible therefore to fully predict how two or more people will interact, how they will get on, what sort of relationship will emerge. The nature and development of the relationship are seen as emergent and evolving rather than as determined by the individual characteristics of the people involved. Each and every interaction is therefore seen as to some extent unique even though it may superficially appear to share similarities with other relationships.

Circularities

Systems theory stresses the interdependence of action in families and other relationships. Each person is seen as influencing the other/s and their responses in turn influence them, which influences the first person's responses and so on. Any action is therefore seen as also a response and a response as also an action. Watzlawick *et al.* (1967, 1974) coined the term *circularities* to capture these essentially repetitive patterns of interaction. This represented a fundamental shift from how relationship difficulties had previously been explained. In effect the question of looking for a starting point – who started it – is seen as unproductive. Even if we can identify who appeared to start a particular family sequence (such as an argument), this may in turn have been a response to a previous episode. Related to this is the common pattern found in families and other relationships, when, as a result of an escalating conflict between two members, a third person is drawn in. This may occur at a largely unconscious level so that all of them may be unaware that the third person is repeatedly involved in this way. These repetitive patterns, these circularities, stress a continual, mutually determined pattern of action over time. The following exchange is a common circularity identifiable in many families:

Sandra: Can I stir that, Mummy?
Diane [mother]: Not just now, be careful, you'll burn yourself.
Sandra: [climbing on to a chair near the cooker] What's that? Can I put some sugar in?
Diane: You can cut up some pastry, don't drop it . . . all right, don't worry, don't wipe it, we'll use some more . . . [exasperated] John, do you think you could do something with Sandra?
John [father]: Doesn't she want to help you?
Diane: Look, she is going to burn herself . . . I've asked you before.
John: Come here, Sandra, get down . . . let's go out to the workshop, we can do some hammering. [Ten minutes later, Diane thinks she has heard Sandra cry and comes to the workshop.]
Diane: Oh god, John, she's cut her finger, can't you see? I thought you'd watch her.
John: It's just a scratch. She's OK . . . I couldn't get this screw out.
Diane: It's all right sweetie. Come on, I've made some more pastry.

The behaviour of this family can be seen to be repetitive and we can predict how they might interact in a variety of different situations, such as bedtime, bathing, going to the park and so on. The presence of these regularities in behaviour makes it look, to an outsider, as if the family is following a set of rules which seem to be necessary to maintain some form of equilibrium (Jackson 1957).

As observers, we can see regularities in the actions of members of a family and we can go on to infer a set of rules that might give rise to such regularities. These are, however, only inferences in the minds of us as observers. The examples in Figure 1.1 illustrate the different ideas of causation inherent in systemic thinking.

Participants in the relationship may explain their own and each other's actions in linear terms, as in Figure 1.2.

Within a circular explanation each partner's behaviour in the examples in Figures 1.2 and 1.3 is maintained by the actions of the other. So John's inability to express his feelings may serve to fuel Mary's demands for a show of feelings and affectionate behaviour which in turn leads to more of the same from John. Likewise, Mary's dependent actions and demands may serve to fuel attempts by John to withdraw and become detached.

Linear explanations are often couched in terms of invariant personality traits, such as John's avoidant or introverted personality, or Mary's dependency. Whether Mary is more or less insecure than other people is less relevant than the fact that her level of insecurity may be

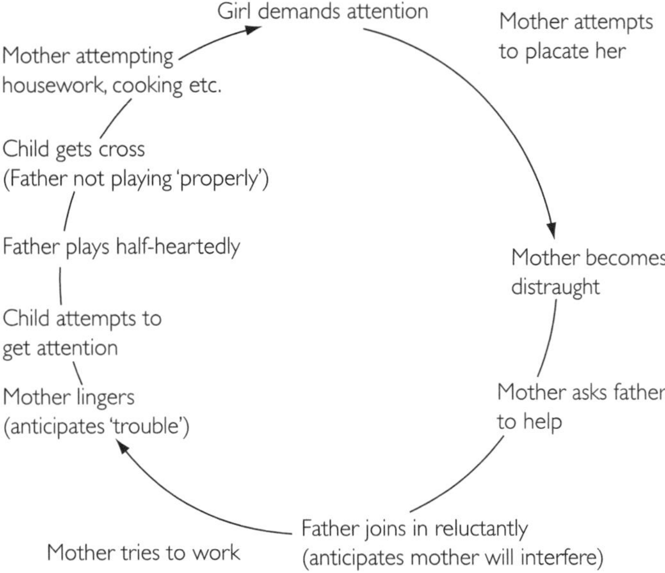

Figure 1.1 Circularity encapsulating a 'peripheral' father role

Linear causality
John, due to his childhood experience of rejection, has a fear of expressing his feelings, which makes Mary feel rejected and hurt.

Circular causality

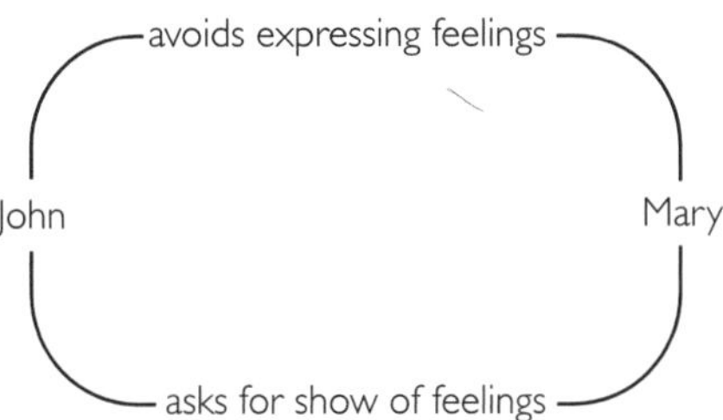

Figure 1.2 Linear vs circular causality I

maintained by the interaction between herself and John. Likewise, John's level of detachment is maintained by Mary's seemingly demanding behaviour. Although the gender positions reflected in these examples may be reversed in some couples, these are common gender patterns. This suggests that, though interpersonally maintained, such cycles are also shaped by dominant cultural gender roles.

Bateson (1972) employed evolutionary metaphors to argue that biological and human systems developed on basic stochastic or 'trial and error' processes. Thus a family system is seen as continually adapting to its ecological context. That is, a family is situated within its extended family network, the local community and culture which place various

Linear causality

Mary might say that the way John withdraws makes her feel vulnerable and that is why she acts in a dependent way.

John might say that Mary is so dependent and demanding that it makes him feel suffocated so he has to withdraw

Circular causality

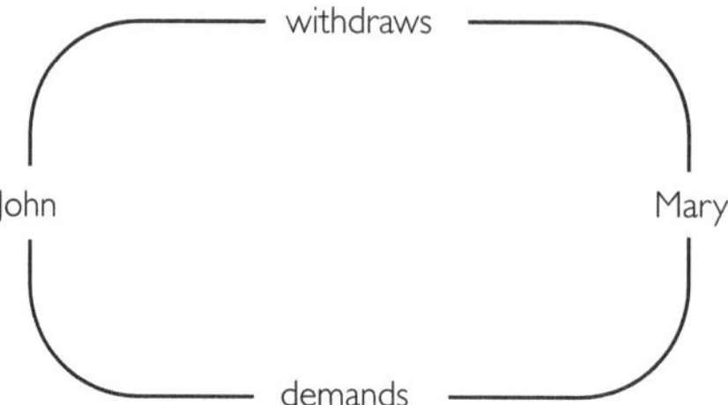

Figure 1.3 Linear vs circular causality II

and shifting demands upon it. A variety of actions or responses may be emitted as a response, but only some fit the demands and are allowed to endure. A typical example is of a young couple with a new baby experiencing various pressures and conflicts where a variety of actions may emerge, such as the couple avoiding each other, arguing, talking to others, the baby becoming distressed, crying, sick, not sleeping. Distress in the baby may have the effect of temporarily distracting the couple from their conflict but may evolve over time into a pattern whereby the distress in the baby functions to stabilize the family system. Arguably systems theory is essentially a theory of stability rather than change and development. The models describe how patterns can be maintained and suggest that once patterns are established homeostatic tendencies compel a system to remain the same.

Triads, triangulation and conflict detouring

A key step in the development of systems theory was to move from a study of individuals and pairs to an exploration of triads (three-person interactions). An analysis of the dynamics of triads helped to illustrate how the twin concepts of closed and open systems could operate side by side in such a way that overall a stability or *homeostasis* could be preserved. For example, escalating conflict (open system) in a pair might be offset by the involvement of a third person. Such a repetitive dynamic could thereby preserve stability (closed system). In effect, such a system displays a rule along the lines of 'if the conflict between two persons escalates beyond a critical point then involve the third person to restore stability'.

Importantly, it was suggested that if the involvement of the third person was through a symptom then the system overall was functioning so that this symptom helped to maintain the balance or homeostasis of the triad:

> When therapists observed that what one spouse did provoked the other, who provoked the first in turn, they began to see that a dyad was unstable and it required a third person to prevent a 'runaway'. For example, if two spouses competed over who was most ill, total collapse could only be prevented by pulling in a third party. Rivalrous quarrels that amplified in intensity required someone outside the dyad to intervene and stabilize it. If a third person is regularly activated to stabilize a dyad, the unit is in fact not a dyad but is at least a triad. With this view, the unit becomes a unit of three people. Similarly if a husband and wife regularly communicate to each other through a third person, the unit is three people instead of a married 'couple'.
>
> (Haley 1976a: 153)

Similar triadic patterns can occur in other, various relationships, for example between colleagues or friends, as shown in Figure 1.4.

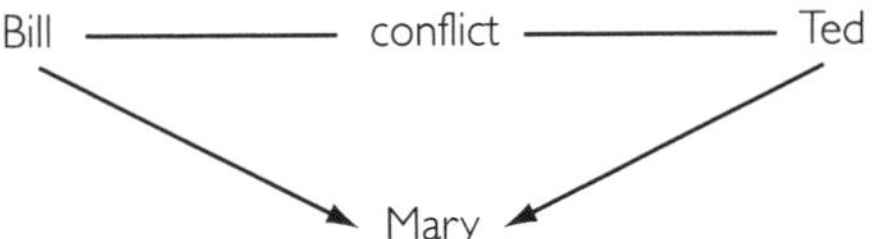

Figure 1.4 Conflict detouring in a work setting

Mary, a young assistant, may respond to the conflicts between her superiors Bill and Ted by making some minor errors and becoming emotional herself. Her 'symptoms' may temporarily distract the men from their conflicts. The focus may then move to Mary and 'her problems', leading the men perhaps initially to try to protect her and possibly accuse each other of upsetting her. However, if they are stressed, overtired and irritable they may find it hard eventually to avoid blaming her for being 'overemotional' or 'weak'. Mary's distress consequently may escalate to the point where she develops a 'problem', perhaps taking time off work and so on. The focus of the difficulties may now move firmly to Mary's problems, perhaps even more generally about the 'difficulties of working with women', 'women's high level of emotionality' and so on, and the conflict between Bill and Ted becomes submerged, except perhaps over disagreements about how to deal with the situation, whether Mary should be replaced and so on.

A person in a conflict detouring position becomes drawn into the relationship between another two people but then their involvement can also serve to prevent resolution of their underlying problems and conflicts. Related to the emotional processes are likely to be changes in perceptions, for example Bill and Ted above come to see themselves as similar, that is, as male, less emotional and more free of problems than Mary.

In social interaction the functioning of groups of people made up a pattern, a meaningful whole which was greater than the sum of its individual parts. By analogy, family dynamics are like a piece of music or a melody which we hear as a combination of notes but where each individual note gains its meaning in the context of the others – the total gestalt or whole. The concept of homeostasis was employed to describe the tendencies of systems to preserve a balance or stability in its functioning in the face of changing circumstances and demands. A system was seen to display homeostasis when it appeared to be organized in a rule-bound, predictable and apparently stable manner. As an example Hoffman (1976: 503–4) cites a triadic family process:

> The triangle consists of an ineffectively domineering father, a mildly rebellious son and a mother, who sides with the son. Father keeps getting into an argument with son over smoking, which both mother and father say they disapprove of. However, mother will break into these escalating arguments to agree with son, after which father will back down. Eventually father does not even wait for her to come in; he backs down anyway.

A pattern of actions can be discerned here, but how do we draw this as a system? One version might be to focus on the smoking as the trigger, which, when it is perceived, leads to the activation of a set of beliefs and rules leading to further actions (see Figure 1.5). However,

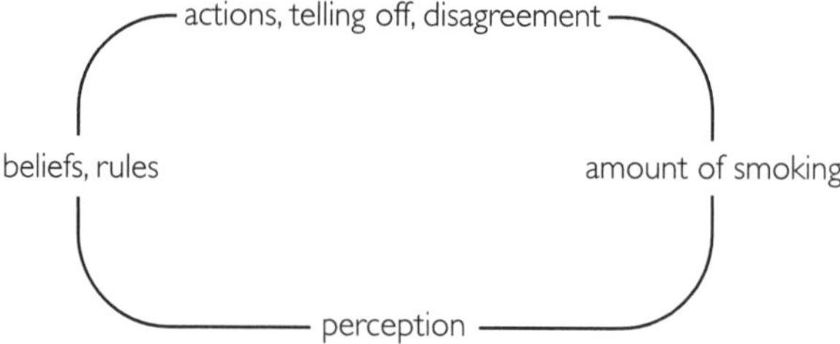

Figure 1.5 A simple cybernetic system

there are potentially an infinite number of other ways we could describe this system, for example focusing on father's level of dominance, or the level of collusion between mother and son, or even on the son as a system – his nicotine intake, arousal level, level of addiction and so on. A system is not static but always in motion, ever changing. In the example above, what we are seeing, arguably, as homeostasis is patterning over time. We can even call this a narrative or story about how these people interact over a period of time. However, during this period the system will look different at any given point, that is, the son does not always have a cigarette in his hand, at times the parents are not discussing his smoking but doing something totally different and unconnected to it, going to work, making love and so on.

> No behaviour, interaction, or system . . . is ever constantly the same. Families, for example, are perpetual climates of change – each individual varies his behaviour in a whirlwind of interactional permutations . . . a 'homeostatic cycle' is a cycle that maintains constancy of relations among interactants through fluctuations of their behaviour.
>
> (Keeney 1983: 68, 119)

Rules, pattern and process

Families do of course have explicit rules, such as the children's bedtimes, manners at the dinner table and so on, but the more interesting rules were seen to be the implicit ones that we, as therapists, could infer, for example that when the mother scolds her son, the father usually pretends to go along with it but subtly takes the boy's side. The smoking example given earlier can be seen to contain a covert rule that the mother will take the boy's side in family arguments even over issues where she actually agrees with the father. However, we could suggest various alternative rules depending on where we choose to look, such as the fact that contact between the boy and his father is initiated through his smoking. In practice what constitutes a system is always a construction, a belief or an idea in the mind of the observer. Keeney (1983) had suggested that within a cybernetic epistemology we can depict a family in terms of as many cybernetic systems as we can formulate distinctions about the system. Which view we adopt is partly a question of choice and usefulness. However, some versions may certainly appear to make more obvious sense than others.

Feedback

The concept of feedback, as applied to human systems, encapsulates the idea of *reflexivity* – a system has the capacity to monitor or reflect on its own actions. It is possible to build simple mechanical systems to demonstrate some adaptability (e.g. a central heating system) but in human relationships the notion of a system contains the idea of assessing what the needs of a particular situation or relationship are and adjusting to deviations from attaining these.

> Feedback is a method of controlling a system by reinserting into it the results of its past performance. If these results are merely used as numerical data for the criticism of the system and its regulation, we have the simple feedback of the control engineers. If, however, the information which proceeds backwards from the performance is able to change the general method and pattern of performance, we have a process which may be called learning.
>
> (Weiner 1967: 84)

An important point to note, though, is that because people in a relationship are capable of reflexivity this does not mean that the most effective, functional or 'healthy' course of action is always pursued. The experience of various forms of therapy reveal that insight into problems does not always guarantee the ability to change them. As we will see later, reflexivity is based upon a set of underlying premises or beliefs that we hold and these may function in a self-fulfilling way so that problems are maintained or even aggravated.

Family coordination through communication

Returning to a biological metaphor, systems theorists suggested that the body could be seen as a set of components which operated together in an integrated and coordinated way to maintain stability (see also homeostasis, p. 35). The coordination was seen to be achieved through *communication* between the components or parts of the system. Bateson (1958) was one of the first to suggest that a variety of social relationships, rituals, ceremonies and family life could be seen as patterns of interactions developed and maintained through the process of *feedback*. This became a key concept in family therapy, namely that some information about the effects or consequences of actions returns to alter subsequent action. Rather than focusing on how one event or action causes another, it was suggested that it is more appropriate to think of people as mutually generating jointly constructed patterns of actions based on continual processes of change.

Double-bind concept

The influence and importance of family communication sequences was highlighted by Bateson and his colleagues in their research on the causes of schizophrenia. They asked in what context schizophrenic behaviour would make sense. One of the answers they proposed was that it made sense in an interpersonal context characterized by repeated contradictory and confusing communications. In particular, they employed the concept of levels of communication and 'logical types' to explain the nature of some characteristic forms of communication that were apparent in the families of young people with a diagnosis of schizophrenia. The following is a now famous example cited by Bateson (1972: 216).

> A young man who had fairly well recovered from his acute schizophrenic episode was visited in the hospital by his mother. He was glad to see her and impulsively put his arms around her shoulders, whereupon she stiffened. He withdrew his arm and she asked, 'Don't you love me any more?' He then blushed, and she said, 'Dear, you must not be so easily embarrassed and afraid of your feelings.' The patient was able to stay with her only a few minutes more and following her departure he assaulted an aide and was put in the tubs.

Relationships are seen to proceed through successive attempts to make sense of what is happening. At times people communicate directly about this by phrases, such as 'what do you mean?', 'you don't seem too happy about that' and so on. A feature of the double-bind phenomenon is that such meta-communication is not allowed, apparently due to unconscious fears of provoking anxiety. 'According to our theory, the communication situation described is essential to the mother's security, and by inference to the family homeostasis' (Bateson 1972: 221).

Meta-communication

Communication takes place at two levels – at a surface or content level, and at a meta-communication or qualifying level. These higher-order communications or meta-communications play a significant role in managing relationships (Watzlawick *et al.* 1967, 1974). In fact this multilayered appraisal may be one of the distinguishing features of long-term relationships. The reflexivity or meta-communication in a relationship system can be seen to be at ascending levels, with each higher level defining those below.

Bateson subsequently revised the double-bind theory to suggest that the process is a reciprocal one, with the child also engaged in double-binding communication. Even less attention appears to have been paid to Weakland's (1976: 29) suggestion that it can in fact be seen as a three-person process: 'The three-person situation has possibilities for a "victim" to be faced with conflicting messages in ways that the inconsistency is most difficult to observe and comment on that are quite similar to the two-person case.'

At a verbal level parents may express unity – 'we want you to be independent' – but may negate this by how they individually express this message to the child or how they act, that is, overt agreement and covert disagreement. For example there may be an overt message from the father that he disapproves of hostility and that everyone in the family is happy. Though appearing superficially to support this, the mother frequently criticizes the father's dislike of physical activities. Further, she may offer justification for her difference to him, not in terms of her disagreement with him but in terms of a 'benevolent' interest in the welfare of the children – thereby laying responsibility for parental differences of opinion on them. Weakland (1976: 33) offers the following example of a family with a schizophrenic son:

> The father and mother insisted for some time that they were in agreement on all matters and that everything was right in their family – except of course, the concern and worries caused by their son's schizophrenia. At this time he was almost mute, except for mumbling 'I dunno' when asked questions. During several months of weekly family interviews, the therapist tried to get the parents to speak up more openly about some matters that were obviously family problems, such as the mother's heavy drinking. Both parents denied at some length that this was any problem. At last the father revealed himself and spoke out with only partially disguised anger, accusing his wife of drinking so much every afternoon with her friends that she offered no companionship to him in the evenings. She retaliated rather harshly, accusing him of dominating and neglecting her, but in the course of this accusation she expressed some of her own feelings much more openly and also spoke out on the differences between them . . . In the following session the son began to talk fairly coherently and at some length about his desire to get out of hospital and get a job, and thereafter he continued to improve markedly.

Open and closed systems

An open system is one with boundaries that allow a continuous flow of information to and from the outside world, while a closed system is one with more rigid boundaries that are not easily crossed. Early theorists (Jackson 1957; Bateson 1972) suggested that relationships could be described as reflexive systems which operated on the basis of two types of feedback: *open systems*, in which feedback serves to produce escalation (e.g. an argument between two people which runs out of control and leads to physical conflict and perhaps the termination of a relationship); and *closed systems*, which employ feedback to correct any deviations from a setting or a norm. The latter therefore tend to reinforce stability and the maintenance of existing patterns. In order for a relationship to function or be viable as a social unit, it needs to show both patterns. Functioning as an open system allows change and adaptation to alterations inside or outside the system (as long as the escalation did not proceed so far as to destroy the system). Alternatively, a system that is rigidly closed would be unable to adapt to new demands and changes in the environment.

In order for a relationship to function or be viable as a social unit, it needs to contain and be able to alternate between these two patterns. Functioning as an open system could bring about change and adaptation to alterations inside or outside the system, as long as the escalation did not proceed so far as to destroy the system. Alternatively, a system that was rigidly closed would be unable to adapt to novel demands and changes in the environment. Positive examples of mutual escalation in relationships are also possible, for example mutual joking or sexual arousal or flattery.

Family homeostasis

The body has an automatic tendency to maintain balance or equilibrium, and this homeostatic tendency can also be seen in family systems. Jackson (1957) proposed that a symptom in one or more of the family members develops and functions as a response to the actions of the others in the family, and in some way becomes part of the patterning of the system. Attempts to change the symptom or other parts of the system were seen to encounter 'resistance' since the system operated as an integrated whole and strove to maintain homeostasis. By 'resistance' Jackson implied not a conscious but a largely unconscious pattern of emotional responses to change in one or other family member. For example, 'a husband urged his wife into psychotherapy because of her frigidity. After several months of therapy she felt less sexually inhibited, whereupon the husband became impotent' (Jackson 1965a: 10).

Jackson (1957) suggested that relationships containing 'pathology' could be seen to function as closed systems. These operated so that any change in the symptomatic member would be met by actions in the others which would have the sum effect of reducing, rather than encouraging, change. Despite family members expressing a desire to change, it was argued that in some sense the symptoms had been incorporated into the relationship dynamics and the habitual behaviour in relation to the symptoms served to maintain rather than change the problems. Jackson borrowed the term homeostasis to describe this process and added the idea that relationships could be seen as if governed by a set of largely unconscious rules, which guided people's actions and embodied the homeostasis.

Family life cycle

An influential model of change and development was proposed in the concept of the family life cycle. This emphasized how development and change in families followed common patterns which were shaped by the shifting patterns of internal and external demands in any given society. Families may at times be faced with massive demands for change and adaptation. This may be the result of changes in family composition – the birth of a child, a divorce or remarriage, a death – or perhaps due to changes in autonomy within the family – children becoming adolescents, a woman going back to work after childrearing, retirement. It was argued that the emergence of problems was frequently associated with these life cycle transitions and their inherent demands and stresses. However, less was said about the possible positive effect of external inputs, for example, the arrival of a child possibly uniting a couple or a bereavement drawing family members closer together. Without an analysis of the meanings such events contained for family members, accounts of change tended to be merely descriptive.

A key issue for any family was how to maintain some form of identity and structure while at the same time needing to continually evolve, adapt, change and respond to external stimuli. There may also be community demands such as local social upheavals and major cultural changes (see Figure 1.6a). Duvall (1977) extended the idea of the individual life cycle model to the idea of a family life cycle. The implications of this model for the practice of family therapy were first set out by Haley (1973) in his book describing the therapeutic techniques of Milton Erickson (see Chapter 2).

Haley (1973) describes how Milton Erickson had noted that problems were often associated with critical periods of change and transition in families. For example, psychotic episodes in late adolescence were seen to be related to difficulties for the family over the departure of the young person about to leave and set up his or her own home. Haley described six key stages as critical, transitional stages for families (see Figure 1.6b).

Milton Erickson's concept of family development emphasized a lifelong process of socialization, adjustment and learning within families (Haley 1973). Hence socialization did not end with childrearing but involved a reciprocal process whereby parents were also continually learning and adjusting to their children. Haley did not expand greatly on the subject, but he does make clear that the model assumes that there exists a common set of values and norms inherent to Western society and to which families are expected to comply. For example, he describes how young people 'need' to practise courtship skills in order to successfully find a suitable mate. Disruptions with this process, for example through involvement in family conflicts, can

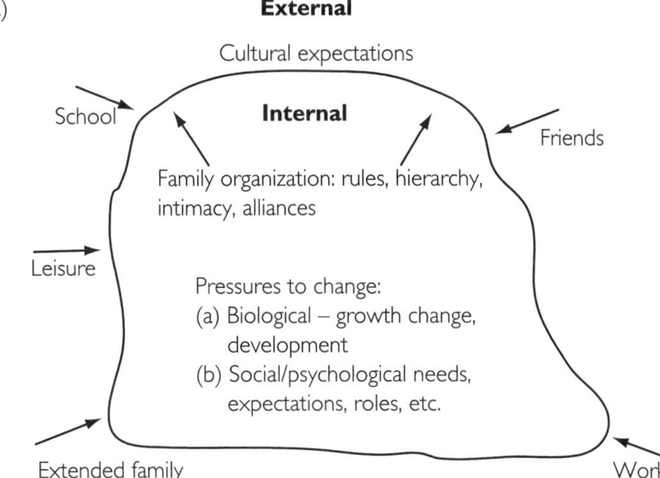

(b) The external and internal demands for change are continuous but become critical at transitional points in the family's life:

Family life cycle stages: transitions
1 Early relationship;
2 Early commitment;
3 Birth of children;
4 Mid years relationship;
5 Leaving home;
6 Retirement and old age.

Attempted solutions
Families need to make changes at these critical transitional points, such as changing the family structure, beliefs or emotional dynamics.

Figure 1.6 The family life cycle: external and internal demands for change (*Source:* adapted from Dallos 1991)

cause problems for the young if it leads to disengagement from their peers.

Carter and McGoldrick (1980) have offered some elaborations of the family life cycle model by additionally noting the significance of intergenerational traditions. They propose a two-dimensional model as shown in Figure 1.7. Carter and McGoldrick (1980: 10) describe their model as follows:

> The vertical flow in a system includes patterns of relating and functioning that are transmitted down the generations in a family . . . It includes all the family attitudes, taboos, expectations and loaded issues with which we grow up. One could say that these aspects of our lives are like the hand that we are dealt: they are a given. What we do with them is the issue for us.
>
> The horizontal flow includes . . . both the predictable developmental stresses, and those unpredictable events, 'the slings and arrows of outrageous fortune' that may disrupt the life cycle process.

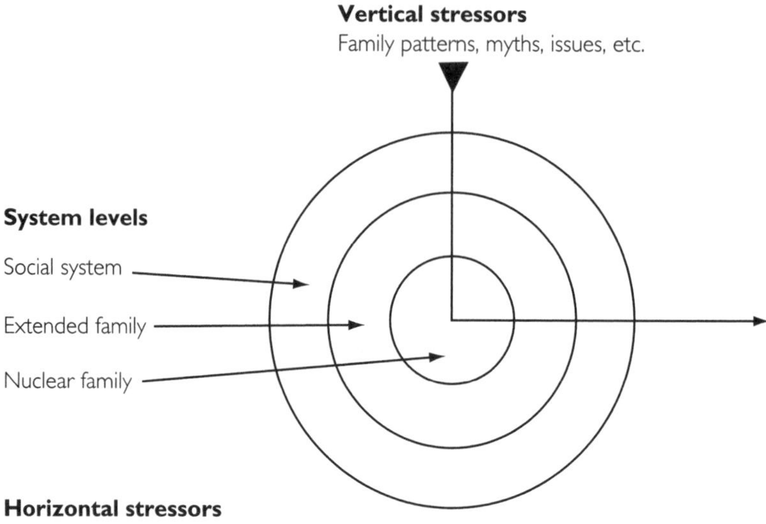

Figure 1.7 Developmental influences on the family

Feminist therapists argued that in fact such patterns represented wider cultural factors, such as expectations about gender roles and opportunities for work outside the family. Attempts to simply fix such patterns in families without due recognition of the cultural factors were seen as potentially oppressive and as implicitly endorsing such inequalities. Most importantly, it was argued that first-order cybernetics often contained, in a concealed form, a range of normative assumptions about healthy family functioning. Structural models most clearly contained assumptions about appropriate organizations, parental control, appropriate closeness and so on. Objective, systemic neutrality, it was argued, was not possible and disguised a range of patriarchal, middle-class, white assumptions (McKinnon and Miller 1987).

Practice

Structural family therapy

At this point, theoretical assumptions were: families are regarded as evolving and capable of change but at any given time a set of rules can be discerned that govern the nature of the family organization. Central aspects of the family organization are seen to be the hierarchical structure – who is in charge, how decisions are made regarding various issues and difficulties which inevitably arise. Particularly significant to this was Minuchin's (1974) view that clarity regarding decision-making was vital: 'Salvador Minuchin and his colleagues in the 1960s and 70s made a simple and enduring point about families: that children thrive when parents, or other caregivers, can collaborate in looking after them' (Kraemer 1997: 47).

This fundamental observation has many related strands. For example, it is intimately related to the concept of *triangulation*, whereby a child may be drawn or invited into the conflicts or distress between parents. Part of the resulting difficulty may be that the child may be enticed to take sides; for example, by taking their mother's side against the father they may be drawn into an adult role and appear to gain power. As a result the power balance may become skewed, for example with the father opting out or becoming peripheral, and the child increasingly being asked to adopt an inappropriate adult role as opposed to receiving the guidance and support that they may need from their parents.

Related structural concepts included the idea of clear boundaries between family members and between subsystems. Most families contain various subsystems, such as the parental/couple subsystem, the sibling subsystem, the grandparent subsystem, adult/children subsystem and other extended family members. Clarity between these different subsystems is regarded as important and a particular problem was seen in cross-generational problems or coalitions, for example where the grandparents exercise inappropriate power over their grandchildren by undermining the parents' authority and wishes.

This theme of clarity about decision-making was also evident in the notion of boundaries. Minuchin (1974) suggested that family members could range from being too close (overinvolved or enmeshed) to too distant (disengaged, detached and overrigid) with each other. Enmeshment could be seen in interactions and ways of relating where, for example, a parent continually spoke on the child's behalf or acted as if they knew more about what a child was 'really feeling or thinking' than the child did. At the opposite end, family members could be too aloof and cold towards each so that they had little idea of or apparent interest in each other's feelings and thoughts. This could lead to a sense of isolation and inability to work together on decisions. Either pattern could be seen to incapacitate the family's ability to work together, to effectively deal with problems in a consistent and constructive manner.

Beliefs and structures

Though structural approaches are seen to be focused on the organizational patterns in a family, these go hand in hand with alterations in the family's belief systems. In fact, as we saw earlier on page 11,

Minuchin gives an example of a family therapy session where he begins by posing a challenge to the father's (and the family's) dominant construction of the difficulties as residing in him. When Mr Smith states that 'I think it's my problem', Minuchin immediately contests this saying, 'Don't be sure. Never be so sure.'

Minuchin goes on to explain that his statement, 'Don't be so sure', challenges from the outset of the therapeutic encounter the dominant view of the problem as residing in Mr Smith. In fact in defining his theory of change Minuchin (1974: 119) makes it clear that alteration in a family's beliefs is regarded as fundamental to change:

> Patients move for three reasons. First, they are challenged in their perception of reality. Second, they are given alternative possibilities that make sense to them, and third, once they have tried out the alternative transactional patterns, new relationships appear that are self-reinforcing.

The ways of challenging beliefs, however, may take various forms depending on the apparent ability or otherwise of the family to incorporate advice and insights. In some cases it is presumed that beliefs will only change as an accompaniment to changes in behaviours – seeing is believing.

Therapeutic orientations

The fundamental view is that alterations made to the organizational structure of a family will change the symptomatic behaviours. Once the rules of the family system alter, so too will the behaviours; for example, if instead of enlisting a child into coalitions against each other the parents start to work together, then the child will no longer display various symptoms. The implications are that as the structure of the family changes, each and every member of the family also changes in terms of their roles, experiences and identities.

Underlying the therapeutic orientation are a set of assumptions about 'healthy' family functioning. It is proposed that certain forms of family organizations are dysfunctional and inevitably lead to problems. At times this may be latent, for example a family may manage reasonably well despite a child being drawn into the parental conflicts, but the inherent instability of the system may become exposed when the child reaches the age at which he or she is expected to leave home and disengage from the family to find an occupation and a mate. The combination of cultural requirements and biological changes requires that the family develops ways of accommodating these demands for change. Since the changes will involve all the members of a family, there is a requirement for joint and concensual decision-making which may not be possible if the family is organized triangularly. Arguably such a structural view is not simply normative and moralistic but acknowledges the cultural realities in which families operate. It has been argued that the approach stigmatizes non-standard family forms, such as single-parent families. However, it is possible to see that, for example, a clear adult decision-making subsystem might equally consist of a mother and a close friend or her parents. The important point is that the child experiences support, a sense of co-operation and clarity from the adults placed in charge of her or him.

Directive stance

Since the fundamental assumption of a structural approach is that families have an objective structure, it follows that therapy involves a process of assessment and mapping of this structure, followed by clear attempts to alter it where necessary. The therapist therefore adopts a sympathetic but nevertheless expert role in which he or she takes on the responsibility of initiating changes. These may be interventions or manipulations that are essentially outside the family's awareness. We can examine three techniques briefly.

Escalating stress and creating a crisis

Minuchin (1974) used this technique in an experiment designed to offer a demonstration of the interconnection of actions and feelings in a family where both the daughters suffered from diabetes. The intention was to explore how changes in the relationships in a family are experienced at a physiological level and how these changes are stabilized by the patterns of family dynamics.

In order to demonstrate this, Minuchin employed a physiological measure of emotional arousal, the free fatty acid (FFA) level in the bloodstream, as changes in FFA levels have been found to relate closely to other measures of emotional arousal, such as self-reports and behavioural evidence.

Both of the children in the family were diabetic; Dede (17 years old) had had diabetes for three years, while her sister Violet (aged 12) had been diabetic since infancy. There was no obvious difference in the girls' individual responsiveness to stress, but Dede suffered much more severely from diabetes and had been admitted to the hospital for emergency treatment 23 times. Violet had some behavioural problems that her parents complained of, but her diabetes was under good medical control.

Minuchin interviewed the parents for one hour (9–10 a.m.) while the girls watched from behind a one-way mirror. From 9.30 onwards he deliberately encouraged the parents to discuss an issue of conflict between them, which led to some experience of stress, in order to see how this affected the children. Although the children could not take part in the conflict situation, their FFA levels (stress levels) rose as they observed their stressed parents. At 10 o'clock the children joined their parents and it became apparent that they played different roles in the family. Dede appeared to be trapped between her parents, each parent trying to get her support, so that Dede could not respond to one parent's demands without seeming to side with the other. Violet's allegiance was not sought. She could therefore react to her parents' conflict without being caught in the middle. The effects of these two roles can be seen in the FFA results (Figure 1.8). Both children showed

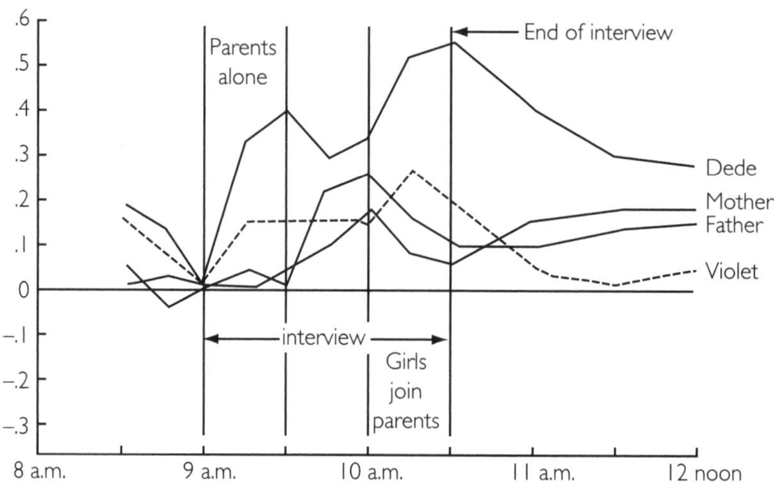

Figure 1.8 Change in free fatty acid (FFA) levels, the Collins family (*Source:* Minuchin 1974)

significant increments during the interview, between 9.00 and 10.00, and even higher increments between 10.00 and 10.30, when they were with their parents. At the end of the interview, however, Violet's FFA returned to baseline promptly, but it took an hour and a half for Dede's level to return to normal. The parents' FFA levels increased between 9.30 and 10.00, confirming that they were experiencing stress, but their FFA decreased after the children had come into the room. It appeared that their conflict was reduced or detoured through the children. However, the children paid a price for this, as shown by their increased FFA levels and Dede's inability to return to baseline.

The Collins family were seen to be organized in terms of a central pattern whereby the parents would triangulate the older daughter Dede into their conflicts by changing the subject to her diabetes problem whenever they discussed any area of disagreement between them as a couple. Children typically become caught up in this process and can be seen to sacrifice themselves for the sake of preserving family harmony by manifesting a symptom when the conflicts start to escalate. Minuchin blocked this pattern by removing the children from the room and continually prompted the parents to discuss their areas of conflicts. He also blocked attempts to change the subject onto the children by bringing the parents back to the conflicts in order to break up the typical pattern.

An underlying assumption of structural techniques is that people are more amenable to making changes when they are emotionally engaged and expressing rather than suppressing their feelings. However, this is not to be confused with simply encouraging conflict in families. Instead, inducing some emotional upheaval is seen as preparing the ground for directing the family to develop some more authentic and productive ways of communicating and relating to each other.

Enactment

Rather than simply talking about or describing situations and problems that occur at home or elsewhere outside of the therapy room, a family is invited to display the patterns there and then. For example, Minuchin *et al.* (1978) developed the technique with families with a child displaying eating disorders, such as anorexia. The therapy sessions would be held over lunchtime and the family would be invited to have a meal together. This could vividly highlight the patterns in the family, such as the inability of the parents to agree and work together on encouraging a girl to eat, and a shifting pattern of coalitions between each parent and the girl. It could also enable a broader discussion of control and independence. For example, through the conflict that might ensue the girl might be able make clear that her not eating was partly an act of defiance and an attempt to assert some independence from being tied up in the struggles between her parents.

Unbalancing

This involves the therapist in using himself or herself in a deliberate way to alter the dynamics of a relationship. For example, many couples attempt to pull the therapist onto their side, to try to convince them that the other partner is insensitive, abusive, awkward, stupid, uncaring and so on. Attempts to stay neutral and to offer a reasonable, impartial point of view may be met with further attempts at enticing the therapist to take sides. The therapist may then deliberately side with one partner against the other in order to break up this repetitive cycle.

For example, a woman who had been hospitalized with depression expressed great pessimism and hopelessness at the start of a session. The therapist, however, encouraged her to voice her distress at her husband's failure to protect her from his intrusive family who were undermining and critical of her. As she gave vent to her feelings she appeared to grow increasingly less depressed and more empowered. The therapist then started to side with her husband in sympathizing with his predicament at trying to keep everyone happy but questioned whether he would be able to construct some clear boundaries between his family of origin and his new family. It was also suggested that the couple go out together to discuss how they might be able to work out some way of solving this dilemma. The wife wanted to solve this in the session, saying she did not trust her husband to do anything about this. They left the session with the wife appearing determined rather than depressed and the husband saying that he had heard clearly what she wanted and that he felt they could come to some decision about it themselves. Subsequently her husband took matters in hand and told his family to back off and give them more space.

Unbalancing can be seen as operating over time such that the therapist can acknowledge that each person is contributing to the interactional pattern but may at one point appear to side with one family member in order to produce a change. However, it is important to be aware of the investment that members have in their relationships.

Strategic family therapy

One of the sources of inspiration for strategic approaches was the work of Milton Erickson who developed a rich variety of techniques, some of which have been developed as strategic techniques and others as forms of hypnotherapy (Haley 1973). Erickson frequently worked with families but also with parts of families or individuals. One of his guiding premises was that problems apparently residing in one person are frequently associated with the difficulties resulting from a family's need to change and reorganize at key transitional stages, such as the birth of a child or when children are about to leave home. In work with young adults, for example, he described a key task as one of 'weaning parents from their children'. In this he recognized that frequently the parents may have a hidden interest in a child remaining at home, for example in order to help them to avoid conflicts in their own relationship. Hence he might sometimes work individually with a young person and assist them in finding ways to become more confident and prepare to become free of their symptoms. However, he would be very aware that improvements in the youth might lead to the parents attempting to 'sabotage' the therapy, perhaps by withdrawing him or her from the therapy on some pretext. Consequently he would also work with the parents. For example, in one case, involving a young woman who was suffering from acute schizophrenia, he arranged for the girl to stay in town near to him while the parents went back some distance to their home on the coast. In Erickson's view it is important to encourage and enable the normal separation at this age to happen rather than to get all the family together to try to talk things through before a young adult moves out.

He also encouraged the young woman to express her resentment of the 'bad ways' in which her mother had treated her by deliberately siding with her and apparently agreeing with her complaint that her mother had treated her badly and that she should not stand for this any longer. In fact he deliberately encouraged anger but at the same time employed hypnotic techniques, such as prompting her to simultaneously notice how her arms felt on her armchair. This was part of an attempt to enable her to get in touch with her feelings, as opposed to the disconnections and denials of feelings that she was experiencing as part of her schizophrenia. At the same time he encouraged her to feel better about herself in various ways; for example, the young woman was very overweight and through direct and indirect comments he encouraged her to accept her body and her 'inner beauty hidden by the layers of fat'.

In conjunction with this individual work he worked with the parents, encouraging them to have a temporary separation which enabled them to renegotiate their marriage without involving their daughter. His interventions were quite forceful:

> I told the father to separate from his wife and live in a different place. Now and then his wife would get agreeable and he would go home and have sexual relations with her . . . The mother was an excellent golfer and a marvellous companion. I arranged that the mother call me regularly while I was treating the daughter. She used me as a sort of father figure . . . When she'd do something wrong she'd call me and tell me about it, and I would whip her over the telephone. So I kept in contact with the parents while seeing the daughter.
>
> (Haley 1973: 271)

Erickson's approach perhaps appears to lack some of the niceties of gender sensitivity and political correctness but at the same time can be seen to reveal a deep compassion and acceptance of human frailty. It also suggests a sense of fun as well as the application of some benevolent trickery to produce profound and rapid changes with quite severe problems.

Strategic approaches encompass a wide range of ideas and tactics. A common feature is the focus on the dynamics of family interaction. Problems are seen as embedded in repetitive interactional patterns or circularities:

> Our fundamental premise is that regardless of their basic origins and etiology – if, indeed, these can ever be reliably determined – the kinds of problems people bring to psychotherapy persist only if

> they are maintained by ongoing current behavior of the patient and others with whom he [the patient] interacts. Correspondingly, if such problem-maintaining behavior is appropriately changed and eliminated, the problem will be resolved or vanish, regardless of its nature, origin or duration.
>
> (Weakland *et al.* 1974: 145)

This view has many overlaps with behavioural approaches, especially in the idea of symptoms as a form of behaviour maintained by the actions of others. However, the others in a family are seen as usually not aware of how their actions are serving to maintain rather than reduce the symptoms. For example, the parents in a family may complain that their daughter is withdrawn and anxious, but every time she tries to haltingly express herself one or other parent tries to 'rescue' her by speaking for her. For her part, when directly asked a question by the therapist, the girl may invite her parents to intrude by shyly looking towards one or other parent before she answers or immediately seeking confirmation once she has started to speak. The parents' actions of 'helping her out' can be seen as an 'attempted solution', an attempt to help her by clarifying what she wants to say. However, this may have quite the opposite effect. It is suggested that these attempted solutions can in fact function to aggravate rather than relieve the problems, leading to a spiral of increasing difficulty.

Less frequently stated perhaps is the central premise of strategic approaches – that people are fundamentally strategic. All of us, including family members and therapists, are involved in making predictions about how others may act, feel and think. Based upon this we make decisions, more or less consciously, about the timing and appropriateness of particular actions and their likely consequences. Haley (1987) perhaps stated this most forcefully in terms of relationships as invariably involving a form of power struggle, for example in terms of how the relationship was to be defined, who was in charge, who initiated decisions and so on. An important implication for therapy was that the therapist and family members were seen as engaged in attempts to influence each other. For example, members of a family typically try to enlist the therapist onto their side, to see things from their point of view and to be an ally to change the others. Hence therapy is inevitably strategic or tactical in that the therapist needs to be aware of these attempts at influence by family members and to act strategically to direct rather than become simply caught up in them.

This is also consistent with a humanistic and existential view that people are fundamentally autonomous, with a desire to be in charge of and make choices in their lives. Invariably this suggests that therapy will involve a clash of wills. Though people may come to therapy to seek help, they also seek to maintain control of their own lives. Strategic approaches recognize this fundamental dilemma and seek ways to enable the therapist to act tactically so that change can occur. Writing about the connections between Western and Eastern psychotherapies, Alan Watts (1961: 55) suggested that connecting is the practice of 'benevolent trickery':

> If I am to help someone else to see that a false problem is a false problem, I must pretend that I am taking his problem seriously. What I am actually taking seriously is his suffering, but he must be led to believe that it is what he considers as his problem.

Beliefs and premises

Though the emphasis is on exploring and helping to change problematic cycles of behaviour, strategic approaches also emphasize the central role of beliefs and cognitions. Problems can be seen to develop in two characteristic ways: people may come to see and treat relatively trivial or ordinary difficulties that we may all face as examples of a serious problem, or alternatively they may 'bury their heads in the sand' and treat difficulties (sometimes quite serious ones) as no problem at all. The first of these can be seen as what Watzlawick *et al.* (1974) describe as the 'utopia syndrome' – a belief that the inevitable difficulties and stresses of life can be avoided. Alternatively, but with equally serious consequences, problems can arise from a denial of obvious difficulties. Failure to take remedial action can lead to initially relatively small difficulties escalating to a point where eventually they become so serious that the situation may come to look catastrophic and hopeless.

The premises or beliefs that family members hold shape both what is seen or not seen to be a problem. Furthermore, these beliefs also shape the 'attempted solutions', such as continual concern, anxiety and desperate attempts to solve matters, as opposed to denial and avoidance of facing issues. The importance of beliefs, or punctuations as described by Watzlawick *et al.* (1974), was therefore seen as fundamental. Interestingly, there was also an early recognition of the importance of cultural and societally shared beliefs:

> Over- or under-emphasis of life characteristics is not entirely a matter of personal or family characteristics; this depends also on more general cultural attitudes and conceptions. While these often may be helpful in defining and dealing with the common vicissitudes of social life, they can also be unrealistic and provoke problems. For example, except for the death of a spouse, our own culture characterizes most of the transitions . . . as wonderful steps forward along life's path. Since all of these steps ordinarily involve significant and inescapable difficulties, such over-optimistic characterization increases the likelihood of problems

> developing – especially for people who take what they are told seriously.
>
> (Weakland *et al.* 1974: 149)

Strategic approaches appear not to hold a view of the family apart from seeing it in terms of a set of local interactional dynamics between family members and between the therapist and the family. An exception is the model of the family life cycle that offers a picture of family development through a series of key transitions and how these may be related to the onset of difficulties, which then can become aggravated by pernicious interactional dynamics. In contrast, structural approaches do have a view of the family as organized in terms of a set of roles and rules that are embodied in the overall family hierarchy, subsystems and boundaries. Furthermore, assumptions are made about 'healthy' family structures, such as a clear parental system with parents capable of working together to make mutual decisions.

However, neither of the approaches appears to recognize that the structures and dynamics are not simply created inside the family but constrained and constructed within the constraints of gender inequalities inherent in society. To take an example, to simply encourage a couple to have an equal role in decision-making about the children may fail to recognize that this is one of the few areas of validation and power that the woman possesses. Similarly, establishing a closer or 'overinvolved' relationship with the children may be a result of the fact that the woman has to carry more of the childcare. Also, she may feel a need to have the children on her side to gain some semblance of influence over her partner who otherwise holds the economic and physical power.

As implied by the term 'strategic', the orientation is one that focuses on problems and contemplations about how to solve these. The underlying theoretical orientation (similar to structural approaches) is that family life invariably presents people with various difficulties. These difficulties may be perceived in various ways and these perceptions guide what steps are taken to solve the difficulties:

> One of our main stated aims is to change overt behavior – to get people to stop doing things that maintain the problem and do other things that will lead toward the goal of treatment . . . it is often just that behavior that seems most logical to people that is perpetuating their problems. They then need special help to do what will seem illogical and mistaken.
>
> (Weakland *et al.* 1974: 157)

Strategic approaches are best known for offering a relatively brief approach which focuses on the core problems and attempts to break up the pattern of maintaining behaviours and failed solutions. This is usually attempted without the family being fully aware of what the therapist is up to. In effect, this represents an 'expert' position with the therapist and the team in charge of effecting changes. Strategic approaches involve the following key stages:

1 Detailed exploration and definition of the difficulties to be resolved.
2 A formulation of a strategic plan of action by the therapist designed to break up the sequences of interactions within which the problem is embedded and maintained.
3 The delivery of strategic interventions – these frequently involve a task or 'homework' that a family is requested to carry out between sessions. These tasks are designed specifically to disrupt the problematic sequences.
4 Assessment in terms of feedback regarding the outcome of the interventions.
5 Reappraisal of the therapeutic orientation or plan, including continuation or revision of tasks and other interventions employed.

To illustrate strategic approaches we can look at strategic, directive and paradoxical tasks (details are provided in the topic reading lists at the end of this book).

Strategic tasks

Strategic tasks can be seen to fall broadly into two categories depending on whether family members are likely to carry out instructions offered or will fail or refuse to do so: *directive* tasks, asking families to do something that the therapist hopes will alter problematic sequences of interactions; and *paradoxical* tasks, where they are asked to do the opposite of what the therapist intends to happen.

Directive tasks

These usually consist of pieces of homework that family members are asked to carry out. Wherever possible it is seen as most effective to involve all of the members of a family in such tasks. The following extract from Haley's work is illustrative:

> In an actual case in which the grandmother is siding with her ten-year-old granddaughter against the mother, the therapist sees mother and child together. The girl is instructed to do something of a minor nature that would irritate grandmother, and the mother is asked to defend her daughter against the grandmother. This task forces a collaboration between mother and daughter and helps detach grandchild from grandmother . . .

> When a husband and wife, or parent and grandparent, are at an impasse over who is correct in the way the child should be dealt with, a therapist can provide a behaviour modification programme. One person may be excluded by this arrangement, or they may be brought together. For example, the parent can say to the grandparent that this is a new procedure being learned at the clinic and from now on parent and not grandparent is to be the authority on what to do with the child with this new procedure. Or parents who have fought over different ways of dealing with the child can reach agreement on this new way and so resolve a parental conflict that has been maintaining a child problem.
>
> (Haley 1987: 70)

Frequently directive tasks can appear quite obvious and commonsensical, but nevertheless the intention behind the task will be focused on disrupting pernicious patterns. Many parents, for example, spend little time together as a couple and have become fixed in their views of each other. A task can be to request that they purchase each other some small gift that the other would not expect. In order to do this they must both think about each other carefully. Sometimes tasks can be employed in a metaphorical way, for example a couple who are experiencing sexual difficulties may be asked to discuss and plan a meal together. They may talk about going out for a meal and what they would have and also discuss where and what they used to eat when they were in the early courtship period of their relationship. The discussion may range over the setting, candles and romantic settings, preparation, choice of wines, length of the first course, who finishes the main meal first and so on. Following a discussion about their preferences they may be asked to arrange such a mutually satisfying meal together.

Paradoxical tasks

These are employed when families find it difficult to comply with directives offered by the therapist. Early systemic therapists referred to families frequently being 'resistant' to change. The concept of resistance has been extensively criticized (Dell 1982) as overtly implying a positivist and mechanistic view of families. Instead inability to comply with directives can be seen in terms of the family's exasperation and sense of failure which make it hard for them to trust straightforward directives. Weakland *et al.* (1974: 159) described the rationale for paradoxical tasks as follows:

> [a paradoxical task] is used most frequently in the form of case specific 'symptom prescription', the apparent encouragement of symptomatic or other undesirable behavior in order to lessen such

> behavior or bring it under control. For example, a patient who complains of a circumscribed, physical symptom – headache, insomnia, nervous mannerism, or whatever – may be told that during the coming week, usually for specified periods, he should make every effort to increase the symptom. A motivating explanation usually is given, e.g., that if he can succeed in making it worse, he will at least suffer less from a feeling of helpless lack of control. Acting on such a prescription usually results in a decrease of the symptom – which is desirable. But even if the patient makes the symptom increase, this too is good. He has followed the therapist's instruction, and the result has shown that the apparently unchangeable problem can change. Patients often present therapists with impossible-looking problems, to which every possible response seems a poor one. It is comforting, in turn, to be able to offer the patient a 'therapeutic double-bind' which promotes progress no matter which alternative response he makes.

Paradoxical tasks can sometimes involve an element of humour which may be helpful. De Shazer (1982) described a paradoxical intervention where a family complained that they were forever bickering and sniping at each other so that people felt upset, hurt and uncared for. In effect, their family life was a form of war where no one could feel safe from unexpected attack. The suggestion was made to the family that it may be important for them to keep on acting like this but it may also be useful to explore further what it felt like when they sniped at each other and also how it was likely to lead to escalating cycles of counter-attack and retaliation. The therapist then asked the family to buy a set of water pistols and for each member to use their pistol to squirt at the member of the family who they felt was sniping at them. The family returned for the next session saying that they had done as requested but found themselves dissolving in laughter very quickly the first time. Subsequently it had helped them to see the futility of what they had been doing, and they were now bickering much less with each other.

Commentary

Systems theory has received considerable criticism for the implication that *all* problems are essentially interpersonal. In particular, the stance of neutrality was severely criticized for implying that, for example, child abuse, domestic violence and emotional abuse should be seen as interpersonal. Central to this was an unwillingness to contemplate inequalities of power within families as significant and to recognize that these were related to wider cultural patterns of inequality, for example the disadvantages commonly experienced by women. In turn it was argued that many of the characteristic patterns were not simply developed from within the family but reflected these wider cultural factors. For example, a commonly observed pattern was that many fathers occupied a distant, disengaged position in families, with the women making repeated attempts to involve them and criticizing their lack of involvement. Rather than simply seeing this as an example of family 'dysfunction', correctable by an 'expert' therapist, it was suggested that, particularly in Western cultures, this pattern was a direct product of patterns of gender and family socialization.

Similarly, the family life cycle has attracted critical attention, especially on the grounds that it takes an overly normative view of family development and focuses on the nuclear family which, in its pure form, is not now the most common arrangement. The experiences of step-families, for example, can involve complex overlapping of life cycle stages. A new couple may find themselves in a courtship phase while at the same time having to deal with adolescent children from previous marriages. There is also the danger of ignoring the diversity of choices people may feel are available about forms of family life. It is possible that adults may choose to live in a single-parent arrangement or a commune, but such choices are less available to a child and, as Haley (1973) argues, in extreme cases the parents' 'eccentric' choices can have considerable ramifications for the child in terms of being rejected by his or her peers and becoming stigmatized and labelled in various destructive ways.

Gender and shifting inequalities of power

Relationships in families may be considered a matter of give and take – but who gives and who takes will vary during the course of a relationship. The balance of power can be seen to be determined by global considerations, such as the general balance of power between men and women, access to jobs, education and so on and also by local conditions – the relative balance of power between partners. One way of conceptualizing power is in terms of the resources that each partner possesses (Blood and Wolfe 1960; Homans 1961). The most obvious and objective resources are income, education, physical strength and occupational status. But there is also a range of relative resources, such as skills, physical attractiveness, love, affection, humour and emotional dependency. These are more open to negotiation and are to some extent constructed within the relationship, so that one partner may have considerable power because the other is deeply in love with, is emotionally dependent upon, or feels inferior to them, or even greatly enjoys their cooking. Which resources are dominant and how they are to be employed is, however, also to some extent dependent on culturally shaped sets of obligations. For example, partners are 'supposed' to provide for each other financially, emotionally and physically. Failure to provide, or withholding or abusing these basic resources may be taken as grounds for complaint or for ending the relationship.

Gender differences in resources are also partly culturally determined. For example, in Western cultures women have generally been valued if they possess beauty, charm, and nurturing and supportive attributes. However, many of these not only have little exchange value but are short-lived. Beauty especially has been and perhaps continues to be seen as a central resource. Consequently women have been encouraged to emphasize their looks in contrast to substantial abilities and skills. Western culture tends to define female beauty as youthful, fit and slim. As women age this resource inevitably diminishes. Likewise, a woman's 'resource' is determined by her role as a wife and mother, but as children grow up she is less needed to care for them. The value of the role of wife may also be transient and lost through separation or divorce, in that it is contingent on being in a relationship and being appreciated in that relationship. Indeed, many women who have described their relationships as egalitarian are shocked to realize the extent of their inequality and dependence when that relationship disintegrates. At this point they may become painfully aware that much of their power was contingent on the wishes of their partner, and the particular nature of their relationship (Williams and Watson 1988; Dallos and Dallos 1997).

A number of researchers and therapists (Homans 1961; Haley 1976a; Madanes 1981) have suggested that satisfaction in relationships is related to an equitable distribution of rewards in the relationship. The power each partner possesses lies in the range of resources they have available and which can be applied to influence their partner or other members of the family. It is suggested (Haley 1973; Carter and McGoldrick 1980; Hesse-Biber and Williamson 1984) that the distribution of power in a nuclear family alters during the family life cycle. Not only do men and women have access to different resources, but this changes during their lives. Typically, it can be argued that men and women have relatively equal power during courtship. Even if there are differences, their effects may be less marked since structures of dependence arising from living together have not been established. With the birth of a first child, and incrementally with the birth of each additional child, a woman's power is likely to decrease. It is common for a woman to stop working or reduce her commitment to work. She thus becomes increasingly dependent upon a husband, and the more children she has the longer she may need to withdraw from a job or career, thus losing out on experience, promotions and so on. In contrast, a husband is likely to be based outside the home. He may take on extra work to help with the finances and this may even help his career to develop, thereby exacerbating the power inequalities in the relationship. As the children start school, and when they leave home, a woman's power may increase if she is able to return to work. At the same time a man's career may be starting to level off. As a couple move towards retirement the balance of power may become more equal, but cultural norms may still perpetuate power inequalities.

Normative assumptions of life cycle models

Families exist within a cultural context and one of the key ways in which this regulates family life is through a set of normative assumptions about how family life should progress through a number of key stages. The family life cycle model suggests an image or norm of what people believe family life 'should' be like. Inherent in this image are beliefs about the form that the family should take: how a family should develop, solve problems, communicate with each other, how the members should feel about each other and when it is appropriate for children to leave and start a new family of their own. In one sense the concept of the family life cycle merely maps out a formal set of assumptions that people in a given society hold about a particular form of family life.

At the same time the concept of the family life cycle embodies the ideological assumptions and imperatives that designate the nuclear family as a goal to be striven for, especially in terms of offering the most satisfactory form of nurturance for children. Given the high rates of divorce now prevalent in most Western societies, this model potentially serves as a form of implicit condemnation for many stepfamilies who may feel obliged to contort themselves into a nuclear family configuration. As with many models in the social sciences, attempts to describe and categorize phenomena, such as the stages that families are likely to proceed through, can lead to the model becoming prescriptive. It has been proposed, in contrast, that we fully acknowledge diversity and talk of life cycle*s* plurally rather than of one superior or normal version. This necessitates that we recognize that events such as divorce be 'viewed as normal rather than abnormal phases of the family life cycle and that this can be reframed in positive terms, such as a couple being "ready for a new relationship" or children "being the lucky possessors of two families instead of one" ' (Morawetz 1984: 571).

Key texts

Ackerman, N. (1956) Interlocking pathology in family relationships, in S. Rado and G. Daniels (eds) *Changing Concepts of Psychoanalytic Medicine*. New York: Grune & Stratton.

Ackerman, N. (1958) *The Psychodynamics of Family Life*. New York: Basic Books.

Ackerman, N. (1966) *Treating the Troubled Family*. New York: Basic Books.

Bandler, R. and Grinder, J. (1975) *The Structure of Magic, Vol. I*. Palo Alto, CA: Science and Behavior Books.

Bateson, G. (1972) Double-bind, in G. Bateson *Steps to an Ecology of Mind*. New York: Ballantine Books.

Bell, J. (1961) *Family Group Therapy* (Public Health Monograph No. 64). Washington, DC: US Government Printing Office.

Bowen, M. (1960) A family concept of schizophrenia, in D.D. Jackson (ed.) *The Etiology of Schizophrenia*. New York: Basic Books.

Buckley, W. (1967) *Sociology and Modern Systems Theory*. Englewood Cliffs, NJ: Prentice Hall.

Framo, J.L. (1976) Family of origin as a therapeutic resource for adults in marital and family therapy. You can and should go home again. *Family Process*, 15(2): 193–210.

Haley, J. (1963) *Strategies of Psychotherapy*. New York: Grune & Stratton.

Haley, J. (ed.) (1971) *Changing Families: A Family Therapy Reader*. New York: Grune & Stratton.

Haley, J. (1973) *Uncommon Therapy: Psychiatric Techniques of Milton H. Erickson, M.D.* New York: W.W. Norton.

Haley, J. (1976) *Problem-Solving Therapy*. San Francisco, CA: Jossey-Bass.

Haley, J. and Hoffman, L. (1967) *Techniques of Family Therapy*. New York: Basic Books.

Kantor, D. and Lehr, W. (1975) *Inside the Family*. San Francisco, CA: Jossey-Bass.

Lidz, T., Cornelison, A.R., Fleck, S. and Terry, D. (1957) The intrafamilial environment of schizophrenic patients: II. Marital schism and marital skew. *American Journal of Psychiatry*, 114: 241–8.

Minuchin, S. (1974) *Families and Family Therapy*. Cambridge, MA: Harvard University Press.

Minuchin, S., Montalvo, B., Guerney, B.G. Jr, Rosman, B.L. and Schumer, F. (1967) *Families of the Slums: An Exploration of Their Structure and Treatment*. New York: Basic Books.

Satir, V.M. (1964) *Conjoint Family Therapy*. Palo Alto, CA: Science and Behavior Books.

von Bertalanffy, L. (1968) *General Systems Theory: Foundation, Development, Application*. New York: Brazillier.

Watzlawick, P., Beavin, J. and Jackson, D. (1967) *Pragmatics of Human Communication*. New York: W.W. Norton.

Wynne, L.C., Ryckoff, I., Day, J. and Hirsch, S. (1958) Pseudo-mutuality in the family relationships of schizophrenics. *Psychiatry*, 21: 205–20.

Wynne, L.C. and Singer, M.T. (1963) Thought disorder and family relations of schizophrenics, I & II. *Archives of General Psychiatry*, 9: 191–206.

SKILL GUIDES

The following skills or techniques can be seen to be derived from the first phase of systemic family therapy. They are included because they embody some of the core contributions of that phase and also because they are of enduring value. Many therapists continue to employ these skills, perhaps adapting them to suit their own styles and to fit with their contemporary views and preferences.

Family sculpting

Background

Family sculpting is a technique developed by David Kantor and Fred and Bunny Dahl and used extensively by Virginia Satir, Peggy Papp, Maurizio Andolfi and others whereby a physical arrangement of family members is made (either by a family member or by a therapist) symbolically depicting how the one sculpt director thinks and feels relationships are or have been, or how, at a given time, the family sculpt director would like them to be in the family.

Usefulness and relevance

The process of sculpting can be used to show existing relationships or change communication patterns and/or as an attempt to restructure family relationships. Sculpting is thus a tool enabling family members to comment on past, present and future relationships – how relationships are experienced, what changes family members or therapists would like to achieve – and to get in touch with the psychological distances and the feelings and emotions they arouse. Sculpting is a useful and powerful tool which can be used in a number of different ways according to the needs of the therapeutic processes. It is useful both in therapy and in training therapists.

Exercise

A family member or therapist is invited (or a therapist negotiates permission) to sculpt the family (to make a living picture of relationships) at a time when symptoms emerge or at a future time when symptoms have disappeared. People are asked to remain silent, to notice their feelings as they are arranged in the sculpt. Family members are then invited to comment on what feelings they have about the positions they have been allocated or chosen. When everyone in the sculpt has had the opportunity to say how they feel, the director of the sculpt then invites everyone to move to a position they would prefer and find more comfortable in relation to other family members. The exercise ends with each person being invited to comment on changes they and others would have to make to become and remain more comfortable both physically and emotionally with themselves and in their relationships with other people in the sculpt.

Sculpting of the family situation can be undertaken by the client/s only or in collaboration with the therapist – or the therapist may wish to sculpt how they experience the family situation as described by the client.

Sculpting with stones – an alternative to sculpting with people

The stones (or other objects, such as sea shells, marbles, pieces of fruit, etc.) may be selected to represent family members according to their size, colour, texture and so on. They may be given names and then arranged and discussed in an analogous way to the work with actual family members. The objects and their arrangements may be interspersed with some humour and all members of the family invited to participate and manipulate the stones according to their ideas about the relationships between the family members. Sculpting with stones involves touch and can arouse powerful feelings with the client/s. It is important to ensure trust is established in the client–therapist relationship and that the clients know there will be sufficient time to work with and through any intense feelings that may be aroused.

Further reading

Goldenberg, I. and Goldenberg, H. (1980) *Family Therapy: An Overview*. Pacific Grove, CA: Brooks Cole.

Kantor, D. and Dahl, B.S. (1973) Learning space and actions in family therapy: a primer of sculpture, in D. Block (ed.) *Techniques of Family Therapy: A Primer*. New York: Grune & Stratton.

Papp, P. (1973) Family sculpting in preventative work with 'well' families. *Family Process*, 12: 197–212.

Satir, V. (1988) *New Peoplemaking*. Palo Alto, CA: Science and Behavior Books.

Family tree and time line

Background

The challenge of organizing often vast amounts of information about family members gleaned by practitioners during sessions when family members are encouraged to share their stories has led to the development of family trees and time lines as a way to record significant information in formats that are accessible and usable for clients and therapists alike.

Family trees, or genograms, are maps providing a picture of family structure over several generations, with schematic representation of the main stages in the family life cycle. The format most generally used was established by Murray Bowen (Carter and McGoldrick 1980) and includes names and ages of all family members, dates of birth, marriage, divorce, separation and death information about three or more generations.

Time lines (see Figure 1.9) can be used to ensure family trees remain useful and uncluttered and to show changes in occupation, location, life course, illness and other predictable and unpredictable life events.

Usefulness and relevance

Family trees and time lines are useful diagnostic tools and can provide a benign shared experience for family members often disclosing, for the first time, information with high emotional intensity. Thus working together on a family tree or time line can also be both cathartic and therapeutic for family members, providing an opportunity for the sharing of ideas, thoughts and feelings hitherto undisclosed.

As with any effective therapeutic intervention, therapists need to be sensitive to nuances of family members' verbal and non-verbal behaviour indicating their vulnerability while involved in creating family trees or time lines.

Exercise 1

Therapists and clients are invited to identify a time in family life that is a snapshot of family process; this should be at a significant point, for example at the point of referral for professional help, at a life cycle transition point such as leaving home, death of parent or spouse, etc.

Date commenced: ____________

Client no./Name: ____________ *Significant others** ____________

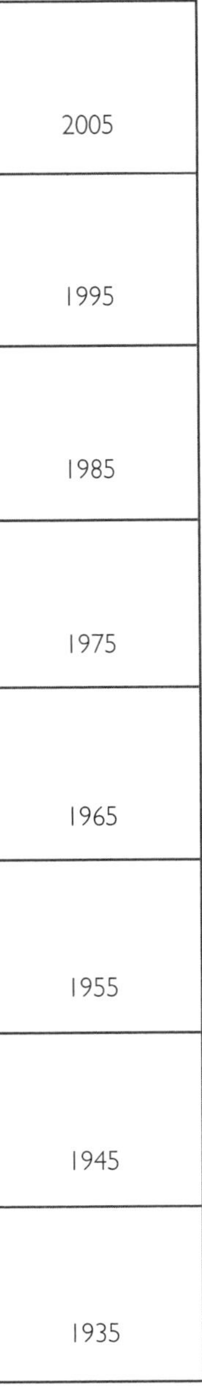

* network of family, friends, professionals and others

I keep six honest serving men,
(they taught me all I knew)
Their names are What and Where and When
And How and Why and Who.

(R. Kipling, *Just So Stories*)

Figure 1.9 Time line

The family tree is drawn showing, where possible, up to three or four generations. Themes to look for and explore may include separation, loss, conflict, closeness, communication, power and family beliefs, myths and legends; explanations and responses to crises and life changes can be described. Using large sheets of flip-chart paper for this exercise enables (if necessary) many people to work together, and the sheet can be saved for later therapy sessions and new information added as appropriate.

Exercise 2

Therapists can complete a time line or ask clients to do so showing the flow of events and crises in a client's life that influence or contribute to symptom formation. Information will be provided on:

1 the client's view of and feelings about significant events;
2 the client's responses to professionals' views/enquiries;
3 the discrepancies between 1 and 2;
4 for the professionals, data for assessment of symptoms and indicators for treatment.

Useful questions to ask are:

What is the problem?
brings you here today?
are the consequences of the problem for the client's life and relationships?
Where do you think it comes from?
can we look for explanations?
When did you first notice it?
How would you like us to be able to help?
Who else knows about the problem?
else understands about the problem?
is affected by the problem?
Why is it happening now?

Further reading

Bowen, M. (1972) Differentiation of self in one's family of origin, in J. Framo (ed.) *Family Interaction*. New York: Springer.

Byng-Hall, J. (1995) *Rewriting Family Scripts: Improvisation and Systems Change*. New York: Guilford Press.

Carter, E.A. and McGoldrick, M. (eds) (1980) *The Family Life Cycle: A Framework for Family Therapy*. New York: Gardner Press.

Framo, J. (1976) Family of origin as a therapeutic resource for adults in marital and family therapy. You can and should go home again. *Family Process*, 15(2): 193–210.

Lieberman, S. (1979) *Transgenerational Family Therapy*. London: Croom Helm.

McGoldrick, M. and Gerson, R. (1985) *Genograms in Family Assessment*. New York: W.W. Norton.

Reframing

Background

Reframing is an important art and skill associated with many therapeutic approaches whereby alternative and equally plausible explanations for the symptomatic or complained about behaviour are offered to clients in order to introduce a difference in communication patterns and open up possibilities for more choices for clients. Thus a teenage father can be blamed for impregnating a girl or praised for his potency; an anorexic girl can be relabelled as strong and determined rather than sick. A classic example of the opportunities offered by reframing is Langbridge's adage, 'Two men look out through the same bars: one sees the mud, and one the stars'. Similarly, the optimist says of a cup that it is half full, while the pessimist says it is half empty.

Usefulness and relevance

Since therapists deal with clients' subjective images of reality, the possibility of investing a dire and depressing situation with new meanings so that clients begin to believe there is a way out of their impasse is an invaluable skill. The ability to reframe or develop new and different and acceptable meanings for and with clients is what enables therapists to create a context for change and work with clients towards developing an understanding of the underlying meaning of their problem.

Exercise

Therapists form a group, trio or pair and give one another several examples of the most dreaded blaming statements from clients. Each person in turn has to think of three non-critical and preferably humorous reframes for each of the statements made. Fluency in this exercise can lead to playfulness in social conversation. So, for example, the statement, 'I had great difficulty getting here today because there was a train strike' can be reframed as 'I am someone who perseveres and overcomes obstacles when I want to get somewhere'.

Further reading

Bandler, R. and Grinder, J. (1981) *Reframing*. Moab, UT: Real People Press.

Haley, J. (1973) *Uncommon Therapy: Psychiatric Techniques of Milton H. Erickson, M.D.* New York: W.W. Norton.

Watzlawick, P. (1978) *The Language of Change*. New York: Basic Books.

Watzlawick, P., Weakland, J.H. and Fisch, R. (1974) *Change: Principles of Problem Formation and Problem Resolution*. New York: W.W. Norton.

2 The second phase – mid-1970s to mid-1980s

Cultural landscape

The second phase can be seen to reveal some important movements in the family therapy field away from the pragmatic and somewhat behaviourist emphasis of the first phase towards a rationalist philosophical approach more central to European traditions of thought. In particular, the ideas of Kant, who stressed that our knowledge of the world was inevitably a construction and questioned the notion of objective reality, inspired the growth of humanistic psychologies in the USA. There were also the wider cultural movements towards individualism, personal growth, inner exploration, creativity and individuality, for example as seen in alternative movements, such as the hippies, ecology groups, gay rights movements and anti-racist movements. In psychotherapy constructivist ideas had a profound effect, for example the work of George Kelly (very much inspired by Kant's ideas) and Carl Rogers, which led to person-centred forms of therapy and counselling. These took as a central aim the establishing of empathy by attempting to understand the client's world from his or her perspective, rather than that of an expert therapist. More generally, there was a movement in psychology away from behaviourism and positivism towards cognitive approaches that focused on how people actively attempted to form versions of the world which shaped their actions. Earlier, Bateson had also been influenced by humanistic and existential ideas and linked his idea of epistemologies, for example, with George Kelly's notion of construct systems (a personal but organized set of interconnected constructs or beliefs).

Outside the USA one of the most significant developments was that of the Milan team in the 1970s. Palazzoli *et al.* (1978) turned to Bateson's ideas, especially his emphasis on families as centrally concerned with the formation of shared meanings or 'epistemologies' through multi-layered communicational processes. Possibly Bateson's interest in ecology, cultural and spiritual beliefs also connected with the importance of religious life in Italy. More generally, Italy has also been identified with a strong emphasis on the family through Catholicism and with a dedication to family ties and honour.

Key people, places and events (bird's-eye view)

The shift to second-order cybernetics heralds an important change in the beliefs about the role of the therapist. The zeal for helping families to change inevitably led to experiences of so-called 'resistance' in families, which in turn led to questions about both the nature of change (**Dell** 1982; **Keeney** 1983; **de Shazer** 1982) and debates about first- and second-order change (**Watzlawick** *et al.* 1974). An awareness developed that grasping the 'emotional logic' in each distressed family situation was crucial if family 'rules' were to alter and transformational change to occur. The use of the 'positive connotation' demonstrated in the work of the **Milan Associates** led to Milan systemic therapy, as it came to be called in the early 1980s, being associated with the therapist's quest for an understanding of a family belief system as a fundamental part of the process of change. Their exploration also supported the work of **Maturana** and **Varela** (1980) and the constructivist position that challenged the assumption that the therapist could be an objective observer outside a family system. Instead, as the therapist became involved with a family system, he or she became part of that system.

By the mid-1980s there were two strands to therapists' beliefs about therapy: those who believed change was instrumental and that intentionality on the part of the therapist was bound to work; and those who were more cautious and could take a position of uncertainty and question the effect of their presence on the family system and were profoundly influenced by **Bateson's** (1972) emphasis on meaning and pattern. Brief therapy (de Shazer 1982) has emerged, alongside the work of the Mental Research Institute (MRI) of Palo Alto, as an approach that appeals to many therapists. Alongside and inextricably linked was the emergence in this phase of postmodernism as the dominant view of the world. The fit between a constructivist view and the questioning of postmodernism is obvious.

This second phase takes us from the development of the team and use of the one-way screen with predominantly first-order modernist ideas to the beginnings of a questioning in the mid-1980s of the implications for family members of unseen therapy teams sending expert messages to family members.

An important factor may also have been the contemporary development of the work of the psychiatrist Basaglia. He promoted a radical revision of psychiatric services in Trieste and other areas which was inspired by Marxist and humanistic perspectives. For example, a radical community-based provision of services for patients and their families was developed which challenged the medical orthodoxy of treatments through medication and confinement. Likewise the Milan team's non-pathologizing and liberating views of problems and families were a challenge to psychiatric orthodoxy. Developments were also occurring in Canada in the work of Karl Tomm and elsewhere, for example the UK and Germany.

In Britain there were a number of interesting developments. The writings of R.D. Laing in the early 1970s promoted a critique of traditional psychiatry and also drew upon Bateson's ideas, such as the double-bind theory, which were developed to describe the processes of the construction and destruction of children's experiences and identities in families. Laing drifted away from the emerging family therapy movement in the UK which he saw as lacking political sensitivity. He also saw the movement as overconcerned with manipulating and 'fixing' families without fundamentally questioning some of the abuses that families inevitably perpetuated from their internalizations of the materialist values of external society.

An imaginative approach linking personal construct theory to systemic ideas was also developed by Harry Procter (1981, 1985). In the early 1980s the Milan approach had a major impact on family therapy in Britain. However, the family movement in Britain remained relatively eclectic, with many practitioners continuing to be influenced by earlier strategic and structural ideas and also by psychoanalytic traditions, especially Bowlby's important ideas regarding the importance of early attachments in families.

Influential people and ideas

> Mental illnesses are indeed mental, in that they are at least 90 per cent made up of blame, or causal attributions that are felt as blame.
>
> We do not 'discover' the world-out-there but, on the contrary, 'invent' it.
>
> (Hoffman 1993: 391, 390)

Second-order cybernetics

A popular view of the shift from first- to second-order cybernetics is that it represents a radical departure and resulted from a number of important critical reappraisals of systems theory (Dell 1982; Keeney 1983). An alternative story is that the shift occurred gradually over a period of time and that the basic principles, notably an emphasis on the construction of meanings, were evident in early writings but were subjugated in the enthusiasm to apply, in an instrumental way, systemic ideas to help distressed people and their families.

The shift to second-order cybernetics has been seen as centred on a critique of the first applications of systems theory, which were seen as offering an overly mechanistic view of families as composed of people actively co-creating meanings. Though the observation of behaviour patterns was still seen as an important starting point, the emphasis moved to an exploration of the meanings, beliefs, explanations and stories held by family members. Inherent in the shift to second-order cybernetics was an important shift in the perceived role of the therapist. In first-order cybernetics the therapist was largely seen as an 'expert' – a scientist who was seen to be able to accurately diagnose the problems in the family, identify the functions that symptoms were serving and intervene to alter these so that the unhealthy function that the symptoms were serving could be remedied. In contrast, in second-order cybernetics the role of the therapist is less of an expert and more of a collaborative explorer who works alongside a family to co-create some new and hopefully more productive ways of the family seeing their situation. Furthermore, this represented a move towards an increased sensitivity to therapeutic relationships. Rather than trying to adopt an 'objective' stance, the therapist is encouraged to be continually reflective – to monitor his or her perceptions, beliefs, expectations, needs and feelings, especially in terms of how these may in turn have an influence on the family.

In effect, early writing (Bateson *et al.* 1956; Watzlawick *et al.* 1967) stressed that what we hear in any given communication is in part determined by what we expect and want to hear and by the history of the relationship (context). Likewise, some extreme critiques and rejections of systems theory (Anderson and Goolishian 1988) can also be seen to be based on a distorted, oversimplified and mechanistic vision of systems theory. This can make for neat and tidy arguments but may not do justice to or represent the depth and complexity of the original ideas.

First-order cybernetics largely adopted a functionalist view of problems: families were seen as interacting systems in which symptoms functioned to preserve stability. Perversely, painful and distressing symptoms, rather than threatening family life and stability, were often seen as holding families together. In effect, symptoms were seen as distracting from or diverting conflicts, anxieties and fears (often unconsciously held) from other areas of the family's experience. Second-order cybernetics challenged this view, predominantly on the grounds that such a functional view was merely an inference in the mind of the observer. The function of a symptom was not there to be discovered, and in fact different therapists often formulated dramatically different functional explanations.

There was a shift away from pathologizing notions of the family to viewing family life as *inevitably* posing difficulties which might or might not lead to distress for some families, depending on how those difficulties were handled. In turn how difficulties were handled – the attempted solutions – were seen as linked to the wider ecology of the family. In particular, families were seen as presented with various developmental hurdles or transitions, such as children leaving home, which needed to be negotiated.

Meta-communication

Watzlawick *et al.* (1974) proposed that confusions in our thinking could occur because meanings are hierarchically structured. One aspect of this is that not only can we communicate but also communicate about our communication. For example, if a friend says, 'Yes, I like this', and I reply, 'Oh, do you? But you don't sound very sure', I am communicating about communicating and my communication in effect alters or gives another meaning to what they were saying. There are various ways that we can engage in such communication; for example, I may communicate displeasure non-verbally but verbally say, 'Oh, yes I do like it'. Table 2.1 shows some examples of how there can be contradictions between various verbal and non-verbal combinations in our communications.

Table 2.1 Varieties of contradictory levels of communications

	Verbal	**Non-verbal**
Verbal	'Don't listen to me' 'I'm a liar, so don't believe me'	'Yes, I like it' Posture showing displeasure
Non-verbal	Sad body posture 'No, I feel fine . . .'	Stroking in a heavy aggressive manner

Watzlazick *et al.* (1967) described many examples of paradoxes that could occur within language itself, some evident from earliest writings:

All Cretans are liars. (Epimedes the Cretan)
IGNORE THIS SIGN
'Oh, all right just ignore me.'

In all these examples, to follow the instruction of the message means to break the injunction. So, if someone says 'ignore me', in order to ignore them I first have to attend to their message which means I have failed to ignore them. But if I do not attend to their message I do not ignore them. These paradoxes can be fun but they are also serious in that they may be found in creative and humorous communication, but arguably also play a more pernicious role in pathology.

The verbal part of a message can at times be relatively ambiguous without the non-verbal component to clarify intention. When there is ambiguity or incongruence between the verbal and non-verbal components an attempt at clarification or meta-communication (communication about communication) may be attempted; for example, a mother might say to her child, 'You don't seem very enthusiastic' or 'You seem a bit fed up'. Young children, lacking the verbal ability and power to engage in such clarification, may therefore become confused and disoriented in times of emotional upheavals in a family.

Communication

Communication is simultaneously an act and a message. Put even more simply, speaking for example is not only a comment or a description but an action in itself – our communications can make things happen. For example, if I say, 'All generalizations are nonsense', my act of saying this is in itself a generalization and therefore invalidates itself. More generally, we have the capacity to engage in ever higher schemes of reflections – I can act, think about my action, think about my thinking about my action and so on. This is not merely a philosophical diversion, since in relationships these processes can be seen to be very problematic. When one partner says, 'Oh, don't hassle me, you're always doing that', this communication contains a classification of the action, it labels it in a particular way – 'hassling' – and contains a general statement about the place of this in the relationship over time. The receiver of the message therefore has a complex task in responding, for example whether to dispute the classification of the act, or the generalization of how often it occurs, or both, or to treat and respond to the communication itself as an act of criticism, aggression or attack. Whether it is treated as an attack is further indicated by the non-verbal features, the voice tone, posture and so on and also the history or context of the relationship. This may be the immediate history, whether they have been in conflict or kidding, and the long-term history, what kind of a relationship they think they have. In addition, other contextual factors, such as where they are – before an important exam, in a supermarket, at an airport, in bed – may also influence how the communication is interpreted.

For communication to occur there must be both a sender and a receiver. Just how a message is interpreted depends not only on the disposition of the sender or the receiver, but on the interchange between them. The meaning of the communication is seen as arising from a process of negotiation involving a further exchange or meta-communication.

The process of communication requires the development of meta-perspectives (Laing *et al.* 1966; Watzlawick *et al.* 1974; Hoffman 1993) or ideas about how each person sees the others, their motives, intentions and how they see their relationships with each other. Through discussions, comments and disclosures the people in a relationship may form a set of shared beliefs, assumptions, explanations and concerns which in turn come to regulate their interactions, produce predictable patterns of actions and also patterns of emotional responses and thoughts. However, the development of such coordinations of action and meanings is seen to be inevitably prone to problems of misunderstandings, confusions and contests over meaning. Partners may hold competing explanations and stories about the meaning of what is going on between them or what should be going on. Problems and difficulties in families are therefore seen as inevitable 'struggles over meaning' (Haley 1963, 1976a; Watzlawick *et al.* 1967, 1974). Meanings, like actions, can be seen as interactional and potentially as escalating, for example an interaction that involves a negative frame of 'blaming' can be seen to escalate to a dangerous degree so that a more positive frame is introduced to protect the group from collapsing into bitter dispute. In second-order cybernetics, problems therefore are seen not simply in terms of patterns of actions but as the patterns of attempts to give meanings to actions.

Though communication is a central feature of systems theory, the somewhat mechanistic models that characterized first-order cybernetics regarded communication as the flow of information as in engineering systems, rather than as the creation and exchange of meanings. Increasingly it became recognized that human communication was complex and involved potentially multiple interpretations of any given communication. People in families did not simply act on the basis of feedback but reflected on the meanings of each other's communications. Specifically, first-order cybernetics played down the importance of language.

One of the earliest and most significant attempts to consider how the process of mutual construction of meanings in communication occurs was the concept of *punctuation* in communicational exchanges. Watzlawick *et al.* (1967) suggested that the flow of communication and action in relationships is divided up into meaningful units or chunks. The term 'punctuation' was coined to describe how people develop a set of *self-fulfilling* perceptions or beliefs about their relationship which can interlock, like the pieces of a jigsaw puzzle, to produce repetitive patterns (Figure 2.1). The concept of punctuation introduces the idea

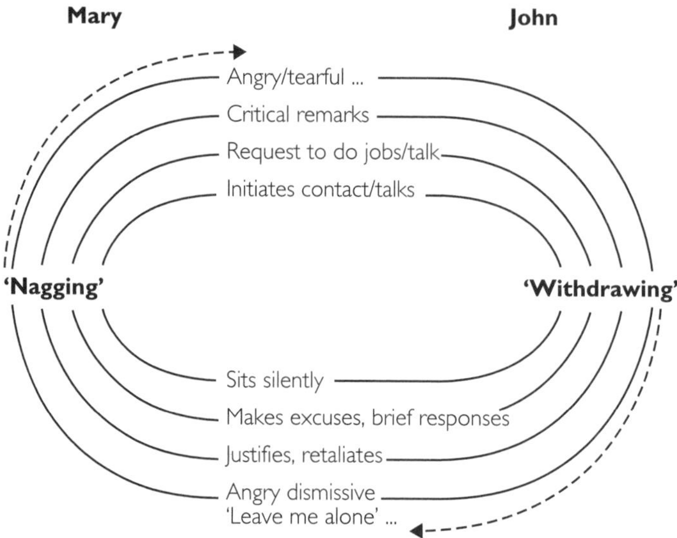

Figure 2.1 Punctuation

of systems as not simply mechanistic, but as governed by patterns of beliefs or constructs. Over time members of a family come to form predictions, not only of each other's actions, but also of each other's thoughts, beliefs and feelings. Since they spend considerable time together, share similar experiences and communicate continually with each other, they come to form a web of mutual anticipation. This serves not only to explain and predict each other's behaviour and thoughts, but also to construct and maintain them. Members of a family might be surprised if, for example, one of them expresses beliefs or shows emotions that they regard as unusual; these signs of surprise will serve to attenuate such deviations.

In second-order cybernetics personal choice becomes a central issue. Family life is seen to proceed on the basis of each person's beliefs or punctuations of events. However, a picture of individual members of families simply acting on the basis of their personal beliefs and intentions loses the important ideas of patterning and predictability that have been a feature of systemic thinking. A significant contribution to what can become a sterile debate about choice and freedom was the concept of punctuation, which suggests that though two or more members of a family may appear to be acting autonomously, their choices can become interwoven such that in fact they become caught in repetitive patterns of action. A relatively unexplored idea that follows from this is that choice in families can be seen to be *contingent*; what each person decides to do is shaped and constrained by what the others do and by what we think they will do. Specifically, each member may be involved in making conscious or semi-conscious calculations about the likely consequences of a possible line of action – whether it will produce a rebuke, admiration, agreement and so on. We will develop this idea of shared action in the next section.

The person as a private 'biosphere'

The cognitive biologists Humberto Maturana and Francisco Varela (Maturana 1978; Maturana and Varela 1980) developed the more extreme versions of constructivism which have characterized second-order cybernetics – namely that individuals and systems can only act or respond on the basis of their internal cognitive structure, their personal map of the world. They termed this 'structural determinism'. Likewise, Kelly (1955) and Bateson *et al.* (1956) had also suggested that each person possesses a unique epistemology, a way of making sense of or explaining the world. Maturana and Varela had in a sense suggested that people are largely informationally closed, that much if not most of the information and meanings available do not reach us in interactions because we are largely filtering material out according to our expectations.

Intention

The widely quoted phrase 'it is impossible not to communicate' emerged from the systems theory view of communication (Watzlawick *et al.* 1967: 193). However, this side-steps the important questions of intention, misunderstanding and unconscious communication. The frequent experience of communication is that we are trying to get a particular message across. We are probably all aware that sometimes we fail in our intention to communicate or that we 'give off' some message, such as lack of confidence, which we do not wish to, but nevertheless that we have some agreement of control over our communications.

It is perhaps possible that intentions may be attributed to us, for example when someone is intent on picking a fight by saying, 'What are you looking at?' A paranoid and aggressive expectation can conclude that a provocative message was being sent. To attribute some communication on the part of the 'victim' in this situation is tantamount to ascribing some blame to them, which is not too dissimilar to ascribing blame to any victim, essentially for being there.

Perhaps Watzlawick's axiom should be redefined slightly as 'it is difficult to engage in action or non-action which cannot potentially be interpreted as a communication'.

Beliefs and actions in triads

Second-order cybernetics offered a different view of some of the processes described in first-order cybernetics. For example, the concept of *conflict-detouring* or *triangulation* (Minuchin 1974; Haley 1976a) can be seen in terms of a movement between actions and meanings, and also in terms of a construction of individual experience.

The development of conflict detouring was seen to involve a form of learning by trial and error. A young child might experience the stress and tension between their parents and respond to the raised voices, banging of doors or violence by crying, losing their concentration on what they are doing and getting hurt, feeling sick and so on (Figure 2.2). One or other of these behaviours may be enough to capture the

Figure 2.2 Triangulation: parental conflict detouring through a child

parents' attention and distract them from their struggle to focus on the child. This temporarily produces a cessation of conflict between parents; following several repetitions of this process, the child's behaviour or symptoms can become programmed into the family dynamics and function to maintain the situation. This basic pattern can be constructed in a variety of ways and circumstances. The parents may not be in conflict with each other but may be stressed, tired or depressed due to pressures at work or from unemployment. The conflict can cut across generations, for example between a single mother and her mother or in-laws, between the parents and the child's school and so on. The child's symptoms can in a sense be seen as benevolent, for example offering a distraction for stressed parents from their own worries.

Triangulation also involves the construction of an agreement about the situation in a family. There is likely to be an agreement that the child is the main cause of the family's current concerns and difficulties. The construction of such an explanation is an example of a family 'myth' (Ferreira 1963; Pollner and Wikler 1985). This is in effect a falsification or distortion of reality since the child's problems can be seen as resulting from, not as causing the conflict.

The belief that the child is the source of the family's problems has resonances with psychoanalytic concepts in that the distortion can be seen to serve as an emotional defence. Once established, this myth can become increasingly painful to confront. For example, if the child's symptoms become severe the parents may feel extremely guilty and to blame by the implication that their conflicts have in a sense been the cause. However, this picture tends to minimize the child's role as merely responding to the conflicts. In reality, most young children at some stage discover the power that a symptom of illness confers, such as being able to avoid school or unpleasant duties, gain sympathy and attention and so on. Therefore a child may start to collude with this state of affairs and continue to display symptoms in part because of the apparent advantages he or she gains. This in turn can serve to confirm for the whole family (including the child) the belief or myth that he or she is the source of the problems.

There may be a variety of constructs to describe the child's problems but the net effect of these is that the parents are described as similar to each other, and different from the child, in not having or being the cause of the 'problem'. In reality, the situation is often more complex than this. The parents may disagree on how to treat the child (e.g. discipline or sympathy) and may shift positions, taking turns to side with the child. These shifting coalitions can be extremely confusing for a young child and have been implicated in causing or aggravating more severe problems, such as anorexia and schizophrenia (Palazzoli *et al.* 1978). Psychiatric and other agencies may also perpetuate conflicting views about such conditions, which families then come to internalize and act out in their internal dynamics.

Ecological perspective – multiple systems

Though it was a fundamental axiom of systems theory that any given system should always be seen as interlinked with others, this became a more central feature of second-order cybernetics. It became recognized that the very process of therapy involved an interaction between two systems – the family and the therapist. Over time these could be seen as a new third system – the therapist–family system. Rather than thinking that we could observe and analyse families in any detached and objective manner, it became increasingly clear that the therapist/observer inevitably perturbed or changed the family system by the very act of observing it. A therapist in effect came to be seen as partly seeing his or her own reflections or the ripples they had made in the new therapist–family system. Another therapist with the same family might see quite different things partly because they were having a different kind of effect on the family. Taken to its extreme, this suggested that there was no such thing as the real family dynamics, only our various perceptions of it.

Observing systems

The emphasis on subjective meanings in terms of the perceptions and punctuations of family members came to be encapsulated in the idea of observing systems. Not only was punctuation regarded as what was going on in families but as inevitable in therapy. As therapists our perceptions and explanations of a family were invariably seen as our own constructions and a punctuation of the process between the therapist and the family. This view gave additional emphasis to the importance of live supervision in family therapy. The therapist needed the supervision team to enable him or her to gain some ability to reflect on their joint dynamics. In turn, it was argued that the supervision team could also only offer their punctuation of the therapist–family system and attempts needed to be made to reflect on this in turn. Regular external consultation was therefore also seen as necessary to reflect on these various levels of interacting systems.

Practice

Hypothesizing

The concept of punctuation was incorporated by the Milan team (Palazzoli *et al.* 1978) into the idea of therapy as inevitably progressing through a process of hypothesizing. There could be no objective truth about a family, only our subjective perceptions as observers. The best we could achieve therefore was to formulate hypotheses (hunches) about what was going on, which could be more or less helpful in our ways of working. This view broadly encapsulates the pragmatic position of the Palo Alto MRI group in that communication needed to be considered in terms of not only what was intended to be communicated but also what its consequences were. Hence a hypothesis was to be judged in terms not of its ultimate truth or falseness but of how effective it was in facilitating some positive change.

Constructivist approaches have repeatedly drawn attention to the fact that family members may disagree, sometimes violently, about their explanations and narratives. These have been seen as essentially interpersonal disagreements or struggles over the punctuation of events. More recently this has been discussed in terms of the competing stories family members hold and which define previous and future events. The analysis of questions about the meaning of a problem or symptom is similar to the processes of deconstruction employed in the analysis of literature and the social sciences. Deconstruction involves taking constructs apart, analysing and tracing their historical origins, examining their inner logic, exploring their contradictions and inconsistencies, exploring the situations in which concepts are employed and considering what implications there are for action. When we engage in this process with families it is not unusual to find that the conflicts are not so much about disagreements as about different uses of a concept. Deconstruction can be employed as an activity that invites alternative meanings to be considered, which by opening up the definition of a concept can encourage or at least lay the groundwork for some mutually acceptable definitions to emerge.

Reframing

A key technique or orientation was that of reframing problems (previously mentioned in Chapter 1). Initially it was seen that therapists would offer new or different ways of seeing a problem as an intervention. Preferably this would be a second-order perspective, that is, a new view which completely changed the sense of a problem. For example, conflict in a couple could be discussed as showing a fiery passion and as something that could eventually make their relationship stronger.

Reframing involves offering some fundamentally different ways for a family to see their difficulties, enabling some patterns of actions or attempted solutions to emerge. A reframe requires some profoundly new ways of seeing the situation rather than relatively minor shifts:

> To reframe, then, means to change the conceptual and emotional setting or viewpoint in relation to which a situation is experienced and to place it in another frame which fits the 'facts' of the same concrete situation equally well or even better, and thereby changes its entire meaning.
>
> (Watzlawick *et al.* 1974: 95)

For example, Harry, a young boy aged 7, was referred with worries about his strange thoughts, nightmares, bizarre images and refusal to go to sleep at night on his own. There were some concerns that he might be displaying some form of childhood schizophrenia. His mother had recently started a training course and was spending more time away from home, possibly leading Harry to worry that the family was disintegrating. It also appeared that both parents had experienced nightmares when they were children and continued to be worried, especially the father, about any indications of unusual internal states.

As a reframe it was suggested that rather than seeing Harry as potentially ill, he could in fact be seen as a very imaginative and sensitive boy. He was also following in the parents' footsteps in being sensitive in this way. Furthermore, this sensitivity perhaps made him concerned about the changes that had occurred in the family and his thoughts symbolized these. Perhaps Harry also hoped that his symptoms might ensure that his parents stayed together in order to look after him, rather than fulfil his fears that they might be going their separate ways. The reframe of Harry as creative and sensitive rather than odd and ill was accepted by the family and they started to notice confirming views, for example when one of his teachers commented that she thought Harry was an imaginative boy.

Watzlawick *et al.* (1974: 123–4) offer an example of the impact of reframing even when the problems have become more acute:

> A twenty-five-year-old man who had been diagnosed as schizophrenic and had spent most of the past ten years in mental hospitals or intensive psychotherapy was brought into treatment by his mother, who thought that he was at the verge of another psychotic break. At the time he was managing to live a marginal existence in a rooming house, taking two college courses in which he was failing. He was manneristic in his behaviour and often 'politely' disruptive during sessions. As far as he was concerned, the problem was a long-standing disagreement between him and his parents about his financial support. He resented their paying his rent and other bills 'as if I were an infant'. He wanted his parents to give him an adequate monthly allowance, out of which he could take care of his obligations himself. His parents, on the other hand, felt that past history as well as his current demeanour indicated that he could not handle these responsibilities and would grossly mismanage the money. They, therefore, preferred to dole out the money on a week-to-week basis, with the amount apparently depending on how 'good' or how 'crazy' their son seemed at the time. This, however, was never clearly spelled out, just as the son never directly expressed his anger about this arrangement but retreated into a sort of psychotic clowning around which his parents took as further evidence that he was incapable of managing his own affairs. It also increased the mother's fear that yet another expensive hospitalization might soon be inevitable.
>
> In the presence of his mother it was pointed out to the son that since he felt outnumbered by his parents, he had every right to defend himself by threatening to cause a far greater expenditure by suffering another psychotic break. The therapist then made some concrete suggestions as to how the son should behave in order to give the impression of impending doom – these

suggestions being mostly reformulations of what the son was engaging in anyway.

This intervention reframed the son's 'crazy' behaviour as something over which he had control and which he could, therefore, use to his advantage, but the same reframing allowed his mother to see it as just that and be less intimidated by it. One of the results was that during their next quarrel the mother simply got angry with him; told him that she was tired of having to manage his affairs, acting as his chauffeur, etc.; and established an adequate allowance for him, with which he could sink or swim as far as she was concerned. In the follow-up interview, this arrangement turned out to be working well, so much so that the son had meanwhile managed to save enough of his allowance to buy a car, which made him less dependent on his mother.

Co-construction of shared histories

One specific example of an attempt to explore the construction of meanings over time and from different levels of influence is Pearce and Cronen's (1980) model. They proposed that the history of a relationship is seen to provide a context within which current actions are interpreted. So the attempts by one partner to be 'nice' may be distrusted if there has been a history of conflict. On the other hand, some unpleasant behaviour may be tolerated if the relationship is defined as 'good'. A problematic situation can occur when there is a fine balance between these definitions, that is, there has been considerable conflict but also some satisfaction. An ambiguity may occur so that a particular action, such as teasing, can be defined as vindictive if the negative aspects are focused on or, alternatively, seen as fun. However, a couple may also attempt to use the current action to define the relationship, for example, we are having fun so our relationship must be good. Each person may also define the present action and the relationship differently. People seem to refer to such states as 'not knowing where we're at' or 'being at a crossroads'. The higher levels of contexts – the family and cultural scripts – can help stabilize such reverberation, but for people who have had contradictory and ambiguous experiences in previous relationships and in their families (life scripts), the reverberation may continue to the higher levels, so that problems in their relationship may imply that the world cannot be trusted. Possibly this offers another way of explaining so called 'insecure' personalities and relationships.

An important contribution of Pearce and Cronen's (1980) model is that it starts to offer a way of integrating meanings created within relationships with wider societal beliefs, attitudes, norms and values.

People in relationships are seen as creating meanings with one eye on the meanings, definitions, expectations of relations prevalent in their local and wider societal context.

Commentary

Second-order cybernetics involved a shift towards embracing *constructivism,* a growing body of theory and research in psychology and other disciplines. At its strongest, constructivists argue that there is no objective reality or truth out there but instead we each see the world through our personal, subjective lenses (Watzlawick 1978). One version of this view emerged from cognitive biology (Maturana and Varela 1980). This resulted from research, particularly on the biology of perception, which consistently failed to be able to identify any straightforward correspondence between, for example, electrical and chemical responses in the retina to various inputs and the experience of perception. This led to the constructivist view that the brain was actively computing patterns internally but that these were not simply determined by external input. In effect the brain could not be 'instructed' by the external input what to experience but actively decided what to experience based on an internal model of the world that had been developed over time.

There had been several moves in the direction of constructivism evident in the development of cognitive psychology, which focused on the nature of internal computing processes involved in memory, perception, attention and learning. Earlier, Piaget (1955) had made major inroads into the study of how children actively learn to make sense of the world. For example, he argued that even our most basic experiences, such as the permanence of physical objects, is based upon a set of assumptions that develop for a child. Initially the world may appear extremely non-permanent since the same object can, for example, look totally different depending on whether we are seeing it from the front, sideways or from the back. To see physical objects requires complex inferences based upon our prior experience of the world.

Moral and political implications

Second-order cybernetics shares with some of the humanistic psychologies a somewhat unrealistic view of the potency of the individual and families. On the one hand there was generally little consideration of the influence of structural factors, such as poverty, unemployment and education, or of the ideological factors, such as the ways in which dominant culturally shared views shape family beliefs. For example, there was generally little recognition that men and women have been socialized into different ways of seeing themselves, their abilities, their emotions and their roles in relationships. Similarly, there was little elaboration of the influence of prevalent ideas about family life and roles, especially gender roles and ideas about parenting, childhood and so on. This lack of concern arguably turned some of the more apparently liberal aspects of second-order cybernetics into a potentially oppressive framework which by implication blamed families (or therapists) for not being able to change themselves. This criticism of course applies to much of psychology in the excessive emphasis that it has placed on the individual or, at best, on relationships while disconnecting them from the cultural context (Hollway 1989). This slippage away from a consideration of the ecological context is perhaps surprising considering that Bateson (1980) and other biologists (Maturana and Varela 1980) were also immersed in evolutionary metaphors which stress the interdependence of organisms and systems with their environment.

Second-order cybernetics challenged the visions of first-order cybernetics of what constituted a 'normal' or 'healthy' family (families in which symptoms functioned in order to preserve homeostasis were in essence regarded as pathological and in need of remedial intervention) and argued that it was the way family members saw their difficulties that in part resulted in problems. The problems did not have an objective existence as such, but by seeing their situation differently change could be produced. The goal of therapy shifted from attempts to remove symptoms as the first priority to encouraging more productive ways of seeing things.

A criticism of second-order cybernetics, especially the constructivist dictum that there is no reality but only our perceptions, is that it can lead to a therapeutic approach that plays fast and loose with truth. Since there is no reality, then, in effect we can invent anything and say anything in therapy as long as it works. However, we cannot even be conclusive about anything 'working' since this also involves adopting a position of truth which cannot be sustained. The best we can hope for is that family members tell us that they think things are better and we choose to accept this.

At its furthest extent, the extreme relativism of second-order cybernetics and constructivism leads us into some impossible dilemmas regarding problems such as physical violence, sexual abuse, emotional abuse and so on in families. Also a whole range of structural factors, such as poverty, racial and sexual discrimination are reduced to being seen simply as perceptions rather than real factors which shape and constrain people's experience. Do we end by saying that these do not really exist but we just have beliefs about their existence? There is a great danger in adopting a naively pluralistic and liberal political standpoint which ultimately condones the political status quo and patterns of inequality and oppression in society.

Power

Constructivist approaches and systems theory more broadly can give the impression that each member of a relationship has equal power to determine how relationships shall be defined, what meanings are given to particular actions. However, this may not be true. Children, for example, may be at the mercy of their parents in forming a view of themselves and important events in the world. The power of parents may not be total in this but nevertheless it can be very naive and oppressive to children not to be aware of the ways that their perceptions and beliefs may be 'programmed' for them. Likewise, the more powerful person in a relationship may be better able to impose his or her views, perhaps in subtle ways through the use of their prestige, educational status, greater experience of the world and so on. Moreover, as we will see in the next chapter, power to define the relationships in ways that privilege one partner is also partly conferred by virtue of our location in society. For example, societally shared views about gender roles, children, race and so on can be enlisted to define the relationship. One powerful tactic, for example, is for one partner to make reference to what is 'normal' and expected.

Milan approaches

The style of the Milan team was extremely elegant, complex and has continually evolved. Our inclusion of it here as a strategic approach perhaps is representative of its early appearance in the field.

A team of therapists in Milan dramatically adapted strategic approaches, particularly in terms of paying much greater attention to the underlying beliefs held by family members. Arguably the approach that was developed is distinct in many ways and should be considered separately. We suggest that originally it shared the most fundamental premise of strategic approaches which is that therapists act tactically towards families. They do not share their analysis of the problems nor volunteer their therapeutic orientations or plans.

We have suggested that both structural and strategic approaches described so far are based on a systemic model in emphasizing how symptoms in one or more members need to be seen as arising from and maintained by the patterns of actions of the members of a family. However, the Milan group utilized one of the purest forms of a systemic approach. Most importantly, they suggested that it was conceptually wrong and therapeutically futile to allocate any sense of blame for the actions of the non-symptomatic members of the family. They argued that a systemic view fundamentally regards the actions of all of the family members not as negative, but as the best that they can do. Another way of seeing this is that the intentions may be positive even if the outcomes are not. A key to this approach was that they developed a strong interest in the underlying premises and beliefs that guided families' actions. Rather than seeing these as merely relevant but in some ways peripheral to therapy, the underlying beliefs or premises held were seen to be of central importance:

> Our interest moved from symptoms and behavioural patterns to epistemological premises and systems of meaning and from the present to a time framework that included past, present and future. The therapist's job became that of creating a context for deutero-learning (i.e. learning to learn) in which the client could find his own solutions.
>
> (Boscolo and Bertrando 1996: 10)

Positive connotation

This technique, which shares features of reframing, was developed to encourage the therapist to view and subsequently reflect back to the families a positive reason for all of their actions. As such it was a fundamental adjunct to paradoxical directives. Rather than simply offering a directive to a family to maintain or even increase a symptom, such a suggestion was supported by providing a rationale for why each and every member was acting in the way they were. This neutral, non-judgemental position also placed the actions of all of the family members on an equal footing and militated against the tendency to see members as victims or victimizers. The positive connotation might commence with a global statement, such as 'All the observable behaviours of the group as a whole appeared to be inspired by the common goal of preserving the cohesion of the family group' (Palazzoli *et al.* 1978: 56). Subsequently there would be an elaboration in terms of the roles each of the family members was playing in ensuring this cohesion.

For example, Mr Bailey, now in his fifties, had been repeatedly hospitalized for a form of depressive illness. The dominant family story about this was that his problems resulted from having experienced shell-shock in the Second World War. The family consisted of Mr Bailey and his wife, two adult daughters (Kathy and Pat) who had recently left home but visited to see their mother every day, and the youngest child, also adult but who was still living at home (he refused to attend any of the sessions). In therapy they complained of interminable bickering – a 'family at war' – and mainly put this down to Mr Bailey's problems and awkward personality. The story of the home situation was that Mr Bailey was excluded from all aspects of family life and was regarded with some contempt, especially since his wife was the bread-winner. This exclusion was confirmed in the session with the women, especially the daughters making faces and laughing when Mr Bailey talked, which was usually in a characteristically rather forceful and emotive manner.

A positive connotation was introduced through a discussion of the roles that the various members of the family played:

Therapist: Can you tell me about the roles that people play in the family? Who is the artistic one? Who is the scientific one? Who makes the decisions? Who gets most upset? Who has the worst temper?

Mr Bailey Well, Kathy is the intelligent one, with her qualifications and everything.

Mrs Bailey: And Pat is the artistic one.

Kathy: I think Dad has the worst temper, but I'm a bit like him.

Mr Bailey: Mum makes the decisions.

Therapist: So, who is the peacekeeper?

Mr Bailey: Well, there isn't one. That's why we are here . . . We are like a boat with a hole in it that's sinking.

Therapist: But someone must be putting their finger in the hole. Otherwise it would have sunk . . . I wonder whether Mr Bailey puts his finger in the hole sometimes?

Mrs Bailey: Perhaps tries to keep the peace in his own way?

Pat: Well I'm more confused than ever now. I always thought Dad was the reason we had all the problems.

Therapist: Well, the boat would have sunk by now if no one had put their finger in the hole, but you've been together a long time. I think that you are trying your best to keep the boat afloat in your own ways.

Key texts

Andolfi, M. (1979) *Family Therapy: An Interactional Approach*. New York: Plenum.

Bateson, G. (1979) *Mind and Nature: A Necessary Unity*. New York: E.P. Dutton.

Bowen, M. (1978) *Family Therapy in Clinical Practice*. New York: Jason Aronson.

Campbell, D. and Draper, R. (eds) (1985) *Applications of Systemic Family Therapy*. London: Academic Press.

Carter, E.A. and McGoldrick, M. (eds) (1980) *The Family Life Cycle: A Framework for Family Therapy*. New York: Gardner Press.

de Shazer, S. (1985) *Keys to Solution in Brief Therapy*. New York: W.W. Norton.

Dell, P.F. (1982) Beyond homeostasis: toward a concept of coherence. *Family Process*, 21: 21–42.

Fisch, R., Weakland, J. and Segal, L. (1982) *The Tactics of Change: Doing Therapy Briefly*. San Francisco, CA: Jossey-Bass.

Gilligan, C. (1982) *In a Different Voice: Psychological Theory and Women's Development*. Cambridge, MA: Harvard University Press.

Haley, J. (1979) *Leaving Home: Therapy of Disturbed Young People*. New York: McGraw-Hill.

Haley, J. (1984) *Ordeal Therapy: Unusual Ways to Change Behavior*. San Francisco, CA: Jossey-Bass.

Hare-Mustin, R.T. (1978) A feminist approach to family therapy. *Family Process*, 17: 181–94.

Hoffman, L. (1981) *Foundations of Family Therapy*. New York: Basic Books.

Keeney, B. (1983) *Aesthetics of Change*. New York: Guilford Press.

Keeney, B.P. and Ross, J. (1985) *Mind in Therapy*. New York: Basic Books.

Keeney, B.P. and Sprenkle, D.H. (1982) Ecosystemic epistemology: critical implications for the aesthetics and pragmatics of family therapy. *Family Process*, 21: 1–19.

MacKinnon, L.K. (1983) Contrasting strategic and Milan therapies. *Family Process*, 22: 425–40.

Madanes, C. (1981) *Strategic Family Therapy*. San Francisco, CA: Jossey-Bass.

Maturana, H. and Varela, F.J. (1980) *Autopoiesis and Cognition: The Realization of the Living*. Dordrecht: D. Reidel.

Minuchin, S. (1984) *Family Kaleidoscope*. Cambridge, MA: Harvard University Press.

Minuchin, S., Rosman, B. and Baker, L. (1978) *Psychosomatic Families: Anorexia Nervosa in Context*. Cambridge, MA: Harvard University Press.

Napier, A.Y. and Whitaker, C.A. (1978) *The Family Crucible*. New York: Harper & Row.

Palazzoli, M.S. (1974) *Self-Starvation*. New York: Jason Aronson.

Palazzoli, M.S., Cecchin, G., Prata, G. and Boscolo, L. (1978) *Paradox and Counter Paradox: A New Model in the Therapy of the Family in Schizophrenic Transaction*. New York: Jason Aronson.

Palazzoli, M.S., Boscolo, L., Cecchin, G. and Prata, G. (1980) Hypothesizing–circularity–neutrality: three guidelines for the conductor of the session. *Family Process*, 19: 3–12.

Pirrotta, S. (1984) Milan revisited: a comparison of the two Milan schools. *Journal of Strategic and Systemic Therapies*, 3: 3–15.

Satir, V.M. (1988) *New Peoplemaking*. Palo Alto, CA: Science and Behavior Books.

Varela, F.J. (1979) *Principles of Biological Autonomy*. New York: Elsevier North-Holland.

von Foerster, H. (1981) *Observing Systems*. Seaside, CA: Intersystems Publications.

Walrond-Skinner, S. (1976) *Family Therapy: The Treatment of Natural Systems*. London: Routledge & Kegan Paul.

Watzlawick, P. (1978) *The Language of Change*. New York: Basic Books.

Watzlawick, P., Weakland, J.H. and Fisch, R. (1974) *Change: Principles of Problem Formation and Problem Resolution*. New York: W.W. Norton.

SKILL GUIDES

As with the skill guides offered in Chapter 1, the following have been selected to offer a flavour of the nature of therapeutic techniques and approaches evolving from this phase. In addition, the approaches chosen in our view continue to be extensively employed by many therapists and adapted to fit contemporary orientations.

Teamwork

Background

With the publication in English in 1978 of *Paradox and Counter Paradox* by Palazzoli *et al.* in which the ritual five-part session was described, teamwork assumed greater importance in the field. The key element of teamwork is the synergy developing from team members sharing ideas, based on feedback. This process requires a certain rigour and individual willingness to give up one's beloved ideas (for hypotheses or interventions) and contribute instead to letting new ideas emerge in team discussion.

Usefulness and relevance

Teamwork could be said to embody second-order cybernetic and co-constructionist practices and thus is an important skill, not least because it demonstrates a congruence between theory and practice. For individual practitioners and therapists, good teamwork provides uniquely creative and supportive experiences with colleagues, in addition to promoting good practice.

Exercise: the sequential discussion

This exercise was designed to develop the rigour required for good teamwork and to encourage co-working rather than individualism.

1 In a group (say four to eight persons) a topic is chosen for discussion in sequence. Group members do not have to speak in any order (e.g. in turn, clockwise or anticlockwise) but the group must

ensure everyone has a turn to express an opinion or ask a question in round one, before the group moves on to a second round of discussion.

2 Whenever a group member speaks they must first comment on what the previous person has said and then add only one new idea of their own to the discussion.
3 Each group member's comment should be brief and allow the discussion to go round the group four or five times.
4 Group members are encouraged to offer their ideas to the group and let the discussion develop through the group's process rather than through individual group members developing their own ideas.
5 After 10 minutes, the discussion ends and group members spend 5 minutes or more reflecting on the experience.

Further reading

Andersen, T. (1987) The reflecting team: dialogue and meta-dialogue in clinical work. *Family Process*, 26: 415–28.

Cade, B.W., Speed, B. and Seligman, P. (1986) *Working in Teams: The Pros and Cons*. London: Hawthorn Press.

Selvini, M., Selvini, B. and Palozzoli, M. (1991) Team consultation: an indispensable tool for the progress of knowledge. *Journal of Family Therapy*, 13: 31–52.

Hypothesizing

Background

While it is our view that we all hypothesize consciously or unconsciously as we make therapeutic decisions about how to intervene, we recognize that the work of the Milan associates from the mid-1970s onwards introduced a more explicit hypothesis-making activity to the field of systemic practice.

Usefulness and relevance

The Milan associates carefully distinguished between the use of hypothesis in the scientific sense or a hypothesis to be proved (a self-fulfilling prophesy) and hypothesizing in the context of systemic therapy, which was a way of organizing information and feedback to provide a guide for the therapist's activity in conducting an interview. Because a hypothesis can be more or less useful and not true or false, a hypothesis allows the therapist to hold on to a view of the family's behaviour that is different from the family's and thus potentially challenging and useful to family members looking for change.

Exercise

In order for practitioners to learn the art of generating and appreciating the usefulness of many possible diverse hypotheses (or possible meanings for problem behaviour) the following exercise introduces some ritual and rigour to the process of hypothesis making.

Participants are asked in respect of a family/client problem to complete the sentence:

A I have a hunch that ______________________________
(Inserted here are one or more of the practitioner's ideas for explaining the presence of problem/symptoms.)

Then participants are asked to complete sentence B:

B And therefore I am interested in finding out more about__________
(Inserted here are several possible avenues of inquiry the practitioner can think of which must be different from what is stated in A.)

We give below an example regarding Johnny, a school-refusing 12-year-old boy:

A *I have a hunch that* Johnny does not go to school because he worries about his mother being alone and lonely at home without him.

B *And therefore I am interested in finding out more about*

1. how much time Johnny's mother and father normally spend relaxing together;
2. what the family patterns are for achieving independence;
3. what interests Johnny's mother has in her life apart from childrearing;
4. how Johnny's father and mother negotiated independence from and with their parents;
5. what kind of relationships Johnny has at school with his peers and what out-of-school friendships he has.

These five possible areas of exploration demonstrate the possible richness of disciplined inquiry based on hypotheses providing a focus but not seen as a foregone conclusion.

Positive connotation

Background

Positive connotation is a therapeutic device most usually associated with the Milan associates and originally designed to provide a 'logic' for symptomatic behaviour that would be consistent with therapists' declared recognition of the value for all family members of the status quo and which included the symptomatic behaviour. According to Palazzoli *et al.* (1978: 86),

> it thus became clear that access to the systemic model was possible only if we were to make a positive connotation of both the symptom of the identified patient and the symptomatic behaviours of the others, saying, for example, that all the observable behaviours of the group as a whole appeared to be inspired by the common goal of preserving the cohesion of the family group.

Usefulness and relevance

This is an important skill for therapists wishing to successfully join with families as it enables an appreciation of the way symptoms can fulfil a stabilizing function (however temporary) for families to be shared. Recognition and appreciation of the usefulness of symptoms is the first step towards dissolving a symptom. As a development of reframing, positive connotation requires the therapist to explicitly appreciate the logic and noble intentions of family members' behaviour, thus reducing the family members' need to resist the therapist's attempts to offer the family alternative meanings. It is widely recognized that nobody ever changes under a negative connotation.

Understanding how to positively connote family situations and relationships is indispensable when attempting to prescribe the symptomatic behaviour and/or offer families a paradoxical intervention. It can be said that positively connotating symptomatic behaviour is a paradoxical intervention in action.

Exercise

Each step is to take no more than 5 minutes.

1 In trios, practitioners A, B and C take it in turns to describe a client family situation in which they find themselves frustrated and feeling negative towards family members.
2 A then listens, while B and C discuss what might be ways to begin to appreciate how family members are attempting to care for one another by certain behaviours; B and C may also choose to speak as if they were family members.
3 A then attempts to describe how she or he is developing an appreciation of the logic of the family behaviours and to make a positive connotation of the symptomatic behaviour.

Further reading

Burnham, J. (1986) *Family Therapy: First Steps towards a Systematic Approach*. London: Routledge.
Hoffman, L. (1981) *Foundations of Family Therapy*. New York: Basic Books.
O'Brian, C. and Bruggen, P. (1985) Our personal and professional lives. Learning positive connotation and circular questioning. *Family Process*, 24: 311–22.

Circular questioning

Background

Asking questions in this way radically changes the process of therapy. Circular questioning is an original feature of the Milan associates' systemic model, which enables therapists to become genuine inquirers and to ask questions of family members on the basis of feedback to the information solicited about family relationships and therefore about difference and change. The differences asked about are various family members' perceptions and beliefs about the meaning of events, relationships, etc.

Usefulness and relevance

To be a genuine inquirer and not to 'know' but to believe the conversation developed using circular questioning, thus illuminating distressing situations and leading family members to see new options and possibilities is a valuable skill for therapists. The style of interviewing can have the effect of empowering family members and therapists alike.

Exercise

Participants are asked to work in trios (A, B and C).

A chooses a neutral topic to be questioned about, for example weather, holidays, food, travel. B asks questions based on feedback and attempts to establish the relationship between A's beliefs and behaviour on the topic as well as to map a system of significant relationships around the topic and the effect these all have in A's life.

After 10 minutes, B and C discuss, with A listening, a focus for the second half of the interview which C then conducts while B observes.

At the end of the second 10-minute interview, A is invited to share any ways in which his or her beliefs have altered, been challenged or become more certain.

Each member of the trio (A, B, C) has the opportunity to observe, be interviewed and interview. There can then be a discussion about the experiences in each of the different positions.

Further reading

Cecchin, G. (1987) Hypothesising, circularity and neutrality revisited: an invitation to curiosity. *Family Process*, 26: 405–14.

Palazzoli, M.S., Boscolo, L., Cecchin, G. and Prata, G. (1980) Hypothesizing–circularity–neutrality: three guidelines for the conductor of the session. *Family Process*, 19: 3–12.

Penn, P. (1982) Circular questioning. *Family Process*, 21: 267–80.

Tomm, K. (1985) Circular interviewing: a multifaceted clinical tool, in D. Campbell and R. Draper (eds) *Applications of Systemic Family Therapy*. London: Academic Press.

Transformational change

Background

Throughout the 1970s and 1980s there was debate about so-called first- and second-order change and how changing the 'rules' that governed family members' behaviour was the transformational change sought by systemic therapists for their clients and not merely a change due to the relief or the catharsis of being listened to by a sympathetic professional person. Examples in everyday life of transformational change are learning to walk, swim, drive or fly; after such experiences, the world for the toddler, swimmer, driver or pilot will never look the same again. Thus we say with clients the 'rules' of behaviour have changed.

Usefulness and relevance

Without an understanding of transformational change, practitioners are not able to identify when family 'rules' do change or recognize when something changes in a family but the 'rules' remain the same and thus relationships too stay the same, leaving a family vulnerable to symptoms returning or new symptoms developing.

Exercise

Participants are asked to bring a pear to a class and are invited, one by one, to describe their experience of selecting and bringing the pear to the group and any other thoughts and feelings they care to share. Invariably someone in the group says, 'After this pears will never be the same again'.

The group leader, having heard the group's pear stories, invites the group to hear about a different kind of *PAIR* (Practice, Application, Ideas, Reflection and Reflexivity) as he or she talks to the group about the elements of learning and change in their professional development. The elements of the PAIR in this case represent elements in teaching the learning processes, and the group leader changed the rules, that is, spelling in order to illustrate the importance of transformational change.

Further reading

Watzlawick, P., Weakland, J.H. and Fisch, R. (1974) *Change: Principles of Problem Formation and Problem Resolution*. New York: W.W. Norton.

3 The third phase – mid-1980s to 2000

I sometimes think that 99 per cent of the suffering that comes in through the door has to do with how devalued people feel by the labels that have been applied to them or the derogatory opinions they hold about themselves.

(Hoffman 1993: 79)

Cultural landscape

The shift from the first to the second phase of systemic therapy saw a movement from an emphasis on pattern and process to an emphasis on beliefs and personal meanings. Importantly, there was also a move towards seeing the therapist as necessarily influenced by his or her own beliefs and prejudices. In the third phase there is a growing awareness of the social and cultural contexts that shape both families' and therapists' beliefs. The seeds for this movement had been germinating especially in the work of therapists inspired by feminist perspectives and more broadly in the emerging social constructionist theories. These were articulated, for example, in the USA by Ken Gergen, Lynn Hoffman and others, in France by Michael Foucault and in Australia by Michael White. Outside family therapy the roots of social constructionism lay in attempts to explain the phenomena of prejudice, racism, gender stereotypes and sexualities. Inspired by feminism in the USA, there was an increasing sensitivity to and interest in the way language contained the heritage of ideas and assumptions of any given culture, for example in the hitherto unquestioned usage of terms such as 'housewife', 'chairman', 'primitive culture', 'neurotic' and 'mentally ill'. The accumulation of critiques of family therapy led to a realization that family life, including the development of 'problems', was fundamentally shaped by language. Just as feminism had raised awareness of the nature of sexist conversation in the workplace and in education, similarly awareness increased of the power of conversations in families to create experience.

The development of this third phase has come from both inside family therapy from observations of therapists in the USA, UK and Australia in particular and also from outside family therapy in the tide of social constructionism and its powerful impact on the social sciences. Possibly the development has been most apparent in countries, such as the USA, UK, Scandinavia and Australia, where there has been a strong feminist movement. In France, though the writing of Foucault has been important and widely recognized, the context is more exclusively linked to Marxist and existentialist theory than to feminism and family therapy.

Theoretical perspectives

The third phase of systemic family therapy represents a move towards social constructionist theory. In fact some have argued (White and Epston 1990; Hoffman 1993) that what is involved here is not just a development but the end of systemic theory and therapy! We will first outline social constructionist ideas and suggest that, as is often the case, the cult of 'disposability of ideas' – a 'social amnesia' for the relevance and continuity of ideas (Jacoby 1975) – is mistaken and unhelpful.

Social constructionism proposes that commonly seen patterns of actions in families are not just produced by the idiosyncratic dynamics of each family but necessitated by the demands of the wider society that a family is located within. Frequently observed patterns, such as that of the 'over-involved' mother and 'disengaged' father, need to be understood more broadly as being determined by the wider societal structures and ideologies which shape family life, especially the relations between men and women:

> The pattern of family behaviour so frequently encountered by family therapists, that of the 'over-involved' wife/mother and disengaged and absent husband/father, suddenly appears in a new light: as a necessary form. That necessity derives from its ability to reproduce the personality characteristics, relationship patterns and behavioural orientations that are functional for continual operation of the contemporary social formation.
>
> (James and McIntyre 1983: 126)

Despite social changes, women are still more likely than men to carry the burden of care for children and to be more centred around the home. This is not simply a personal choice but one shaped by a variety of economic and practical necessities dictated by the society they live within. However, associated with any given society are a web of discourses or ideologies, such as that women are 'naturally maternal' since they are seen to be more emotionally responsive, nurturing, non-competitive and so on. In this way a set of roles and beliefs about family life are reproduced across the generations.

General systems theory does not take account of the wider societal factors that shape the patterns of interactions observed by family therapists, and this has been seen by some as a major indictment and testimony of its failure (James and McIntyre 1983; Williams and Watson 1988). However, it has been suggested in contrast that in fact second-order cybernetics can be utilized to take such factors into account:

> The second-order cybernetic view argues, in a manner similar to that of the feminist critics, that it is the observer (or therapist) who draws distinctions that 'create the reality' . . . By including the observer as part of the system observed, second-order cybernetics acknowledges that the system considered relevant is a construction of the observer drawing the distinctions . . . Drawing distinctions is thus not only an epistemological act, it is a political act.
>
> (McKinnon and Miller 1987: 148)

As therapists become increasingly aware that the 'reality' they observe is a construction, they may also become aware that their perceptions are shaped by their culture. However, though seemingly obvious, this step to a cultural awareness was, as McKinnon and Miller argue, not an inevitable one. Instead, many therapists became distracted by an emphasis on subjectivity – that what was seen was part of their personal baggage. One of the contributions of social constructionism has been to draw attention to the fact that such subjectivity can only be partial since even the words we employ in our 'private' internal conversations are soaked in the legacy of meanings of our cultural contexts.

A variety of societal influences may shape people's experiences in families, including institutionalized structures and practices. Adequacy of housing, income, type of locality, and educational opportunities are determined by the family's position in the socio-economic pecking order. Dominant shared beliefs or ideologies define expectations, ideas of identity, gender and other family roles, and a system of perceived rights and obligations. These beliefs may shape not only the practical, more obvious aspects of life but even the most intimate, supposedly 'private' moments, such as expressions of sexual intimacy and moments of family sorrow and joy. Even in our moments of solitude our private internal reflections consist of verbal dialogues and images which are imported from our cultures. For example, the words and phrases that we use in speaking with our self connect us to our immediate and historical cultural legacy of ideas and meanings. Feminist analyses have been particularly helpful in drawing attention to how language itself contains and perpetuates a variety of assumptions, directs our attention and may perpetuate ways of thinking which support inequalities, for example in terms like housewife, 'good' mother and single-parent.

The production of dominant systems of ideas and meanings – ideologies – is regarded in social constructionism as shaped and maintained according to distributions of power. As a telling example, people of the lowest socio-economic groups and ethnic minorities generally have poorer physical and mental health: put simply, they die younger and appear to have generally more tormented lives. However, until recently it has not been acknowledged that these differences are due to basic inequalities in our society but due to 'poor health habits', 'fecklessness' and so on. The crushing effects of poverty and stress have been frequently minimized in terms which extol the virtues of personal autonomy and choice. Such conceptualizations can be regarded as systems of knowledge or ideologies which serve to disguise or justify the privileges of the most powerful groups. In short, the dominant classes have privileged access to a variety of means, education, the media, commerce and industry to promote systems of thought which maintain their superior opportunities and position: 'The ideas of the ruling class are, in every age, the ruling ideas . . . the class which has the means of material production has the means of mental production, so that in consequence the ideas of those who lack the means of mental production are, in general, subject to it' (Marx and Engels 1970: 35).

Foucault (1975) has been highly influential in pointing out that in any given culture there can be seen to be dominant narratives or discourses. In the early days of psychotherapy, for example, the dominant narrative had been that problems were due to individual factors or disorder. With the advent of interactional approaches the dominant narrative has moved, to some extent, to a view that problems are due to a variety of transactional processes within the family. Though family therapies have argued for a 'neutral' approach, a systemic approach has been seen more critically from the outside, for example by parents' rights groups, as accusative, blaming and implying that family dysfunctions cause the pathology.

Connections and links to the second and first phases of systemic family therapy

Social constructionism contains a number of premises which can be seen to be closely related to systemic ideas. These include an emphasis on context and interpersonal processes in creating joint actions and mutually constructed meanings, strategic interaction, an acknowledgement of the importance of power and on the exchange of ideas or feedback. Social constructionism argues that meanings are jointly created through the dynamic processes of conversations. Rather than focusing on individual characteristics or traits, the focus is on how individual experience is fundamentally social and interpersonal. Individual identity and the self are not seen as stable or monolithic, rather identity is seen as fragmented and distributed across social contexts. For example, a child may act and feel like a different person according to whether he is with his parents, siblings, mother or father, the therapist, at school and so on. We are shaped by the interactions across different contexts in which we are involved.

These interactions are seen to be recursively shaped by the use of language which is regarded as active and *strategic*. People are seen as continually employing 'rhetorical devices' in the use of language to achieve particular ends and goals – to persuade, accuse, justify, solicit sympathy or admiration, seduce and so on. A variety of linguistic strategies are seen to be employed to achieve these ends, such as humour, presenting arguments *in extremis*, emphasizing one's honourable intentions, use of metaphor and reference to stereotypes (Potter and Wetherell 1987). In effect this emphasizes that we are all strategic interactants and that therapy therefore needs to be able to take this into account. This connects with the emphasis of strategic therapies that recognize the need to consider the therapist–family encounter as inevitably a strategic one (Haley 1963, 1976a). Related to this is an emphasis on power. Social constructionism emphasizes that interactions are invariably connected to power and that language use defines power, for example by our sophistication with language, our accents, our access to specialist knowledges inherent in different languages, such as specialist scientific and medical languages.

Importantly, social constructionism also emphasizes that meanings and identities in interactions are dynamic and prone to escalations. For example, in a family there can be an escalating process or polarization whereby people are ascribed increasingly divergent meanings and identities. Typically this may mean that one person is increasingly assigned to an identity as the 'ill' member, in contrast to the others who are 'well'. These processes of polarization can be seen similarly in systemic terms, such as escalation and feedback. In social constructionism conversations can also be seen as proceeding on the basis of mutual influence or feedback. An important difference is that, unlike the early systems theories, this feedback is not described in terms of 'information' but as an exchange of meanings. However, the emphasis on meanings was evident in Bateson's (1972) writing, rather than the more mechanistic analogy of families as simply exchanging information which gained some ascendancy in the first cybernetics. However, the emphasis on meanings with the greater possibility of transformation of systems through, for example, 'reframing' was central to second-order cybernetics.

Both systemic theory and social constructionism also emphasize the importance of contexts and how these are internalized into the dynamic of family interactions. Perhaps systemic theory has until recently paid less attention to the wider social and cultural contexts, though the importance of the wider social contexts and family dynamics has been explored, for example by feminist systemic therapists who have developed detailed analysis of the links between subjective experience in families and dominant cultural discourses and structures (Goldner 1991; Hare-Mustin 1991). Goldner (1991) convincingly described how patterns of abuse and violence in couples' relationships embodied a range of cultural expectations about gender roles and male and female identities which helped to construct and legitimize patterns of abuse. Similarly, an analysis of child abuse revealed the operation of pernicious patriarchal assumptions, including expectations of men's right to dominate in families and to employ violence to ensure compliance.

In summary, there can be seen to be much in the way of links between social constructionist and systemic perspectives which invite us to consider the potential of viewing social constructionism as offering some ideas which extend but also connect with systemic theory.

Influential people and ideas

Social constructionism has a lengthy and extended history in the social sciences. It is based in sociology but overlaps with social psychology in its interest in interaction and the study of group (e.g. family) processes. Rather than adopting a broad or macro level of analysis as sociological theories had predominantly been interested in, social constructionism was interested in developing theories about the links between individual experience and society. Perhaps one of the most vivid metaphors used was that of the 'looking-glass self'. Mead (1934) and Cooley (1922) proposed that our identities, our sense of self, were constructed from the social interactions that we take part in. In these interactions others act like a mirror in presenting us with images of our self. People are seen as fundamentally social: without others to interact with we cannot have a self. The myriad of reflections over time serve to build up some consistent or enduring sense of who we are, an identity. Others, especially parents at first, also initiate us into the common values, beliefs, expectations of our culture. We gain not just a sense of a specific

Key people, places and events (bird's-eye view)

An influential view in this phase is seeing families as 'problem-determined' systems (**Anderson** and **Goolishian** 1988). This means that it is not the dynamics which cause the problems but more that the problem-saturated ways of talking about difficulties can produce problems. Conversations which focus on families' experiences as evidence of illness, inadequacy, blame and failure keep them locked into narrow ways of seeing their actions and experiences and produce and maintain pathology. Though family conversations are seen as key to this process, blame is not ascribed to families. Instead, it is suggested that these conversations are shaped by the built-in assumptions inherent in the language that they have available to discuss their relationships.

It is acknowledged in the third phase that there is a pernicious influence of factors outside the family's control so a more neutral view of problems follows. In effect, pathology is seen as inevitable, for example, where ethnic minorities experience racial abuse and discrimination, or where women are confined to drudgery, or where poverty and deprivation are seen to strip people of their self-respect and foster a sense of hopelessness. Families are viewed as a microcosm which reproduces rather than causes these difficulties.

The 'problem-determined' system (Anderson and Goolishian 1988), *The Reflecting Team* (**Andersen** 1990), the work of **Michael White** and **David Epston** with narrative therapy and the Just Therapy Group provide a framework for understanding developments in theory and practice during this third phase. The importance of the 'self of the therapist' also becomes a dominant theme. The debate between intrapsychic and interpersonal approaches then focuses more on integration and a 'both and' perspective rather than on 'either or' as previously.

The social constructionist perspective brings into focus a number of questions:

1. Are disagreements in relationships fundamentally interpersonal or related to wider conflicts and contradictions within and between competing societally shared beliefs or discourses?
2. Is it possible that some narratives, by virtue of being different from the dominant societally shared ones, are seen as deviant and are marginalized, excluded or punished?
3. To what extent do family members create their own narratives or predominantly draw from and adapt narratives from a societally shared pool?
4. Do some of the distortions or fabrications occur because of attempts to contort personal experiences into common socially acceptable ones?

self which would reverberate with every new interaction but a more general sense of self in terms of how we compare with images of what it is, for example, to be a man or a woman, a teenager, black or white, a brother or a sister, a mother or a father.

> Social constructionism presents [family therapy] with a range of new distinctions . . . [it] turns to . . . the intersubjective influence of language and culture . . . it references knowledge neither in the observer nor the observed, but rather in the place between the two, in the social arena among interpreting subjects.
>
> (Pare 1995: 221)

Social constructionist approaches overlap with but also differ from the constructivist approaches outlined in the previous chapter in proposing that the beliefs held by family members are not simply personal or familial. Instead, it is argued that people in families absorb the beliefs or discourses which are common to the particular culture within which they exist. In particular, these common beliefs are seen to be embedded in the common currency of language. Rather than seeing language as relatively passive and as used to describe the world and family experiences, language instead is seen as involved in creating this world. Language is seen to constitute social experience, and the way that people speak about events constructs them. Furthermore, it is suggested that it is not simply the way families communicate that is central but that language contains with it, often implicitly, the 'history of ideas' of our culture. To take some simple examples, the terms available to describe family roles carry implications about who performs them, such as mothering. Terms such as neurotic and hysterical have been predominantly applied to women and shape their personalities and family roles. Even more broadly, Palazzoli *et al.* (1978) have pointed to the dearth of language available to describe interpersonal as opposed to personal processes. Language habits also draw us into particular ways of making sense of events; for example, saying that someone 'is angry' rather than that they may be 'showing' anger. Frequently we are not even aware of how these linguistic conventions implicitly lead us to particular ways of explaining events. Most obviously this leads to the tendency to define problems in personal rather than interpersonal terms. Accompanying this is also the danger that we ignore these wider cultural assumptions contained in language and other forms of symbolic representations.

However, just as second-order cybernetics represents a significant shift in the field, the third phase, characterized by social constructionism, does not represent a complete rejection of the influence of general systems theory or constructivism on systemic and family therapy practice. Social constructionism is, after all, fundamentally an interactional, interpersonal model. The second-order cybernetics view is that problems arise from the personal, idiosyncratic perceptions and beliefs held by family members.

Constructivist approaches have been invaluable in highlighting how the beliefs that family members hold serve to shape their actions, choices and attempted solutions to what are perceived to be the problems. They also add an important dynamic component in stressing how disagreements between members of families are often at the root of relationship struggles and failed patterns of attempted solutions to problems. Also, the idea of preferred views is helpful in revealing how the struggles over meanings can be seen in terms of attempts to remain true to a positive, desired narrative about one's life, or a narrative in which the self is located in a positive valuable role. However, these preferred views can be seen as not simply personal preferences but as shaped by shared societal values, norms and ideologies.

Arguably the foundations of social constructionism and the feminist influences in family therapy can be traced to the influence of Marxist theory, in particular the proposition that dominant groups in society have the power to produce and sustain dominant beliefs or ideologies. The dominant sections of society – predominantly white, male and upper-class in Western societies – are seen as able to disseminate and enforce by a variety of practices beliefs which suit and maintain their positions of dominance. These ideologies may also serve to distort, as in the popular and pernicious view that society is structured according to fundamental abilities and that the poor are in that position because they have less ability, are less intelligent or do not want to work.

View of the person – construction of experience

The dominant narratives can be seen to both shape our futures – what we expect, aspire to, images of existence – and at the same time shape the past – how we make sense of what has happened. Like buying clothes off the shelf, we attempt to fit our experiences into the narratives that are available:

> There exist a stock of culturally available discourses that are considered appropriate and relevant to the expression or representation of particular aspects of experience . . . persons experience problems which they frequently present for therapy when the narratives in which they are storying their experience, and/or in which they are having their experience storied by others, do not significantly represent their lived experience, and that, in these circumstances, there will be significant aspects of their lived experience that contradicts this dominant narrative.
>
> (White and Epston 1990: 27–8)

These narratives may in turn shape our aspirations and dreams, they map what we believe to be possible and desirable – for example, spontaneous romance and mutual compatibility, harmonious family life – and we may experience distress when our experiences do not appear to fit or match up to these ideal narratives. As another example, childbirth is surrounded in narratives of joy, self-fulfilment, closeness of the parents and so on, but the reality for many may involve elements which do not fit – tiredness, irritability, self-doubt, distance and lack of intimacy between the parents. The more strongly this ideal version or narrative is accepted as the 'truth' of how things should be, as normal, the more distress and guilt people may experience if their experience appears to fit this (La Rossa 1986; Carter and McGoldrick 1989). Such ruptures between our preferred narratives, or societally sanctioned dominant narratives, and what we are actually experiencing can, as we saw in the last chapter, set in motion patterns of failed attempted solutions which are driven by attempts to reconcile our preferred views with a view of ourselves as incompetent, abnormal or deviant.

Social constructionism shares with systemic theory an emphasis on the centrality of relationships. We only become people through being involved in a social world of meanings through our interactions with others. It also shares with constructivism a view of people as actively engaged in formulating meanings, attempting to understand, predict, plan and reflect on their own and each other's actions (Gergen 1985; Goldner 1991; Hoffman 1993). In addition, it emphasizes that all aspects of our existence are fundamentally social; from the moment of birth we can be regarded as immersed in a social world which offers us not only a view of the world but also epistemological orientations, ways of knowing or thinking about this world. Rather than predominantly starting with a perspective on how the individual is actively making sense of his or her world, this process of making sense is itself seen as socially constructed and mediated activity.

In social constructionist theory, 'madness' is not an objective phenomenon but a construction – it is a label given to certain actions within a particular culture. Arguably in another culture the same actions might well be defined in alternative ways.

This emphasis on culture and ideology or discourse starts to separate social constructionism from constructivism. In effect, though interactions are central they are seen as also shaped by commonly held ideology and discourse – sets of interconnected beliefs held in common in any given culture. Early social constructionism, however, could be seen as pluralistic in that society was seen to be composed of a range of competing or contested discourses. However, fuelled by input from feminist theories, which in turn were based in Marxist analysis, social constructionists have argued (Foucault 1975; White and Epston 1990) that the discourses that are available in a given culture at any time are intimately linked to structures of power. As an example, until recently men have had the power to define what were acceptable female identities; women could not vote, they were supposed to stay at home with their children, were not expected to enter professions, or to be sexually aggressive. Similarly, inequalities between races have been maintained by a combination of structural power, which in turn can shape ideological power. Such an analysis represents some stark contrasts to constructivism. Rather than seeing people as inevitably free to construe the world in their personal and subjective ways, social constructionism proposes that in any given culture there are common materials, building blocks, from which identities and relationships are constructed. Further, some members of our society have more power than others to design and construct identities, for example members of the medical profession have the power to assign a variety of labels, such as schizophrenic or anorexic, to people. In turn, members of the medical profession are required to act in certain ways as part of their position in the social order, they are not simply free to do otherwise.

Some key family therapy concepts, such as the idea of family life cycles (Carter and McGoldrick 1980), strike chords with social constructionist ideas. For example, the family life cycle embraces the idea that each of us is simultaneously involved in a variety of social groups, for example, a woman in a family may simultaneously be a mother, a worker, a daughter, a lover, middle-class, white and most generally a woman. Our sense of self is therefore seen as fragmented, complex and multiple. At any given moment and in different contexts one aspect of our identity may dominate over another. There may also be strains and conflicts between these different identities which are defined by the various social systems that we belong to, for example, the identity of a mother and career woman. These societally constructed identities may themselves shift and leave us with ambivalent or contradictory images of our self, for example the shifting ideas of masculinity and fathering may leave many men confused about what sort of person they should be. Social constructionism suggests that our social world is actively created by the interactions between and within groups of people in society. What is created is a set of ideas, or shared beliefs, ideologies which lead to various practices, including ideas about what the structure and behaviours comprising families should be like. More widely, the practices or regimes that follow define our access to money and housing, work opportunities, educational structures and a variety of intrusive measures, such as surveillance of the care of children, acceptable behaviour inside and outside the home.

An important difference between constructivism and social constructionism is that the latter takes as its central point that there are social realities. It is not simply suggested that there is a 'real', objective world 'out there' but that there are dominant beliefs, explanations, ways of thinking about the world, and in particular a shared language which construct how we see the world. The fact that these socially constructed views continually change does not mean that at any given moment or point in history they do not have a real existence as influential shared ideas. This sensitivity to how families are immersed in the reality of their culture highlights how constructivism, in contrast, tends to isolate families from society. Instead of simply exploring new narratives, a social constructionist approach to therapy tries to consider how a family's creativity is shaped by dominant narratives, and what is co-constructed in therapy must engage with this wider societal system of beliefs. Such therapy often includes an explicit discussion of these societal beliefs, as in the approach of Goldner *et al.* (1990), where couples are encouraged to critically discuss how their ideas are shaped by the commonly held expectation of gender roles and male–female relationships.

White and Epston (1990) argue that it is this fundamental view that a scientific approach can establish the objective 'truth' of disorders that is a central political issue in therapy. More specifically, this view also regards societal or even relational factors as secondary if not irrelevant. Many families can be regarded as having been immersed or indoctrinated into such a view and therefore see their problems in such a 'problem-saturated' way. However, this scientific view of problems is related to power, for example, the power invested in the medical profession or the power of dominant sections of society to define problems as signs of personal weakness rather than as indications of social inequalities. To challenge these definitions is also, in effect, to challenge the existing structures of power:

> In joining with persons to challenge these practices, we also accept that we are inevitably engaged in a political activity. (We would also acknowledge that, if we do not join with persons to challenge these techniques of power, then we are also engaged in political activity.) This is not a political activity that involves the proposal of an alternate ideology, but one that challenges the techniques that subjugate persons to a dominant ideology.
>
> (White and Epston 1990: 29)

Social constructionism is not a simple and systematically organized theory. At least two strands can be detected. On the one hand it can be employed to offer a view of human experience as a 'top-down' process, whereby we are shaped by our internalization of dominant discourse (Hollway 1989). This in turn is seen to be related to structures of power in any given culture so that until recently, for example, in Western societies male discourses had come to be dominant. A more 'bottom-up' slant is offered by Foucault (1975), who stressed that discourses are reproduced, transformed and have their impact in local, day-to-day interactions and conversations. Hence, discourses are not easily identifiable, objective entities, but continually shifting waves of meanings.

Nevertheless, both slants suggest that there are dominant ideas which have powerful consequences. White (1995), in particular, argues that medical discourses of mental health have had a consistently negative impact in shaping people's experiences and, most importantly, in legitimizing practices, such as exclusion and confinement and creating 'spoilt identities' through the processes of diagnosis, leading to labelling and stigmatization.

Practice

The third phase is much less characterized by techniques of family therapy as much as orientations to working with families. However, a number of what might be described as techniques include:

- reflecting teams and processes,
- externalizing the problem and narrative therapy,
- interviewing the internalized other,

as well as what are better described as therapeutic stances or orientations:

- feminist perspectives,
- Just Therapy,
- therapy as conversation,
- the self of the therapist and resource-focused therapy.

The role of the therapist in the third phase (as in the second phase) continues to be that of a non-expert. Therapy is seen as a collaborative process, involving a co-construction of new ways of seeing problems. This need not necessarily involve new perspectives as such, but can be inspired through validation of family members' difficulties and struggles. Although the therapist and the supervision team are seen as taking a non-expert position, nevertheless it is arguable that there is an expectation that they have sophisticated awareness. Therapy requires a sociological awareness of issues of power: both structural inequalities and the potentially oppressive impact of dominant cultural discourses. Added to this, the therapist is expected to be aware of and to continually monitor their own political dilemmas and prejudices – potentially oppressive assumptions and practices inherent in their privileged position of power and status in relation to the family. This may include their cultural class and gender status and the privileges, as well as assumptions and expectations, of their own professional organizations.

Brief solution-focused therapy

This approach has perhaps some of the closest connections to all three phases of the development of systemic therapy. It has connections with strategic therapies but has evolved to be more collaborative and oriented around ways of facilitating a family's own reshaping of meanings. The overall stance is that of a non-critical position of acceptance and validation. Rather than starting with a framework of looking for and healing pathology, the emphasis is on encouraging families to recognize their competencies. As such the approach challenges prevailing discourses of 'illness', 'pathology' and 'dysfunction'. This is consistent with a social constructionist approach with its emphasis on how 'problem-saturated' ways of talking about difficulties serves to reinforce and escalate them into problems. By focusing on competence the family is encouraged to change how they talk and think about their difficulties.

> Unlike the accepted view of family therapy that the family unit operates on a principle of a pressure to maintain a homeostatic balance and maintain its boundary, Solution Focused Therapy views change processes as inevitable and constantly occurring. Like the Buddhist view that stability is nothing but an illusion based on a memory of an instant, it views human life as a continuous changing process.
>
> (Berg 1991: 10)

Like strategic approaches solution-focused approaches are concerned with the patterns of attempted solutions that family members have been employing to attempt to solve their problems but which have been failing. However, they adopt the view that in fact families have often been attempting a range of actions which have been solutions.

Focus on solutions, not problems

The emphasis of the approach is to move to a *focus on solutions*, rather than just the problems. For example, parents might describe a child who 'fights all the time' or lies all the time'. However, they may also be able, if prompted, to recall some examples of when the child was 'co-operative' and 'honest'. Often these exceptions are seen by the family as insignificant and unimportant. Instead of predominantly attempting to focus on and dissolve the problems, the focus of the therapy is on paying attention to these exceptions and the interactional patterns around them – what mother and father do at these times, how the child starts to be co-operative, where this occurs, the role of other children. From such a detailed exploration of the exceptions some clues may emerge suggesting what the family could 'do more of' in order to encourage the exceptional behaviour. There is a related focus on changes that families may already have started to make prior to commencing therapy – spontaneous recovery. Rather than ignoring such changes, which are said to be common, the therapist draws the family's attention to such changes and works with them to maintain and build on such changes. Where families find it hard to think of exceptions or changes prior to the sessions they can be invited to imagine possible solutions, or solutions that they have seen work in their families of origin and elsewhere.

When asked to report exceptions families appear to describe two types: deliberate exceptions where they can see that they have done something differently, for example made an effort to discuss their feelings about a problem rather than become drawn into assumptions of bad intentions that lead into patterns of mutual accusations; and incidental or chance exceptions where things have been different but for external reasons. For example, a couple might have got on better while on holiday, or while the man was ill and vulnerable.

Goal setting

A central feature of the approach is to collaboratively formulate clear goals with families. These should be described specifically and be relatively concrete so that change and progress are visible to all. One elegant technique that is employed to clarify goals is the 'miracle question'. Families are asked the following question:

> Suppose there is a miracle tonight while you are sleeping and the problem that brought you to the attention of [this service] is solved. Since you are sleeping you do not know that a miracle has happened. What do you suppose you will notice that's different the next morning that will let you know that there has been a miracle overnight?
>
> (Berg 1991: 13)

The aim of this question is to help identify specific behaviours and actions that indicate change, instead of the abstract and potentially unattainable goals that families often articulate, such as wanting to be happy or like a normal family. The process of setting goals is collaborative in that the therapist follows the family's goals.

Overall the approach can be summarized in terms of three rules:

1 *If it ain't broke, don't fix it.* Even the most chronic problems show periods where the troublesome patterns or symptoms are absent or reduced. The therapist needs to have a broad and tolerant view of what 'ain't broke' – what are competencies. These can be built on so

that therapy does not become bogged down into attempting to build a utopian family.

2 *Once you know what works, do more of it.* Once exceptions and competencies have been discovered, families are encouraged to do more of these. This can lead to a self-reinforcing cycle of success which will start to replace that of failure, incompetence and desperation.
3 *If it doesn't work, don't do it again; do something different.* Families often become involved in cycles where they cannot see that they have any alternative but to continue to act in the ways that they have, or in fact to do more of the same. For example, a couple who argue may consider that they need to get their point across more forcefully or to withdraw. However, with exploration of the pattern they might notice that this escalation does not occur if they are holding hands at the time or if they listen for longer and do not jump in and interrupt each other continually. This alternative pattern is built on and hopefully will eventually replace the more negative sequence.

The approach assumes that one of the hardest tasks for people in families is to stop behaviours. This tends to imply blame, and there is a tendency for us to become defensive and to attempt to justify our actions. By avoiding this reaction (or resistance) change can occur more easily.

Rigid beliefs – pre-emptive construing

Also underlying the approach can be seen to be an awareness that problems and negative interactional patterns are held in place by constrictive patterns of beliefs. Typically families describe problems in all-or-nothing terms such as always, never, only and nothing, which serve to narrow thinking and produce a kind of 'tunnel vision' (Dallos 1991, 1997). Kelly (1955) termed these pre-emptive constructs, and Beck (1967) in his cognitive theory of depression saw them as rigid and constraining cognitive schemas. Exploring exceptions serves to challenge these rigid beliefs and allows some new ways of seeing the relationships and the problems (Eron and Lund 1993). From these new perceptions it is possible to generate further new solutions or exceptions. Interestingly, this idea of exceptions is also evident in the most contemporary approaches, such as White and Epston's (1990) emphasis on 'unique outcomes' or family stories showing exceptions of competence to their dominant stories of incompetence.

Reflecting teams

One of the ways that attempts have been made to avoid these contradictions is by the use of reflecting teams (Andersen 1987). Instead of consulting in relative secret with an anonymous and potentially oppressive supervision team, the discussions between the therapist and the team are held openly in front of the family. Arguably in this way they are not simply imposing interventions, including new beliefs and meanings, on families, but are sharing their thoughts and concerns with them. Through the team's discussion the family is invited to consider alternative stories, explanations and attributions regarding their lives together. At times the reflecting team may disagree and debate different possible explanations or ideas among themselves. This may allow different family members who are holding opposing views to feel understood and perhaps enable them to move on to more constructive stories. Importantly, the reflecting team enables family members to hear and perhaps internalize a different conversation rather than simply different explanations. By being able to internalize different conversations they are perhaps, in Bateson's terms, 'learning to learn' or being encouraged to become more creative. The therapy thereby becomes less concerned with content and is less in danger of becoming marooned in attempts to offer families a 'better' view or story.

Some therapists (White 1995) also engage in more or less open discussion of political issues, such as the oppressive nature of discourses of mental health, and assist family members to resist through 'externalizing' their problems. Instead of viewing problems as due to their personal failings, people are encouraged to resist, with the therapist's assistance, the dilemmas and contradictions contained, for example, in dominant notions of mental health (unemotionality, self-sufficiency, non-vulnerability, independence, aggressiveness, stability and so on).

Narrative therapies

> Experience is not what happens to you. It is what you do with what happens to you.
>
> (Aldous Huxley)

The meanings that people give to events serve to explain but also to shape and constrain choices about what are seen to be possible courses of action. Narrative therapies recognize the natural ability that people have to possess, to generate and evolve new narratives and stories to make sense of their experiences. In doing this we draw on culturally shared narratives or ways of interpreting events and also our own family traditions (White and Epston 1990; Freeman *et al.* 1997). There is less of a split between therapeutic and natural everyday activities which produce change. Both therapeutic and natural change are seen to centre on conversation; there is not seen to be a fundamental difference in how change occurs naturally and therapeutically. It is suggested that, for example, the natural process of change involves the development of personal accounts of narratives which make sense of experience. However, the reactions of others, especially family members, to each person's account-making are central (Harvey 1992). Validation and confirmation of these attempts is seen as essential to change and development. Similarly, therapy is seen as a mutually validating conversation from which change can occur. Specifically, therapy is seen to consist not just of offering new perceptions and insights but also of the processes of reflection – the nature of the conversation, the way issues are considered and how questions are raised and answered. Therapy can in a sense appear to be 'just talking', though in fact it is these processes of reflection which are being stimulated and which for many families have become extremely difficult, being disrupted by conflicts and anxieties. (Of course, when 'just talking' and 'just therapy' are taken to mean talking about justice and acting justly no credible disqualification can be made.) Perhaps one of the most significant techniques to emerge is the reflecting team (Andersen 1990). The discussions in front of a family offer not only some new stories but also an opportunity to hear different ways of talking about their situation – a different conversational process:

> Narrative therapy employs a linguistic practice called externalization, which separates persons from problems. Separating the problem from the person in an externalizing conversation relieves the pressure of blame and defensiveness. Instead of being defined as inherently *being* a problem, a young person can now have a *relationship* with the externalized problem.
>
> (Freeman *et al.* 1997: xv)

Externalizing problems

White and Epston (1990) suggest that problems are derived from the internalization of oppressive 'problem-saturated' ways of seeing ourselves. Part of the process of problem formation and maintenance is a process of internalization so that difficulties are seen in terms of individual or family 'faults', something deficient in individual personalities and their relationships:

> 'Externalising' is an approach to therapy that encourages persons to objectify and, at times, to personify the problems that they experience as oppressive. In this process the problem becomes a separate entity and thus external to the person or relationship that was ascribed as the problem.
>
> (White and Epston 1990: 38)

The techniques for doing this include treating or speaking about the problem as an object or entity outside of the person or the family. As an example they cite how a person supposedly suffering from schizophrenia may be encouraged to resist the all-embracing, 'totalizing' nature of such a definition of their identity by discussing how she could combat or resist the 'voices' which were harassing her. Discussions may focus on some successful instances of how she had been able to 'defy the voices' influence'. White and Epston's approach appears to have the effect of reducing the all-pervasive nature of the labelling associated with problems. Instead of discussing problems with a totalizing narrative in which they totally encapsulate the person so that the symptoms become the defining part of their identity or their relationships (e.g. Jim *is a* schizophrenic, or Debbie *is an* anorexic) they can be identified as just one part of their identity. This approach also fits with the increasing attempts to define problems more specifically in terms of profiles of competencies and deficiencies (Boyle 1990). Therapeutic discussion invites people to look at the ways that they may have been 'conscripted' into pathological identities. One part of this can be to explore how they have come to enforce the oppression inherent in such labels on themselves by engaging in self-criticism, self-blame and self-accusations. A related aspect is to explore with family members how they may be imposing these on each other and also conscripting the whole family into a pathological identity – that they are a pathogenic or a 'problem family'.

Externalizing problems is not so much a technique as an orientation or philosophy of therapy. Rather than regarding problems as inherently personal and a central part of the person, they are seen as unwanted invasions which spoil the nature of experience and can promote a sense of failure and inadequacy. In externalizing problems the therapist proceeds not so much by simply identifying this process but by raising questions which invite the person and family members to explore it and to create ways of resisting it. For example, Paul, aged 7, was constantly and apparently uncontrollably soiling himself. Through playful conversations with the therapist, he coined a name for the problem – 'sneaky poo'. Subsequently he explored how and where 'sneaky poo' caught him; for example, he said that he was most likely to be caught when he was distracted – playing or on his computer: 'I think how I tricked him was when I rushed to the toilet, he thought I was still standing there playing' (Freeman *et al.* 1997: 100). Discussions ensued about the power of mind Paul possessed which enabled him to gather knowledge about the deceptive tactics of 'sneaky poo' and find ways to resist and outwit it.

Writing

In addition, therapy can involve the use of various forms of writing, such as letters from family members to each other, autobiographical accounts, stories and so on, to facilitate the ability to engage in internal dialogues and reflecting processes (Dallos 1997; Papp and Imber-Black 1996). The use of writing is seen to have a range of functions. To start with it is an activity which carries high status in many societies, and encouraging clients to be able to express themselves in a written form can be seen as empowering. Writing can also encourage the development of reflection and 'internal dialogues' since we can continue to engage with – to have a conversation with – something that we have previously written. For family members it can also serve to help avoid the compelling patterns of mutual attack and blaming that may be initiated when they start to discuss issues (see the Introduction). Writing to each other may enable a full and uninterrupted statement of their thoughts and feelings about each other. Communication in written form can also enable a more considered and less immediate, reflex emotional reaction than speech. For example, the therapist may write to a family or some members to share her thoughts before a session. The family has time to consider her written words carefully and may come to the next session with some clear ideas which can facilitate a collaborative process of creating some new narratives.

Feminist therapies

Feminist practitioners have offered major contributions to defining a form of therapy that attends to the individual, the relationship and the wider social context. Williams and Watson (1988) supply us with three central principles in the growth and development of feminist practice:

1 commitment to equality within therapy – therapy characterized by

- a demystified and explicit therapy process,
- a demystified therapist,
- strengthened clients' rights in therapy,
- the client as expert about his or her life,
- the therapist's use of power minimized,
- client and therapist having equal worth,
- temporary power inequalities;

2 commitment to bringing the social context into therapy – to working explicitly with women's experiences of sexual and other social inequalities;

3 commitment to power redistribution within society – to political, economic and social equality between the sexes.

An influential example of the application of a social constructionist perspective has been the analysis of power and gender relations in families (Goldner 1991; Hare-Mustin 1991). This reveals all aspects of family life – from the daily routines to the most profound experiences – to be shaped by culturally shared discourses of gender. Work with families where there has been violence between couples reveals that, rather than being deviant, these relationships may more accurately be seen as embodying *in extremis* the dominant assumptions in society about relations between the genders. The men seem to be caught in attempts to establish a culturally sanctioned view of themselves as dominant, in control and invulnerable and the women as nurturing, sensitive, responsive to and needing others. Though not excusing or encouraging a denial of responsibility for the violent partners, the feminist systemic perspectives emphasize the processes of unconscious internalization by men and women of these dominant discourses of gender which shape their 'personal' beliefs and narratives. These filter our perceptions of self and others and shape what kind of relationships we expect and attempt to create. When there is a rift between these expectations, then frustrating attempts to coerce others to fit into the prescribed roles may lead to threats and ultimately to violence (mainly by men). Women too may in some cases stay in such relationships predominantly because of their socialization and induction into ideas, such as that men are naturally more aggressive, women more nurturing, and most importantly that the violence is an indication of their failure to manage the relationship. The previously dominant view of the family as being women's domain carries with it the responsibility for managing everyone's feelings, including their anger.

Power and the construction of reality

Knowledge and power are seen to be inextricably intertwined, and a prime aspect of this is the rise of influence of scientific thought, medicine, technology, economic analyses and so on. These forms of knowledge make claims to 'objectivity', that is, to be fundamentally true; a good example here is the idea of the organic, 'scientifically verified' nature of psychotic disorders. Access to these bases of knowledge is regulated, for example the selection processes for training for medicine or to gain entry into the higher levels of the political domain where confidential knowledge is guarded. In turn these knowledges have important implications for practices – what is done. Medicine is a good example, with a wide range of institutions, hospitals, equipment, assessment procedures, legal rights and so on which can be employed to control what is done to people. However, Foucault clarifies that knowledge or discourses do not simply operate in this fairly straightforward way. Instead, he argues that discourses operate in both positive and negative ways. By positive he does not mean 'good', but that they operate to construct ways of thinking about the world: 'Positive . . . in the sense that power is constitutive or shaping of people's lives . . . in "making up" persons' lives . . . negative . . . contributes a theory of repression' (Foucault 1975, quoted in White and Epston 1990: 20).

Culturally available stories

Foucault proposed, then, that society contains a repertoire of dominant narratives which shape our thinking and experience, how we think about ourselves, our inner conversations and how we interact with each other. Not all stories have equal status. In fact he argues that some are made peripheral or subjugated; examples are narratives which are relegated as historical, no longer relevant, such as attempts to frame Marxist ideas as out of date and no longer applicable to modern society. Also, local or subcultural narratives may be dismissed as naive, simplistic or superficial within the dominant scientific/logical framework. This can apply, for example, to racial differences so that until recently many Third World cultures were referred to as 'primitive' societies. Another example may be the common references to young people's views and enthusiasm for change being labelled as idealistic or unrealistic fantasies, and women's arguments regarded as 'hysterical' or over-emotional.

Foucault's ideas point to a view of society as containing a hierarchy of narratives, with some relegated to the periphery: 'There exists a stock of available discourses that are considered appropriate and relevant to the expression or representation of particular aspects of our lived experience' (White and Epston 1990: 27). In contrast to constructivist views, this suggests that narratives and their formation are not simply or predominantly personal. Families do not have an infinite number of ways of viewing events, instead there is a limited array of narratives which have been made available to us through our socialization or immersion in our culture. This sets limits to our thinking and serves to constrain our perceived domain of options or avenues of action. Significantly, this analysis also suggests that people attempt to employ these dominant narratives to fit their experiences. Family members can be seen to have unique patterns of experiences and histories, but they will attempt to select a dominant narrative to embrace these.

A young couple, Julie and Damian, discussing their sexual problems, offers an illustration:

Julie: Is it you get frustrated because you think you should be doing it once a week ? . . . I don't . . . we don't sit down with other couples and ask them how often they have intercourse . . . it's only what society says . . . I think he's governed by what things should be, or driven by desire.

Damian: Both . . . not just because I feel we should. . . . I've got to feel right . . . I'm not just a machine.

Julie: I think he would do it everyday if I wanted to.

Damian: I don't think so . . . I know deep down that if she wanted sex I would but it's never been tested that there is a limit for me.

(Foreman and Dallos 1992)

This brief extract reveals several dominant discourses that have been identified as common themes in heterosexual relationships. One of the most common is a biological male sexual drive discourse which suggests that men have a greater physiological need for sexual 'release'. In contrast, this suggests that women have less of a need for sex and are more interested in relationships and emotional intimacy. A more 'modern' or permissive discourse suggests that sex is fun and a good physical activity (like aerobics or jogging) which is essential for good health, and regular sex also helps to cement the relationship. These can be seen to operate in this extract overtly and covertly. Julie suggests that Damian is like other men in needing it and he implies he at least partly agrees with this: 'I don't think so' but 'its never been tested'. Julie says she does feel a need to do it so often, which fits with the discourse that women need it less. She also implies that the permissive discourse, 'what society says', sets norms or expectations which drive Damian but not her. In effect, Damian and Julie can be seen as contemplating alternative explanations or stories of their relationship and sexuality, but this contemplation is constrained by the wider domain of available discourses – the dominant narratives. They can attempt to wander outside the perimeters of this domain but then risk a variety of subjugating processes, such as being seen and seeing themselves as eccentric, weird, odd, deviant or perverted.

An awareness of these discourses does not necessarily inevitably mean that people can easily transcend them. White and Epston (1990: 29) suggest that developing 'resistance' or a subversive position in relation to such discourses is an essential part of therapy:

> In joining with persons to challenge these techniques of power . . . we are inevitably engaged in a political activity . . . (if we do not join with persons to challenge these . . . then we are also engaged in political activity) . . . not a political activity that involves the

proposal of an alternative ideology, but one that challenges the techniques that subjugate persons to dominant ideology.

Commentary – feminist orientations

A variety of important critiques and developments in family therapy have been inspired by feminist ideas and included important observations regarding the nature of power and abuse in families. Specifically, it was argued that not all members of a family should be seen as having equal responsibility for the problems, and the adoption of a 'neutral' position by family therapists regarding some kinds of problems, such as abuse, could be seen as condoning such actions. In this section we want to explore feminist orientations not just as a critique of systemic approaches but, most importantly, to draw out some core comparisons and contrasts between structural and strategic approaches and also to prepare the way for a discussion of the second wave of applications in Chapter 4.

Feminist approaches take a wider lens and focus not only on the patterns of interactions in families but also on the wider social context. They argue that families should be seen not simply or predominantly in terms of patterns of interactions between the family members but as shaped by the prevalent ideas in society about family life. They also argue strongly that these ideas are largely based upon patriarchal notions which tend to confer a lower status on the activities and roles of women. Within the family it has been traditionally expected that men should be the 'breadwinners' and women responsible for the nurturance of the children and domestic duties. This was seen to cut both ways in that women's supposed natural qualities, such as greater emotional sensitivity, were seen as fitting them to take care of the children. On the other hand these emotional qualities are typically undervalued in contrast to the more 'rational' scientific qualities that are seen to be valued in the external world of work, for example. However, it was also argued that this arrangement produces a context in which men are burdened with the felt responsibility for the family's economic well-being and are deprived of the experiences that encourage them to be nurturant or emotionally responsive.

Family therapy which did not address these traditional sex roles and expectations was seen as potentially colluding with or reinforcing them (Urry 1990). Blindness to these issues was highlighted in some of the directives and tasks employed by family therapists. For example, Warner (1980) described how a typical intervention such as asking parents to reverse roles could inadvertently serve to further disempower a woman in a family:

> Arnold was an eight-year-old boy who was soiling himself especially when he was at school or away from home. He came at first with only his mother who was encouraged to bring along the step-father and Arnold's two older sisters for the second interview.
>
> Whenever Arnold was soiled and his mother ordered him to the bathroom to wash himself, Arnold had resisted and gone into a temper tantrum. The step-father had not been involved.
>
> A major change in the family functioning was effected by asking the step-father to take a more active part, and by encouraging the mother to allow this to happen. By the time of the third interview soiling was still occurring but the tantrums were no longer taking place. The step-father was directing Arnold to wash whenever he was soiled and this happened without any fuss.
>
> > . . . a considerable lessening of the soiling was reported. However, it was noticed that the mother appeared depressed . . . A paradoxical type of comment was made by the therapist that with the upheavals of her past life and current worries, it was a wonder that she was not more depressed. All the children were asked to carry minor domestic chores for their mother, for which they were to be financially rewarded.
> >
> > (Warner 1980)

Though no doubt well-intentioned, this intervention can be seen as not recognizing that men and women in families are expected to play different roles and, importantly, that for women their self-esteem and respect may largely be based on their success in the domestic sphere. Regarding the above example, Urry (1990: 108) suggests that the woman

> is being viewed in a framework of having failed, whilst her husband is presented as the solution of her incompetence. The support she is given by the therapists with their 'paradoxical type of comment' offers some understanding to the woman. However, it falls far sort of recognising her strengths and encouraging her competences. This therapy is exemplary in the way it maintains myths of male supremacy and reflects a society organized around financial reward.

This critique embraces both a specific point about systemic therapy as having failed to consider images of family life – how families are viewed in different cultures – and the values and expectations that follow. Related to this, it is argued that there is a reality 'out there' which is independent of the observer. Families can be seen as displaying real structures which contain patterns of inequalities and gender roles. Furthermore, it is argued that these patterns are not simply constructed within families but are shaped by the very real structural and ideological forces in society.

Key texts

Andersen, T. (ed.) (1990) *The Reflecting Team*. New York: W.W. Norton.

Andersen, T. (1995) Clients and therapists as co-researchers: enhancing the sensitivity. *Fokus Familie*.

Anderson, H. (1990) Then and now: from knowing to not knowing. *Contemporary Family Therapy Journal*, 12: 193–8.

Anderson, H. (1997) *Conversation, Language and Possibilities*. New York: Basic Books.

Anderson, H. and Goolishian, H. (1986) Problem determined systems: towards transformation in family therapy. *Journal of Strategic and Systemic Therapies*, 5: 1–13.

Anderson, H. and Goolishian, H. (1988) Human systems as linguistic systems. *Family Process*, 27: 371–93.

Boscolo, L., Cecchin, G., Hoffman, L. and Penn, P. (1987) *Milan Systemic Family Therapy: Conversations in Theory and Practice*. New York: Basic Books.

Boszormenyi-Nagy, I. (1987) *Foundations of Contextual Therapy: Collected Papers of Ivan Boszormenyi-Nagy*. New York: Brunner/Mazel.

Burck, C. *et al.* (1998) The process of enabling change: a study of therapist interventions in family therapy. *Journal of Family Therapy*, 20: 253–68.

Capra, F. (1996) *The Web of Life*. New York: Anchor Books.

Carr, A. (2000) *Family Therapy: Concepts, Process and Practice*. Chichester: Wiley.

Carter, B. and McGoldrick, M. (1989) *The Changing Family Life Cycle: A Framework for Family Therapy* (2nd edn). New York: Gardner Press.

Cecchin, G. (1987) Hypothesizing circularity and neutrality revisited: an invitation to curiosity. *Family Process*, 26: 405–14.

Cecchin, G., Lane, G. and Ray, W.L. (1994) *The Cybernetics of Prejudices in the Practice of Psychotherapy*. London: Karnac.

de Shazer, S. (1985) *Keys to Solution in Brief Therapy*. New York: W.W. Norton.

de Shazer, S. (1991) *Putting Differences to Work*. New York: W.W. Norton.

Dell, P. (1989) Violence and the systemic view: the problem of power. *Family Process*, 28: 1–14.

Flaskas, C. and Perlesz, A. (eds) (1996) *The Therapeutic Relationship in Systemic Therapy*. London: Karnac.

Framo, J. (1992) *Family-of-Origin Therapy: An Intergenerational Approach*. New York: Brunner/Mazel.

Freedman, J. and Coombs, G. (1996) *Narrative Therapy; The Social Construction of Preferred Realities*. New York: W.W. Norton.

Friedman, S. (ed.) (1993) *The New Language of Change: Constructive Collaboration in Therapy*. New York: Guilford Press.

Friedman, S. (1995) *The Reflecting Team in Action: Collaborative Practice in Family Therapy*. New York: Guilford Press.

Furman, B. and Ahola, T. (1992) *Solution Talk: Hosting Therapeutic Conversations*. New York: W.W. Norton.

Gergen, K. (1985) The social constructionist movement in modern psychology. *American Psychologist*, 40: 266–75.

Gergen, K. (1988) *Feminist Thought and the Structure of Knowledge*. New York: New York University Press.

Gluck, S. and Patai, D. (1991) *Women's Words: The Feminist Practice of Oral History*. London: Routledge.

Goldner, V. (1985) Feminism and family therapy. *Family Process*, 24: 31–47.

Goldner, V. (1988) Generation and gender: normative and covert hierarchies. *Family Process*, 27: 17–31.

Hardy, K. and Laslotty, T. (1995) The cultural genogram: key to training culturally competent family therapists. *Journal of Marital and Family Therapy*, 21: 227–37.

Hare-Mustin, R. (1987) The problem of gender in family therapy theory. *Journal of Marital and Family Therapy*, 26: 15–27.

Harré, R. (1986) *The Social Construction of Emotions*. New York: Basil Blackwell.

Hoffman, L. (1985) Beyond power and control. *Family Systems Medicine*, 3: 381–96.

Hoffman, L. (1993) *Exchanging Voices*. London: Karnac.

Hoffman, L. (1998) Setting aside the model in family therapy. *Journal of Marital and Family Therapy*, 24: 145–56.

Imber-Black, E. (1988) *Families and Larger Systems: A Therapist's Guide through the Labyrinth*. New York: Guilford Press.

Jones, E. and Asen, E. (2000) *Systemic Couple Therapy and Depression*. London: Karnac.

Kaplan, A. (ed.) (1988) *Postmodernism and its Discontents*. New York: Verso.

Luepnitz, D.A. (1988) *The Family Interpreted: Feminist Theory in Clinical Practice*. New York: Basic Books.

Masson, J. (1990) *Against Therapy*. New York: Fontana.

McGoldrick, M., Anderson, C. and Walsh, F. (eds) (1989) *Women in Families*. New York: Norton.

McNamee, S. and Gergen, K. (1992) *Therapy as Social Construction*. London: Sage.

McNamee, S. and Gergen, K.J (eds) (1999) *Relational Responsibility. Resources for Sustainable Dialogue*. Thousand Oaks, CA: Sage.

Minuchin, S., Yai-Yung, L. and Simon, G. (1996) *Mastering Family Therapy*. New York: Wiley.

Nicholson, L. (ed.) (1990) *Postmodernism and Feminist Theory*. New York: Routledge.

Pilgrim, D. and Reimers, S. (2000) The real problem for postmodernism. *Journal of Family Therapy*, 22: 6–28.

Ray, W. and Keeney, B. (1993) *Resource Focused Therapy*. London: Karnac.

Real, T. (1990) The therapeutic use of self in constructionist systematic therapy. *Family Process*, 29: 255–72.

Shotter, J. and Gergen, K. (1989) *Texts of Identity*. London: Sage.

Tomm, K. (1987) Interventative interviewing: Part I. *Family Process*, 26: 3–13.

Tomm, K. (1987) Interventative interviewing: Part II. *Family Process*, 26: 167–83.

Tomm, K. (1988) Interventative interviewing: Part III. *Family Process*, 27: 1–15.

von Glaserfeld, E. (1987) *The Construction of Knowledge*. Seaside, CA: Intersystems Publications.

Waldegrave, C. (1990) Just therapy. *Dulwich Centre Newsletter*, 1: 5–46.
Walters, M., Carter, B., Papp, P. and Silverstein, O. (1989) *The Invisible Web: Gender Patterns in Family Relationships*. New York: Guilford Press.
Weingarten, K. (ed.) (1995) *Cultural Resistance: Challenging Beliefs about Men, Women and Therapy*. New York: Harrington Park Press.
White, M. (1995) *Re-authoring Lives*. Adelaide: Dulwich Centre Publications.
White, M. and Epston, D. (1990) *Narrative Means to Therapeutic Ends*. New York: W.W. Norton.
Wynne, L., McDaniel, S. and Weber, T. (eds) (1986) *The Family Therapist as Systems Consultant*. New York: Guilford Press.

SKILL GUIDES

Consultation

Background

With the recognition of systemic practices as offering core skills for a variety of professional activity, practitioners have increasingly applied skills to non-therapeutic contexts. Most usually this has meant practitioners becoming consultants to one another, other welfare or mental health organizations or commercial organizations.

Relevance and usefulness

For practitioners to be able to appreciate and demonstrate the generic nature of systemic practices is extremely important as an underpinning of the new theoretical paradigm. The development of skills that enable practitioners to be useful in conversation with colleagues in turns helps to develop their own credibility and that of the approaches that they employ.

Exercise

Participants are asked to organize themselves in trios (A, B and C): A takes the role of a representative of an organization in trouble, B takes the role of a consultant and C takes the role of an observer. Using the following format, B explores A's problem:

1 What is the problem?

2 What does the problem enable people in the organization to do/not to do?
3 Which roles and relationships in the organization are affected by 1 and 2?
4 How does 3 represent a dilemma for the organization?
5 How does this pattern of relationships enable the organization to manage change?
6 What are the gains and losses of 5 to A and for the organization?
7 What does 6 enable A and the organization to do and not to do?
8 A, B and C share their experiences and learning.

Further reading

Campbell, D. (1995) *Learning Consultation*. London: Karnac.

Campbell, D., Coldicott, T. and Kinsella, K. (1994) *Systemic Work with Organisations*. London: Karnac.

Campbell, D., Draper, R. and Huffington, C. (1991) *A Systemic Approach to Consultation*. London: Karnac.

Campbell, D., Draper, R. and Huffington, C. (1991) *Teaching Systemic Thinking*. London: Karnac.

Externalizing the problem

Background

An original contribution from narrative therapists Michael White and David Epston, externalization is a sophisticated practice based on the premise that exploring a problem or difficulty as if it were a separate 'something' from the person with the difficulty can promote new agency in previously disempowered clients.

Integral to using this approach is a belief that practitioners can see the client as separate from their problems. Practitioners using this skill need to develop genuine empathy and curiosity about the client's struggle with their symptom as if it were an unwanted visitor in their lives.

Relevance and usefulness

Narrative therapy and practices identify some political implications of the context of therapy, and externalizing conversations help practitioner and client alike to rename the dominant stories in people's lives and thus to empower clients to develop new and different stories about themselves. This 're-authoring' may include clients dissociating themselves from dominant, oppressive discourses in the political, economic, social and therapeutic context.

Skills that enable clients to rediscover their agency for life are invaluable for practitioners but none more so than those (like externalizing conversations) that are embedded in respectful collaborative practices.

Exercise

Participants are asked to organize themselves in trios (A, B and C): A is a person with a difficulty, B is an explorer or investigative reporter and C is an observer.

Part I

A selects a difficulty or problem he/she wants help with. B inquires about A's problem to ascertain:

1 the problem's influence in different areas of A's life;
2 the strategies, deceits, techniques and tricks the problem uses to intimidate A;
3 particular qualities possessed by the problem for undermining A;
4 problems, aims and goals for A's life;
5 who supports the problem and its schemes;
6 what destructive actions the problem will resort to in A's life should the problem's dominance in A's life be shortened.

Part II

This part involves B interviewing A to ascertain ways in which the externalized problem is incompetent, fails to achieve its goals and can be undermined and hindered.

In addition, B seeks to identify what techniques and strategies have been developed by A to undermine and disqualify the problem, as well as any network of relatives, friends and professionals who A feels are available to help deny the problem's wishes.

Then B summarizes with A the ways in which the problem can be successfully demoralized.

Part III

Here A talks about their experiences of Parts I and II, and then B and C discuss their reactions to A's experience as described.

Finally, A, B and C have the opportunity to discuss their learning experiences.

Further reading

Freedman, J. and Combs, G. (1996) *Narrative Therapy*. New York: W.W. Norton.
Freeman, J., Epston, D. and Lobovits, D. (1997) *Playful Approaches to Serious Problems*. New York: W.W. Norton.
White, M. (1988–9) The externalising of the problem and the re-authorising of lives and relationships. *Dulwich Newsletter*, Summer: 3–20.
White, M. (1995) *Reauthorising Lives: Interviews and Essays*. Adelaide: Dulwich Centre Publications.

Collaborative inquiry

Background

As constructivist ideas have permeated the field and discussions about power inequalities between therapists and clients have impinged on practice, more and more attempts have been made to develop collaborative approaches to therapy. Generally collaboration carries with it the idea of more than just lip-service to working 'with' clients and presumes the therapists will seek to create a context for genuine inquiry and exploration from a position of 'not knowing' the reasons for the presence of symptoms.

Relevance and usefulness

Because we all create our own experience, the client is indeed the 'expert' about their own life experiences, and a collaborative non-expert approach by the therapist recognizes this client expertise at the same time as offering an authentic invitation (in response to the client's request for help) to explore unfamiliar and uncharted emotional territory in the hope that useful new possibilities for action will emerge. More than any other therapeutic style, collaborative approaches promote client autonomy while offering a non-invasive experience of interdependence with the therapist during the inquiry (therapy) process.

Exercise

Participants are asked to take one of three positions: explorer, presenter or observer.

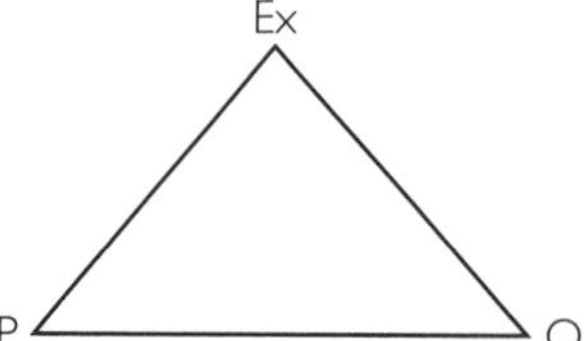

Figure 3.1 Collaborative inquiry triangle

The explorer is given the following guidelines for a conversation:

1 Keep the inquiry within the parameters of the problem described.
2 Allow yourself to hear multiple and contradictory ideas at the same time.
3 Choose co-operative rather than uncooperative language.
4 Use the same words and language as your conversation partner.
5 Ask new questions which are based on the answers to previous questions.
6 Be a respectful listener, and do not understand too quickly.
7 Create a conversational context which allows for mutual collaboration in the problem defining and dissolving process.
8 Keep a conversation going with yourself in your head about what you are hearing from your conversation partner.

Similarly, the observer is offered guidelines for listening and watching the three stages of the conversation:

1 Ask the presenter to describe a problem, complaint or worry. (This can be work-related or personal.)
2 Find out how describing the problem in this way creates a problem for the presenter. For example, how does it lead the presenter to organize his or her relationships or behaviour? Map how his or her important relationships are affected by the way he or she (the presenter) is describing their problem. Clarify who are the key players and what they are doing in relation to the problem.
3 Find out what different explanations the presenter holds and others who are affected by the problem. Clarify what effect the different explanations have on the relationships described by the presenter.

After 10 minutes of exploration, the explorer and observer discuss what has interested them in the conversation and speculate about ways forward in the presenter's situation, while the presenter listens without participating.

The presenter is then invited to comment on what they have heard and suggest a direction in which the conversation could usefully develop.

Following another 10 minutes of conversation between the explorer and the presenter, the observer joins for a three-way conversation about the learning and the experience.

Each member of the trio takes a turn in each of the positions.

Further reading

Anderson, H. (1996) *Conversation Language and Possibilities*. New York: Basic Books.

Hoffman, L. (1993) *Exchanging Voices*. London: Karnac.

Reflecting processes

Background

Since the late 1980s, reflecting team processes have become an important aspect of clinical practice. The method arose originally from the development by Tom Andersen of the reflecting team, in which the family and the behind-the-screen observing therapists switch places during the therapy session so that family members have an opportunity to observe therapists talking about them and then offer the therapists feedback.

The intervention was intended to provide an opportunity for *réflexion* (the French equivalent of reflection), meaning that something heard is taken in, thought over, and the thought is given back. This way of working aims to promote more egalitarian relationships between clients and therapists.

Relevance and usefulness

It is our belief that in the context of more collaborative and egalitarian relationships, clients are likely to be more receptive to new ideas and therefore to the risks of change.

Authentic feedback from clients and therapists in training who have experienced reflecting processes is unanimously that being able to listen without having to justify, explain or set the record right, while still knowing there will come an opportunity to speak, provides an unusual space in which other new ideas can surface and a different kind of listening takes place. Clients also acknowledge an intense interest in hearing what other people have to say about them.

It is also clear from client feedback that experiencing reflecting processes conveys to clients how much thought and attention is being given to their situation by professionals who simultaneously are perceived as more authentically caring and more professionally useful.

Exercise: reflecting team discussion

1 Participants are asked to get into groups of three, four or five. One person is asked to present a case or situation he or she is feeling stuck with and to say something about the therapy, why he/she feels stuck, and what he/she has done to get 'unstuck'. This should not go on for longer than 10 minutes.
2 The others in the group then discuss the case or situation together, and the presenter becomes an observer, forbidden to speak or even correct any misunderstanding. The group aim to arrive at some systemic understanding of why this person is stuck with this case. This should take about 10 minutes. We often ask the group to use the sequential format described earlier for their discussion.
3 The presenter is then invited to comment on the discussion. He or she usually has views about what seemed accurate or inaccurate, helpful or unhelpful but is asked to refrain from trying to explain his/her views and invited to comment on the discussion he/she has just heard in step 2.
4 Again the group turn to each other to discuss the comments made by the presenter. These comments should be used as information to enable the group to develop further their systemic formulation about the case. They can ask themselves, 'What does it tell us about this system/situation that the presenter has chosen to comment on these particular aspects of our discussion?' This takes about 5 minutes.
5 The presenter can then be invited to comment on this second discussion.

Further reading

Andersen, T. (1987) The reflecting team: dialogue and meta-dialogue in clinical work. *Family Process*, 26: 415–28.

Andersen, T. (1991) *The Reflecting Team: Dialogues and Dialogues about the Dialogues*. New York: W.W. Norton.

Andersen, T. (1993) Reflections on reflecting within families, in K. Gergen and S. McNamee (eds) *Therapy as Social Construction*. London: Sage.

Hoffman, L. (1990) Constructing realities: an art of lenses. *Family Process*, 29: 1–12.

James, S. *et al.* (1996) Using reflecting teams in training psychology students in system therapy. *Journal of Systemic Therapies*, 15(4): 46–58.

4 Ideas that keep knocking on the door: emotions, attachments and systems

Introduction

The role of emotions in systemic practice has been much debated. In the first phase there were clear connections with psychodynamic models in terms of the importance of unconscious emotional processes. As we saw in Chapter 1, there was a rejection of what was seen as the essentially individualistic understanding of problems in psychodynamic theories. Some practices, such as the emphasis on the importance of 'joining', a concept very sympathetic to the notion of the therapeutic alliance, were also central to systemic therapies. Following a lengthy separation, the two approaches are increasingly showing signs of a process of rapprochement. Importantly, this is being fuelled not only by shifts amongst systemic therapists towards a greater interest in the nature of the inner worlds and, especially, the emotional world of family members, but also by dramatic shifts in psychodynamic theorists' narrative ideas (Larner 2000: 61; Flaskas 2002), so that therapy has come to be regarded as a more collaborative and mutually constructed process (Bion 1961, 1970; Winnicott, 1971) in contrast to the more 'expert' interpretative stance of earlier psychodynamic approaches. Running alongside the connections with psychodynamic approaches has been a long-standing relationship with attachment theory. Though also concerned with how internal worlds develop, attachment theory fundamentally adopts a social-interpersonal approach to examine how attachments are formed in families. In fact Bowlby (1973) argued that attachment must be seen systemically as a self-corrective process between the infant and the carer. Together they maintain a homeostatic balance of security and arousal in the relationship.

Returning to the role of emotions, in systemic practice, as we mentioned earlier in Chapter 1, Haley (1987) and others regarded struggles fuelled by unconscious emotional needs as one of the key features of family dynamics. The direct exploration of emotions in therapy, however, was discouraged for pragmatic reasons. Haley (1987: 125), for example, argued that asking families about their feelings was not likely to elicit new information or lead to change:

> If a person is caught up in a sequence . . . expressing his emotions is not likely to cause change . . . For example, if a man gets red in the face and is silent every time his wife criticizes him, the therapist may arrange for the man to express his anger in words instead of by changing the colour of his face. If the man does so, the wife must respond differently, and a new system is being generated. Asking 'How do you feel?' about something is the least likely way to bring out emotions . . . It is better to provoke him to more anger, perhaps by sympathising with him, to shift the way he is communicating.

Systemic therapists like Haley argued that emotions were driven by interpersonal events and experiences, and their expression served interpersonal functions (Ray 2004). In terms of therapy, it was seen as more pragmatic and efficient to alter the interpersonal patterns and communicational sequences than to engage in explorations of intra-psychic emotional states. Similarly, Palazzoli *et al.* (1978) argued that in Western culture our language tended to reify emotions. Phrases such as 'Mary is angry' or 'John is jealous', they argued, imply that these states are strictly intrapsychic rather than transient states that ebb and flow as part of relationship dynamics.

The inclusion of emotions in systemic practice is important for a number of reasons. The first is that, without being addressed, the model is necessarily incomplete and loses the opportunity to connect with other perspectives and research into the nature of emotions, problems and change. We will also argue that rather than emotions being a sort of add-on, they are fundamental to family relationships and in particular to children's development in families and therefore to systemic theory and practice. Secondly, systemic practice has encountered considerable criticism for being unable to offer convincing models of aberrant emotional states in families, especially in relation to physical and sexual abuse. As we saw in Chapter 1, systemic concepts of escalating processes, such as symmetry and complementarity, offer an important description and analysis but say little about the nature of emotional experience in such escalations, and they also appear to miss the important 'common-sense' observation that such escalations are generally suffused with emotionality.

Finally, it is important to note that most if not all systemic and family therapists have taken account of and utilized emotional issues in their work with families. For example, most therapists are sensitive to the first impressions of a family's emotional atmosphere. Whether they appear hostile, anxious or confident is likely to influence how the therapist decides to approach them. Subsequently, in attempting to gain the co-operation and trust of a family (joining), attention is paid to the general emotional atmosphere. Generally, attempts are made to encourage a positive and warm working relationship with a family.

Therapists of all schools are likely to pay attention to the emotional atmosphere of a family and individual members as they discuss important issues. Working alongside family members and helping them to manage their emotional reactions in more productive ways may be one of the core outcomes of family therapy. As we saw in the Introduction, families' experience of what is useful about therapy emphasized the importance of providing a situation which helped them to express and also to contain their feelings (see page 3).

Most therapists have ideas about the likely progression of emotions in a family; for example, a sense that a particular emotional sequence is likely to follow will influence the therapist's choice of particular questions to family members.

Family members usually have a set of beliefs and explanations about the role of emotions in their lives. How emotions are expressed and dealt with will differ, and these beliefs may vary from family to family. However, families and their therapists also can be seen to share some common assumptions or discourses about emotions. For example, in the Taylor family of the Introduction there was a belief that it was important to get their feelings out in the open and that this had been difficult in the past, especially for Mr Taylor. This can also be seen as part of a wider cultural belief that men are 'naturally' less emotionally articulate than women, along with a common assumption that therapy should be concerned with exploring feelings. This assumption is also most certainly a legacy of psychodynamic theory and we can find evidence of the influence of Freudian ideas in most of our conversations with families in clinical and everyday contexts. Psychodynamic ideas about the centrality of emotions and the need to access and release unconscious emotional conflicts and anxieties are now a fundamental feature of Western cultures.

Systemic theorists had, as we have already indicated, made for a variety of important reasons a decision not to place emotions at the centre of systemic theory. Haley (1987) has articulated many of the reasons for this, and we offer a combined summary:

1 A focus on emotion distracts attention from the interactional dynamics and patterns in families.
2 There had been an assumption that emotions are essentially private, personal, intrapsychic phenomena. A discussion of these in therapy can steer the therapy away from looking at interpersonal dynamics.

3 Therapeutically a discussion of feelings often generates little new information. For example, asking someone how they feel about their difficulties often simply produces little change and tends to keep the focus on the identified patient, reinforcing rather than challenging their assignation to the sick role.
4 Perhaps most importantly, the study of emotions had been so totally colonized by psychodynamic theory that their exploration in therapy almost invariably veered towards speculative formulations about unconscious processes. This tended to propel the analysis of the problems and focus of the therapy progressively further into the client's past. Consequently, the discussion and therapy often became largely disconnected from present processes and events, which might be contributing to the problems.

Our suggestion is that though many of Haley's reasons were at the time valid in creating a distinctive alternative to psychoanalytic theory, it is no longer necessary to exclude an analysis of emotions from a central position in systemic thinking.

Susan Johnson (1998) argues that

> emotion is not a within phenomenon that falls outside the bounds of system theory. It is a leading element in the system that organizes interactions between intimates. To leave emotion unaddressed is to miss a crucial part of the context of close relationships. Emotional expression is the main route by which partners and family members define their relationships and influence each other's behavior.

We want to offer an overview of some interesting developments in the study of emotions and also to look at some of the elaborations of psychodynamic perspectives which complement a systemic perspective. An analysis of emotions in fact can be seen to offer an interesting example of the value and necessity of integrating the three phases (Flaskas 2002).

Emotions and the first phase of family therapy 1950s to mid 1970s

Despite some of the reservations shared by systemic therapists about the emotions and their centrality in therapy, in fact many of the early formulations were centrally concerned with emotional processes. Two key ideas, triangulation and the double-bind, which made a significant contribution to early systemic therapy both revolved around emotional processes.

Triangulation

As described in Chapter 1, triangulation was seen as a process whereby emotional tensions and conflicts occurring between a pair in a family result in a third person being drawn in to ameliorate the level of tensions:

> The basic building block of any emotional system is the triangle. In calm periods, two members of the triangle have a comfortable emotional alliance, and the third, in the unfavoured outsider position, moves either toward winning the favour of one of the others or towards rejection . . . In tension situations, the outsider is in the favoured position and both of the emotionally over-involved ones will predictably make efforts to involve the third in the conflict.
>
> (Bowen 1971: 172)

Bowen, like other systemic therapists, proposed that triangles represented one of the primary emotional units in families. The emotional levels, tension, conflicts and fear could escalate between a pair in a family and the emotional balance could be restored by drawing in a third person. Again as we saw in Chapter 1, Minuchin (1974) described how this process was also involved in conflict avoidance. The experience of conflict for a pair, for example a couple, could be extremely aversive and a way of avoiding this is to draw in a third member. In his therapeutic approaches Minuchin (1974) included the technique of intensification whereby he blocked such triangulating avoidance manoeuvres and insisted that a couple address and try to resolve their conflicts. Much of the early writing in family therapy stressed this notion of families attempting to sustain an equilibrium or homeostasis in their emotional reactions.

The double-bind

In their studies of schizophrenia, Bateson *et al.* (1956) reversed the usual causal question about what makes people act in disturbed and crazy ways, typically labelled as schizophrenic. Instead, he asked in what situation schizophrenia would make perfect sense, in fact would in a sense be adaptive. This line of thinking led to the concept of the double-bind. In short, this proposed that serious disturbance arises from situations in which conflicting and contradictory messages are given and there is no apparent possibility of escape.

In the Gregg family, for example, Mrs Gregg continually smiled as she recounted stories of how inconsiderate, aggressive and even violent her son Hugh had been towards her. When he reacted with anger towards her criticisms she smiled further and explained that this was an example of Hugh's behaviour. Similarly, if Hugh tried to be pleasant or loving towards his mother he was reminded of what he was really like. For much of the time in the sessions Hugh's solution was to act in a 'silly' way which allowed him to be neither angry nor loving (see Dallos 1997).

An important question is what drives or causes such patterns of ambivalence on the part of parents in the first place. Bateson *et al.* (1956) strongly implied that the ambivalent and contradictory communication arose out of a deep fear of potential rejection. For example, Mrs Gregg perhaps feared that if she were to show her true feelings some catastrophe, such as rejection, might occur. Bateson (1972: 215) suggested in his description of 'double-bind' situations that these were driven by anxieties and insecurities:

> The need of the mother to be wanted and loved also prevents the child from gaining support from some other person in the environment, a teacher for example. A mother with these characteristics would feel threatened by any other *attachment* of the child and would break it up and bring the child back closer to her with consequent anxiety when the child became dependent on her.

Unfortunately, the impressions formed from the early descriptions were that the model was mother-blaming, which obscured later reformulations as a mutual and even a triadic process. Weakland (1976) argued further that such patterns could be better seen as a triangular double-binding process, typically where the mother is or feels disempowered. Mrs Gregg reported that she often 'feared for her life' in the face of the periodic coalition that arose between Mr Gregg and Hugh. Though alternately criticizing Hugh, Mr Gregg also tended to take his son's side and undermined Mrs Gregg's attempts to gain some control. Later it turned out that the couple had attempted to keep secret from Hugh the fact that they did not like each other, had both had affairs and were living a lie, staying together purely for economic reasons and because they had nowhere else to go. In fact it seemed clear that the parents both felt extremely vulnerable and frightened at the prospect of being on their own, despite their dissatisfactions with their marriage. In addition, such insecurities can be seen to be transgenerational, as attachment theory reveals. Hence, though a parent may appear to be acting in a destructive way, this needs to be seen in the context of how they have learnt to survive emotionally in their own family of origin. This typically reveals, returning to Bateson's emphasis on 'fit', that their behaviour makes sense and fits with their own early experiences. For example, both Mr and Mrs Gregg had themselves experienced difficult and insecure relationships with each of their parents.

In summary, therefore, double-bind theory, like the concept of triangulation, appears to be based on the assumption that emotional processes, which may be largely unconscious, lead to the emergence of problematic behaviour patterns in families. This also reveals the legacy of psychodynamic theory in early systems theory models of families and therapy.

Attachment theory

Bowlby (1973) suggested that attachment to adult caregivers is a fundamental aspect of child development. He drew upon naturalistic (ethological) studies of a variety of animals which showed that the young have an instinct to become attached predominantly to their mothers. However, a number of ethologists, such as Lorenz, discovered that young geese could become attached to *him*, not just to their mother. Later he discovered that they could even become attached to his wellington boots or even a cardboard box as long as it was associated with providing nurturance such as physical contact, food and affection. A variety of other studies had also shown that the essential ingredients of the attachment were not simply due to the fulfilment of basic needs such as food. Harlow and Harlow (1962) showed that young monkeys could forgo food from a wire surrogate mother in favour of the opportunity to have physical contact with a comforting furry surrogate. Attachment was seen to have evolved in order to protect infants from danger by keeping them in close comfort to the mother.

Bowlby (1969, 1973) noted in his observations of the behaviours of children who were separated from their mothers for prolonged periods that these infants go through a predictable set of emotional reactions. The first stage involves protest, consisting of crying, active searching and resistance to others' attempts to soothe them. The second stage appears to be despair, in which the child becomes passive and sad. And the third stage is detachment, in which the child appears to actively ignore and angrily reject the mother if she returns. This last stage was seen as a form of defence to limit the possibility of being hurt further by mother's departure. However, infants who experience a consistently available mother or carer and appear to become securely attached become more able to tolerate their mother's absence. Also, they are able to move away from her as a secure base to explore their environment and establish relationships with others (Winnicott 1971).

Apart from the detachment stage, remarkable similarities were observed between human infants and primates. Bowlby (1973) went on to suggest that though the attachment process in humans closely resembled the apparently largely instinctual processes in animals, it also involved the child developing an internal 'attachment model'. By this he meant that children develop a set of meaningful representations about whether and how much they can trust others, based on their early experiences. He went on to classify children as developing largely different styles or patterns of attachment: secure, anxious and avoidant (Bowlby 1969, 1973). The secure style is characterized by an ability to tolerate absence from the parents, to operate independently and generally to possess a basis of trust and confidence about one's self and the world. Children with anxious and avoidant styles are generally much less secure and do not expect others to be trustworthy. These children generally cope less well on their own and may develop ambivalent – close but also rejecting or overly clingy – relationships. The sense of self is central to Bowlby's ideas. The different experiences of these children lead them to develop a sense of self-worth, as opposed to inadequacy and insecurity about their worth. Consequently, attempts may be made by the child to secure or enhance self-esteem but this may be within a sense that any such acceptance cannot be relied upon and ultimately the child will be rejected. Bowbly (1973: 238) argued that the sense of attachment and security experienced came to depend on two factors:

(a) whether or not the attachment figure is judged to be the sort of person who in general responds to calls for support and protection;
(b) whether or not the self is judged to be the sort of person towards whom anyone, and the attachment figure in particular, is likely to respond in a helpful way.

He went on to say that although these perceptions of the attachment figure and the self are logically independent, they are aligned; for example, children who have had rejecting or abuse experiences come to see themselves as not worthy of love and affection.

Once established, these patterns are regarded as relatively stable and enduring. Evidence has started to accumulate that in fact these patterns of emotional attachment learned in childhood extend into adult relationships (Ainsworth *et al.* 1978; Main *et al.* 1985; Fonagy *et al.* 1993). It has been suggested that the children's attachment patterns tend to be reproduced in relationships with other adults and also carried to the next generation with the relationships between the adult and his or her child.

Attachment theory has revealed that there can be strong escalating patterns between children and parents; in insecure (anxious or avoidant) attachment, the child will increasingly demand care and attention or increasingly withdraw. The notions of 'comforting' and 'soothing' are central in attachment theory such that the level of arousal and anxiety is maintained at a balance: not too much arousal so that the child is over-anxious, and not too little so that a child is bored and listless.

We assert that Bowlby's work is relational and therefore systemic.

Emotions and the second phase of family therapy

Attachment theory: the move to internal representations

Attachment theory has continued to adapt and evolve, and there are emerging explicit connections and collaborations between family therapists and attachment specialist workers. There has been a powerful turn to an emphasis on exploring the links between early attachment experiences and people's narratives. Mary Main (1993) has developed an important research tool – *the adult attachment interview*. This is a detailed structured interview that invites people to tell the story of their childhood attachment experiences, including the nature of their relationships with each parent, patterns of comforting, danger, loss and threat from parents or others. The interview is transcribed and then analysed for both the *content* and the style or *form* of the responses. The interview can be classified in terms of the *coherence* and amount of *insight* or *integration* that people show in their 'narratives'. Such classification has been seen to be effective in predicting people's childhood attachment experiences and also their relationships with their own children (Fonagy *et al.* 1993). These narrative styles appear to be able to predict adult romantic attachments (Hazan and Shaver 1987; Crittenden 1998; Feeney 1999). As an example, the processes involved in reproducing adult relationships may be that someone who as a child develops an insecure and ambivalent attachment style may enter adult relationships hoping to find the security that they lacked as a child. However, since they are likely not to trust the affection they may be lucky enough to find, a self-fulfilling prophecy effect may be set up so that eventually their clingy ambivalence does lead their partner to become exasperated and even to reject them. It is also argued that insecure individuals seek other vulnerable people as partners since they do not regard themselves as 'good enough'. Such pairing based on combined vulnerabilities may be unstable. There is evidence to suggest that separation and divorce are more likely with such couples if they do not have the means to heal vulnerabilities and to grow (Hendrix and Hunt 1998).

One of the most interesting aspects of the work on adult attachment has been the development of models of people's internal worlds. It is argued that the nature of our early experiences and attachments is held as memories of interactions, feelings, conversations and images. As the child develops these develop into characteristic styles of internal dialogues. For example, some people frequently give themselves a hard time, punish themselves, perhaps using their parents' or voices from their past (and possibly still present) who have previously hurt them or each other. It is also argued that when the experiences have been predominantly negative or when children have been abused they find it painful to remember or contemplate these voices from the past or speculate on how these people might have seen the world. The ability to reflect, to consider one's own and others' thoughts, may therefore be impaired (Crittenden 1998). Fonagy *et al.* (1993) have developed the *reflective functioning scale* which they argue suggests that children who have insecure attachment styles do appear less able to reflect on their own and others' thoughts. This of course has powerful implications for family life. Managing relationships may be difficult when family members find it hard to contemplate each other's or their own actions. This is an important idea, suggesting that the ability to understand and develop narratives regarding our experiences is a learnt *skill* which may fostered or held back by family experiences. This has substantial implications for all forms of therapy, not least the forms of narrative and family therapy, when family members are required to listen and reflect on reflecting team discussions!

Attachment theory models of emotions may appear to present a somewhat static and pessimistic view of emotions, implying that we are prisoners of our emotional histories and doggedly repeat and reproduce these in adult relationships and subsequently with our own children. A systemic perspective hypothesizes about these patterns but suggests that intimate adult relationships are much more open to negotiation and change, with attachment patterns not so rigidly determined by past events, and that they are open to continual negotiation and change, offering opportunities for growth and healing:

1 *Natural account-making processes.* Harvey *et al.* (1992) suggest that one of the ways that people deal with destructive emotional experiences such as abuse is by a process of forming accounts of their experiences. Through repeated internal dialogue and repeated presentation of accounts to others people eventually are able at least partly to transcend their abusive experiences. A key ingredient they suggest is that others, such as friends, relatives and colleagues, validate this process by responding in a positive way by listening rather than rejecting or criticizing people's attempts to make sense of their traumatic experiences. This work also suggests more broadly that particular attachment styles may alter according to the nature of positive (or negative) relationships as we progress into adulthood.
2 *Multiple attachment models.* It is suggested that people may have different attachment styles, reflecting the presence of various significant other people in their lives (Crittenden 1998). As we develop and mature we may be able to draw on these different attachments to alter our earlier primary patterns.

3 *Resilience*. Increasing interest in how individuals manage to resist apparently damaging emotional experiences in childhood also indicates that attachment is a dynamic and ongoing process. Some personal qualities, such as a sense of humour, intellectual abilities and the presence of at least some positive and validating input can help children to resist difficult emotional experiences (Walsh 1996; Dallos *et al.* 1997):

> All studies world-wide of children of misfortune have found the most significant positive influence to be a close, caring relationship with a significant adult who believed in them and with whom they could identify, who acted as an advocate for them, and from whom they could gather strength to overcome their hardship.
>
> (Walsh 1996: 266)

Family life cycle approaches suggest that family members are faced with varying emotional stresses throughout their lives. These include stresses associated with the birth of children, departures such as children leaving home, and bereavements. These require families to organize themselves in different ways at different times. It is possible that at times it is functional for family members to be extremely close or even to appear over-dependent on each other. At other times it may be appropriate to be more emotionally distant. When children are leaving home it may even be expected that parents slow some ambivalence: on the one hand encouraging their child to become an independent adult, and on the other being concerned and feeling sad at their departure. Emotions and family dynamics are interdependent.

Emotions inform how difficulties are perceived, and subsequent attempted solutions may serve to ameliorate or aggravate anxieties (Dallos *et al.* 1997). A range of factors, including external stresses on the family, the quality of interpersonal relationships, and health, in turn shape the emotional resources that are available at any given time. We will return to this point later in this chapter.

Attachment styles and couples' dynamics

Some attempts have been made to integrate an analysis of emotional attachment styles with an analysis of the interactional processes in couples. Pistole (1994) suggests that the relationships that develop in couples may be shaped by but cannot simply be predicted from their attachment styles. It is possible, for example, that in some cases the interactional dynamics serve to aggravate each person's characteristic style and in other cases to effect change. Couples' attachment styles shape the beliefs and expectations that each partner holds as they interact and, in turn, the solutions to relationship problems that emerge. Couples frequently display cycles of closeness–distance (Byng-Hall 1985, 1995) where a frustrating process appears to take place in which attempts by either partner to become close are met by withdrawal from the other and vice versa. In such cases a couple may eventually find it extremely difficult to move from an unpleasant stalemate and feel that their relationship is disintegrating since neither can take the risk of showing intimacy for fear of rejection. Pistole (1994) suggests that such stalemate cycles may be linked to an interlocking of each partner's attachment styles and needs. Anxieties may be generated by some unexpected external changes, which in turn upset the balance of an established relationship pattern:

> John and Jane's relationship has been stable for 2 years. Jane is promoted to a job that demands more investment from her and also provides her with a greater sense of personal meaning. Perceiving the change in the amount, quality, and direction of Jane's attention and emotional investment (more in her job) as a separation threat, John approaches. Jane, involved in her work, is not attentive and responsive to John's bid for greater closeness. Following a rebuff, which is experienced as an abandonment threat, John experiences separation anxiety and responds with more pressure for closeness and with protest behaviour, that is anger, as a bid for Jane to be responsive and emotionally available. Jane in turn feels both unduly pressured and attacked; she backs off or responds with anger designed to distance John. A pursuit cycle had begun and may continue until sufficient anger from both parties results in an argument followed by some sort of contact (perhaps 'kissing and making up'), which calms John's attachment system and allows the couple to re-balance their distance.
>
> (Pistole 1994: 151)

Later it is possible that stress and demands may lead Jane to wish to gain more reassurance and contact from John. However, he may still be smarting from the rejection he perceived earlier from Jane, leading him to avoid showing affection. If John and Jane have anxious attachment styles then such disturbances may lead both of them to feel abandoned and uncared for but unable to make the first move for fear of further rejection. Of course it is also possible that partners become aware of their own histories and are able to transcend their immediate emotional reactions. This may in some cases require some 'luck' in finding understanding partners and friends or, alternatively, therapeutic input.

Emotions in couples' interactions

Gregory Bateson (1972) proposed that dynamics in families and couples also displayed patterns of escalating emotions. He also argued that possibly one of the important functions that sexual intimacy played in relationships was that it could provide a release of feelings and tension, especially through sexual orgasm:

> If there be any basic human characteristic which makes men prone to struggle, it would seem to be this hope of release from tension through total involvement . . . [there is an] obvious relationship of these interactive phenomena to climax and orgasm . . .
>
> (Bateson 1972: 111)

It would be contentious to suggest that sexual orgasm simply functions to defuse escalating conflicts in relationships, but Bateson (1972) did point to the centrality of emotional arousal in relationships and the need to establish a pattern of managing this which, like the case of a child with a parent, was comfortable. Through focusing on sexual intimacy he also indicated that pleasurable emotions are a central ingredient. Of course sexuality is complex and shaped by a variety of personal and cultural factors, but the nature of emotion and mutual arousal may be extremely important.

Work by Gottman (1979, 1982) has specifically attempted to explore links between emotional arousal and dynamics in couples. In a range of studies Gottman (1979) and Gottman *et al.* (1977) took physiological and psychological measures of emotional arousal in couples engaged in requiring negotiational tasks. The method he developed was to videotape couples engaged in discussions and negotiations of areas of conflict. Subsequently each partner in turn viewed the replay of the interaction on videotape and a range of measures was taken. This was more convenient than, in effect, wiring the couple up while they were interacting, and the measures have been found to agree closely with the actual emotional changes in the original interactions. Gottman discovered that each partner's emotional arousal at any point was related to that of the other. However, Gottman *et al.* (1977) also found interesting differences between couples who generally described their relations as satisfactory as opposed to unsatisfactory. Dissatisfied couples tended to display much greater mutual escalation of negative emotional responses. This was not simply in what was said but in the non-verbal aspects of their utterances. Furthermore, these patterns of mutual responding appeared to be very predictable or stuck. In contrast, in satisfied couples negative emotional arousal and action in one partner might be met by a positive response and validation which often had the effect of halting any potential escalation.

Gottman (1979) suggested that the patterns of mutual emotional responsiveness to each other become learned or programmed in time. Each partner responds to the other's emotional tone in a largely conditioned and unconscious manner. In effect, this seems to confirm the common-sense observation that partners come to be able to 'press each other's emotional buttons'. He went on to describe how patterns of emotional avoidance can also be mutually constructed; for example, one finding was that generally patterns of negative emotional reactions are likely to be terminated when a woman becomes angry. At this point men are more likely to withdraw. Over time this pattern of a show of anger by one partner followed by withdrawal can lead to avoidance so that issues are not resolved. Significantly, he also found that as emotional escalation proceeds women are more likely to experience this as fear and men as anger. He suggests that men generally experience emotional arousal in relationships as more aversive than women and attempt to withdraw. When this strategy is blocked, excessive frustration and anger may develop. Hence both personal and culturally shared gender factors may play an important role in shaping the emotional patterns.

There is considerable evidence to suggest that emotional arousal and problem-solving abilities are closely related. When couples are caught in such escalating emotional patterns there is a tendency for thought processes to be become limited, inflexible and ineffective. Therapeutic approaches which just focus on the cognitive aspects may underestimate the difficulties that partners have in overcoming their learned patterns of mutual emotional arousal. Again as we saw in the quotes from families in the Introduction, an opportunity to discuss issues without becoming drawn into these patterns is typically seen as a key ingredient of what family members find useful in therapy:

Mrs Taylor: I thought what was most useful was hearing Barbara talking about things . . . to hear what was going on in her head . . .

Barbara: Yeah, getting my point of view across rather than getting into an argument.

Over time therapy may also allow an opportunity to learn or develop some less rigid tit-for-tat patterns of emotional arousal.

Alongside systemic therapies there has been a massive upsurge in cognitive therapeutic approaches inspired by the work of Beck (1967) on depression and previously George Kelly's (1955) personal construct theory. A revolution in individual psychotherapeutic work has followed, especially in the area of work with disorders of depression and anxiety (Brewin 1988). There are links with these approaches in systemic family therapy especially in the constructive approaches of the second phase, for example the applications of techniques such as reframing which bear a similarity to Beck's ideas of cognitive restructuring. In Britain we have also seen the influence of the work of Harry Procter (1981, 1985) which developed George Kelly's personal construct theory into the idea of family belief systems or shared constructs.

Specifically, Beck had proposed that various problems, such as depression, were maintained and possibly caused by patterns of negative thought processes. This featured a generally pessimistic view of the world. It was suggested that some people in effect suffered from an information-processing deficit in that all aspects of experience were seen as reflecting a triangle of negative cognitions; that their lives demonstrated personal failure, that they were powerless to alter events and that the future was bleak and beyond their ability to change things. It was argued that some people exemplified a dysfunctional view of the world, and therapy required discussion and confrontation of their negative ideas through activities and therapeutic 'experimental tasks' designed to disprove their faulty theories of the world.

George Kelly's (1955) work shared this emphasis on the importance of ways of seeing the world, but he cautioned against evaluations such as implying dysfunction, arguing that people adopted what appeared to be the best ways of making sense of events. He proposed that each person is like a scientist attempting to make sense of and to predict and anticipate events in the world. However, each person was seen as possessing a unique set of beliefs, a personal construct system, about the world. A core aspect of this was a set of beliefs or constructs about the self. In particular, positive and negative feelings were seen to be associated with validation and invalidation of our desired self. Change involved working in a collaborative way with people to discover alternative ways of making sense of the world, but this required an understanding of how and why they had come to develop certain views. Similarly, Kelly suggested that emotional states were intimately connected to patterns of beliefs. For example, he argued that anxiety arises when we feel that we do not have an adequate understanding and ability to predict situations, when we feel out of control.

There is considerable literature on both these approaches, but central to both is the idea that emotions and our beliefs are inextricably intertwined. There has also been a burgeoning of experimental and clinical research on the relationship between emotions and cognitive processes (Brewin 1988). Cognitive therapies have been predominantly individually focused though more recently they have developed to include a developmental perspective regarding what kinds of early interpersonal experiences produce core schemas that shape people's thinking (Young 1990). This idea both encourages an exploration of early systemic processes and reintroduces the idea of unconscious processes (schemas). Like systemic therapy, the cognitive therapies also share a pragmatic and collaborative approach, for example in the use of tasks and homework designed as experiments to gather information and to confront the validity of beliefs. Increasingly, it is also acknowledged that this requires clients' engagement and the development of a good therapeutic relationship.

Emotions and the third phase of family therapy

In the third phase there is emphasis on the importance of wider cultural factors, such as dominant values, expectations and beliefs in any given culture. Emotions and their role in family life can be seen to be highly influenced by such societal factors. An example from our own work (Dallos and Dallos 1997) may help to reveal some of these processes. In particular, our example serves to highlight some important differences in assumptions about gender and what is seen to be legitimate emotional expression.

Simon and Deidre had been married for 10 years and were reporting difficulties in their marriage. Deidre had become anxious and unable to engage in sexual intimacy. She complained that she could not feel warm towards Simon since he was continually attempting to get away from her – apart from complaining about lack of sexual intimacy. Simon generally appeared to have a predominantly avoidant attachment style. He described how his parents had frequently argued and that the emotional atmosphere at home was generally cold. He reported that he generally had difficulty expressing his feelings and tended to go off by himself on outdoor pursuits. Deidre on the other hand reported that her family background had been warm and affectionate, that people were generally able to express their feelings and their vulnerabilities. Her background appeared to be secure, though she described herself as rather insecure at college and entered into counselling to help her deal with some issues. When she and Simon first met she said that she admired his independence – he was a lecturer and rode a motorbike. On the other hand Simon admired Deidre's warmth and felt she might enable him to become more emotionally expressive. However, as their relationship developed it appeared that Deidre became seen as increasingly 'neurotic' and 'clingy' because she wanted to spend time with Simon, whereas he continued with his solitary outdoor pursuits. Rather than seeing Simon's actions as indicative of his avoidant and anxious attachment style, the relationship increasingly became portrayed as Simon being secure and normal and Deidre as insecure with Simon but not in other relationships.

This example serves to illustrate not only how attachment styles both shape and are shaped by the relationship dynamics but also how they point to the important influence of wider cultural factors. In particular, it indicates the widely held values in Western cultures of independence, self-sufficiency, avoidance of displays of vulnerability and emotionality (White and Epston 1990; Rogers and Pilgrim, 1997). Arguably these are also predominantly regarded as male characteristics which have been valued in patriarchal cultures. In Deidre and Simon's case it is possible that these cultural values won out so that despite Deidre probably being better adjusted and more in touch with her feelings at the start of the relationship she became increasingly construed as 'neurotic' and inadequate.

The language of emotions

> We might consider how emotions came to be constituted in their present form, as physiological forces, located within individuals, that bolster our sense of uniqueness and are taken to provide access to some kind of inner truth about the self.
>
> (Abu-Lughood and Lutz 1990: 6)

Third-order or social constructionist approaches invite us to question not only our conscious, overt beliefs but also our implicit assumptions or 'common sense'. This is particularly relevant to a discussion of emotions and feelings. Talk about feelings pervades much of social interaction as well as our private internal dialogues. However, it is possible that much of the time we are unaware of some of the dominant assumptions or discourses that shape such talk and our beliefs about emotions. Lutz (1990) suggests that a range of culturally shared assumptions regarding emotions not only shape our beliefs about emotions but also serve to construct our experiences, including what we regard as legitimate feelings and what courses of action are acceptable once particular feelings arise. These culturally shared assumptions are regarded as shaping the terrain of internal experience, but importantly they also exclude other possible assumptions, for example that emotions are not simply private, internal and biologically driven but socially constructed both in the flow of personal interactions and conversations. The meanings ascribed to our own and others' internal states and feelings are in turn shaped by the range of possible meanings – the discourses about emotions available in our culture.

Specifically, some of the shared meanings include the views of emotion as:

> Natural rather than cultural, irrational rather than rational, chaotic rather than ordered, subjective rather than universal, physical rather than mental or intellectual, unintended and uncontrollable, and hence often dangerous.
>
> (Lutz 1990: 69)

Perhaps most significantly emotions are regarded as generally inferior to intellectual and rational thought. In most professional spheres of activity, for example, it is seen to be necessary to be able to contain and control one's emotions in order to be able to work effectively and rationally. However, emotions are also contrasted with 'cold' and lifeless logic. Here emotions are seen as embodying more primitive states, closer to nature, free, authentic and unshackled states of being.

However, this juxtaposition between feelings and rationality may not be inevitable. In fact the separation between feeling and rationality is in itself a culturally shaped device. More specifically, the experience of an emotion can be seen to be based upon beliefs which in turn invariably involve feelings. Cultural changes indicate some of the issues here, for example the emotion of 'melancholie' featured strongly in medieval times but has largely become an obsolete term (Jackson 1985). Furthermore, melancholie was more likely to be experienced by men and implied refinement and brave suffering. In contrast, the modern concept of depression tends to focus more on women and portrays the condition as implying a deficiency, for example a biologically based disorder or a distorted and dysfunctional view of the world. Similarly, it can be suggested that the widely accepted differences in emotions between men and women are not in fact natural and inevitable but in fact part of a process of social construction.

Typically, the distinction between emotions and rationality can be seen as embodying the differences between the positive and largely male values in Western societies – rationality, coolness, control – as opposed to the less valued features of impulsivity, lack of control, weakness and vulnerability. Running through these assumptions about emotionality can be seen to be a theme of control. The notion of control is in turn a necessary part of the idea of emotions as being fundamentally biological, an essential inner state that each person has to wrestle with, more or less successfully, and bring under control. A related idea is of emotions as building up like a dam that may burst if feelings are not expressed. This biological premise, however, diverts attention away from the possibility that the experience and expression of emotions may be predominantly socially and culturally shaped. An important example here is that though men are generally seen as less emotional, more in control, the exception is anger, which is generally accepted as a more legitimate, in fact desirable, male emotion.

Culturally shared discourses may therefore serve to define our internal states, what meanings we give to them and what are legitimate ways of acting. The classic study by Schachter and Singer (1962) also illustrates these points. Participants were administered dosages of either a stimulant drug or a placebo and the effects of the drug were found to be related more to social effects of being with another person who acted in an angry as opposed to silly way. The actual physiological arousal effects of the stimulant drug as opposed to the placebo were mediated and could be counteracted by the social situation. This and other studies suggest that, rather than some simple correspondence between internal physiological states driving emotions, there is a complex process of attributions made about our internal states which is based on the immediate social context that we are in and more broadly the wider cultural one.

Lutz (1990) also argues that dominant assumptions about the nature of emotions pervade not only everyday ideas but also scientific research. An important example is the work on attachment inspired by the work of Bowlby (1969). His work, inspired, as we saw earlier, by animal studies, is founded on the notion of a fundamental biologically based bond between mothers and infants. Feelings of love towards the child from the mother are seen as natural and instinctual, as are the child's emotional responses. However, arguably this is not simply based on empirical discoveries:

> Bowlby-style bonding theory naturalizes the connection between women and affect through evolutionary theory and is continuous with earlier theorizing about the elevated moral status of women achieved through divinely assigned and naturally embedded mothering skills.
>
> (Lutz 1990: 82)

The importance of women for the bonding in early childhood follows from the view of women as more emotionally aware and sensitive. Elsewhere there are studies which suggest that women are superior at decoding facial expressions (Hall 1978); this is explained in evolutionary terms, for example that they have become better at this because of their historical role of being the ones to care for infants and therefore needing to be sensitive to their expressions. However, in many of these studies the actual superiority of women's performance is small and the evolutionary explanations are dubious. For example, arguably it was also necessary for men as hunters to co-operate and thus to be able to read each other's expressions accurately.

Despite these widely reported differences between men and women, especially in the supposed greater concern that women have with feelings, analysis of everyday conversations does little to bear this out. For example, cultural stereotypes might suggest that men distance themselves more and talk about how others feel or how they have felt in the past and talk about the causes of their feelings in abstract terms. Analysis of men's and women's talk about emotions (Shimanoff 1983; Lutz 1990) suggests that in fact men and women tend to be similar in the extent to which they place themselves at the centre of talk about emotions, and there is little evidence of these cultural stereotypes. Nevertheless, it seems likely that men's and women's talk is still regarded as different. Likewise, evidence from attachment theory using the adult attachment interview suggests that differences in the style of people's talk about their early experiences, including how able they are to process difficult emotional experiences, reflect on their own and others' internal states and relate their experiences of interpersonal processes more to the nature of their early family experiences than simply to gender differences (Crittenden 1998; Cassidy and Shaver 1999).

Returning to our example of Simon and Deidre, it is possible that their differences in emotionality were less than either of them perceived them to be. However, possibly they both adopted different positions in that Simon was struggling to be more emotionally expressive while not losing his male 'control', whereas Deidre was struggling to control her feelings without losing her feminine 'sensitivity'. It is interesting to consider that systemic approaches in many ways anticipated some of the core concepts of social constructionism, including an analysis of emotions; rather than seeing these as somehow fundamental intrapsychic states they came to be seen as a product of interpersonal processes. However, the contribution of third-order cybernetics and social constructionism has been to reveal how these interpersonal exchanges are themselves shaped by culturally shared discourses. Here it is not just that actions and experiences are assigned particular emotional labels in interactions but assumptions are carried, often implicitly, about the very nature of what emotionality is. Simply put, when we ask someone, 'How do you feel?' we are not just asking politely about their feelings but perhaps perpetuating assumptions that the answer reflects some aspects of the person's real inner state as opposed to reflecting, at least in part, their relationship with us and the wider culture that we share.

Integration with psychoanalytic thinking

The therapeutic relationship

A connecting thread for all of the psychotherapies has been found to be the importance of the therapeutic relationship, with a large number of studies identifying it as the single most powerful predictor of outcome in therapy (Horvath and Symonds 1991; Bergin and Garfield 1994; Sprenkle and Moon 1996). The concept of the therapeutic alliance is generally seen to originate from the psychodynamic therapies (Bordin 1979; Luborsky 1984). When systemic therapists discuss the therapeutic relationship it is with an emphasis on the nature of the emotional or affectionate aspects of the relationship. Bordin (1979) emphasizes that this fundamentally embraces three connected features. In addition to the emotional bonding with the therapist, he suggests that there is an agreement on the goals of the therapy and the tasks this will involve:

- *A therapeutic bond:* This is the client's overall positive affectional

bond to therapist and includes their sense of trust, belief in the therapist's abilities, positive expectations of help from the therapist, collaboration and involvement.
- *Therapeutic goals:* The explicit contract which includes clarity and agreement of overall goals, ways to achieve these and how to monitor progress.
- *Therapeutic tasks:* Clarity and agreement on the tasks of therapy, including ground rules, responsibilities, mutual roles and consent.

The present emphasis in systemic therapy on developing a 'collaborative' approach focuses on therapist and family members working together to determine the goals of therapy and shapes the therapeutic bond. Many families attend therapy with clear ideas (perhaps from information from the Internet) about a diagnosis and what kind of help they want, for example that their child's problems appear to be a symptom of attention deficit hyperactivity disorder (ADHD) and the child needs medication and behavioural treatment. The therapist may be less sure that this is appropriate. Despite a positive initial feeling between the family and the therapist, this is likely to dissolve if they cannot find a mutually satisfactory way of working together. Larner (2000) describes how it is important here to hold a 'not knowing' position where, rather than become sucked into unhelpful impasses (Leiper 2001), the therapist attempts to find out more about what the family believes and feels, and what might be some of the underlying anxieties and feelings which they cannot yet express.

However, it also suggested that, despite collaboration being a 'worthy aim', there will be times in the therapeutic relationship when there are 'ruptures' (Leiper 2001). Since there are difficult and painful issues that need to be aired there will be times when the family is reluctant to air them. It is a delicate question of how much the therapist encourages a family to face some of these complex issues. Arguably at times the family need the therapist to encourage them to face some issues though they may at the same time feel angry and resentful towards her for doing so. Psychoanalytic ideas here emphasize the therapist as using her own unconscious or semi-conscious responses to guide this process (Larner 2000; Flaskas 2002). Likewise, Byng–Hall (1995) describes this as creating a secure base for work with a family and Mason (1993) refers to it in terms of a balance between safety and certainty. The level of uncertainty that families can tolerate will vary as therapy progresses and their trust in the therapist and their relationship with them will change and hopefully grow.

Defence processes and unconscious communication

Underlying the focus on the therapeutic relationship are the core ideas from psychoanalysis that emphasize the unconscious, internal world of family members. Though psychoanalytic ideas have evolved and developed (Larner 2000; Flaskas 2002), one of their substantial contributions is to emphasize these emotional and at times subterranean processes in and between the family members and the therapist. As we stated at the start of this chapter, systemic therapists have from the start been aware of and paid attention to the feelings of family members and their own feelings as important to the process of therapy. However, a schism occurred in the emphasis that psychoanalytic approaches were seen to place on an individualistic focus on these processes and an 'expert' stance where the therapist did the interpreting of unconscious processes of which family members were believed to be unaware. More recently, there has been a shift to a more interactional and collaborative view of these processes in psychoanalytic thinking (Larner 2000). Also, systemic therapists (Flaskas 2002) have been able to describe how some of the core psychoanalytic concepts are compatible with a systemic communicational view. Three of the major concepts in psychoanalytic thinking – transference, counter-transference and projective identification – are all seen as powerful, largely unconscious processes that impact on therapeutic and therapist choice of interpretation. As systemic therapists we maintain that these three concepts can be seen as not just internal processes *in* family members but as interactional processes happening in the therapeutic situation.

Transference and counter-transference
Family members experience the therapist in terms of their own past relationships, perceived similarities and a sense of *recreating* these previous relationships in the therapeutic process. In turn the therapist is seen as bringing his or her past patterns of relating to the therapeutic relationship and *recreating* these in the therapeutic process.

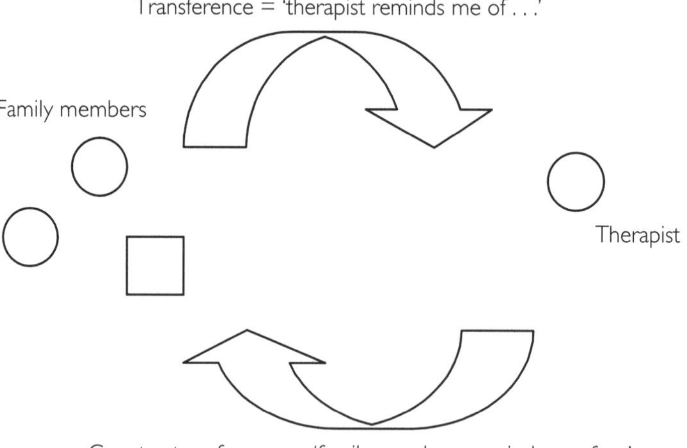

Figure 4.1 A systemic summary of transference and counter-transference.

This can be seen as circular process involving communication at verbal and, importantly, non-verbal levels. (See fig. 4.1.) Simply put, it is often experienced by the therapist as strong feelings of liking or not liking some family members, with a gradual realization that they remind the therapist of someone who has been important in their life. Conversley therapists may recognize that family members' feelings towards therapists may be triggered by family members' own memories of important people in their own lives.

Projective identification

Family members are struggling with unacceptable feelings which are unbearable as conscious thought. These feelings are 'split off' and projected outwards away from the self. In turn the therapist is seen to take on board these feelings since they connect with his or her internal world. The therapist may experience painful, uncomfortable feelings, such as anxiety, anger, threat, chaos, and come to realize that he has identified with some unconscious, unstated feelings in the family.

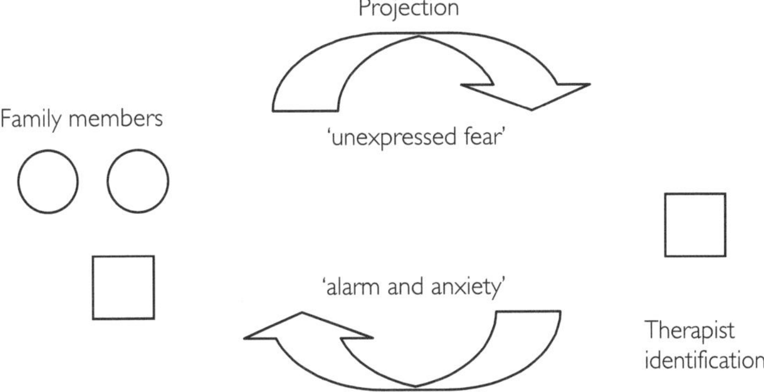

Figure 4.2 A systemic summary of projective identification.

Typically in therapy this is experienced as strong feelings. For example, Flaskas (2002: 147) gives as an example a 7-year-old girl presenting with distress and anxiety:

> the child quickly comes to give up her symptoms, and her mother expresses more distress and I come to feel alarmed and anxious . . . there were no words about fear in circulation in the family, and indeed fear came to be expressed physically by the girl waking up in pain. I came to experience an emotion which was very hard for the family to know about at a conscious level.

We believe psychoanalytic ideas can complement systemic practitioners' work, but they are continuing to have a powerful impact, especially as we have suggested when they can be seen not as somewhat mystical and speculative internal processes but as evident in forms of human communication. This adds to a systemic perspective in drawing attention to unconscious processes and the development of empathy. It also adds to psychoanalytic ideas in helping therapists to explore what it is that they do which helps or hinders these processes. Such research and exploration has been taken up by psychotherapy process researchers and will hopefully lead to further integrations between therapeutic models (Bordin 1979; Horvath and Symonds 1991).

Key texts

Ainsworth, M.D.S. (1991) Attachment and other affectional bonds across the life cycle, in C.M. Parkes, J. Stevenson-Hinde and P. Marris (eds) *Attachment across the Life Cycle*. London and New York: Tavistock/Routledge.

Ainsworth, M.D.S. and Eichberg, C. (1991) Effects on infant–mother attachment of mother's unresolved loss of an attachment figure, or other traumatic experience, in C.M. Parkes, J. Stevenson-Hinde and P. Marris (eds) *Attachment across the Life Cycle*. London and New York: Tavistock/Routledge.

Akister, J. (1988) Attachment theory and systemic practice: research update. *Journal of Family Therapy*, 20: 353–66.

Akister, J. and Reibstein, J. (2004) Links between attachment theory and systemic practice: some proposals. *Journal of Family Therapy*, 26: 2–16.

Behr, H. (2001) In memoriam. The importance of being a father: a tribute to Robin Skynner. *Journal of Family Therapy*, 23: 327–33.

Bergin, A.E. and Garfield, S.L. (eds) (1994) *Handbook of Psychotherapy and Behaviour Change*, 4th edn. New York: Wiley.

Bertrando, P. (2002) The presence of the third party: systemic therapy and transference analysis. *Journal of Family Therapy*, 24: 351–68.

Bordin, E. (1979) The generalizability of the psychoanalytic concept of the working alliance. *Psychotherapy, Theory, Research and Practice*, 16: 252–60.

Bowlby, J. (1969) *Attachment and Loss, Vol. 1*. London: Hogarth Press.

Bowlby, J. (1973) *Attachment and Loss, Vol. 2: Separation, Anxiety and Anger*. London: Hogarth Press.

Byng-Hall, J. (1995) Creating a secure family base. Some implications of attachment theory for family therapy. *Family Process*, 34: 45–68.

Byng-Hall, J. (1999) Family and couple therapy: toward greater security, in J. Cassidy and P.R. Shaver (eds) *Handbook of Attachment: Theory, Research and Clinical Applications*. New York: Guilford Press.

Cassidy, J. and Shaver, P.R. (eds) (1999) *Handbook of Attachment: Theory, Research and Clinical Applications*. New York: Guilford Press.

Cohen, N.J., Muir, E., Lojkasek, M., Muir, R., Parker, C.J., Barwick, M. and Brown, M. (1999) Watch, wait, and wonder: testing the effectiveness of a new approach to mother–infant psychotherapy. *Infant Mental Health Journal*, 20: 429–51.

Crittenden, P.M. (1996) Research on maltreating families: implications for intervention, in J. Briere, L. Berliner, J. Bulkey, C. Jenny and T. Reid (eds) *APSAC Handbook on Child Maltreatment* (pp. 158–74), Thousand Oaks, CA: Sage.

Crittenden, P. (1998) Truth, error, omission, distortion, and deception: an application of attachment theory to the assessment and treatment of psychological disorder, in S.M. Clany Dollinger and L.F. DiLalla (eds) *Assessment and Intervention Issues across the Life Span*. London: Lawrence Erlbaum.

Crittenden, P.M. (1998) Dangerous behaviour and dangerous contexts: a thirty-five year perspective on research on the developmental effects of child physical abuse, in P. Trickett (ed.) *Violence to Children* (pp. 11–38). Washington, DC: American Psychological Association.

Crittenden, P.M. (2000) A dynamic-maturational exploration of the meaning of security and adaptation: empirical, cultural and theoretical considerations, in P.M. Crittenden and A.H. Claussen (eds) *The Organisation of Attachment Relationships: Maturation, Culture and Context* (pp. 258–384). New York: Cambridge University Press.

Crittenden, P.M. (2002) Attachment theory, information processing, and psychiatric disorder. *World Journal of Psychiatry*, 1: 72–5.

Crittenden, P.M. (in press) If I knew then what I know now: integrity and fragmentation in the treatment of child abuse and neglect, in K. Browne, H. Hanks, P. Stratton and C. Hamilton (eds) *Prediction and Prevention of Child Abuse: A Handbook*. Chichester: Wiley.

Crittenden, P.M. (in press) Transformations in attachment relationships in adolescence: adaptation versus need for psychotherapy. *Revista de Psychotherapia*. See www.patcrittenden.com.

Crittenden, P.M. and Claussen, A.H. (in press) Developmental psychopathology perspectives on substance abuse and relationship violence, in C. Wekerle and A.M. Wall (eds) *The Violence and Addiction Equation: Theoretical and Clinical Issues in Substance Abuse and Relationship Violence*. Philadelphia, PA: Brunner/Mazel.

Crittenden, P.M., Landini, A. and Claussen, A.H. (2001) A dynamic-maturation approach to treatment of maltreated children, in J. Hughes, J.C. Conley and A. la Greca (eds) *Handbook of Psychological Services for Children and Adolescents* (pp. 373–98). New York: Oxford University Press.

Dallos, R. (2001) ANT – Attachment Narrative Therapy: narrative and attachment theory approaches in systemic family therapy. *Journal of Family Psychotherapy*, 12: 43–72.

Dare, C. (1998) Psychoanalysis and family systems revisited: the old, old story? *Journal of Family Therapy*, 20: 165–76.

Diamond, G. and Siqueland, L. (1998) Emotions, attachment and the relational reframe: the first session. *Journal of Systemic Therapies*, 17(2): 36–50.

Erdman, P. and Caffery, T. (eds) (2003) *Attachment and Family Systems: Conceptual, Empirical, and Therapeutic Relatedness* (pp. 225–40). New York. Brunner-Routledge.

Feeney, J.A. (1999) Adult romantic attachments and couple relationship, in J. Cassidy and P.R. Shaver (eds) *Handbook of Attachment: Theory, Research and Clinical Applications*. New York: Guilford Press.

Flaskas, C. (1997) Engagement and the therapeutic relationship in systemic therapy. *Journal of Family Therapy*, 19: 263–82.

Flaskas, C. (2002) *Family Therapy: Beyond Postmodernism*. Hove: Brunner-Routledge.

Fonagy, P., Steele, M., Moran, G.S. and Higggit, A.C. (1993) Measuring the ghost in the nursery: an empirical study of the relations between parents' mental representations of childhood experiences and their infants' security attachment. *Journal of American Psychoanalytic Association*, 41: 957–89.

Fonargy, P., Steele, M., Steele, H., Leigh, T., Kennedy, R., Mattoon, G. and Target, M. (1995) Attachment, the reflective self and borderline states, in S. Goldberg, R. Muir and J. Kerr (eds) *Attachment Theory: Social Developmental and Clinical Perspectives*. New York: Analytic Press.

Hazan, C. and Shaver, P.R. (1987) Romantic love conceptualized as an attachment process. *Journal of Personality and Social Psychology*, 52: 511–24.

Hill, J., Fonagy, P., Safier, E. and Sargent, J. (2003) The ecology of attachment in the family. *Family Process*, 42: 205–21.

Hills, J. (ed.) (2002) *Rescripting Family Experiences: The Therapeutic Influence of John Byng-Hall*. London: Whurr.

Horvath, A. and Symonds, B. (1991) Relations between working alliance and outcome in psychotherapy. *Journal of Counselling Psychology*, 38: 139–49.

Hughes, D.A. (1998) *Building the Bonds of Attachment, Awakening Love in Deeply Troubled Children*. Northvale, NJ: Jason Aronson.

Jones, E. and Asen, E. (2000) *Systemic Couple Therapy and Depression*. London: Karnac.

Kobak, R., Duemmler, S., Burland, A. and Youngstrom, E. (1998) Attachment and negative absorption states: implications for treating distressed families. *Journal of Systemic Therapies*, 17: 80–92.

Leiper, R. (2001) *Working through Setback in Psychotherapy*. London: Sage.

Lindegger, G. and Barry, T. (1999) Attachment as an integrating concept in couple and family therapy: some considerations with special reference to South Africa. *Contemporary Family Therapy*, 21: 267–88.

Luborsky, L. (1984) *Principles of Psychoanalytic Psychotherapy. A Manual for Supportive-Expressive Treatment*. New York: Basic Books.

Marotta, S.A. (2003) Integrative systemic approaches to attachment related trauma, in P. Erdman and T. Caffery (eds) *Attachment and Family Systems: Conceptual, Empirical, and Therapeutic Relatedness*. New York: Brunner-Routledge.

McFadyen, A. (1997) *Rapprochement* in sight? Postmodern family therapy and psychoanalysis. *Journal of Family Therapy*, 19: 241–62.

Muir, E., Lojkasek, M. and Cohen, N. (1999) *Watch, Wait and Wonder: A Manual Describing a Dyadic Infant-Led Approach to Problems in Infancy and Early Childhood*. Toronto: The Hincks-Dellcrest Centre/Institute.

Muir, E., Lojkasek, M., and Cohen, N. (1999) Observant parents: interviewing through observation. *International Journal of Infant Observation*, 3: 11–23.

Muir, E., Lojkasek, M. and Cohen, N. (2000) Observing mothers observing their infants: an infant observation approach to early intervention. *PRISME*, 31: 154–70.

Ray, W.A. (2004) Interaction focused therapy: the Don Jackson legacy. *Brief Strategic and Systemic Therapy European Review*, 1: 36–45.

Safran, J.D., Crocker, P., McMain, S. and Murray, P. (1990) Therapeutic alliance ruptures as a therapy event for empirical investigation. *Psychotherapy*, 27(3): 154–65.

Walsh, F. (2003) Family resilience: a framework for clinical practice. *Family Process*, 42: 1–18.

Werner-Wilson, R.-J. and Davenport, B.R. (2003) Distinguishing between conceptualisations of attachment. Clinical implications in marriage and family therapy. *Contemporary Family Therapy*, 25(2): 179–93.

Wood, B.L. (2002) Attachment and family systems. *Family Process*, 41(3).

Young, J. (1990) *Cognitive Therapy for Personality Disorders: A Schema Focused Approach*. Sarasota, FL: Professional Resources Press.

5 Systemic formulation

Cultural landscape

As we have seen, systemic therapy offered a way of looking at problems and distress that differed from other approaches. Instead of starting with the person and his or her internal states as the initial focus, systemic family therapy saw distress and problems experienced as intimately bound up with relationships. As it has evolved there have been changes and shifts with systemic therapy as to how we explain problems, from problems in structures and patterns in the first phase to meanings and culturally shared language processes in the second and third phases. But how does such understanding or theory lead to our clinical practice? Increasingly in the psychotherapies there has been an emphasis on 'formulation' (Eels 1997). This is broadly definable as the process of putting together an understanding of the difficulties, combining information about the problems, observation, conversations with the family together with theory, clinical experience and the therapist's own personal experiences. This formulation essentially puts together a local theory about the causes of the problems, what is maintaining them and what might assist in facilitating change. Formulation therefore helps to offer explanations, but also ideas or guides for action. This emphasis has also been spurred by the various guidelines that have evolved on good clinical practice, for example the National Institute for Clinical Excellence (NICE 2001) guidelines which stress the need for clear assessment and choice of treatment informed by clinical evidence. At a simple level this can become an attempt to match the treatment to the type of problem based on the research evidence. In practice it is much more complex than this and formulation embodies the idea of fitting the treatment closely to a detailed exploration with families of their problems. Formualtion also helps to clarify communication and understanding between various professionals and between them and the family.

Importantly, formulation offers an alternative to psychiatric diagnosis. It offers an understanding based on psychological processes including thoughts and feelings and the impact of environmental events. In part, the roots of formulation can be traced to ideas regarding the 'function' of symptoms, for example in the behavioural therapies and in the process of 'functional analysis' (Slade 1982) and also in psychoanalytic theory, for ideas such as the defensive function that a symptom was seen to be serving (Freud 1958). This attempt to look for active psychological factors in the causation and maintenance of problems offers a contrast to diagnosis and diagnostic systems such as DSM (American Psychiatric Association 1980) and ICD. Though subjected to extensive critiques (Boyle 1990; Johnstone 1993) these still continue to be extensively employed in most mental health settings. This offers the challenge to those of us not wishing to acquiesce to notions of illness or disease as the basis of problems to be clear and convincing in the alternative explanations that we are able to offer.

It is increasingly becoming recognized that formulation needs to be a collaborative process whereby the therapist and family work together to co-construct a shared understanding of the difficulties. In effect, both the therapist and the family have their formulations. For example, many families come to us with forceful ideas influenced by medical theories, for example that their child 'has' ADHD and this is what is causing the problems. Moreover, as we will also see in the next chapter, formulation typically takes place in a context where colleagues work together who may hold quite different theories and ideas about problems. For example, psychologists, psychiatrists and social workers frequently work alongside each other in clinical work with children. In order to facilitate communication it is important to be clear and explicit about what their different understandings and explanations may be. Often in family therapy teams our experience has been that though we share a systemic perspective there are layers of differences shaped by our particular professional base. Formulation allows each team member to hold their own variation of a formulation regarding a family or system but also to move towards an understanding of points of agreement and, importantly, disagreement. The latter can then be employed as useful and creative tensions rather than covert feelings and later obstacles to co-operative work.

In this and the following chapter we want to outline a model of systemic formulation that offers a map to guide and encourage systemic thinking. As we will discuss in the following chapter, systemic thinking is not predominantly the application of specific techniques but a way of thinking about problems and difficulties. One of the major developments of systemic therapy has been the extension of such thinking not only to different family problems and configurations but also to the relationships within and between organizations and agencies.

Systemic theory: assessment and formulation

The initial model guiding systemic family therapy came from general systems theory, especially the notion of self-governing systems. The key concepts in the model were of problems as resulting from processes over time, of circular as opposed to linear causation, escalation and interconnected systems and subsystems. The emphasis in the first and second phases was on making 'objective' and 'scientific' assessments and formulations. The family was seen as an entity 'out there', which could be accurately described and assessed. The purpose of formulations was to be able to map the nature of the dysfunction and subsequently develop corrective interventions.

A range of standardized tests measuring family function were developed, among them the McMaster, Family Adaptability and Cohesiveness Evaluation Scales (FACES) and circumplex models (Olson *et al.* 1979). The aim was to assess 'dysfunctions' of family structure and process. For example, a family might be seen as lacking a clear hierarchy and decision-making capacity in the parental subsystem. Alternatively, they might be seen as caught up in a process whereby attempts by either parent to take control would be met by the other parent siding with the child. These formulations of dysfunctional structure and process would then guide the interventions specifically targeted to correct these.

Systemic theory has evolved since its inception in the 1950s from a theory centred on a biological metaphor of families as homeostatic systems to one of families as 'problem-saturated' linguistic systems. Symptoms are seen as problems in interaction and communication between people rather than as existing within persons. Importantly systemic approaches have increasingly come to regard all aspects of therapy as interactional and collaborative processes. Formulation, therefore, is not seen as something that the therapist *does to* the family but as something that he or she *does with* the family. The process of formulation is seen not as an objective process but as a set of perturbations which starts to change the family system. The questions that are asked, when and how they are asked and ensuing conversations can potentially prompt significant changes in families. Systemic therapists thus make less of a distinction between assessment, formulation and intervention.

It is tempting to aspire to promote schemes of assessment and formulation which set out clear and detailed guidelines that clinicians can follow, especially when the dictionary definition of *formulate* is 'to express clearly and exactly'. While it may be helpful to contemplate developing such maps, efforts to produce clear maps reveal the complexity of the task involved. However, we suggest that formulation contains within it core conceptual, psychological and philosophical issues relating to therapy. Most fundamentally, we are compelled to consider the meaning of what we consider to be a problem or symptom. Historically, family therapy has been critical of medical models and instead offered an interpersonal model of the causes and maintenance of problems. Significantly, it has also become increasingly critical of medical and pathologizing processes (White and Epston 1990; Hoffman 1993; Dallos and Draper 2000). Within this framework family therapy offers a critical position in that it endeavours to question the potentially oppressive assumptions that may be made about family members and which family members may have been 'conscripted' into holding about themselves.

The first phase

Function of a symptom

A cornerstone of early systemic thinking was that symptoms in families served a *function* of stabilizing a family system. In many ways this appeared a counter-intuitive idea since the established view was that the symptoms were the very thing that was causing the distress and unhappiness in the family. Don Jackson (1957) was the first to state clearly that a family with serious problems could be seen as if it was a rigid or homeostatic system. Examples of this could be seen in accounts of how the removal of a patient from a family into a psychiatric unit could be followed by another member of the family developing some difficulties as if to maintain the status quo of the family dynamics. The classic example came from work with children where it was suggested that, for example, a symptom shown by a child could serve a function of distracting attention from the parents' conflicts with each other and thereby stabilizing the marriage. As the child's symptom grew more intense the definition of the situation as the child having or being the problem would become increasingly dominant. In a sense family members were seen to be acting as if they had an investment in keeping the symptomatic member in that role despite overtly stating that they wanted them to change. It is possible to see connections here with psychoanalytic ideas, with the family as acting on the basis of the collective unconscious needs of its members (Ferreira 1963).

Attempted solutions

One of the most enduring and helpful ideas from the first phase is the model of formulation proposed by the MRI team. This consists of the elegantly simple idea that many problems arise from the failing solutions that are applied to ordinary difficulties:

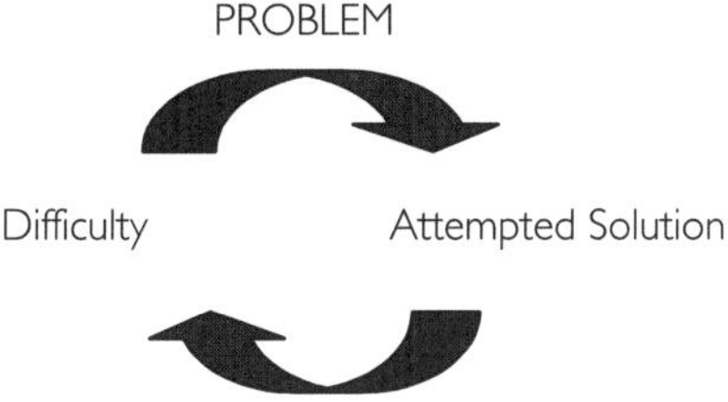

In this approach to formulation the focus is on an identification of what is seen as the problem and how this is linked to difficulties which the family has attempted to overcome. The formulation consists of the following steps:

- Deconstruction of the problem – when did it start, who first noticed, what was first noticed?
- Linking the problem to ordinary difficulties.
- Exploration of what was attempted to solve the difficulties.
- Beliefs about the difficulties and what to do about them.
- Discussion/evaluation of what worked and what did not work.
- What decisions were made about whether to persist with the attempted solutions and which solutions to pursue.

As we can see, this model bears a resemblance to a behavioural functional analysis (ABC) and cognitive behavioural analysis in that attempted solutions in effect represent *b*ehaviours, *c*onsequences are the effects of the attempted solutions and *a*ntecedents are in effect the difficulties or triggers that set off the attempted solutions. Like functional analysis, this model assumes that there is a recursive cycle in play so that the attempted solutions can serve to construct a vicious cycle whereby there is an escalation of the difficulties.

The second phase – progressive hypothesizing

The Milan team (Palazzoli *et al.* 1980) influentially articulated the idea of family therapy as inevitably progressing through a process of hypothesizing:

> By hypothesising we refer to the formulation by the therapist of a hypothesis based upon the information he possesses regarding the family that he is interviewing. The hypothesis establishes a starting point for his investigation as well as verification of the validity of that hypothesis based upon scientific methods and skill.

> If the hypothesis proves false, the therapist must form a second hypothesis based upon the information gathered during the testing of the first.

The process of developing hypotheses, they argued, was fundamental not only to the process of formulation but also to the practice of clinical work. A hypothesis could help to cut through the potential chaos of overwhelming amounts of information and help to organize the information into a manageable structure. A hypothesis can help the therapist to actively engage the family by pursuing issues and asking questions to explore and test the hypothesis and can offer a direction to the work, reducing therapist and family anxiety. A hypothesis was not to be seen as necessarily being true but as being more or less useful as a tool for eliciting new information.

The Milan team went on to note a number of other important aspects of this process:

- Explicitly forming and stating our hypotheses can help to reflect on our implicit assumptions, which if left implicit may get in the way of therapeutic progress.
- Articulation of hypotheses can help to reveal differences and agreements within the therapy team, which again might impede therapy if left unstated.
- There is less pressure on the therapist to 'get it right', which can reduce anxiety especially in the early stages of therapy.
- As the engagement with the family is less of an 'expert' position it may make it easier for the therapist and the team to remain curious and interested as opposed to trying to develop a correct formulation.

In the second phase it could seem as if the Milan team made statements about their hypothesis being 'correct' in providing an explanation for family dynamics. The team created hypotheses, and not the team and the family collaboratively.

The third phase

Systemic family therapy began to move towards constructivism – mutiple lenses, narratives and language. Families were no longer seen as objectively 'out there' and the task of the therapy team as being to accurately assess their dysfunctional patterns. It was recognized that we could only see a family through our own constructions – our personal lenses. Consequently, descriptions and formulations were seen as having an 'as if' quality – they were propositions rather than truth. As such these propositions could be more or less useful in guiding our work with families. The value of the propositions was essentially in terms of the extent to which they facilitated positive change. Instead of assessment and formulation being seen as a one-off scientific activity, they came to be seen as a continual process of developing, testing and revising formulations. This has much in common with George Kelly's (1955) notion of 'man the scientist' – that science and human experience are similar in essence in that both are engaged in a process of inquiry in which ideas about the world are formed, tested and revised where necessary (Hoffman 1993; Procter 1996; Dallos 1997).

Exploration of meaning and explanation

The work of the Milan team showed a significant shift in that the focus of the hypotheses and formulations was the belief systems of family members. Increasingly the emphasis was on the meanings that family members ascribed to each other's actions. For example, they describe a case of an adolescent boy who was displaying delinquent problems. The boy was living alone with his 'attractive' divorced mother. Their first hypothesis was that his behaviour was intended to draw his father back into the family. However, this was rapidly disproved and a more accurate hypothesis suggested itself: 'The mother was an attractive and charming woman, and, perhaps after these years of maternal dedication, she had met another man, and perhaps her son was jealous and angry, and was showing this through his behaviour' (Palazzoli *et al.* 1980: 2).

Two members of the Milan team (Luigi Boscolo and Gianfranco Cecchin) developed a more social constructionist view of formulation, which emphasized 'curiosity' as the cornerstone of systemic formulation rather than the analogies with the scientific process of hypothesizing and hypothesis testing (Cecchin 1987)

Systemic practice since the mid-1980s has shown a significant move towards social constructionism encapsulated in narrative approaches to therapy, which emphasize the idea of socially constructed realities and the centrality of language. Interestingly, this emphasis reconnects with its roots in communications theory, which emphasized that families were communicational systems, so that each and every action is seen as a potential communication. Likewise, symptoms were seen as attempts to communicate what was too difficult or too dangerous to say in any other way (Jackson 1957, 1965a, 1965b; Haley 1987).

Social constructionism shares these roots in communications theory in emphasizing that language is not fundamentally used to convey inner beliefs of the family members but that talk is in itself an action. How talk happens shapes the experiences, feelings and beliefs of family members. The idea is that when families increasingly or predominantly talk to each other in terms of problems and pathology, this creates problem-saturated systems (Anderson *et al.* 1986).

Another important feature of social constructionist approaches in current practice is the consideration of the role of dominant ideas or discourses that are shared in different cultures. For example, ideas such as that of mental health, satisfactory family life and normal transitions are seen to be embedded in language and shape the expectations and actions of family members. Therapy in part consists of raising these discourses to consciousness in order to assist families to be less trapped. Formulation attempts thereby to be a shared activity rather than predominantly conducted by the therapist (White and Epston 1990).

The phases of systemic family therapy emphasize different aspects of the formulation process, but we suggest there are a number of common threads. We propose the following model of systemic formulation:

1 *The problem – deconstruction*
2 *Contextual factors*
3 *Beliefs and explanations*
4 *Problem-maintaining patterns and feedback loops*
5 *Emotions and attachments.*

As we have suggested, family therapy has moved through a number of phases which are reflected in the formulation process. The phases have seen a shift from an emphasis on patterns and processes to cognitions and language and cultural contexts. These phases are also reflected in the scheme for formulation which has been proposed by Alan Carr (2000a):

1 Repetitive problem-maintaining behaviours
2 Constraining belief systems and narratives
3 Historical, contextual or constitutional factors.

By this he refers to factors, such as family scripts, economic and social support and, importantly, the cultural values and norms.

Our proposed formulation scheme shares many features of this model, but we offer some additional points of focus. In addition, we suggest that it is important to think about assessment and formulation in terms of two interconnected processes: *analysis* and *synthesis*. Analysis entails exploration with the family of the nature of the family, its members and their problems. This features prominently in the early sessions, and continues throughout therapy. Synthesis may follow or run alongside the assessment and analysis, and involves starting to integrate the strands of information into preliminary hypotheses or formulations of the problem. This distinction between analysis and synthesis is consistent with a constructivist view which regards observation and gathering of information as an 'active', 'selective' and 'interpretative' process. In starting afterwards to analyse the problem we are inevitably making assumptions and interpretations, for example about what evidence from the analysis is relevant, what further material we need, selectively attending to some factors and less to others. In recognizing this distinction it may be possible to adopt a reflexive stance and be less vulnerable to becoming limited by our implicit assumptions.

Example of systemic formulation

The formulation is presented partly in the present tense to convey a sense of active curiosity. The details of the case are outlined in the form given by the professional (social worker, nurse) 'keyworking' the case thus reflecting the 'hard' data/information a family therapist/team has available at the point of referral. In any one case there may be more or less information available. The aim in our example is to give a flavour of a systemic formulation for a complex case.

Genograms

Frequently a systemic formulation starts with a visual depiction or *genogram* of the immediate family and consideration of connections with external systems. The genogram (see Figure 5.1) offers a map of the family system in terms of relationships and sources of support, and helps to promote further therapists' questions which help to direct the gathering of further information.

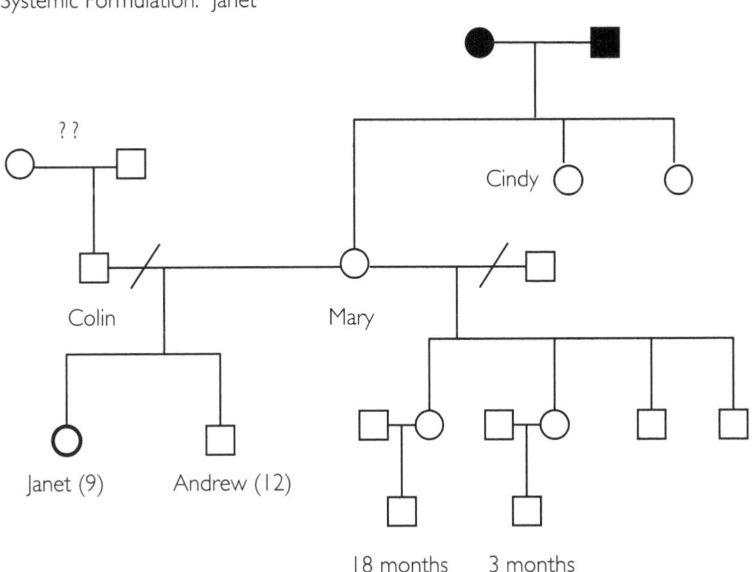

Figure 5.1 Janet's family genogram

Janet, aged 9, was referred by the school nurse to the primary care therapy service serving GPs in an inner-city locality. The school nurse reported an accumulation of concerns about Janet's weight and her behaviour at home, expressed by her mother.

Social Services files documented concerns about contacts with accident and emergency services at the local hospital, including an admission for a 'straddle injury' to Janet's groin at the age of 4. Several such incidents had occurred and Social Services had been alerted. Janet's mother, Mary, had also contacted Social Services, for example to ask for a wheelchair to assist Janet who she felt was experiencing difficulty with mobility. The accumulation of this evidence, plus Mary's anxieties, led to a referral to Child and Family Services. Mary and the school nurse had also expressed concerns about Janet's low weight.

Earlier, worries about Janet's development as an infant had been brought to the attention of the paediatric services. She was currently being reviewed at yearly intervals by the paediatric consultant. Mary reported having found it hard to 'bond' with Janet when she was born, and felt sad and depressed for a long time after her birth. At times she wished Janet would be taken away, though she did not feel like this towards her other children. She feels guilty about this now and cannot really understand why she felt this way. However, she was able to describe feelings of exhaustion and a deterioration in her marital relationship, with an eventual separation from her husband when Janet was 3. There had been a history of domestic violence from Janet's father towards Mary, which she attributed to his excessive drinking. He now lives alone in close proximity to the family, and until recently had overnight contact with Janet at his home. More recently Janet has said she does not want to stay overnight, but is still in contact with him.

Mary has a close relationship with her sister, Cindy, who lives locally and has no children of her own but has a special relationship with Janet and takes a close interest in her. Mary is very involved with her infant grandchildren. One of her older sons attended a school for children with learning and behavioural difficulties. Mary views him as possibly 'autistic'. One of her other sons has done well educationally and is a school teacher. This success is important to her.

The family have always lived in a very poor, socially deprived location in local authority accommodation, alongside some of the most 'difficult' families in the area. The area is due to be demolished, and the family have been waiting to be rehoused for the last 2 years. They are a Romany family from several generations back, and this is a central part of their identity. They express this in terms of a strong interest in spiritualism and clairvoyance. Mary's clairvoyant had mentioned a 'white car' which Mary connected with Janet's nightmare about a 'white van' and her fears of transport. Mary was in her late forties and at the time of the referral is awaiting a heart operation, having suffered from angina and arrhythmia for a number of years. This meant she easily becomes physically exhausted.

The referral

A recent specific development is Janet's refusal to travel in any form of transport. This started with her refusing to go on a school outing. However, she is willing to walk, for example to school, town and therapy sessions. Hence, she was attending a primary care service instead of the more distant secondary one. There are concerns that this is resulting in her becoming socially excluded and withdrawn. In parallel with this, her mother's limited mobility has resulted in her also becoming more excluded and withdrawn, especially from her extended family, for example on family holidays.

At home Janet cannot sleep in her own bed, has night terrors and loses control of her temper. She has also set the family dog on her mother. She is refusing to eat food prepared for her by Mary and is seriously underweight. At school Janet participates quite enthusiastically. She has friends and is achieving just adequately for her age; there are no substantial concerns regarding a learning disability. Mary describes Janet as being a prisoner in her own home.

Deconstructing the problems

Mary has a number of concerns about Janet's behaviour and fears. She appears to be worried that Janet is not eating properly and that she is becoming socially withdrawn and isolated as a result of her fear of transport and hence inability to see her friends or her family. It is also likely that Mary regards Janet's temper as a problem, especially her anger towards her. In addition, Mary has concerns about her own feelings about Janet, having found it difficult to bond with her and having felt that she wanted her taken into care. She links these feelings with the deterioration in her marriage and her fatigue. It is quite possible that, given the concerns of Social Services and school, Mary feels a failure as a mother and possibly that she is 'under the microscope' in relation to suspicions of abuse or neglect of the children.

Mary's clairvoyant appears to support a supernatural belief that a vision of a 'white van' is connected to Janet's fear of transport.

Mary's father's views are unclear, but it may be that he feels rejected by Janet and possibly feels under scrutiny from Mary and Social Services.

Janet appears to be angry with her mother and may see the problems as mainly to do with home since she is able to go to school and has friends there. It is possible that she is frustrated by her mother's loss of mobility and ill health and is in a sense copying her.

Social Services appear to have serious concerns that Janet may be either suffering some abuse or physical neglect since there are documented concerns about hospital admissions for injuries. This includes one for a prior straddle (groin) injury at age 4 which might be raising anxieties regarding sexual abuse. This concern has also been voiced by the school nurse who was worried at Janet's loss of weight.

Various exceptions and competencies are worth drawing out. Janet has friends and is achieving adequately at school. Mary appears to have a close relationship with Cindy, who seems to be fond of Janet. Mary has had success as a mother, one of her sons having become a school teacher, and she appears to be proud of this achievement.

Contextual factors

Mary and her family live in a socially deprived area. Mary has poor health and has no parents to support her. Janet's father has been violent, alcoholic and is possibly still being abusive towards her. It is also quite likely that financially the family are finding life very difficult. In addition, they have a Romany identity which might also contribute to their feeling marginalized. The professional agencies may have a high degree of suspicion about the family and about Mary's abilities as a parent. This may contribute to her anxiety, distress and sense of failure and self-blame. The involvement with Social Services has extended over a considerable period of time, at least since Janet was 4, and it might be that Mary has become dependent on Social Services and professionals to give her advice and direction, or that she feels her authority as a mother is undermined leaving her feeling depressed and incompetent:

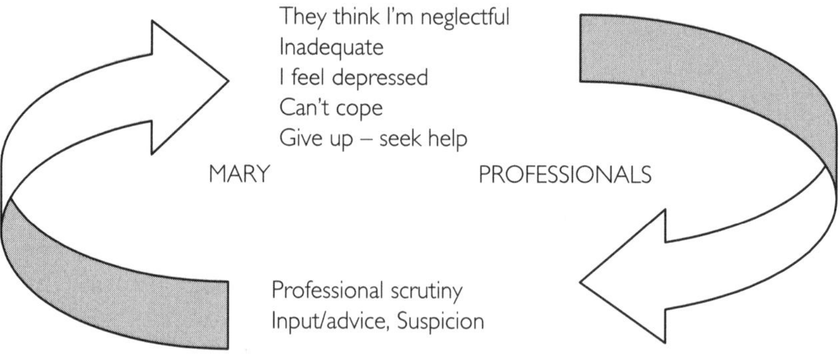

Beliefs and explanations

Mary appears to hold a belief that Janet's problems are caused by the difficulty she had in bonding with her – in effect, that perhaps she is a 'bad' mother. She tempers this view with a mitigating one that this was caused in turn by exhaustion and the deterioration of her relationship. It is also likely that she sees Janet's father as partly to blame because of his violence, though she has tried to enable contact to occur between him and Janet. Since her children have achieved differently, one a school teacher and the other with possibly 'autistic' problems, it is likely that Mary partly believes that there may be something medically wrong with Janet. Alongside such an organic view, Mary may believe that Janet has inherited tendencies, such as a bad temper, from her father. It is also possible that Mary may at times hold a belief that the problems are that she is exhausted, living in a poor area, coping with keeping contact with a violent ex-partner, and coping with ill health.

Janet may believe her mother does not care about her and may be frustrated with her mother's ill health. She may have some anger or anxiety towards her father, perhaps seeing his living situation as 'unsafe', and has decided not to stay with him overnight.

Outside the family, Social Services appear to hold a belief that there may be some abuse in this family which is at the basis of Janet's anxieties. This belief might be supported further by the fact that Janet seems to be performing reasonably well at school and has friendships.

Turning to socio-cultural beliefs and discourses, the dominant discourses shaping the beliefs of the family members and professionals are likely to be those of problems due to neglect and abuse or some form of organically based problems for Janet. More subjugated discourses might be that their social conditions are destructive – socially deprived area, difficult families and also that the family are marginalized due to their Romany origins.

Another dominant discourse in play may be that of the 'naturalness of motherhood': despite the conditions that she is in, Mary, as a good mother, ought to feel positive and loving towards her children rather than having 'bad', 'unnatural' thoughts such as having wanted to put Janet into care, despite experiencing violence from her father, etc.

Finally, due to their Romany origins, the family appear to hold beliefs about supernatural causes of the problems which also place them outside the cultural norms.

Problem-maintaining patterns and feedback loops

It does appear that there is a pattern of both rejection and dependency between Mary and Janet. Certainly Janet displays a need for her mother, while also venting her anger on her mother. Importantly, not eating and her fear of using transport mean her illness and dependency are maintained. For her part, Janet also appears to show a mixture of caring and negative feelings towards Janet. It is possible that their interaction shows a dynamic of Mary attempting to be patient, caring and considerate, which eventually exhausts her and leads to angry rejection. Janet is also the last of Mary's children and again this may involve a mixture of desperate exhaustion that she was the 'last straw' but on the other hand also the last baby and some feelings of regret.

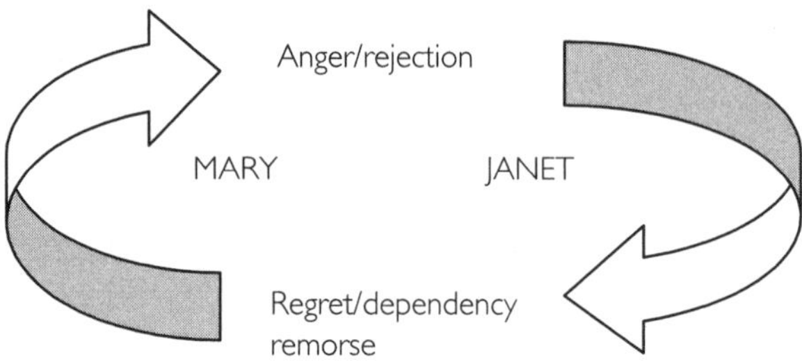

This pattern may be fuelled by the violence that Janet may have witnessed from her father towards her mother so that Janet imitates this. It might also be that Mary finds it hard to be consistent since she feels both angry and responsible about the painful events that Janet has experienced and her early feelings of wanting to reject her.

Emotions and attachments

It seems likely that there were early problems in the attachment between Mary and Janet. She felt sad and depressed and this may have induced an insecure attachment state in Janet. This could explain in part the pattern of Janet now engaging in clingy behaviours which ensure that she remains close to her mother, for example sleeping with her, and the anxiety about transport may represent a fear of being taken away from her. It is not clear what Mary's attachment history is, though she appears to have a close relationships with her sister. Certainly she has experienced the loss of her parents and the ending of her relationships with the fathers of her children. It is not clear when her parents died, and this may be connected to the attachment problems with Mary. It is also not clear wheher Mary's first relationship was abusive, but women who are abused in relationships often have had a history of insecure childhood relationships, and have witnessed or been a victim of violence. Usually this is accompanied by a sense of inadequacy and low self-esteem which makes them vulnerable to enter into abusive relationships on the basis of feeling they do not deserve any better.

Synthesis

The above framework may help to direct our attention to the complex web of factors that have shaped and maintain the problem/s. However, it is easy to see that even the brief examples that we have offered regarding Mary and Janet can quickly come to appear like an overwhelming kaleidoscope of factors. Somehow this mass of information needs to be combined into a manageable formulation. This requires that we engage in a process of selection of what is seen to be key as opposed to peripheral to our understanding of the problem. In effect, this can be seen as an example of a fundamental psychological process – the construction of a narrative which embraces events, actions and contexts into a story or 'pattern that connects'. The Milan team initially referred to this as 'hypothesizing' but, as we saw earlier, this was in the sense of seeing a hypothesis as an attempt to construct frameworks of meaning rather than to objectively test the real causes of the problems in a family.

Formulations: Mary and Janet

We offer two examples of systemic formulations of this case. Neither of these claims to be exhaustive, but each attempts to offer a view which fits with the available information. In practice this means that some features or details may be given more attention than others.

The difficulties may have arisen from the early experiences with Janet. Mary was experiencing abuse and the family were probably in difficult circumstances. Janet is the last of Mary's six children and it may be that she was exhausted physically and emotionally and felt she just did not have the energy for Janet. Also she was the second child with Janet's father, and Mary may have lost the hope that she perhaps had for the relationship with the first child, Andrew. It seems that Janet's father may not have made many positive contributions, leaving Mary feeling overwhelmed, abused and exhausted so that she found it hard to bond with Janet. This may have set in motion a pattern whereby she felt guilty and less able to manage her. For example, when Janet sleeps with her it may be harder for her to set clear rules about this since she feels guilty at having felt rejecting towards her when she was little. This sense of guilt may pervade a considerable proportion of her interaction with Janet. In turn Janet may respond to and aggravate this pattern by making greater demands for reassurance from her mother and finding ways of becoming dependent but also hostile towards her. Hence there may be patterns of comfort/rejection between them which are self-maintaining but also gradually escalating. This pattern may also be fuelled by the self-doubt that Mary may have about her abilities as a parent and low self-esteem resulting from the domestic abuse and her deprived living conditions.

A second formulation is concerned more with the relationships between Janet and her father and between the professional systems and Mary. Janet has recently refused to stay overnight with her father and it is possible that she has some fears about this situation. At home she is showing fears of sleeping on her own which might be connected to possible abusive events with her father. Also refusal to eat can be associated with sexual abuse, for example with oral sexual acts that the child may have been forced to perform. In addition to this, it might be that Mary is reluctant to think about this possibility since contact with the father has given her some occasional respite from Janet and also as a responsible mother she appreciates that Janet needs to have a relationship with her father. She may also be aware of the suspicions of Social Services and feel that to admit her concerns about this would further support a view of her as being to blame, at fault for not having drawn attention to the abuse earlier and so on. She may even fear that her children might be taken away from her, which makes her reluctant to voice her concerns. This lack of action might in turn engender anger from Janet for her mother 'not protecting her'. An escalating pattern may be fuelling mutual suspicions and concerns:

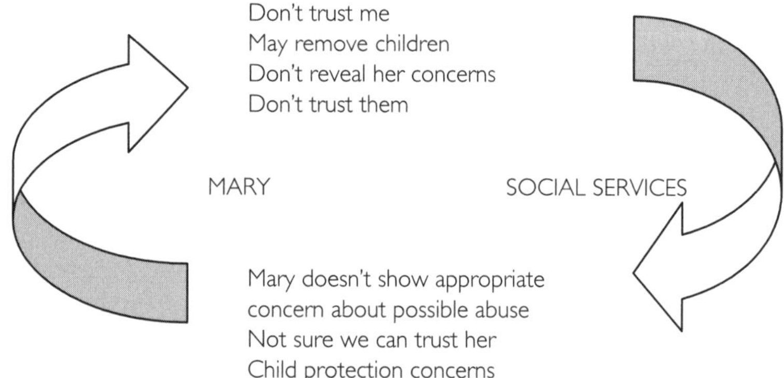

These two formulations are not exclusive and can be seen as complementing one another. In the case of the second there is an element of blaming involved in the suspicions regarding Janet's father. Rather than allocating blame it might also be possible to see Janet's father as caught in a process where he is seen as an 'abuser', alcoholic, violent and irresponsible. This is very tempting with families who live in such deprived social contexts, but it is important to remember that this is not the only context where abuse occurs and it can be discriminatory to assume that, because a family is poor and living in a deprived area, abuse is occurring. However, in the context of a history of injuries such a hypothesis would at least need to be considered. Importantly, though, a systemic hypothesis attempts to consider how the family–professional system can escalate and make matters worse as well as potentially better. Potentially escalating cycles of suspicion can fuel a sense of failure and eventual hopeless passivity for mothers like Mary.

Commentary

In the present culture in health and welfare professions 'formulation' is a much used word. Whether professionals from different disciplines have a shared understanding of the concept we would question, yet within the profession of systemic and family therapists there is a commitment to creating a shared language with colleagues in the interests of good practice and effective multidisciplinary working.

A systemic approach to formulation in 2005 takes into account the cultural context of the profession in Great Britain. For example, this fits with the guidelines that have been developed (NICE 2001) which emphasize comprehensive formulation as a cornerstone to offering the best treatments for various forms of distress and difficulties. However such guidelines can be over-prescriptive and ultimately unhelpful. Instead systemic formulation celebrates the uniqueness of each case by a sensitive analysis (see Skill Guide p. 169).

The emergence of children's trusts where professionals from education, health and social work are mandated to create an integrated service reflecting collaborative practice so that shared language for formulation is necessary.

Other clinicians working systemically with families find themselves in a variety of complex positions regarding formulation:

- As an employee of the state we may feel pressure to offers formulations which contain elements of social control, for example to enable a child in a family to become 'less disruptive' and return to school.
- We may be critical and sensitive in our formulations of patterns of inequalities and oppressions which have shaped the problems in the first place.
- We may be aware of the competing perceptions and definitions of the 'problem' – the individual's view, the family view, differences of opinion within the family, the view of various agencies, such as the police and Social Services involved with the family, school, the legal system, cultural systems and the therapist's professional system.

Key texts

American Psychiatric Association (1980) *Diagnostic and Statistical Manual of Mental Disorders*, 3rd edn. Washington, DC: American Psychiatric Association.

Anderson, H. and Goolishian, H. (1992) The client as expert: a not-knowing approach to therapy, in S. McNamee and K. Gergen (eds) *Therapy as Social Construction*. London: Sage.

Anderson, H., Goolishian, H.A. and Windermand, L. (1986) Problem determined systems: toward transformation in family therapy. *Journal of Strategic and Systemic Therapies*, 5: 1–13.

Boyle, M. (1990) *Schizophrenia: A Scientific Delusion?* London: Routledge.

Carr, A. (2000) Evidence-based practice in family therapy and systemic consultation I. *Journal of Family Therapy*, 22(1): 29–60.

Carter, E. and McGoldrick, M. (1988) *The Changing Family Life Cycle: A Framework for Family Therapy*, 2nd edn. New York: Gardner.

Cecchin, G. (1987) Hypothesizing, circularity and neutrality revisited: an invitation to curiosity. *Family Process*, 26: 405–13.

Dallos, R. (1996) *Interacting Stories: Narratives, Family Beliefs and Therapy*. London: Karnac.

Dallos, R. and Draper, R. (2000) *An Introduction to Family Therapy: Systemic Theory and Practice*, 1st edn. Buckingham: Open University Press.

Eels, T.D. (1997) *Handbook of Psychotherapy Case Formulation*. New York: Guilford Press.

Eron, J.B. and Lund, T.W. (1993) How problems evolve and dissolve: integrating narrative and strategic concepts. *Family Process*, 32: 291–309.

Ferreira, A.J. (1963) Family myths and homeostasis. *Archives of General Psychiatry*, 9: 457–63.

Haley, J. (1973) *Uncommon Therapy: The Psychiatric Techniques of M.H. Erickson*. New York: Norton.

Hoffman, L. (1993) *Exchanging Voices: A Collaborative Approach to Family Therapy*. London: Karnac.

HMSO (2000) *Assessing Children in Need and Their Families*. London: HMSO

Jackson, D. (1957) The question of family homeostasis. *Psychiatry Quarterly Supplement*, 31: 79–99.

Johnstone, L. (1993) Are we allowed to disagree? *Forum*, 56: 31–4.

National Institute for Clinical Excellence (2001) *The Guideline Development Process: Information for National Collaborating Centres and Guideline Development Groups*. London: NICE.

Olson, D.H., Sprenkle, D.H and Russel, C.S. (1979) Circumplex model of marital family interaction. *Family Process*, 18: 3–28.

Palazzoli, M.S., Boscolo, L., Prata, G. and Cecchin, G. (1978) *Paradox and Counter Paradox: A New Model in the Therapy of the Family in Schizophrenic Transaction*. New York: Jason Aronson.

Palazzoli, M.S., Boscolo, L., Cecchin, G. and Prata, G. (1980) Hypothesizing – circularity – neutrality: three guidelines for the conductor of the session. *Family Process*, 19: 3–12.

Procter, H. (1981) Family construct psychology, in S. Walrond-Skinner (ed.) *Family Therapy and Approaches*. London: Routledge & Kegan Paul.

Rustin, M. and Quagliata, E. (eds) (2000) *Assessment in Child Psychotherapy*. Tavistock Clinical Series. London: Duckworth.
Rutter, M. (1999) Resilience concepts and findings: implications for family therapy. *Journal of Family Therapy*, 21(2): 119–44.
Slade, P. (1982) Towards a functional analysis of anorexia nervosa and bulimia nervosa. *British Journal of Clinical Psychology*, 21: 167–79.
White, M. and Epston, D. (1990) *Narrative Means to Therapeutic Ends*. London: Norton.

SKILL GUIDE

Systemic formulation

We have suggested that systemic formulation involves a number of components. Though we have placed these in order, it is not necessary that you follow this. However, we do suggest that taking time to explore each of these areas can be helpful in the initial stages of formulations. Furthermore, we suggest that the process involves an interconnected process of analysis and synthesis. It makes sense for analysis to come first, but in reality often cases come to us already formulated to some extent, for example in a referral letter from a medical colleague or social worker. In effect, the synthesis phase has already begun and may have an effect of pre-empting the analysis phase. For these reasons it may be useful to adopt a propositional, curious, 'not knowing' position to formulation (Anderson and Goolishian 1992). We may move between analysis and synthesis in a repeated, 'recursive' manner, coming to form what appear to be convincing ideas or theories which we may revise in the face of new information. Likewise, our lack of clarity about our formulation may lead us to actively seek further information.

Formulation is also a collaborative process, and the components that we outline below will be things that the family has already thought about. Often there are disagreements within the family about their formulations and they feel confused about 'what is going on' and 'why the problem is happening'. Therefore, how much we share our formulation with a family at any particular point in time is a sensitive decision. Some families may initially be seeking support and advice, and may feel confused by premature theorizing. Formulations can be shared with families through reflecting team processes, and it may be helpful for teams to bear the five areas below in mind so that their conversations embrace these, though the balance may vary from session to session as therapy progresses.

Analysis

1 *The problem – deconstruction*. What is seen to be the problem and by whom? How did the family come to us, who initiated the referral and why? The role of professionals in defining the problem. The role of others, for example extended family and friends, in defining the problem.
2 *Contextual factors*. Family structure and genograms, family life-line, history of the problem, environmental factors, family resources, cultural factors, role and history of other agencies
3 *Beliefs and explanations*. The meanings that different family members hold about the problem, agreements and disagreements in their beliefs, values and expectations in the family, impact of community, religious and cultural beliefs and attitudes.
4 *Problem-maintaining patterns and feedback loops*. Structures: exploration of the organization of the family in terms of boundaries, hierarchy, subsystems and other systems connected to the family. Process and feedback loops: repetitive patterns of behaviours, thoughts and feelings and possible examples of escalating patterns.
5 *Emotions and attachments*. This involves exploring the emotional life of the family, especially the attachments and emotional dependencies between family members and across the generations. This may be a reflexive process whereby the therapist's own initial feelings about the family and the impact of the family on him or her are explored to guide thinking about the family's view of the world, trust and anxieties.

Synthesis

It is a considerable task to weave together this mass of information. Therefore synthesis is inevitably selective and to some extent intuitive. It is not about being correct but about helping us to stay curious and active in our thinking rather than stuck, for example, in negative ways of seeing the family. The following we suggest may also help this process:

- *Reflexive position*. An attempt to consider our own beliefs and assumptions and how these are shaping our formulations. Recognition that we are engaged in 'formulating' – that it is an active ongoing process and the relationship we are developing with the family is influencing this process. For example, if we are beginning to feel disappointed in the lack of progress some more negative tone to our formulations may start to creep in!
- *Levels of analysis*. It is possible to think about synthesis as moving

between more local and immediate analysis of the family dynamics and beliefs and wider organizational and cultural factors. It can be helpful to map the patterns initially alongside the wider contextual factors to try to see how they fit together. For example, we can draw with a family a diagram of some of the core patterns surrounding the problem and look at what sense other professional agencies, with their religious or cultural values, make of these patterns.

- *Collaboration*. Formulation is not just something we do. The family has its own ideas and also ideas about our ideas, and we may have ideas about their ideas, about our ideas and so on. Reflecting team discussions can be helpful in facilitating mutual understanding and the feedback from a family may help us to co-construct joint formulations. Inevitably, if our formulation is significantly different from the family's own understanding then stuckness, lack of trust and loss of co-operation are likely to follow.
- *Engagement/authenticity*. For both the therapy team and the family thinking and formulation are more productive, free and creative when there is a sense of trust and a mutually secure base or sense of safety. There is no magic recipe for fostering this, but an attempt to be honest and authentic is important. This may involve open discussions with the family about some differences in opinions and feelings. Left unstated these can leave a sense of unspoken judgements and criticisms which get in the way of developing a collaborative formulation. A typical example is when a family returns to a descriptive cataloguing of the problems and the therapy team feels exasperated that they have moved no further in their understandings. However, this may reflect the fact that the family feels that their views of how serious and difficult things are have not been heard and taken account of in the formulation of the problems.

6 Current practice development 2000–2005

Conversations across the boundaries of models

Cultural landscape

In the previous chapters we have described how systemic family therapy has evolved from the original experimentation with meeting together with family members to the development of a variety of family therapy models. We have also looked at how systemic approaches offer a way of formulating problems and difficulties which is different from other approaches, such as cognitive, psychodynamic and behavioural models.

Since its birth in the 1950s we have seen systemic thinking and practice develop from a precocious infant into a deviant and marginalized adolescent and then finally into a fully fledged and respected member of adult society. Politicians now even refer to 'systemic' problems and processes in everyday language. It is this wider impact on both popular and professional consciousness that we wish to have as a starting focus for this chapter.

Possibly in its early rebellious adolescent period systemic family therapy was more resistant to embracing integrations. Haley (1987), for example, argued that systemic and psychoanalytic ideas were largely incompatible, since systemic ideas locate problems in the transactional patterns between people whereas psychoanalytic ideas locate them firmly within individuals' psyches. But nowadays systemic family therapists can be seen in conversations across the boundaries with psychodynamic, cognitive and behavioural colleagues.

In much contemporary practice systemic therapists find themselves working alongside colleagues using different approaches, but having similar organizational demands and rules. Good work with a family can be neutralized if communication and co-ordination between the different professionals involved in a case is poor or ineffective. In fact we suggest that it is as important to manage these interprofessional relationships as it is the work with a family, if not more so! Systemic and family therapists, with their emphasis on different levels of context, are well placed to facilitate 'connections' across the boundaries of models.

Systemic theory has increasingly moved towards a self-reflexive approach in that an essential part of the analysis moves from 'out there' – an analysis of the family – to a more internal analysis 'in here' – in which the focus is on how the therapist and the family are experiencing each other (Flaskas 2002)

The plenary sessions at the annual conference of the British Association of Family Therapy and Systemic Practice in October 2004 provide a useful measure for the self-reflexive capacity of the profession: plenary speaker Sheila McNamee spoke on the theme of promiscuity in the practice of family therapy; Pam Ryecroft talked about wading through the 'swampy lowlands' of practice when theory abandons us; and Bebee Speed's presentation, with its emphasis on collaborating with colleagues who use different approaches, was entitled 'All aboard in the NHS' (see *Journal of Family Therapy*, 26(3): 224–79).

Systemic approaches are increasingly used in various settings and with a variety of problems where the work does not simply or predominantly involve meeting with family members but instead consists of the application of a systemic perspective or systemic thinking to the dynamics of various organizations and issues. In this chapter we describe examples of how systemic practitioners work creatively in a variety of contexts such as mental health units, forensic settings, educational settings, multi-disciplinary mental health teams, residential homes for children and therapeutic work with individuals.

Practice

As we have seen in the previous chapters, systemic family therapy can be seen more as an approach or orientation than as a set of specific techniques. The central idea of feedback drives a pragmatic approach to problems and difficulties. Perhaps this was most explicitly articulated in the MRI team's definition of problems as arising from failed attempted solutions to problems (Watzlawick *et al.* 1967, 1974). This elegantly simple approach provides a way of thinking about problems and difficulties in a variety of situations. This chapter will employ the model of systemic formulation described in the previous chapter (see Skills Guide) to look at some important developments and conversations across the boundaries with models outside systemic family therapy. Of course, deciding where a model ends and another begins is not always so straightforward. As a starting point we suggest that it is possible to see some paradoxes in contemporary thinking in systemic family therapy, and likewise in other therapies. On the one hand post-modernist thinking eschews the notion of reality and truth and argues that instead there are competing ideas or narratives about the world, including families and the role of their dynamics in relating to problems. For example, Harlene Anderson does not locate problems in terms of family dynamics as such but in terms of conversational patterns (Anderson *et al.* 1986). But alongside such postmodern views there is also an increasing recognition of the value of some modernist ideas such as patterns of family attachment (Doane and Diamond 1994; Byng-Hall 1995, 1998; Dallos 2004) or patterns of expressed emotions (Leff and Vaughn 1985; Leff *et al.* 2003). The latter approach has prompted wider psychoeducational approaches to severe conditions such as schizophrenia, depression and eating disorders. These focus on the structure of the emotional connections between family members in an unashamedly modernist manner.

The examples we have chosen illustrate applications of systemic ideas in situations which do not obviously lend themselves to typical systemic family therapy as well as attempts to integrate with other models of intervention. The relevant key elements of systemic formulation appear in each case discussion in *italics*.

Working with addictions

Vetere and Dallos (2003) comment that the application of systemic approaches has been slow in the addiction field, including mainstream alcohol treatment services. Typically treatments have emphasized group therapy approaches, individual therapy, including behavioural and psychodynamic therapies and medical approaches focusing on dealing with attendant health problems. The approach adopted by Vetere and Henley (2001) is an excellent exemplar of how systemic thinking can be woven in and used alongside other approaches, for example in multi-modal and multi-professional work in adult and child mental health services in the NHS and in work in social services.

Analysis

The problem – deconstruction

The starting point of Vetere and Henley's (2001) *analysis* was that it is not only the drinker who has a problem. Clearly there is usually one person in the family who is identified as the 'alcoholic'; however, drinking problems have an impact on family relationships:

> They include disruption to family members' roles, routines, and communication, disruption to family celebrations, and adverse

> effects on social life and family finances. For example, there may be difficulties for children in bringing friends home, or being collected safely from school, when a parent is drinking; family celebrations may be spoiled by drunken behaviour; opportunities for socialisation may be constrained because of shame and embarrassment . . .
>
> (Vetere and Dallos 2003: 167)

In addition to these problems, there may be changes in the roles taken by family members, with the alcoholic parent unable to carry out tasks such as working to financially support the family. There may also be violence. The family may become organized around the drinking, with concomitant social withdrawal and depression for other members as well as the drinker. In short, a systemic analysis of the problem recognizes that family members also need help at least to enable honest communication among family members about the impact of drinking, for example, and in some cases to escape from the trap of a mutually destructive relationship.

More broadly, there is also a great problem for alcohol services. Progress is often slow, with relapse frequent, and staff may come to feel exasperated and angry with clients' apparent unwillingness to change.

Systemic practice allows co-dependency issues to be addressed more effectively.

Contextual factors

Community alcohol services have typically had an individual focus, offering medical advice, individual behavioural and cognitive therapies, as well as group therapy approaches during rehabilitation. The Alcoholics Anonymous movement has also had an impact with its 12-step programme, which emphasizes abstinence and the need to admit defeat – 'hitting rock bottom' as a precursor to a form of religious conversion to sobriety. More recently, the services have been stimulated by models of motivation, for example motivational interviewing (Miller and Rollnick 1991) and the cycle of change model (Prochaska and DiClemente 1992). The latter model was adopted as the context for service delivery and development. It emphasizes that change is cyclical, progressing through precontemplation, contemplation, motivational interviewing, preparation, action and maintenance, and importantly that relapse is expected and is seen as part of the cycle of change. It is also recognized that people may go through the whole or parts of the cycle several times before they manage to maintain abstinence or controlled drinking.

In relation to drinking there is a recognition that problems occur in a variety of contexts. For example, people describe how some of their excessive drinking takes place in work or leisure contexts. For many couples it was initially an activity they enjoyed together. Even more broadly, the problems can be located within a wider cultural context in which heavy drinking is associated with fun, sexuality and, especially for men, potency. Alcohol producers invest a vast amount of money in advertising drink through images promoting such associations.

Beliefs and explanations

Paradoxically the dominant beliefs amongst families are typically that drinking is an involuntary illness, perhaps inherited from parents, but also an irresponsible behaviour. It may have been learnt, perhaps from parents and friends, but this more social view also implies that the person should be able to do something about it 'if they really wanted to'. These two beliefs can be seen to contradict each other and associated beliefs about what actions follow from this. If it is an illness, then the belief may be that they deserve sympathy and support, whereas if it is irresponsible behaviour, then family members feel it is appropriate to be angry and to condemn the behaviour. Family members may also feel responsible for causing the drinking, for example that they have been too critical, uncaring and so on, but then again that they cannot have positive feelings towards the person.

The beliefs held by the person with the drinking problem reflect these beliefs but also frequently a sense that they are more able to cope, more relaxed and able to control it. Bateson (1972) described this as a 'symmetrical struggle with the bottle' in that the person believes that they can beat it. These are also reflected in dominant professional models and explanations that mesh with a family member's thinking, for example the learned behaviour models. Vetere and Henley (2001) describe how in addition the community alcohol service had incorporated the cycle of change model which offers a map of the characteristic beliefs that people hold regarding their drinking (though they may not be aware of these beliefs):

- *Precontemplation* – this typically involves denial, a view that 'I do not have a problem' and 'I do not see why I have to change my behaviour'.
- *Contemplation* – there is a recognition that they have a problem but they do not believe they can really do anything to change it. This is often a pessimistic, depressive state where the recognition of problems is medicated away with drink – it is seen as the only viable solution.
- *Preparation* – a belief that something can be done, and the formation of a plan for when and how the changes will start.
- *Action* – a belief that the time is right to start to make some changes, to 'get up and do it'.
- *Maintenance* – this involves a belief that though changes have been made, maintaining these will require planning and support.

This model also represents a set of beliefs that inform the professional working in this context and which then are shared with the drinkers and their families.

Problem-maintaining patterns – feedback loops
Vetere and Henley (2001) suggest that the primary relationship for the person with the drinking problem is with alcohol. As other relationships deteriorate, they may feel they have less to live for and therefore need to drink more. Family members may become intensely involved in this process and form strategies to disrupt it, such as searching for alcohol, hiding alcohol, isolating the drinker, keeping the drinker short of money and keeping people away from the family. These strategies may not only shame the drinker but also come to socially isolate and shame the family members. There is also the possibility that other family members gain a moral high ground and some sense of power, for example children may reprimand their father and speak to him in a belittling manner. This can further lead the drinker to feel shamed, a failure, humiliated, to which they respond with anger and or more drinking.

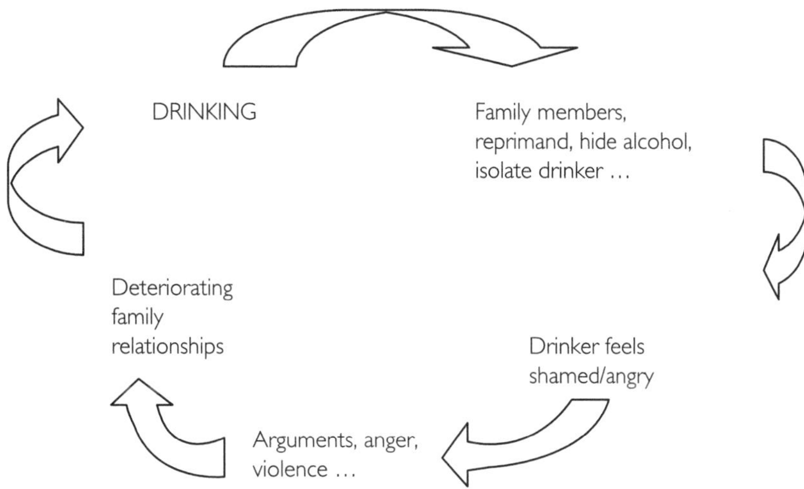

Emotions and attachments
Vetere and Henley (2001) describe how the primary relationship and attachment appears to be with alcohol. It appears to offer more comfort than other relationships in the person's life. This may have arisen as a learned pattern whereby, for example, the drinker has seen his father or mother use alcohol as a way of coping with painful feelings, such as failure, loss and abandonment. In some sense there may even be a sense of loyalty to a parent through drinking. Many young men, for

example, find that the only personal and 'intimate' time they have had with their father has been over drinks in the pub. Even more frequently, alcohol may be a way of medicating away painful feelings of abuse, abandonment and neglect in the family or institutions in which they have lived. A vicious cycle of reflective behaviour is established, it becomes very difficult for the family members to react with much affection, which in turn confirms the drinker's sense of failure and abandonment, and arouses attachment anxieties which are self-medicated away through alcohol.

Family members, for their part, have come to feel inadequate and anxious that they cannot help or deal with the problems. They may not want to raise their hopes one more time, only to have them dashed. Earlier on in the progression of the problem there may be an alternating pattern of hopefulness and bliss that 'everything will now be fine' when the drinker stops for a while. Typically this fails and they may then all feel let down, hurt and eventually move towards giving up hope. This can lead to an avoidant attachment approach where they too find ways of trying to cut off their feelings and act like they no longer care about the drinker. This deterioration may mean that the drinker feels there is nothing left to lose, so why try to make the effort? For many couples sexual intimacy ceases both because of negative feelings and physical inability, and a further potential source of intimacy, contact and attachment is lost. A related danger is that if attempts are made to resume intimacy after periods of separation, for example during a temporary period of sobriety, this may not work or be very satisfying because of the long-standing distrust, anger and sadness between partners. Attempts at intimacy then become highly charged and prone to disappointment, with each partner feeling they have mad a huge effort only to be let down again.

Synthesis

Vetere and Henley (2001) present an approach to working with alcohol problems which offers an integrated formulation combining a systemic approach with the cycle of change model. This involves a recognition that engagement is likely to be a difficult and lengthy process and, in keeping with the cycle of change and systemic theory, that relapse will be very likely to occur. They combine work with the drinker alongside work with the family members.

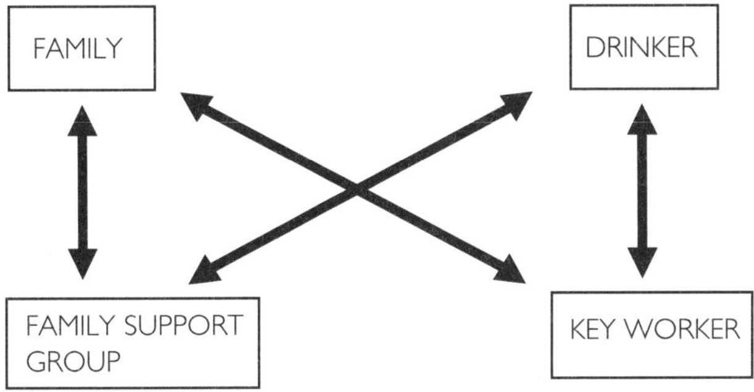

The relationship with the key worker is seen as part of an important triangle. An alcohol service worker attempts to build, through individual contact, a constructive relationship with the drinker. This may be the first positive relationship the drinker has been able to build and experience for some time. Alongside this there is an eight-week relatives support group for the family members. The cycle of change model is employed as a framework, with discussions for both the drinker and family members about the possible implications of changes and how ready they are to contemplate and carry out change.

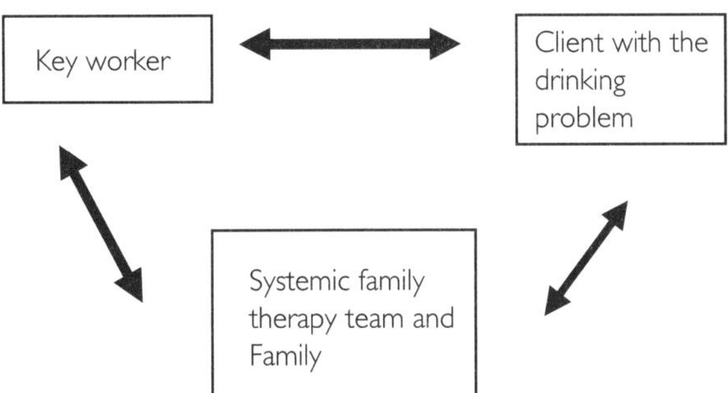

The key worker helps and supports the client to make the changes and also offers encouragement in the face of the difficulties the client may have to face regarding the family work. The family therapy team liaise with the key worker to maintain clear communication in an effort to avoid potential difficulties or sabotaging of the work. In this way support is offered both to the client and to the family as they prepare for and then engage in change processes. The motivational model is used throughout, with the recognition that the client and family need considerable time to engage with treatment and have the opportunity to consult the team and key worker before they actually engage in making changes. Specifically, the approach emphasizes that both family members and the client need to recognize and accept that they need to make changes:

> The legacy of shame and contempt from the non-drinking partner can persist while the drinking partner revolves around the stages of change, seemingly unable to change and reinforcing the idea that they are unable to accept responsibility for their behaviour. In these circumstances it seems to us that the non-drinking partner holds a belief that they do not need to change, almost as if they are in the pre-contemplation stage.
>
> (Vetere and Dallos 2003: 171)

The family have a chance to discuss these issues in the family support group and share experiences with other families. They are also offered consultation with the key worker or the family therapy team as a preparation for the family therapy work. Support from the key worker remains in place during the action and maintenance part of the work. This support can help to deal with disappointments, resentments, anger and loss of hope on the part of both the family and the drinker. Processing these feelings in individuals can make family therapy sessions more productive and focused on change.

Example

Claire, a mother of four, was referred by her key worker, having recently attended a detoxification programme run by the community alcohol service (*contemplation, preparation* and *lapse*). Following this and the previous two programmes, her relationship with Mike went through a blissful period but then plummeted back to previous relationship dissatisfactions. Mike, a businessman, asked for help with their relationship, though Claire was initially less committed to this agenda (*co-dependency*). She described having been multiply abused by her stepfather and confused about why her mother had not protected her. Claire had attended some courses in counselling skills which she had not completed, feeling that Mike had supported her in her efforts. Mike had insisted that Claire attend work-based social functions with him, which she disliked and at which she drank to excess.

The couple were seen for consultation meetings (*preparation, action* and *lapse*) in an attempt to assist them, especially Claire, to move towards a preparation and action phase of change. During these consultations she revealed that she felt Mike treated her like her father and felt subordinate to him. A discussion of issues of empowerment and gender relationships took place and allowed Claire to agree to Mike's wish to resume their sexual relationship.

Following this consultation phase regular three-weekly couples therapy took place (*action phase*) along with a number of individual meetings. The couple's work addressed issues of power and control in the relationship, alcohol as a way of coping with unbearable feelings, communication, physical intimacy and decision-making. Claire stopped drinking and they decided to cease regular meetings though they kept the door open for further meetings. Claire decided she needed a short period of trial separation from Mike. Following this they returned for further work (*maintenance of changes*) in which they discussed Mike's heavy drinking and abusive behaviour early on in the relationship, his insecurity and attempt to control Claire. They accepted that both of them needed to change and to take responsibility for their behaviour. Claire started work with homeless people on a voluntary basis and Mike has promised his support for her to attend college. An important strand of their new understanding was that Claire recognized that she had gone from an abusive relationship in her family of origin into a marriage with Mike in which she was subordinate. These structural shifts, such as Claire's work outside the home and preparation for college, along with a fundamental revision in their joint understanding of the problems, are seen as a necessary part of the *maintenance of changes*. Both Claire and Mike recognize the need for Claire to establish her independence, and they may decide to live separately for some time. Claire continues to be abstinent.

Working with post-divorce processes and contact disputes

In the UK it is estimated that the number of marriages which end in divorce is approaching 40% (Muncie *et al.* 1997). In addition, many children are born outside formal marriage relationships which have a high chance of ending. Sociologically this is quite a profound shift since the start of family therapy fifty years ago and has substantial implications for how we think about our work.

What follows is an account of work in a private practice. The families described have not entered into therapy but made, under some pressure, some small steps to try and resolve issues of access. In their communications to the families and the courts Blow and Daniel (2002) attempt to offer a recognition of each partner's and the children's positions without confronting anybody. However, they do aim to introduce an element of uncertainty – the possibility that there may be other ways of viewing things. Most importantly, a central part of this is 'privileging children's narratives'. They conclude their account with a powerful reflexive note: 'In this context, the meaning of mothering and fathering, the question of children's rights and adults' responsibilities, all become exposed in a raw form which challenges therapists and other practitioners to the core to question their own values and beliefs' (Blow and Daniel 2002: 101).

It is now almost the norm for a child to experience the separation of his or her parents and to grow up in some form of arrangement which involves different levels of contact with them. For many family therapists and of course other clinicians and professionals involved with children and families, a substantial part of the work is dealing with the aftermath of the effects of the separation and, importantly, the continuing contact processes.

Analysis

The problem – deconstruction

Many children show great distress as well as a range of problems which turn out to be related to divorce and its aftermath. Among the manifestations of this are sadness, failure at school, violence and behavioural problems, anger towards parents and loss of contact with parents. Parents also manifest problems, for example increasing animosity towards one another, sometimes culminating in violence witnessed by children.

Professionals working with children in various contexts may be unable to bring about any change in the context of such raging disputes and may experience a real pull to take sides. Each partner's stories may become 'frozen' – for example, stories about harsh and abusive behaviour may become embellished to support their sense of justification. We frequently hear, for example, that a father has been and is abusive and therefore contact with the children should be avoided. Of course, in some cases this may be appropriate but in part the story serves a function of managing the otherwise unmanageable feelings of the divorce. For clinicians there can be difficulties in both striving to hear and understand the underlying pain as well as helping partners to move towards less 'frozen' stories which give the children more space. However, the issues are further complicated when there are new partners, stepchildren and extended family.

Context

The work is carried out as a private therapeutic service which offers systemic therapy to individuals, couples and families. Referrals come from solicitors and court welfare officials. The main reasons for the referrals are contact disputes where previous interventions have been unsuccessful and where there is a request for assessment and recommendations for contact arrangements. The work usually takes the form of ten sessions or so of 'systemic assessment', with family members being seen together and individually. This involves 'exploring connections between the accounts of different participants, testing patterns between the accounts of different participants, testing out the possibilities for change and endeavouring to create a space for new thinking which can lead to different interactions' (Blow and Daniel 2002: 87). A report is prepared for the courts which attempts to offer a new story for all of the participants, connecting together the competing stories.

The wider context is that the legal system can promote an adversarial framework with each partner convinced that the other is attempting to exploit them. Financial, emotional and contact issues may become entangled in legal language and attempts to establish who is really to blame.

Beliefs and explanations
Blow and Daniel (2002) emphasize that it is important to consider not only the content of the beliefs that family members hold but also the form of these stories and the processes or structures that maintain them. In particular, they describe how the parents may have developed dramatically new ways of storying their lives. This may include negative ways of seeing a partner in order to justify the decision to divorce. But these changes may be less positive and acceptable for the children. In addition, there may be pressure to stick to rigid stories in the context of legal battles where consistency is emphasized and to change one's story might imply devastating consequences.

Blow and Daniel (2002) emphasize that in this context there may be intensely different narratives regarding events to the point where the therapist almost feels that they are going 'mad'. Importantly they also emphasize that the explanations and stories that people hold need to be seen in a developmental perspective and in terms of how they are shaped and constrained by the current as well as past dynamics. For example, a child's narrative that she does not want to see her father because he frightens her is both her story and her choice, but is also shaped by her feelings about what her mother wants and needs to hear and by what has happened in the family prior to the divorce.

A number of important and common themes are found in Blow and Daniel's work; for example, a belief that one partner was the cause and decided to separate, leaving the other as a victim. Gender and power are an important related theme with the children predominantly living with the mothers who may take the 'moral high ground' that they are acting out of responsibility for their children's interests. Fathers are seen as more likely to act on the basis of rights and hold a belief that the mother's actions are unfair. Alongside this sense of unfairness there can be a belief for both partners that they are powerless.

Problem-maintaining patterns – feedback loops
Blow and Daniel (2002) say that though parents readily agree that their children's interests come first, each may also believe that only they truly know what the child wants. While the disputes appear to relate to the children and access, they usually represent long-standing power struggles between the couple. Children often experience being told by one parent that they have been brainwashed by the other (non-resident) parent, and while acknowledging the reality that the parent may have tried to influence them, often decide not to see or to see less of a non-resident parent. For children who had once been close to the non-resident parent, this can be seen as an escape from an intolerable

situation into 'certainty', which fails to take into account the complexity of children's thinking.

An important point is that it may be very tempting to see children as passive victims in this process, but the children need to be seen as making decisions, albeit ones constrained by the system they are in. Typically, siblings also take different roles, with one child going willingly to see a parent and the other adamantly refusing. Though this may not be conscious, it can be a way of balancing the system. In our experience the child displaying the greatest apparent difficulty is often the one who is also demonstrating a greater loyalty to the marriage. Sometimes this is shown by conflict, confrontation and refusal to accept a new partner, since such acceptance would mean feeling the finality of the parents' separation.

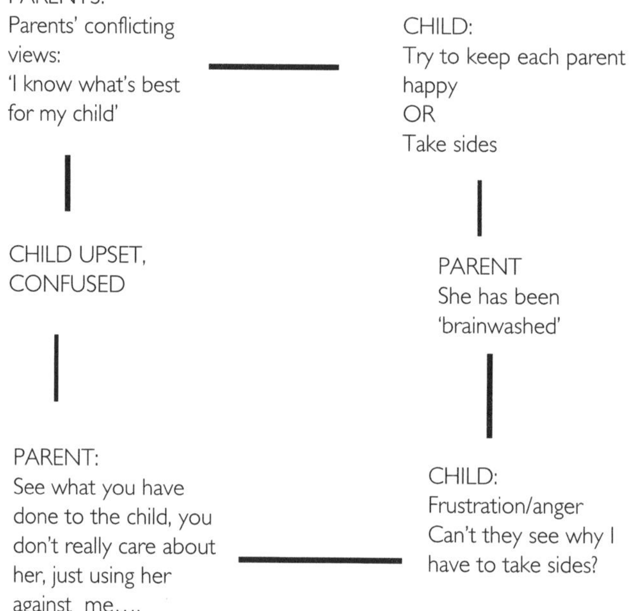

Emotions and attachments

In the context of the emotional chaos of divorce and its aftermath, parents may cling to their children's love as the one thing that they can count on:

> Adult attachments may be seen as increasingly transient and children's love may be felt to be the solution against aloneness. Their presence may give a sense of permanency – the final alternative to loneliness that can be built up against the vanishing possibilities of love.
>
> (Blow and Daniel 2002: 101)

Too often this can develop into role reversal, with the children predominantly meeting parental needs, not the other way round. Blow and Daniel (2002) go on to offer powerful examples of common patterns to suggest that there can be reversals of attachments during the separation and post-divorce process. Parents are often distracted with their own sense of loss, anxieties, anger, and exhilaration about a new romantic relationship. This can mean not only that they are not emotionally available for the children but also that the children may feel that they have to look after their parents and each other (Abbey and Dallos 2004). Importantly, children may feel compelled to edit or distort their stories in order to accommodate the feelings and anxieties of their parents:

> A resident parent may think that her new partner will feel more secure if the children have less to do with the other parent. When the non-resident parent introduces a new partner, this can generate fear in a single resident parent that a 'proper' family might be more attractive to the children. Children are sensitive to such fears and may edit their accounts of visits to highlight only deficits.
>
> (Blow and Dallos 2002: 90)

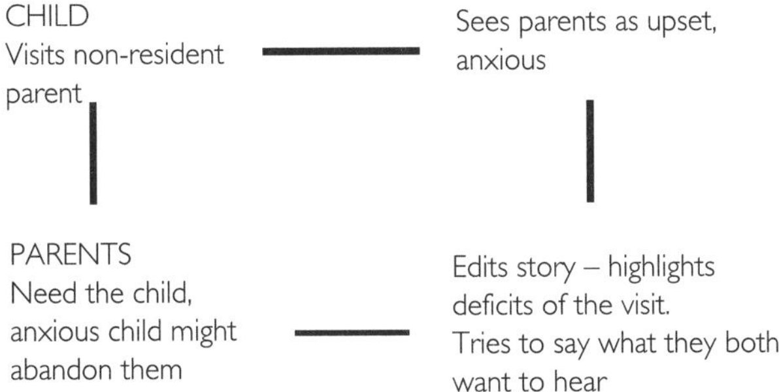

Even when the situation appears more amicable we have also found, for example, that a new partner might feel threatened if the former partners appear to be getting on too well. Children are very sensitive to their parents' feelings and may become drawn in – for example, in this situation apparently perversely acting 'as if' they are trying to make things worse between the parents. This may be because of their anxieties and fears of getting their hopes up for a reconciliation, of getting hurt again but also of seeing their parents exposed to further hurt. In short, the context is typically that instead of getting the support at a time they most need it, they cannot count on being looked after, and often have to take care of their parents. Perhaps it is less than surprising that many children who feel they have sacrificed their own needs to look after their parents then feel angry and betrayed when their parents find new partners and become taken up with them. Furthermore, this can often involve other children who are competing for attention and moreover are the children of the person who appears to have taken their mother or father away. Particularly, we hear of many mothers who feel desperately caught in the middle between balancing the emotional needs of their children, a new partner and a difficult ex-partner. Further examples abound – for example, if a father is more loving and generous in his new relationship than he ever was in the old, this may be seen by the mother as an insult as opposed to an opportunity for the children to benefit from the change in their father. Such traps or paradoxes can be seen to be fuelled by the underlying insecurities of each parent about their failure in relationships and whether they will be 'good enough' in possible future relationships.

Synthesis

The approach recognizes that divorce takes place in the context of a legal system which fuels adversity and certain narratives about blame, responsibility, rights and so on. However, the approach is sensitive to attempting an understanding of how each person's explanations and feelings have arisen. Importantly, it is also sensitive to the massive implications that may be involved in a shift in positions. This involves adopting a reflective position to try to understand what it would feel like to be each member of the family. In turn there is use of one's own experiences regarding relationships and life experiences to connect with existential questions about meaning in life and happiness. This includes the possibility that for some critical life events, such as divorce, there may not be a resolution that the ex partners *need* to hold some negative stories about each other to help make sense of why they separated.

Example

Jenny (13) had at first wanted to see her father, but her forceful younger sister, Hannah (9), had decided not to which made it difficult for Jenny, so she fell in line. There had been many levels of inequality in the relations, with the father, Julian (who was white), having power and control over his wife, Zara (who was black and dependent on him). She had become more independent since the divorce and he saw her concern about her daughters seeing him as vengeful. In turn she saw his expression of concern about his daughters as his desire to dominate them. After seeing their father, the girls communicated to Zara that they were capable of speaking their minds with him. Likewise, they told him that they did not like him implying that everything they said was because of their mother's influence.

The therapists discussed with the girls the history of the choice they had made about not seeing their father and the possible consequences of having so firmly allied themselves to their mother's story. Also, it was made clear that the therapists understood the girls' decision not to see their father as a solution to feeling so caught in the middle of their parents' vicious and unyielding relationship. They discussed whether it was necessary to preserve this decision for the girls to close off any memories of good times with their father:

> We were able to do this without losing sight of other explanations or getting into a symmetrical relationship with them; thus for a rare moment, we created a space where uncertainty about the truth could be tolerated.
>
> (Blow and Daniel 2002: 99)

They go on to say that in the context of therapy such moments could have been built on further, but that this had less chance in this context:

> We disturbed the system, but Zara's vigilance and her response to our feedback reinforced her defences and her need for control. She too understood that, given a truly free will, her daughters might choose to see their father and she feared loss too much to take the risk.
>
> (Blow and Daniel 2002: 100)

Work in forensic contexts

Applications of systemic ideas in the context of work with people who have committed criminal offences pose a number of important questions for systemic therapy. Vivian-Byrne (2001) describes her experience of working within a forensic secure unit and her attempts to integrate systemic ideas into this context. She describes the dilemmas of work with people who have been committed to a secure unit for serious offences such as rape and murder and who are also diagnosed as having severe mental health problems. We will refer to the inmates of such units as 'clients', although the choice of an appropriate term here in a sense encapsulates the nature of the issues. In many ways they are more akin to prisoners, or perhaps between prisoners and patients. However, this locates them in certain ways and narrows the potential relationships they may have with the staff.

Analysis

The problem – deconstruction

What is the problem and for whom? To start with, the issue here is not simply about the offenders and their problems, but also about their families, the staff in the unit and more broadly the unit itself. Among the concerns with regard to clients are their past actions, the future threat they hold, their current behaviour, their conflicts with staff and other clients; of concern with regard to staff are the frustrations they feel, for example a sense of futility and impotence in facilitating any change. Furthermore, there is the wider problem in terms of the relationship that such units have to the Home Office and other government departments and policies.

Vivian-Byrne (2001: 103) locates these questions more broadly in the position that such offenders hold in society: 'I work with members of one of the most reviled group in our society, variously called child molesters, paedophiles or sex offenders, many of whom have been multiply abused in families or care systems'. Implicit in this is that though these clients have done terrible things, they too have been victims and deserve some understanding, perhaps even sympathy. That this is unlikely to happen may be one of the problems that is inherent in such units and may make any change difficult.

Contextual factors

Already in this discussion of the problems we can see the appearance of the central systemic concept of contexts. The staff operate within a particular setting, in this case what has been described by Goffman (1971) as a 'total institution' where all aspects of the clients' lives are controlled. In particular, this locates the unit as needing to serve to protect the public from the risk of these dangerous people. The clients are in custody, on locked wards and not attending voluntarily, and this has immense implications for the power relations between them and the staff members. Furthermore, not only are the clients in custody but they are further disempowered by being labelled as 'ill' and not responsible for their actions. The role of the clinician in such a context is therefore complex, especially regarding their power in that they need to disentangle their involvement with the custodial and statutory responsibilities that other staff have, for example to determine the levels of dangerousness and readiness for entry back into the community. The clinician in such a situation also carefully needs to consider her relationships with other members of staff and, more broadly, the expectations of her role within the system.

Beliefs and explanations

An important contribution of a systemic approach to meanings is to consider the extent to which these are shared in a system, what the differences are and how they regulate practices and in turn become self-fulfilling. According to Vivian-Byrne (2001), beliefs and explanations are typically rigid and absolute in this context. It is clear and incontestable that real and unacceptable actions have occurred and it is very difficult to put alternative, less negative constructions on the actions. She goes on to say that one of the dominant explanations available is a 'simplistic, linear narrative whereby illness causes violence'. In this way the inmates are not seen as *responsible* for the crimes they have committed because they are seen as ill. This boils down to a punctuation of their actions as being either bad or mad. This belief or punctuation has serious implications and, in particular, tends to imply a related punctuation of clients as being either responsible or not responsible. If the crime committed is seen as due to the illness, then they are not responsible. There are alternative explanations possible, as Vivian-Byrne (2001) says, for example that they too have been victims of abuse, violence and neglect or that violence and sexual attack are gendered activities. Nevertheless, the above explanations are seen to prevail perhaps as a consequence of the medical ethos of the units but also in part the preferred personal narratives of many of the staff members.

Located within these beliefs are also related ideas about the role of the clinical team. In accepting the notion of illness, clients and others are seen as looking to staff to be 'experts', to know what to do. This can create a highly unrealistic belief that the clinician can solve all the problems and also locate the blame with them if things go wrong. This connects with an important shared belief that assessment of risk safety is paramount. This implies keeping clients safe but also acting in safe ways such that they do not become more dangerous as a result of interventions. Importantly, this connects with media coverage of horrendous cases where clients have gone on to commit serious offences and this was seen as due to failures of the staff to assess risk adequately and take appropriate protective measures.

Problem-maintaining patterns – feedback loops

These beliefs and explanations both maintain and are in turn maintained by patterns of actions. Vivian-Byrne (2001) describes how one of the patterns revolves around the definition of the clients' as 'ill'; this can lead to a position of not taking responsibility for their actions and in turn giving up attempts to produce any change:

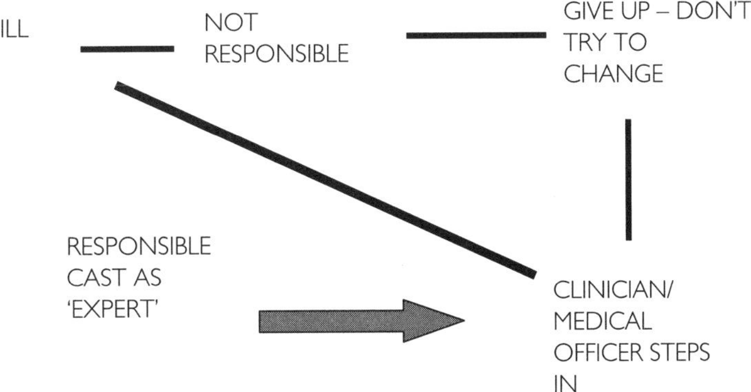

She argues that this is maintained by another influential pattern which is that to resist the definition of one's actions as indicative of an 'illness' typically implies an alternative definition of being 'responsible' for one's actions. Since these have been extreme there is reluctance to do this since it implies great 'badness' or evil. A related pattern is that when clients appear not to accept responsibility the responsible medical officer steps in to take responsibility for treating the client's illness: 'This then has major implications for the patient, other clinicians involved in their care and other agencies embroiled in the network which unfolds' (Vivien-Byrne 2001: 106).

The clinician can become caught in a pattern whereby their expert position can be seductive in offering status when things go well. On the other hand, this can set the clinician up to fail since the clinician, rather than the client, has taken on the *responsibility* for change. The clinician may then also be in a position of being attacked or criticized by colleagues, especially if they have chosen to go outside the boundaries of standard treatment protocols. One of us has also worked in a forensic context and has experienced pressure not to appear 'over-indulgent' or 'soft' on clients. Yet to take an overly critical attitude with the client may endanger any potential of forming a therapeutic relationship with them. Typically this also revolves around the question of treatment versus punishment and reparation for the crime. One approach that can be helpful is to bring these structural issues out into the open, for example issues of trust and confidentiality. Many clients imagine that whatever they will say, regardless of what the therapist promises, can be used against them. This can breed a climate of mistrust since the therapist may likewise think that the client is only saying what they think the therapist wants to hear.

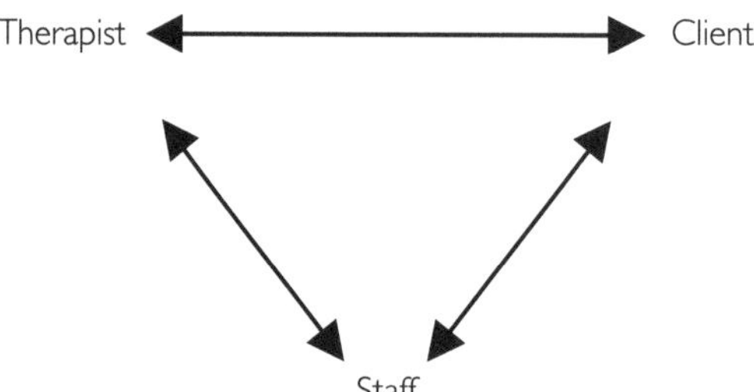

Emotions and attachments

Despite the severity of the crimes committed, family members struggle to find ways of maintaining their relationships and attachments. This can be both beneficial but also minimize the seriousness of the crimes: 'I have been influenced by seeing a woman who has been multiply stabbed and nearly died as a result continuing to go to extreme lengths to maintain the attacker as her partner' (Vivian-Byrne 2001: 103).

Vivian-Byrne (2001) highlights the abuse that many clients have experienced which may make it difficult for them to develop trust and a positive therapeutic relationship with clinicians. Related to this, the nature of their actions and their criminal and mental status are likely to define them as not trustable and hence make it harder for clinicians to form a relationship with them. She also discusses how the pressure to enter into an expert role sets up anxieties and feelings of doubt about clinicians' ability to produce any meaningful and lasting changes in their clients. In terms of emotional support from colleagues, this links to patterns above that in order to feel confident of support from colleagues there is pressure not to deviate too far from acceptable protocols of working. However, this can close down options such that there is less scope for therapeutic creativity. In short, the climate of concern about risk and safety is one where great anxiety may be experienced by staff and the solution may be to adopt conservative approaches and stay close to protocols.

Synthesis

The above illustrates some features of a systemic analysis of the work in such units. In attempting a synthesis there is an attempt to incorporate the therapist's self-reflections, a view of their formulation as prepositional, adopting a collaborative, co-constructive approach and developing an authentic relationship with clients, colleagues and the unit. For Vivian-Byrne (2001) a core issue was what alternatives it might be possible to generate with clients and staff in such a setting which do not distort the reality of what has happened but also offer more flexibility and some potential for change. She drew on Mason's (1993) ideas of safety and certainty which offer a way of facilitating flexibility in this context:

- *Safety* – psychological and emotional containment (in a forensic context also the physical containment and protection of the public and staff).
- *Certainty* – knowing abut the condition to be treated and the means of doing so to lead a client to a 'better place'.

These two constructs can have four combinations:

- *Safe certainty* – the therapist knows what to do to help me.
- *Safe uncertainty* – the therapist will try to help but is not quite sure how and I will have to be active in this.
- *Unsafe certainty* – when people do not feel contained but there is a pressure to be certain, for example to generate a diagnosis or grasp at a solution.
- *Unsafe uncertainty* – the sense of being overwhelmed by the complexity and enormity of the problems and not knowing where to go or what to do.

Vivian-Byrne argues that this formulation (Figure 6.1) can help staff and clients move to a more flexible understanding of the processes that may be in play. Typically, a feeling of unsafe uncertainty may prevail at the start of a piece of work where the staff may feel overwhelmed by the problems and lack of apparent process. This can lead to profound pressures to move to either safe certainty, where staff take on all the responsibility for change, or unsafe certainty, which may involve a negative diagnosis with little future hope or potential for change. Specifically, she offers several case illustrations.

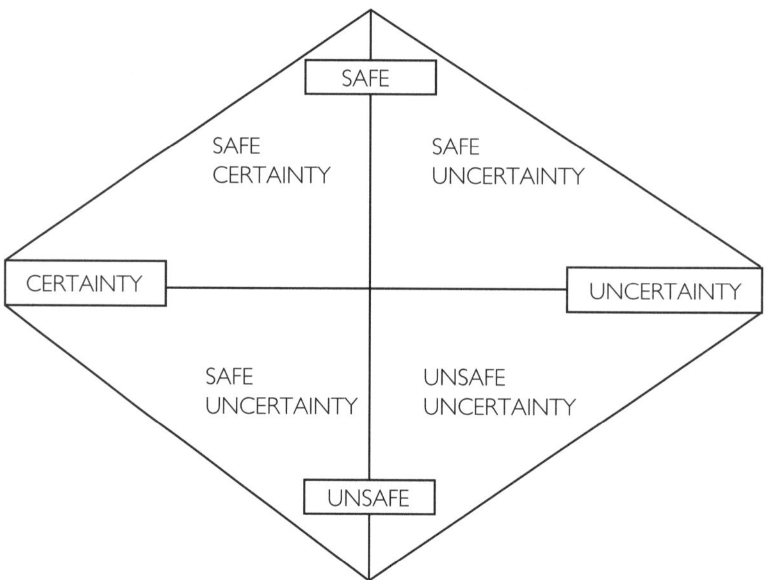

Figure 6.1 Safety/certainty matrix

A young man was convicted of killing an elderly man while he was 'floridly psychotic' and subsequently diagnosed as schizophrenic. He improved greatly with medication, becoming a model patient, and was discharged. However, he has confided in some members of staff that he still held some of his 'psychotic' beliefs, for example extreme coincidences as supporting his spiritual beliefs. He was reluctant to discuss these ideas openly since he realized that as a consequence he could be confined again. In essence he seemed to be caught in a dilemma: to acknowledge some responsibility for his actions was a sign of progress and healing, but also to admit that he thought some of his thoughts at the time were not an 'illness' was an indication that he was in fact still ill and dangerous. This has echoes of a 'catch-22' situation: if you admit you are crazy, you are crazy; if you deny that you are crazy, you must be really crazy.

As we have seen from Vivian-Byrne's (2001) work, systemic formulations, especially regarding positions of safety/certainty, (Figure 6.1 above), helped her to generate some flexibility and creativity in a context which could appear extremely rigid and in which therapeutic change was unlikely.

Commentary

We have looked at three examples of contemporary developments in systemic practice. There are countless more we might have mentioned, but we hope that the three above give a flavour both of departures from and developments of systemic theory and practice but also indicate some of the continuities. We have employed the framework of formulation to highlight further how systemic practitioners think about problems. This shows both the distinctive features of systemic formulations and connections with other approaches to formulation.

Guidance about the possible application of systemic concepts to a variety of contexts is what many new family trainees require. Often they have told us that they do not convene whole families, or work in teams with video equipment. However, they do want some different ways to view their work which can take account of some of the unhelpful behavioural patterns they observe. In entering a variety of different situations systemic theory and practice have also undergone the twin processes of *accommodation* – fitting in and adapting ideas from other theoretical models and practices into a systemic lens – and *assimilation* – developing and transforming a systemic lens in order to absorb other models. At the boundaries, we can see new adaptations or syntheses of models and practice. We do not have the space to attempt to do justice to all of these creative fusions but instead have looked at a sample. We hope that the examples give you some inspiration for thinking about your own contexts, especially in terms of how a systemic approach can allow you more manoeuvrability and creativity. Inevitably, this involves an element of risk; for example, we have both worked in psychiatric in-patient settings for people suffering with eating disorders. These contexts typically combine nursing, psychiatric, medical and psychological inputs. Unlike working with a family, we experienced ourselves as much more inside the system and at times as powerless to effect any change

Formulation

As we saw in the previous chapter, systemic therapies were pioneering in their move to consider formulation as a dynamic, progressive, reflexive and collaborative process. A landmark was the work of the Milan team in their development of the idea of 'progressive hypothesizing'. This encourages a prepositional approach which is able to work alongside or embrace other models since it is not premised on a search for a 'true' formulation but on ways of seeing problems and situations which are elaborative or conducive to change. In the examples we have chosen above the concept of 'uncertainty' was key for the thinking about ways of opening up new, less rigid ways of viewing events – alternative narratives.

Contexts

The examples illustrate the application of systemic ideas in a variety of contexts and where the work does not predominantly revolve around contact with families. Arguably one of the great strengths of a systemic approach is its recognition of the importance of contexts and how these influence the behaviour, thoughts and feelings of people in different situations or organizations, and of thinking about the structures, shared meanings, texts, notes and practices in these various settings. In this we can see some of the core ideas from recent and past phases of family therapy, for example a structural description of hierarchy, rules and shared beliefs.

A significant aspect of working in different contexts is the ability to work alongside colleagues using different models. One of the major contributions of a systemic approach is that it can offer a meta-perspective – a bird's-eye view to help us to look at the contexts we are in. What patterns is our organization caught up in? What patterns am I caught up in with my colleagues? What can I/we do that may allow some change to occur? How might my own actions, beliefs and feelings be contributing to stuckness or unhelpful patterns developing with my colleagues? How does the organization I am working in relate to and communicate with other organizations?

Patterns and processes

The idea of patterns has been a central strand of systemic thinking and arguably is one of the most significant aspects which differentiates it from other models. This involves both an ability to look for existing patterns of actions, beliefs and feelings but also imagination of possible patterns that may arise. Perhaps this is also one of the most contested and debated areas of contemporary systemic thinking. Early systemic thinkers articulated ideas about structure, patterns and rules regulating family life and these came to be contested as 'expert' and modernist views in that they appeared to imply notions of truths which expert systemic thinkers could accurately identify. A contrary position is that of uncertainty, according to which realities are socially constructed and multiple.

We can see in the three exemplars above some very interesting issues relating to this. For example, in Blow and Daniel (2002) we can see some fascinating examples of not just dominant patterns but dominant ideas that seem to shape the actions and experiences of children and parents in the post-divorce experience. Their work also connects with Bateson's (1972) ideas of variety and constraint, that certain explanations and beliefs are allowed to endure whereas others become excluded. Blow and Daniel go on to argue that the structures of the divorce context, along with commonly shared discourses, for example about gender roles, constrain the range of stories that parents are likely to hold. Similarly, in the context of work with alcoholism and in secure units it is clear that one of the core issues is just that the range of possible explanations is severely constrained. Furthermore, the possibility of the survival of alternative stories is also sharply constrained. For example, dominant medical models locate offenders and alcoholics as either 'ill' or 'irresponsible'. These powerful discourses have to be taken into account in thinking of assisting in re-storying experiences. A more structural or social constructionist approach recognizes that there are dominant stories that shape our experiences and that these are related to regimes of power in a given culture.

Perhaps this tension between acknowledging commonality – what families (and other groups and systems) share in terms of patterns and experiences – and uniqueness – what is different, unusual or idiosyncratic for each family – will be a continuing debate for systemic therapists in the twenty-first century. However, our three examples suggest that the further we move from family systems, the greater the rigidities we may see in systems such as prisons and other institutions. Certainly our experience is that it is much easier to facilitate change in so-called 'stuck' families than 'stuck' organizations!

Multiple models

Arguably there has been increasing contact between different models of therapy, with one of the key points of contact being a recognition of the importance across all therapies of the therapeutic alliance (Larner 2000; Anderson 2001; Speed 2004). In our three examples we have seen integrations with a number of models, including attachment theory, medical models, motivational interviewing and the cycle of change model. At times the use of different models is explicit, as in Vetere and Henley's (2001) work; at other times it is more implicit, as in the descriptions of the needs and anxieties of parents and children post divorce. Increasingly we see in various practice contexts, such as the National Health Service, social services and forensic services a use of multiple models. Perhaps one of the most common mixtures is the use of cognitive therapy approaches, which are widespread, alongside systemic family work. Examples of this combination can be found in the work on early intervention in schizophrenia (Burbach and Stanbridge 1998). More informal integrations are extremely common, for example, in child and adolescent mental health services a combination of cognitive and family therapy is the normal package provided to young people and their families. Though of course there are major issues about waiting lists and availability in many services.

There are many issues about the benefits and concerns regarding integrations. Asen (2004) poignantly indicates some issues, for example that a too easy acceptance and blurring of ideas from different models without taking account of important differences can lead us to be lazy and sloppy in our thinking. He also points to an important issue which connects to the basis of systemic therapies:

> I have to confess that I become increasingly irritated by terms and notions such as 'conversational process', 'therapeutic conversations' or 'dialogue together' . . . Language is certainly one activity in which we engage with others to create realities, but is it the only one? . . . There are many creative therapists who make use of non-verbal . . . interventions – including play [and] music, through visuals, through touch. In our ordinary lives we are moved by multi-sensory experiences.
>
> (Asen 2004: 283)

Systemic therapy was inextricably linked with a theory of communication which emphasized the mutli-faceted nature of communication (Watzlawick 1964). It was argued that any action or even non-action carried meaning in an interpersonal context. It is interesting to consider here that systemic theory and therapy seem to have drifted away from this extremely important recognition of the multifaceted nature of communication. However, developmental researchers and attachment theorists, for example, are exploring this rich and fertile territory to map how relationship patterns and personality develop from this web of non-verbal and verbal communication – and most interestingly, how use of language and the ability to place our experiences into narratives is itself shaped by early non-verbal experiences (Crittenden 1998; Dallos 2004).

Key texts

Allison, S., Perlesz, A., Pote, H., Stratton, P. and Cottrell, D. (2002) Manualising systemic family therapy: the Leeds Manual. *Australian & New Zealand Journal of Family Therapy*, 23: 153–8.

Anderson, H. (2001) Postmodern collaborative and person-centred therapies: what would Carl Rogers say? *Journal of Family Therapy*, 23(4): 339–61.

Anderson, H., Gollishian, H. and Winderman, L. (1986) Problem determined systems: towards transformation in family therapy. *Journal of Strategic and Systemic Therapies*, 5: 1–13.

Asen, E. (2004) Collaborating in promiscuous swamps – the systemic practitioner as a context chameleon? *Journal of Family Therapy*, 26(3): 280–6.

Bateson, G. (1972) *Steps to an Ecology of Mind*. New York: Ballantine.

Bentovim, A. and Miller, L.B. (2001) *The Family Assessment*. Brighton: Pavilion.

Blow, K. and Daniel, G. (2002) Frozen narratives? Post-divorce processes and contact disputes. *Journal of Family Therapy*, 24(1): 85–104.

Burbach, F. and Stanbridge, R.I. (1998) A family intervention in psychosis service integrating the systemic and family management approaches. *Journal of Family Therapy*, 20(3): 311–25.

Byng-Hall, J. (1995) Creating a secure base: some implications of attachment theory for family therapy. *Family Process*, 34: 45–58.

Byng-Hall, J. (1998) Evolving ideas about narrative: re-editing the re-editing of family mythology. *Journal of Family Therapy*, 20(2): 133–43.

Crittenden, P. (1998) Truth, error, omission, distortion, and deception: an application of attachment theory to the assessment and treatment of psychological disorder, in S.M. Clany Dollinger and L.F. DiLalla (eds) *Assessment and Intervention Issues across the Life Span*. London: Lawrence Erlbaum.

Dallos, R. (2004) Attachment narrative therapy: integrating ideas from narrative and attachment theory in systemic therapy with eating disorders. *Journal of Family Therapy*, 26(1): 40–66.

Doane, J.A. and Diamond, D. (1994) *Affect and Attachment in the Family*. New York: Basic Books.

Larner, G. (2000) Towards a common ground in psychoanalysis and family therapy: on knowing not to know. *Journal of Family Therapy*, 22(1): 61–83.

Leff, J. and Vaughn C. (1985) *Expressed Emotion in Families: Its Significance for Mental Illness*. New York: Guilford Press.

Leff, J., Alexander, B., Asen, E., Brewin, C.R., Dayson, D., Vearnals, S. and Wolff, G. (2003) Modes of action of family interventions in depression and schizophrenia: the same or different? *Journal of Family Therapy*, 25(4): 357–71.

Miller, W. and Rollnick, S. (1991) *Motivational Interviewing: Preparing People to Change Addictive Behavior*. New York: Guilford Press.

Muncie, J., Wetherell, M., Dallos, R. and Cochrane, A. (eds) (1997) *Understanding the Family*. London: Sage.

Pote, H., Stratton, P., Cottrell, D., Boston, P., Shapiro, D. and Hanks, H. (1999). *Systemic Family Therapy Manual*. Leeds: University of Leeds.

Prochaska, J. and DiClemente, C. (1992) Stages of change in the modification of problem behavior, in M. Hersen, R.M.Eisler and P.M. Miller (eds), *Progress in Behaviour Modification*. Sycamore, IL: Sycamore Press.

Speed, B. (2004) All aboard in the NHS: collaborating with colleagues who use different approaches. *Journal of Family Therapy*, 26(3): 260–80.

Vetere, A. and Dallos, R. (2003) *Working Systemically with Families; Formulation, Intervention and Evaluation*. London: Karnac.

Vetere, A. and Henley, M. (2001) Integrating couples and family therapy into a community alcohol service: a pan theoretical approach. *Journal of Family Therapy*, 23(1): 85–102.

Vivian-Byrne, S.E. (2001) What am I doing here? Safety, certainty and expertise in a secure unit. *Journal of Family Therapy*, 23(1): 102–17.

7 Research and evaluation

Introduction

The relationship between systemic family therapy and research has been an interesting one. Early work in the 1950s was regarded as primarily a research endeavour. Haley (1978: 73) observed that during this era, 'it was taken for granted that a therapist and a researcher were of the same species (although the therapist had a more second-class status)'.

Some of the ideas which became fundamental to systemic theory and practice arose from research interests. For example, in the 1950s Bateson was involved in research into communication processes and learning in mammals, including some fascinating studies of communicational processes in dolphins (Bateson 1972). This led to extensive research on communication in humans and relationships, such as families, and to the seminal book of the Palo Alto group, *Pragmatics of Human Communication* (Watzlawick *et al.* 1967). This not only inspired a plethora of research on 'deviant' communication processes, for example explorations of families with a schizophrenic member, but also a wide range of research into communication in non-pathological contexts. Interestingly, much of this initial research centred on audiotaping of family therapy sessions or interviews with families. The process of family therapy was seen as a potential goldmine of research. Watzlawick *et al.* (1967), Weakland (1962) and others published a fascinating range of studies based on the analysis of transcripts of therapy sessions. With the advent of videorecording these studies expanded to include observations of the interrelationships between modes of communication, for example inconsistencies between verbal and non-verbal messages. Such observational studies led to some important models (e.g. the double-bind theory), and the discovery of the importance of non-verbal communication (e.g. when there is inconsistency between the verbal and non-verbal messages the latter, especially for children, may be given more credit).

Another influential body of research was directed towards exploration of family variables in attempts to identify family 'types', for example family dynamics associated with anorexia nervosa or schizophrenia. It was hoped that such research would reveal important factors related to aetiology and subsequently could be employed diagnostically and to guide treatment. Of central interest were the types of treatment that were appropriate for different disorders. For example, Minuchin *et al.* (1978) gave an account of work with psychosomatic families, Haley (1966) and Weakland (1962, 1976) described work with schizophrenia and the Milan team reported on their work with anorexia and subsequently schizophrenia (Palazzoli *et al.* 1978). The studies range in their methods from detailed attempts to control variables and employ standardized instruments in order to measure family factors, to studies that relied on descriptive case study material. This variety of methods led to criticisms of a lack of vigorous research and evaluation of systemic therapies. Though valid up to a point, these criticisms may also have missed the point that valid research may need to be multi-faceted and explore the intricacies of families' experiences, as well as employing more 'scientific' and 'objective' instruments such as psychological tests and inventories.

Why conduct research?

Despite the legacy of research in systemic therapy, there has also been a considerable backlash against research. Interestingly, one of the strongest articulations of this protest came from Jay Haley (1971, 1976a, 1976b) who, ironically, was also one of the most influential and productive of the early researchers. He argued that the purposes of research were distinct from those of therapy. Specifically he argued, from a pragmatic approach that embodied the strategic and solution-focused approaches which were gaining ascendancy, that the production of change could occur without ultimate understanding of the nature or causes of change. More profoundly, he suggested that therapy was an infinitely complex shifting web of interactions, feelings, beliefs and emotions. These in turn were shaped by the past experiences of each family member, the therapist and the supervision team. To attempt to fully understand and to be able to predict this complexity was, he argued, futile. This view is in fact central to systems theory. Though systems can be seen to display predictable patterns it is argued that it is not possible to predict precisely the effect that interventions or perturbations of the system will have (Weiner 1961; von Foerster and Zopf 1962; Bateson 1972, 1980). Moreover, as we have seen, the second phase suggested that there was in fact no system 'out there' to predict, but that the observer was inevitably part of the equation. The act of observation inevitably produced an element of perturbation and altered the family dynamics being observed.

We want to suggest that, though important, these doubts about the value of research may inevitably be misguided. Perhaps one of the most obvious reasons for this is the very fact that systemic therapies arose from research and that to abandon this might stifle future creativity. Second, it may be that there has until recently been a restricted view of what counts as research. Arguably the daily work of family therapists involves important aspects of what can legitimately be counted as research. For example, the fundamental systemic notion of revising interventions on the basis of feedback is a microcosm of the research process. Third, we agree at least to some extent with the move in psychotherapy and more broadly in all areas of clinical and medical work towards proceeding on the basis of evidence. This emphasis has been described as the need to develop 'evidence-based practice' in which practitioners continually attempt to evaluate the nature and effectiveness of their work. Such data are of course valuable to managers and purchasers in making decisions about what services to support and develop. However, we suggest that what counts as evidence should be considered broadly. Simply counting cases and supposedly objective measures of outcomes may offer scant information and may also at times be misleading if we do not understand the nature of the work undertaken or, for example, some of the subtleties of changes that may be occurring.

We suggest that an interest in research encapsulates the notion of family therapy as motivated by 'curiosity'. Sometimes this may have a direct and instrumental focus, for example the research may be driven by questions about the cost-effectiveness of alternative forms of family treatment and at other times by more conceptual questions about the process of change, or qualitative questions such as how family members experience family therapy. The kinds of questions we may wish to ask can be grouped into the following categories. *Evaluation research* may be concerned with questions about the effectiveness of family therapy:

- comparison of systemic family therapy with other forms of therapy, such as cognitive therapies;
- comparisons between different types of systemic therapies;
- effectiveness of systemic therapies for different types of disorder.

Process research is concerned with more specific questions about how therapy works and what the active ingredients may be:

- the therapeutic alliance – the relationship between the family and the therapist and how this relates to the effectiveness of different types of interventions;
- how change occurs – different stages in therapy, changes in family dynamics, family beliefs and emotional dynamics;
- therapist variables – gender, race, experience of the therapist;
- family members' experience and expectation of therapy and how this relates to change, experiences of different types of interventions;
- supervision, for example comparisons of reflecting team vs consultation approaches.

Family theory research is research that is aimed at exploring family life more broadly than just the therapeutic context:

- family dynamics in relation to different types of disorders and problems;
- family roles, such as gender roles and cultural expectations;
- decision-making in families, power and influence strategies;
- family communicational processes;
- emotions and family dynamics;
- family life cycle processes, transitions and change.

These three broad categories of research are to some extent distinct but also show considerable overlap. Evidence from therapy, for example, informs family theory and in turn theoretical research about family dynamics also offers ideas for the development of practice. Research is associated predominantly with evaluation, and this may not always be the most inspiring. Reiss (1988: 34) argues that in order to 'do family therapy research without dying of boredom' we might wish to concentrate on process and conceptual research:

> Our true passion . . . is reserved for demonstrating to others by what mechanisms we have achieved effectiveness . . . what we cherish and what we believe permits us to be effective is our insight into family life and its relationship to psychiatric symptomology.

In our experience many trainee family therapists share Reiss's view. Evaluation of the effectiveness of therapy is seen as a laudable and worthy aim but also one that under- rather than overwhelms them with enthusiasm. Arguably evaluation on its own provides a bland picture that may be of interest to purchasers of services but ultimately is of little value to clinicians in terms of helping them to improve what they do. Critical to any development of therapy is to develop increasingly sophisticated ideas about the active ingredients of therapy. However, it is also suggested that in order to achieve increases in such understanding it is necessary to develop theories of therapeutic change and family functioning. Pinsof (1988) refers to this as a 'discovery' oriented approach as opposed to a 'confirmatory' one. He also argues that systemic therapy tends to have general rather than specific theoretical principles and there is a need to develop more specific microtheories. An important example is to consider the nature of the therapeutic alliance. A range of studies, both systemic and individual, has indicated that the relationship between client and therapist is critical to the outcome of therapy. For systemic therapy this poses a range of related questions, for example whether the therapist needs to be allied to every family member, the identified patient, various subsystems, the most powerful or influential members of the family and so on.

Research on natural family dynamics and processes can be of considerable interest but also relevance to therapy. Watzlawick *et al.* (1974) examined change processes in a variety of natural settings, and these ideas have been extensively applied to work with families and individuals. However, there has subsequently been a dearth of research on natural processes of change in families:

> There has been relatively little interest among family therapists in systematic observations of families in non-therapeutic settings. In particular there has been surprisingly little interest in the circumstances and processes that lead to major or substantial change in family patterns in natural settings – changes that, in some instances, might truly be called self-healing.
>
> (Reiss 1988: 37)

This lack of attention to natural healing processes is generally evident in psychotherapy research yet is perhaps least explainable for systemic theory since its roots were so firmly in observations of family dynamics. It is as if we have become fixed in looking only at deadlocks in families rather than how the majority, a vast untreated population of families who experience problems, also manage to resolve these problems themselves. However, there is increasing interest in the question of family resilience (Walsh 1996; Dallos *et al.* 1997).

Science, research and systemic therapy

Arguably the practice of systemic therapy is one of the therapies that is most compatible with research. This may seem an odd assertion given that there has been considerable criticism that systemic family therapy has lacked rigorous research. Compatibility with a scientific method can readily be seen both in terms of the process and the practice of family therapy. Modern science does not claim to provide definitive explanations; instead it attempts to produce the best possible explanatory model. Furthermore, science is not seen as the dogged accumulation of facts but as developing on the basis of paradigm shifts (Popper 1962; Kuhn 1970). For example, the move from Newtonian physics to relativity theory involved a creative leap to a new theory which took account of the position of the observer relative to what is being observed. Though this offered a better explanation of the observed facts, it is not seen as a definitive, once-and-for-all theory. Science in its essence involves a continual process of formulating theory, testing and reformulation based on the evidence or feedback. This is consistent with the systemic notion of therapy as guided by a process of 'progressive hypothesizing'. Therapists are not trying to capture fundamental truths about a family but instead are attempting to develop more or less useful explanations.

The practice of family therapy also lends itself to scientific research. For example, the common usage of supervision teams means that it is possible to introduce inter-rater reliability measures into observations about family and family–therapist interactions. In contrast to most other therapies, where the therapist works alone with one client, family therapy is public and less subject to potential personal biases. Likewise, the videorecording of sessions is extremely common and this material also offers scope for structured analysis and, for example, inter-rater observational analysis. It is also possible to transcribe videotaped sessions and engage in detailed analysis of the content of the sessions. The hitherto frequent use of tasks or assignments between sessions can also be seen as offering an opportunity for research investigation.

Systemic therapy is not only compatible with the principles of the natural sciences but also and more so with the profound developments in the theoretical and research bases of the social sciences. It has been acknowledged that the positivist principles of the natural sciences – the reliance on objective, observable data – are not sufficient for an understanding of social phenomena. If it is recognized that a fundamental feature of human beings is that we create meanings rather than just behave, then it is not sufficient to simply attempt exploration through experimental or observational approaches. For example, we need to have some ideas about how families experience therapy and what changes occur in their beliefs and explanations in order to understand more about how therapy functions. Furthermore, in order to develop such understandings we may also need to consider how our own experiences may be colouring what we are able to hear families say about these experiences. In the social sciences such issues have been taken up in a range of research approaches.

Varieties of research

There is a common assumption among trainees and many experienced family therapists that research basically involves a choice between giving families a variety of questionnaires or tests and interviewing them in some way. Despite the fact that family therapy relies fundamentally on observation, this is often not even considered as a research possibility. In fact there are a wide range of research methods that have relevance to research into systemic family therapy. The realization of this potential choice and recognition that much of the practice of family therapy can be turned into research can be quite a liberating experience. However, there can be seen to be a fundamental division between *quantitative* and *qualitative* research methods.

Quantitative methods rest on positivist assumptions about an objective reality, quantification and reliable measurement. The theoretical basis is drawn from the natural sciences and the aim is to be able to create generalizable models from which specific predictions can be made. These are set out in the form of testable hypotheses, and statistical techniques are employed to assess the probability that the observed results could have occurred by chance. Evaluative studies of family therapy tend to be in this mould, with the focus on observable changes in symptomatic behaviours. By and large these approaches are also reductionist in that attempts are made to reduce the phenomena to small, focused and manageable components. In evaluation, therefore, it might be argued that change can be reduced to a measure of some key behaviours rather than looking at the complexity of family functioning over time and the multiplicity of potential influences.

Qualitative methods are largely based on theoretical positions that are concerned with exploring meanings rather than simply observable behaviours. Constructivist and social constructionist approaches to family therapy fall into this category. Families are seen as creating meanings that guide action and it is change in the meanings of their actions, including the 'symptoms', which is of fundamental significance. Simply focusing on the 'problems' is seen as inadequate since this would, for example, fail to take into account the processes whereby they have evolved from the conversations in families and between families and professionals. It is suggested that there is no objective reality 'out there' but that the researcher or therapist is inevitably bringing a set of their own assumptions that colours what they see. In order to conduct research there is a need to engage in a collaborative process of exploration with the family. In effect, the family helps the researcher to form an understanding of the family's world.

Ethnography emphasizes that the understanding of social phenomena involves the researcher becoming immersed in the subject matter. An example would be a study of street gangs in which the researchers join and live with the gangs for a period to gain an idea of what this experience is like, to become immersed in their activities and to learn their language, idioms and vocabulary. Similarly, Vetere and Gale conducted a study which involved the researchers living in with families for several weeks to gain an insight into their lives (see Vetere and Gale 1987: 168–9). On the basis of this immersion the researcher formulates and successively reformulates his or her hypotheses or guiding propositions. Rather than simply attempting to eliminate the researcher's 'biases', ethnography recognizes that this is both a futile and sterile endeavour. Instead, the researcher continually attempts to reflect on how the events being studied impact on him or her and also how these alter and change. Part of this reflection involves a consideration of the researcher's social and cultural contexts, for example how a researcher's white middle-class background may influence their perceptions and reactions to the actions and beliefs of black youths and their behaviour in gangs.

Such conscious use of self is also reminiscent of the therapist's involvement with a family. We will explore a variety of such qualitative methods in some more detail later, but the significant point is that research methods in social sciences parallel the shifts from first- to second- and third-order cybernetics. There is an emphasis on the inevitability of the observing position and also on the observer in turn being influenced by their social and cultural contexts. As in the example of youth gangs, a family therapist or researcher is involved in attempting to understand a family set of beliefs – in a sense, attempting to learn their language.

At the extremes, these two positions are worlds apart. However, it is possible to see considerable overlaps – for example, measurement and quantification may be included in both approaches. The number of times a family employs a particular concept in their descriptions may be meaningful and add to the picture given by an analysis of the meanings of their explanations and stories, for example, how important and central the theme currently is for the family. It is also possible to distinguish the approaches in terms of their technical aspects as opposed to the conceptual differences. For example, interviews are usually regarded as a qualitative approach but the analysis of the content can include quantification into themes or categories. It is our suggestion that it is useful to think of ways of integrating the approaches, especially if we are interested not just in evaluating therapy but exploring the processes of change.

Returning to our three broad categories of research – evaluation research, process research and family theory research – we can see that there is a range of different research methods that are located within these – see Sprenkle and Moon (1996) and Wynne (1988) for very helpful overviews of the variety of family therapy research possible. These are summarized in Figure 7.1.

Case studies
These consist of in-depth explorations of effects of therapeutic treatments, or a family's experiences of different kinds of event, such as changes in their relationships over time. The researcher may employ a variety of methods within a case study – such as observation, interview, asking the family to keep diaries, observations of people outside the family – to build a rich and detailed picture.

Case studies may be individual or multiple case studies, for example a study might consider in depth the experience of a family who have had a positive vs a negative experience of therapy.

Interview studies
These consist of the use of interviews with family members, either individually or together (or both). The interviews are usually transcribed and explored to gain a picture of the nature of people's understandings, beliefs and experiences of various family events (loss, break-up, transitions), or their experience of therapy. Due to the extensive time involved in analysis, interviews usually involve a relatively small number of people, for example, 20 families would be a sizeable sample.

Focus groups are used in an approach where a group of people are interviewed, for example, members of a family support group or a group of therapists. Such interviews allow further information to emerge through the mutual prompting of ideas that surface through discussion.

Questionnaire/survey studies
These involve the use of questionnaires designed to explore family members' beliefs and feelings about various issues, for example, aspects of their lives, experiences of therapy, attitudes to services. Questionnaires may involve a large sample to gain a broad picture, or general attitudes to various issues. They also allow the use of statistical methods to allow predictions to be made, for example about various trends such as gender differences, family attitudes to divorce or support services.

These studies can also involve selecting a particular sample – for example, family therapists working with different approaches – to explore their views and employ a process of feedback to the participants to arrive at a consensual view, for example the key differences between narrative and strategic approaches (Delphi studies).

Experimental or comparative studies
These usually involve some attempts at control or manipulation of certain variables by the researcher. For example, different types of therapy may be compared or attempts made to compare the responses to different types of interventions.

Frequently standardized measures may be employed, such as inventories of family functioning – for example, the FACES measure of family cohesion and adaptability (Olson *et al.* 1989). Statistical techniques may also be employed, for example, to assess significance of differences between types of treatment and to allow generalizable predictions to be made.

Observational studies
These involve various forms of observations of families. The kind of observations may vary from external observations where the researcher attempts to gain a relatively 'objective' picture, for example of family communication patterns, to more subjective or participant observation where the researcher tries to become immersed and fully understand the nature of family experiences. In turn, the observations may vary from structured – using quantifiable ratings of predetermined aspects of family dynamics – to unstructured, where an informal approach is used and particular events are focused on as and when they emerge as important.

Figure 7.1 Varieties of research methods

Evaluation research: does family therapy work?

A much repeated critique of family therapy is that there has been inadequate research designed to evaluate its effectiveness in comparison to other treatments and in terms of types of problems and family variables. Eiser (2002: 129) makes the point that 'there is now considerable evidence that a range of family interventions are effective for most child and adolescent disorders . . . as well as many adult disorders including schizophrenia, depression and drug and alcohol abuse'. This general conclusion is supported by a substantial body of evidence. We need to note here, though, that family therapy takes the position that problems are to do with relationships in families and do not simply reside inside one person. Hence evaluation of effectiveness needs to take both these factors into account. Potentially change in the system means that the long-term changes are more likely to be better since if a person attempts to change while the family system remains the same there is a strong likelihood that he or she will relapse as the system patterns take over. This was exactly the observation that led Jackson (1957) to his initial theory of family homeostasis.

The studies have been summarized in various ways: according to types of problems and also in terms of meta-analyses. Meta-analysis consists of grouping the data from a number of studies together as if they constituted one large study with a substantial sample size, thus increasing the power and generalizability of the findings. These major reviews have concluded that family therapy has been established as of proven effectiveness in a wide range of areas (Hazelrigg *et al.* 1987; Markus *et al.* 1990; Shadish *et al.* 1995; Goldstein and Miklowitz 1995). These findings are based on a substantial number of reviews of research. Tables 7.1 and 7.2 offer an overview of some of the outcome

Table 7.1 Outcome studies of adult problems

PROBLEMS	RESEARCH STUDIES
Alcohol and substance misuse	Stanton and Shadish (1997)
Child abuse and neglect	Brunk *et al.* (1987), Nicol *et al.* (1988)
Chronic pain	Mason (2003)
Schizophrenia	Goldstein and Miklowitz (1995), McFarlane *et al.* (1995), Fadden (1998), Berkowitz (1987), Bennum and Lucas (1990)
Anxiety	Arnow *et al.* (1985), Barlow *et al.* (1984), Baucom *et al.* (1998)
Psychosexual problems	
Depression	Leff *et al.* (2000), Jones and Asen (2000)
Marital distress	Baucom *et al.* (1998), Shadish *et al.* (1995), Dunn and Schwebel (1995)

Table 7.2 Outcome problems of child and adolescent problems

PROBLEM	RESEARCH STUDIES
Adolescent anorexia	Eisler *et al.* (2000), Robin *et al.* (1995)
Adolescent depression	Kolko *et al.* (2000)
Psychosomatic problems, non-organic pain, asthma, etc.	Silver *et al.* (1998), Sanders *et al.* (1994), Gustafsson *et al.* (1986), Lask and Matthews (1979)
Adolescent drug abuse	Waldron (1996), Stanton and Shadish (1997), Hengeller *et al.* (1991)
Emotional problems	
Depression and grief	Black and Urbanowicz (1987), Brent *et al.* (1997), Kolko *et al.* (2000), Simpson (1990)
Anxiety	Barret *et al.* (1996)
Obsessive compulsive disorders	March *et al.* (1994)
Conduct problems	
Temper, tantrums, defiance and non-compliance	Serketich and Dumas (1996), Webster-Stratton and Hammond (1997), Dadds *et al.* (1987)
ADHD	Barclay *et al.* (1992), Ialongo *et al.* (1993)
Adolescent conduct problems	Chamberlain and Rosicky (1995), Gordon *et al.* (1988), Alexander and Parsons (1973), Hengeller (1997)
Obesity (in children)	Hazelrigg *et al.* (1987), Markus *et al.* (1990), Shadish *et al.* (1995)
Chronic physical illness	Hazelrigg *et al.* (1987), Markus *et al.* (1990), Shadish *et al.* (1995)

studies available. They draw extensively on the helpful review of the evidence compiled by Alan Carr (2000a, 2000b)

The studies listed in Tables 7.1 and 7.2 are drawn from a broad spectrum of family treatments, including some that adopt a behavioural as opposed to a narrative social constructionist approach – for example, parent training programmes for children with behavioural problems (Serketich and Dumas 1996). This involves training and coaching parents in applying behavioural principles, such as use of start charts or tokens to increase positive and decrease negative behaviours. It is recognized that these approaches also work because they help parents to function consistently in agreement with each other and to encourage a belief that views the child's problems as linked to external factors rather than as due to their basic 'wickedness'. In contrast, there have been studies using narrative approaches. March and Mulle (1998) developed this into a treatment programme called *How I ran OCD off my Land*, which used the idea of 'externalizing' OCD (obsessive compulsive disorder) by giving it an unpleasant nickname. The child and their family worked together to identify situations which led to the OCD and to find ways of driving it away from their lives. Similarly, Silver *et al.* (1998) found that a narrative family therapy approach was more effective in treating soiling than standard behavioural approaches. Some of these studies are of relatively new programmes but others are tests of long-standing approaches such as Stanton's work (Stanton and Shadish) on integrated family therapy approaches, combining structural and strategic approaches, for alcohol and drug abuse.

Group comparison evaluative studies

These are perhaps the best known of all research designs. The most widely employed method in clinical research had been to compare two groups of clients, for example those undergoing a particular treatment and those who are not receiving any treatment (a control group). The inclusion of a control group is to identify whether change in a group of people may be happening naturally as a result of time spent engaged in any activity. These studies also employ pretest and posttest measures, usually a range of standardized tests and questionnaires, and may in addition include ratings of change based on structured observation. Participants are randomly allocated to either the treatment or control groups so that biases, such as severity of problems, age, abilities and resources, do not obscure or bias the results. Predominantly the focus is on assessing overall average change for the various treatments. Statistical tests are typically employed to determine the probability of whether the changes pre and post therapy could have occurred by chance. A standard benchmark of probability is that if the chances of this are less than 5 per cent it is concluded that the effects due to the treatments are significant. However, there have been occasions where consternation is caused when it is found that non-treatment and the effects of spontaneous recovery can be as good as therapy (Rachman and Wilson 1980).

A drawback of such group-based experimental studies can be that individual differences in response to treatments may be obscured. Also, such studies may tell us little about the active ingredients of a treatment. Reiss (1988) argues that in a climate of competing resources for services the main aim of such studies is often to reassure or convince fund-holders to maintain or increase resources rather than to develop our knowledge of therapeutic effectiveness. This kind of design is also subject to ethical criticisms in that the control group is not allowed the benefit of assistance when they may be in considerable distress. In this section we will examine a number of approaches to evaluative research.

Simpson (1990) attempted to compare the effectiveness of a Milan family therapy approach with other 'routinely employed' treatments in an out-patient child psychiatry department. Eighty-seven families took part in a study in which families were randomly assigned either to a course of Milan family therapy treatment or to an eclectic package of treatments including individual psychotherapy, behavioural and cognitive approaches and non-Milan family therapy. The families contained children displaying a wide range of problems, but families with a child displaying psychotic symptoms were excluded since this was an experimental study. All the families were assessed prior to treatment, at the end of treatment and at a six-month follow-up on a range of measures: semi-structured interviews, the Rutter A and B scales (a measure of disturbance in school-age children), three rating scales on which parents indicated the severity of the presenting problems, satisfaction with current family life, satisfaction with therapy and the Life Event Inventory.

In addition, the therapists completed an assessment schedule at the end of each therapy session including details of the session and, at the end of treatment, the therapist's impression of the amount of change that had occurred.

The results indicated that Milan family therapy was as effective as the other therapeutic techniques employed, even though these had the advantage of being more specifically selected according to the children's presenting characteristics. Milan family therapy was shorter in duration than the other treatments, and families reported greater positive change on general family functioning.

Dare *et al.* (1990) attempted to evaluate the effectiveness of family therapy in comparison to individual supportive therapy for women suffering from anorexia. A sample of 80 women participated in this study, and each was randomly assigned to one of the two treatment groups. Individual supportive therapy (an average of 16 sessions) was a symptom-focused treatment which made use of a broad range of therapeutic interventions including behavioural, analytic and strategic techniques. Family therapy (an average of nine sessions) adopted a range of approaches including structural, strategic and systemic approaches.

The therapy was also adjusted according to the age of the women. With the younger group the first phase was focused predominantly on the eating problem and on encouraging the parents to take charge. Once progress with weight gain was established, other family issues relating to the eating were discussed. Later the sessions moved towards the encouragement of autonomy and enabling the young women to take control of their eating and discussions of their eventual leaving-home transitions and the impact this had on the parents' marriage and so on. Four therapists took part, providing both the family and individual treatments in order to control individual variables. Both groups were intended to have approximately the same number of sessions, though the individual group on average had 16 as opposed to nine sessions for the family therapy group. With the older age group there was no initial attempt to get the parents to take charge. Instead the focus was more on issues of separation and on reducing the use of the eating disorder as a medium of communication.

In addition, the women were divided into four subgroups in order to facilitate exploration of a range of related specific questions:

1 age at onset of the anorexia was 18 years or under, and duration less than 3 years ($n = 21$);
2 age at onset of the anorexia was 18 years or under, and duration more than 3 years ($n = 19$);
3 age at onset of the anorexia was over 18 years ($n = 14$);
4 women suffering with bulimia ($n = 19$).

Seven women in total dropped out of treatment.

Outcome measures were taken immediately after the cessation of treatment and at a one-year follow-up. In addition, the initial assessment included a measure of expressed emotion between the patients and their parents. Progress was classified in terms of three categories:

- good outcome – a weight of more than 85 per cent of normal, resumption of menstruation and an absence of bulimic symptoms;
- intermediate outcome – a weight of more than 85 per cent of normal, but no resumption of menstruation, bulimic symptoms occurring no more than once per week;
- poor outcome – body weight less than 85 per cent of normal or bulimic symptoms occurring more than once per week.

For the first group, aged 18 or less at time of onset and duration less than 3 years, family therapy was found to be significantly superior to individual treatment. There were no significant (statistically) differences for the other groups, though family therapy appeared to be somewhat less effective for the post-18 onset subgroup.

A related finding was that dropout from treatment was significantly related to the level of expressed emotions. For example, in family therapy a high level of critical comments expressed by the mother towards the patient was likely to predict an early dropout from treatment.

Overall the study suggested that family therapy is an effective approach with a younger age group, especially where the symptoms are of relatively short duration. The authors also discuss the nature of the processes of change and conclude that the apparently contrasting techniques of putting the parents in charge of the younger group and of encouraging the parents to disengage from the older group share the function of exploring and clarifying the boundaries between the generations and of accepting the need to consider new ways of coping in the face of the life cycle changes that need to be negotiated.

Evaluative studies may incorporate important conceptual perspectives into the study. For example, the study by Leff *et al.* (1989) is based upon the conceptual framework of expressed emotion which is a measure of the emotional tone and processes in families. This factor is seen to consist of three related aspects: overinvolvement, critical comments and warmth. As we saw in Chapter 4, these factors can be seen as encapsulating some of the key findings regarding family dynamics and pathology, such as schizophrenia, that have been identified repeatedly, for example, Bateson *et al.* (1956), Wynne *et al.* (1958), Weakland (1976) and Minuchin *et al.* (1978).

The work of Leff and his colleagues supported the idea that the level of expressed emotion in the family environment of a person who has suffered from serious mental disturbance is significantly related to the likelihood that they will subsequently relapse. The three factors comprising expressed emotion – high levels of criticism, emotional overinvolvement and lack of emotional warmth – have all been seen as likely to promote relapse following hospitalization and recovery (Vaughn and Leff 1985; Berkowitz 1987). An important question that this study attempted to address was whether family therapy could be employed to alter the family atmosphere by reducing expressed emotion and therefore cutting the risk of relapse. The family therapy provided was eclectic and described as a combination of 'educational, behavioural, structural and systemic techniques'.

The participants were aged between 16 and 65, had been diagnosed as suffering with schizophrenia and were either living with or spending more than 35 hours per week in face-to-face contact with one or more relatives. All of the families were selected on the basis of having high expressed emotion. The participants were randomly assigned to be offered either education plus family therapy (n = 12) or education plus a relatives' group (n = 11). All participants were also still taking neuroleptic medication. Eleven of the 12 families accepted family therapy (conducted in their homes) but only six out of the 11 accepted participation in the relatives' group. The family therapy sessions lasted for about half an hour and the relatives' groups for about an hour and a half. Non-acceptance was generally associated with poorer outcome. The participants' mental state and social activities and the parents' levels of expressed emotion (Camberwell Family Interview) were assessed independently before the treatment, at nine months after the start of treatment and at a follow-up after 2 years.

The relapse over 9 months in the family therapy group was 8 per cent, compared to 17 per cent in the relatives' group. Generally the participants' social functioning also showed 'small, non-significant gains'. Relapse was defined as the reoccurrence of psychotic symptoms that had previously subsided or the increase in symptoms still present. For both groups there was a decrease in expressed emotion. For the family therapy group there was a significant reduction in contact and for the relatives' group a significant reduction in expressed emotion. Reduction in contact occurred in various ways, for example as a result of moving to independent living, more social activity or attending a day centre. Families who did not take part in the relatives' group showed very little change in expressed emotion and no reduction in relapse rates.

The findings overall were taken to suggest that both family therapy and a relatives' group can be effective in reducing relapse in people suffering from schizophrenia and that this reduction is associated with a reduction of expressed emotion and a reduction in face-to-face contact. This reduction in contact in turn may be associated with a reduction in overinvolvement. However, education plus family therapy was seen as the most efficient form of intervention since there was a much lower tendency for families to drop out of treatment.

Evaluative case studies

These have a long tradition in clinical research, spanning the famous case studies of Freud's pioneering work and the early case studies in the systemic literature which, for example, explored the nature of communication and family dynamics in relation to various types of problems, such as schizophrenia and anorexia (Weakland 1976; Haley 1976b; Minuchin *et al.* 1978). These typically involved the presentation of extended pieces of transcripts from therapeutic sessions with families, with a commentary and theoretical analysis. The reports could include details of individual cases or multiple case studies offering comparisons and contrasts across a number of families. The development of systemic family therapy can be seen to owe much to the accumulated knowledge gained by combining such case studies conducted by different therapists in a variety of contexts with families. This produced a form of meta-analysis where the combination of many case studies built a generalizable picture. It also permitted a sequential testing of theories and models through the selective exploration of different cases and examination of the significance of cases which suggested exceptions or inadequacies of the models (Yin 1994). For example, generalizations about anorectic family types as conflict-avoiding and enmeshed might be questioned by description of cases showing family dynamics that do not fit with this generalization. A progressive use of case studies to test theories through 'falsification' is consistent with the pure version of the scientific method (Popper 1962).

Bennum and Lucas (1990) examined the effects of an educational programme for six couples where one partner had a long-standing psychiatric history of schizophrenia. The programme offered information about schizophrenia and systemic family management, including problem-solving and communication training. This was followed by eight sessions of treatment in which the ideas were explored and applied by each couple to their particular concerns. The effects of the programme were assessed by means of a standardized test, the Psychiatric Assessment Scale, and a five-minute sample of speech from the non-clinical spouse about their partner was used to assess the level of expressed emotion. A personal approach to assessing change was also employed by means of a personal questionnaire. Each couple generated four target problems that they hoped would be addressed during the treatment programme. These were then turned into statements such that each partner could rate improvements on a four-point scale. The measures were employed eight weeks before the course, before and after the two-day course, following the eight-week programme of treatment where the skills were applied to specific problems, and at follow-up – 3, 6 and 12 months after treatment had ended.

The results were analysed for each of the six cases to provide an individual profile of change. In addition, commonalities in the changes across the six couples were also drawn out. Positive changes, especially in terms of the personal questionnaire, and problems identified specifically by each couple were found and were maintained over the follow-up period. Partners generally felt more confident about their ability to cope and there were indications of deterioration in symptoms. Individual factors were also examined – for example, the two spouses who had been rated as having high expressed emotion at the start of the treatment and who showed a change to low expressed emotion had become less critical and emotionally hostile to their partners.

Observational studies

Case studies can combine elements of observational studies. Of particular interest for therapeutic work are studies that have explored in detail the processes of change in family therapy. This can involve a variety of methods, but there is a growing interest in qualitative case studies that focus on the processes of conversations in family therapy. Specifically these are concerned with exploring changes in meanings surrounding the problems as therapy progresses. Such studies complement clinical practice and do not necessarily require any additional burden to be placed on the clinician.

Observational studies have been highly important in systemic family therapy. They laid the basis for ideas regarding family dynamics as displaying pattern and predictability. Initially observational studies predominantly took an 'outside' perspective in that families were observed in order to identify 'objective' patterns and structures. Minuchin (1974) and Minuchin *et al.* (1978), for example, conducted studies (see Chapter 2) to investigate the relationships between family dynamics and emotional arousal in family members. A wide range of studies has been conducted to explore causal links between family dynamics and types of disorder. An example of the use of observational measures has been the work on expressed emotion (Vaughn and Leff 1985) and the related concept of parental affective style (Doane *et al.* 1981, 1984, 1985). Expressed emotion (criticisms, warmth or hostility, and overinvolvement) is measured from interviews with each parent on their own. Affective style on the other hand is measured directly from family interactions. Doane *et al.* (1981, 1985) have shown that a high level of expressed emotions, which are found to be associated with relapse in families with a schizophrenic member, is also shown directly in their interactions.

Most observational studies have involved such structured observation and have adopted a quantitative approach. However, participant observation is an interesting alternative. In participant observation the observer includes himself or herself as part of the study. For example, this could involve accounts not only of the therapist's observations of a family but also of their reactions, feelings, memories triggered regarding their own family and so on. Though few specifically participant observational studies have been conducted, arguably most case studies of family therapy involve participant observation since the therapist comments on therapeutic processes in which he or she is integrally involved. An interesting and little repeated study was conducted by Vetere and Gale (1987) in which researchers lived with families for a period and were able to observe family dynamics in their natural setting, for example interactions at meal times, leisure activities, and disputes. A structural framework based on Minuchin's structural family therapy model was employed to categorize the observations but in addition the researchers also commented on their own reactions, possible influences they may have had on the family and so on.

An exploratory study of observations of changes in expressed emotion during family therapy was conducted by Vostanis *et al.* (1992). The study explored changes in expressed emotion displayed in the interaction in 12 families as they progressed through therapy. The families had been referred for child-related problems and varied in composition from nine nuclear, two step- and one single-parent families. The therapeutic orientation was based on the Milan model. Videorecordings of the first, second and last session were analysed by an independent observer using the expressed emotion dimensions and an overall global rating was made of the sessions for emotional overinvolvement and warmth, and the number of instances of critical and positive comments was counted. These measures were based on a combination of the speech of family members. Ratings were made for each family member and then combined to give an overall measure for the family.

The results indicated that all three measures – overinvolvement, critical comments and warmth – changed 'significantly between the beginning and termination of therapy'. The authors also employed the measures to look at the specific patterns of transactions between the family members over the course of therapy, suggesting that specific patterns, such as critical comments between parents about each other or comments directed towards the identified patient, may change to patterns of expressions of mutual warmth as therapy proceeds successfully.

Questionnaire and self-report studies

These formats are perhaps the most common type of research in family therapy. Particularly in relation to evaluation, many studies have been conducted which employ a variety of measures such as satisfaction questionnaires and various tests, such as the Beck Depression Inventory (Beck 1967) and FACES (Olson 1989), to assess change in family therapy. Specifically many studies have been conducted to compare the effectiveness of various forms of family therapy or to compare family therapy to other forms of therapy or treatment. These studies have mostly been quantitative in nature, with the intention of producing 'objective' and reliable information about the comparative effectiveness of family therapy. Such studies, though making strong claims for scientific objectivity, essentially rely on subjective measures in that family members in completing tests and questionnaires are offering self-reports – their view of how they feel and of the family dynamics.

Questionnaires vary in their design, but most contain a balance of closed and open-ended questions. The following is an example of a closed question:

> Please rate each statement according to how well it describes your family, and tick the appropriate box.
>
> We resolve most emotional upsets that come up.

strongly agree	*agree*	*disagree strongly*	*disagree*
☐	☐	☐	☐

In addition, questionnaires may include a range of open-ended questions which invite participants to offer their own views in their own words. It is possible to phrase these in the format of circular questions:

- Who would you say in your family most wanted to go for therapy and who least wanted to?
- Why do you think this was the case?

- What has been the most significant way that therapy has effected your family?

The analysis of responses to such open-ended questions is more complex and less easily quantifiable. However, it is possible to start with a content analysis, for example by attempting to find categories into which the responses fall. This can include a quantitative analysis, such as the number of times certain categories are referred to – for example, if the therapist's personality is mentioned frequently as a key factor by most families, it may suggest that this is seen as important by the family members.

Therapy process research

The aim of process studies is not simply to produce evaluations of therapy in terms of outcome but to reveal more about the nature of the therapeutic process – the active ingredients of therapy. Many therapists write eloquently about what they do and their reasons for conducting the work in various ways. However, it may be the case that our ideas about what works and why may not closely match what, for example, families perceive to be helpful. Process research can be helpful in distinguishing between therapeutic approaches but also in drawing out commonalities. For example, a good, positive therapeutic relationship seems to be central to all forms of family therapy, and even to all psychotherapy. We might also suggest that different forms of family therapy, such as narrative and strategic approaches, share some important features, such as utilizing spontaneous events or changes that families themselves initiate, reframing problems and working with families in a pragmatic and experimental manner. In this section we will review a number of studies that have attempted to explore aspects of the process of family therapy, starting with a study that has attempted to explore the nature of the therapeutic alliance in family therapy.

A therapeutic process study

From a variety of studies in psychotherapy the nature of the therapeutic alliance has emerged as a central feature. Quinn *et al.* (1997) attempted to explore the extent to which this is also true for family therapy. However, in contrast to individual therapies the situation is more complex since there are a range of alliances – each individual member and the therapist, subsystems (e.g. the parents) and the therapist, and the family overall and the therapist.

Quinn *et al.* employed an instrument called the Interpersonal Psychotherapy Alliance Scale (IPAS). This scale, developed by Pinsof and Catherall (1986), assesses the relationships between the client and therapist, therapist and other important family members, and the family group and therapist. The IPAS questionnaire consists of a series of statements, such as 'The therapist cares about me as a person', 'The therapist has the skills and abilities to help me' and 'The therapist and I are in agreement about the goals of therapy' to which a response is made on a seven-point scale ranging from completely agree to completely disagree. This measure was taken at the end of the third therapy session since by then the nature of the relationships between the family members and the therapist would reasonably be expected to have become established.

Seventeen couples undergoing marital or family therapy took part. At the termination of therapy the families and couples were asked to rate how effective the therapy had been in terms of two questions: the degree to which they felt that the goals of therapy had been met and the degree to which they believed the changes would last more than six months.

The results showed strong, statistically significant positive correlations between the ratings of the therapeutic alliance and the family's estimates of success of therapy. The more highly the family members rated the relationship with the therapist, the better the eventual outcome. Some specific findings were that most positive outcomes in therapy were associated with the women, more than the men, feeling aligned with the therapist with respect to the therapeutic task, but also believing that other family members were also working well with the therapist.

In-depth single case process study

Frosh *et al.* (1996) aimed to identify some of the factors that are involved in the process of change during the course of family therapy. Rather than imposing any manipulations, this study explored a piece of family therapy that had already taken place. Hence there was no possible bias effect since the therapist had no idea beforehand that the sessions would be analysed. Permission was asked after the sessions had already taken place.

Videotapes of six out of eight sessions of a programme of family therapy were transcribed and analysed in detail. The parents had recently separated – a decision made by the father and initially resisted by the mother. The analysis was based on a grounded theory (Glaser and Strauss 1967) approach in which themes are allowed to emerge from the analysis rather than imposed *a priori*. The transcripts were initially analysed to elicit themes in the conversations between the therapist and family regarding change. Successive readings were made of the text to refine the categories. From this analysis two predominant themes emerged: managed and evolving change (though other complex issues were also evident). The concept of managed change contained the idea that change occurred through people actively attempting to do things differently, in contrast to evolving change which occurs spontaneously and naturally. These beliefs or discourses about change were seen to be employed strategically in different ways at different times by the family members in order to meet their own needs. The father who had initiated the separation argued that change was spontaneous and talking about things – trying to manage change – was pointless. This seemed to fit with his wish not to reverse his decision to leave as a result of therapy, whereas his wife initially did wish to reverse the separation.

The analysis involved presenting extensive examples of these two concepts of change and mapping how their usage altered as therapy progressed. Over the course of therapy, family members were seen to move from relatively polarized and rigid positions in their views of change, to a recognition that therapy could be helpful in helping them come to terms with their separation. The family conversations gradually showed a greater tolerance of alternative ideas of change.

Exploring the experience of family therapy

Despite the fact that one of the most common applications of family therapy has been in relation to children's problems, there has been little research on how children experience therapy and what this might tell us about ways of making the process interesting and effective for them. Stith *et al.* (1996) explored the experience of 16 children undergoing therapy with their families (12 families in total). One of the children was aged 5, nine were between 8 and 9, five were preadolescents (aged 10–12) and one early adolescent (age 13). Fourteen of the children were white and two were African-American. Ten of the children were in single-parent families (headed by single mothers), four were in nuclear families, one was in a remarried family, and one was being raised by grandparents. Eleven of the 12 families presented with child-focused problems and the remaining family identified marital problems as the main concern.

Therapists were asked to invite families to participate, and the families were then contacted by a researcher. Children were usually interviewed while the parents were seeing the therapist. Each child was interviewed twice and the parents were interviewed once.

A semi-structured interview lasting about half an hour was employed. Children were invited to tell their experience of therapy in their own words, but a number of general questions were included, such as: When you and your family talk about coming here, what do you call this place? What happens when you and your family come here? What do you like or don't you like about coming here? Do you ever wonder about the people behind the mirror? What do you think about them? An attempt was made to compare the children's accounts with their parents' or a teenage sibling's perceptions of the child's experience. These interviews employed a number of questions, such as: What do you think Mary (for example) thinks about coming to family therapy? How does she respond when it's time to come to therapy?

The interviews were transcribed and then members of the team each independently analysed two of the initial transcripts employing a grounded theory framework (Glaser and Strauss 1967). This involved systematically reading through the transcripts and coding each sentence, combining these into preliminary categories, and progressively sifting and recoding these categories. These codes were employed to generate more refined questions for the subsequent interviews. This was an iterative process, with the interviews being successively analysed and refined. The categories were then discussed by the team and refined until no new categories emerged.

The children's experiences were found to fall into four areas or themes:

1 *The reactions of the children to the process of videotaping and live supervision*. All of the children were aware of the mirror and that there were people behind it, but not all were aware of the purpose of this arrangement:

Interviewer: Have you ever wondered who those people are back there? What do you think their job is?

Child: To see what we're doing and to tell the counsellor if they're doing good or if they want to improve things, or like to just see what's going on in families . . . and seeing what their problems are and seeing what their advantages are.

(Boy, aged 9)

2 *How they understood why they and their families came to therapy*. Most children saw the existence of problems that needed solving as the main reason the family had come:

> Mom and Dad get into fights and stuff and they didn't get along.
>
> (Girl, 9)

> We're coming here to make our family a better place . . . a better family, to make us have happier lives.
>
> (Boy, 8)

3 *How they described what happened in therapy*. A dominant theme was the children's desire to be included in the therapy. They generally did not like being left in the waiting room and wanted to be actively involved in talking not just about themselves but about issues in the family more generally. They also preferred to be able to engage in activities, such as drawing or 'games', such as sculpting:

> I feel comfortable when we are talking about someone else, then I can contribute.
>
> (Boy, 8)

> I don't mind the questions. It's just all the time and everything. Like they ask me a question and they make a question out of my answer.
>
> (Girl, 12)

4 *What they said had changed during the time they had been coming to therapy*. The children talked about what had changed in how they felt during the therapy itself and how things had changed at home. Generally they described becoming more comfortable with therapy as time went on. The therapy was generally seen as having helped to solve particular problems:

> Before I had tons of problems, like at school, but now I'm doing OK.
>
> (Boy, 11)

> It's brought everybody closer. Everybody's been able to talk about their problems. They can talk it out and come together. Usually, everybody's apart and they keep their feelings to themselves and just let it happen.
>
> (Brother, 15)

In general, all the children interviewed indicated a desire to be actively included in the therapy. All but the youngest understood the purpose of therapy and reported that talking about problems was helpful to them and their families. The younger children (aged 5–9) enjoyed play activities and found the personality of the therapist to be important. The key conclusion reached was that children wished to be included but did not wish to be the sole focus. They wanted to learn more about the workings of their family, help in the solutions of problems, and not have their own troubles be the focus. However, an hour of 'adult talk' may be too much for many children, and therapists need to find ways of connecting with children through activity and play. The parents' and siblings' responses also suggested that children were more comfortable the more they knew about the reasons why the family had come for therapy. Discussing this and the reasons for the technology may be very useful in the initial sessions. Though initially resistant, the children saw some value in the sessions over time.

Finally, the researchers suggested that therapists who are interested in children, able to express warmth and connection to them, and willing to operate in the children's world will have more success involving them in therapy.

Family theory research

The origins of family therapy arose from research studies into the nature of communication and its relationship to the development of pathology. This quickly developed into a plethora of enthusiastic studies which attempted, for example, to discover causal links between patterns of family dynamics and types of pathology. This led to research on the nature of 'psychosomatic and anorexic' families, 'schizophrenic' families, 'addictive' families and 'delinquent' families. Though of some value, much of this line of research has not proven fruitful, partly since it is extremely complex to classify families and also because such work missed the systemic understanding that family systems inevitably have a uniqueness and unpredictability and evolve and change over time. Nevertheless, studies attempting to explore theoretical models for families can also be valuable, for example in pointing to common tasks and processes that families undergo, how family beliefs are shaped, the impact of the wider culture and the dynamics of families in various contexts. Our first study in this section is an attempt to explore the last question – how families function in settings other than the therapy suite.

A participant observational study

Vetere and Gale (1987) aimed to explore the nature of interaction of families presenting with child-focused problems. Though we know much about how families interact in the context of family therapy suites, we know less about how they actually act in their home situations. Furthermore, less is known about the detailed nature of interactions and what it feels like from the 'inside'. A participant observational approach was employed whereby a researcher lived with a family for 3 weeks. During this time she engaged in the full range of family activities, such as meals, outings, domestic duties and leisure pastimes, including watching television and playing games. The researcher kept detailed notes of the family interaction, primarily using a structural systemic format noting the family structure: family boundaries, subsystems, hierarchy, alliances and triangulations. In addition, detailed notes were kept on the emotional atmosphere, the impact on the researcher and inferences about the possible experiences of the various family members.

The study suggested that family dynamics as observed in the homes were analogous to those typically observed in therapeutic situations. However, the timing and pacing were on a different time scale. For example, arguments, disagreements, sulking and so on could last for days, in contrast to the accelerated pace of events in therapy. The analysis of family beliefs from the repertory grid analysis suggested that the family dynamics were significantly shaped by the nature of the families' beliefs. These had a stability and, for example, were at the basis of patterns of scapegoating that could occur. A wide range of gender stereotyped behaviour and ideas also became evident as part of the observations, such as implicit expectations about domestic roles, duties and obligations.

Interview studies

Next to questionnaire-based studies, interviews are perhaps the most common form of research, especially qualitative research. The purpose of an interview is simply to enable participants to express their views, opinions, explanations, accounts and narratives about something. One of the advantages of an interview is that it enables us to hear what is important to members of a family rather than imposing a set of questions on them. However, interviews may vary in the extent to which they are prestructured – for example, in some cases the researcher will have a large number of specific questions they wish to ask. At one extreme, such an interview may resemble a verbally administered questionnaire. At the other, interviews may be largely unstructured and represent a conversation between interviewer and interviewee. Perhaps most commonly, a semi-structured compromise is employed where the interviewer does have a range of questions but also aims to explore issues as they arise. Some elaborations on interviewing have been suggested; one important addition is to consider the interview a collaborative venture. For example, the interview can be in two parts so that following a break (either during the interview or at a later stage) the interviewer asks the respondent to comment on the process and suggest their own questions, and the interviewer may comment upon some of the key issues that have struck them and invite the reflections. Also, the interviewer can offer a written summary of their impressions to a family and hold a subsequent interview to discuss the family's reactions to these. Another variation based in ethnography is that following each interview the interviewer analyses their data. Based on this analysis they may alter their focus, adding or deleting some questions according to the themes that are emerging. In this way there is a greater sensitivity to focusing on questions that are of relevance to the interviewee than to questions assumed to be important by the interviewer.

Interestingly, though family therapists have developed considerable skills in interviewing families there has been a relative dearth of studies that employ interviews of couples or families. These can of course be complemented by interviews with each individual member. However, conjoint interviews offer the bonus of a wide range of interactional material, including the nature of family conversations regarding different areas, how families jointly remember events, differences in opinions and how these are dealt with. Outside family therapy, interviews with groups of people can be found in focus group studies, the aim of these being that the group processes facilitate opinions and ideas surfacing since members may prompt each other to consider issues and voice a wider range of opinions than they might otherwise.

A conjoint interview study

Dallos *et al.* (1997) aimed to explore processes of resilience in families and, in particular, the accounts that family members offered of how problems had developed. In order to offer some contrasts, two groups were interviewed: a group of young adults who had experienced extended mental health problems and their families, and a group of young people who were not known to have a clinical history. The study employed retrospective interviews which were intended to draw out accounts from both groups of how initial difficulties had been dealt with. One of the key hypotheses was that the nature of the initial perceptions of problems may lead to attempted solutions that can serve to aggravate, rather than alleviate, distress. A semi-structured interview format was developed which included drawing a life-line on which key positive and negative events from the child's birth were plotted. Families were interviewed together. This produced accounts of the key events, early indications of difficulties and details of attempted solutions. In addition, the conjoint interviews gave a picture of how families construct memories, including who is dominant in telling the story, differences in their memories and, more broadly, how memories of key events are constructed for the identified patient.

The interviews were videotaped and transcribed and independent analyses performed to generate common themes in the accounts and the influence of dominant discourses, such as medical models of emotional distress. These themes were successively checked against the transcripts and revised. A count of the frequency of different themes mentioned by the families was also produced. In addition, the videotapes were examined to produce a map of the family dynamics. The summaries of the analyses were discussed by the researchers and also shown to some of the participants to corroborate the analysis. The results indicated that there was surprisingly little difference between the two groups in their accounts of the severity of early difficulties experienced. However, the clinical group's accounts indicated fewer resources, such as emotional 'spare capacity' in the family and practical support available. Also, the clinical group showed less ability to contemplate alternative narratives (negative as well as positive) about how events may have proceeded along different paths.

Case study series

Palazzoli *et al.* (1989) employed a research/therapeutic approach in which the developmental nature of psychosis in young adults and the efficacy of a therapeutic approach were explored simultaneously. Combining detailed notes on the developmental history of the problems in families, the team employed a standard package of treatment to investigate commonalities and differences in 149 families' responses. A feature of their approach was the use of the 'invariant prescription' in which the parents are instructed to go out together on a secret outing; the children are not to be informed of any details of where the couple are going or what they will do together.

The intervention was regarded as both a therapeutic and a research technique. Its aim was to explore the developmental hypothesis that children experiencing psychotic disturbance have become entangled and embroiled in a no-win stalemated struggle between their parents. Over the years it is suggested that one or other child in the family, perhaps as a consequence of some special sensitivity or the timing of their entry into the family, becomes progressively conscripted into siding with one parent against the other and also ultimately betrayed when the parents eventually redirect their attentions to each other, thereby also emotionally abandoning the child.

The invariant prescription is intended to both reveal and help break up this pattern. The responses of the children and their families were seen as providing a test of the developmental hypothesis and of the efficacy of this therapeutic approach. The responses of the families were categorized into various types. For example, a common feature to the invariant prescription was a display of extreme anger by a non-symptomatic sibling, which was seen to reveal and challenge their secret collusion in gaining a favoured and powerful role in the family.

The findings of the team, based on more than 50 families presenting with psychotic symptoms in a young adult, supported the developmental hypothesis and indicated that the invariant prescription provoked significant positive changes in the families. The changes were measured in terms of standard psychiatric measures based on the American Psychiatric Association (1980) family perceptions and on independent observations and ratings by the therapy team members.

Discussion and reflections

As we have discussed, there is considerable pressure from managers and purchasers of therapeutic services to provide evidence of effectiveness. More broadly, this has been described as the need to develop evidence-based practice. This is perhaps especially significant for family therapy since it is seen as a high-cost resource, especially when it is conducted in teams, and also requires more in the way of resources such as video equipment. At times it might appear that an audit of the effectiveness would be sufficient.

In some cases this may be true, but we hope that you have also seen that evaluative studies can and need to do more. Good research helps to reveal the nature of the therapeutic process and also to develop general theory about family functioning. Without knowledge of what aspects of therapy were significant and the nature of the experience for families, evaluation may just become a sterile activity. Given the limited time that most clinicians have available for research, they may therefore be more reluctant to undertake such activity. One of the challenges for research into family therapy, and into other forms of psychotherapy, is for the research to be compatible with the process of clinical work. Qualitative research, for example the kind of study conducted by Frosh *et al.* (1996), points towards such a compatible approach.

As we indicated at the start of the chapter, family therapy, with its techniques of videorecording and live supervision, lends itself readily to the collection of material that can subsequently be analysed and presented as good qualitative research. In turn, it may be that such qualitative studies can be pursued as larger studies including some quantitative measures. However, we do feel that the traditional view that research must involve quantitative measures is no longer tenable. Further, we suggest that research that does not include qualitative aspects, such as attempts to consider family members' views and experiences, is seriously limited.

There follows a list of some key reference texts relating to family therapy research. In addition, we have included some papers relating more broadly to psychotherapy research which you may find interesting to follow up, such as work on readiness to change, the therapeutic alliance and explorations of clients' perceptions of significant events in therapy.

Key texts

Varieties of research

Aveline, M. and Shapiro, D.A. (eds) (1995) *Research Foundations for Psychotherapy Practice*. New York: Free Press.

Barkham, M., Shapiro, D.A. and Firth-Cozens, J. (1989) Personal questionnaires in prescriptive vs. exploratory psychotherapy. *British Journal of Clinical Psychology*, 28: 97–107.

Bennum, I. and Lucas, R. (1990) Using the partner in the psychosocial treatment of schizophrenia: a multiple single case design. *British Journal of Clinical Psychology*, 29: 185–92.

Berkowitz, R. (1987) Rating expressed emotion from initial family therapy sessions (a pilot study). *Journal of Family Therapy*, 9: 27–37.

Elliott, R. (1986) Interpersonal Process Recall (IPR) as a process research method, in L. Greenberg and W. Pinsof (eds) *The Psyhotherapeutic Process: A Research Handbook*. New York: Guilford Press.

Elliott, R. and Shapiro, D.A. (1988) Brief structured recall: a more efficient method for studying significant therapy events. *British Journal of Medical Psychology*, 61: 141–53.

Fonagy, A. and Roth, A. (1997) *What Works for Whom? A Critical Review of Psychotherapy Research*. London: Guilford Press.

Friedman, M.S. and Goldstein, M.J. (1994) Relatives' perception of the interactional behaviour with a schizophrenic family member. *Family Process*, 33: 377–87.

Frosh, S., Burck, C., Strickland-Clark, L. and Morgan, K. (1996) Engaging with change: a process study of family therapy. *Journal of Family Therapy*, 18: 141–61.

Llewelyn, S.P., Elliott, R., Shapiro, D.A., Hardy, G. and Firth-Cozens, J. (1988) Client perceptions of significant events in prescriptive and exploratory periods of individual therapy. *British Journal of Clinical Psychology*, 27: 105–14.

Martin, G. and Allison, S. (1993) Therapeutic alliance: a view constructed by a family therapy team. *Australia and New Zealand Journal of Family Therapy*, 14: 205–14.

Miklowitz, D.J., Goldstein, M.J., Falloon, I.R.H. and Doane, J.A. (1984) Interactional correlates of expressed emotion in families of schizophrenics. *British Journal of Psychiatry*, 144: 482–7.

Olson, D.H. (1989) Circumplex model of family systems viii: Family asssessment and intervention, in D.H. Olson, C.S. Russel and D.H Sprenkle (eds) *Circumplex Model: Systematic Assessment and Treatment of Families*. New York: Haworth Press.

Pinsof, W.M. and Catherall, D.R. (1986) The integrative psychotherapy alliance: family, couple and individual scales. *Journal of Family and Marital Therapy*, 12: 132–51.

Prochaska, J., DiClemente, C.C. and Norcross, J.C. (1992) In search of how people change: applications to addictive behaviours. *American Psychologist*, 47: 1102–14.

Quinn, W.H., Dotson, D. and Jordan, K. (1997) Dimensions of therapeutic alliance and their associations with outcome in family therapy. *Psychotherapy Research*, 7: 429–38.

Sprenkle, D.H. and Moon, S.M. (1996) *Research Methods in Family Therapy*. London: Guilford Press.

Stith, S.M., Rosen, K.H., McCollum, E.E., Coleman, J.U. and Hetman, S.A. (1996) The voices of children: preadolescent children's experiences in family therapy. *Journal of Marital and Family Therapy*, 22: 69–86.

Vostanis, P., Burnham, J. and Harris, W. (1992) Changes of expressed emotion in systemic family therapy. *Journal of Family Therapy*, 14: 15–27.

Wynne, L.C. (ed.) *The State of the Art in Family Therapy Research*. New York: Family Process Press.

Family therapy outcome studies

Alexander, J. and Parsons, B. (1973) Short-term behavioural interventions with delinquent families: impact on family processes and recidivism. *Journal of Abnormal Psychology*, 81: 219–50.

Arnow, B., Taylor, C., Agras, W. and Telch, M. (1985) Enhancing agoraphobia treatment outcome by changing couple communication. *Behaviour Therapy*, 16: 452–67.

Barclay, R., Guevremont, D., Anastopoulos, A. and Fletcher, K. (1992) A comparison of three family therapy programs for treating family conflicts in adolescents. *Journal of Consulting and Clinical Psychology*, 60: 450–62.

Barlow, D., O'Brien, G. and Last, C. (1984) Couples treatment of agoraphobia. *Behaviour Therapy*, 15: 41–58.

Barret, P., Dadds, M. and Rappee, R. (1996) Family treatment of childhood anxiety: a controlled trial. *Journal of Consulting and Clinical Psychology*, 64: 333–42.

Baucom, D., Shoham, V., Mueser, K., Daiuto, A. and Stickle, T. (1998) Empirically supported couple and family intervention for marital distress and adult mental health problems. *Journal of Consulting and Clinical Psychology*, 66: 53–88.

Black, D. and Urbanovicz, M. (1987) Family intervention with bereaved children. *Journal of Child Psychology and Psychiatry*, 28: 467–76.

Brent, D., Holder, D. and Kolko, D. (1997) A clinical psychotherapy trial for adolescent depression comparing cognitive, family and supportive treatments. *Archives of General Psychiatry*, 54: 877–85.

Brunk, M., Hengeller, S. and Whelan, J. (1987) Comparisons of multisystemic therapy and parent training in the brief treatment of child abuse and neglect. *Journal of Consulting and Clinical Psychology*, 55: 171–8.

Carr, A. (2000a) Evidence-based practice in family therapy and systemic consultation. *Journal of Family Therapy*, 22(1): 29–61.

Carr, A. (2000b) Evidence-based practice in family therapy and systemic consultation II. *Journal of Family Therapy*, 22(3): 273–96.

Chamberlain, P. and Rosicky, J. (1995) The effectiveness of family therapy in the treatment of adolescents with conduct disorders and delinquency. *Journal of Marital and Family Therapy*, 21: 441–59.

Dadds, K., Schwartz, S. and Sanders, M. (1987) Marital discord and treatment outcome in behavioural treatment of child conduct disorders. *Journal of Consulting and Clinical Psychology*, 55: 396–403.

Dunn, R. and Schwebel, A. (1995) A meta-analytic review of marital therapy outcome research. *Journal of Family Psychology*, 9: 58–68.

Eiser, I. (2002) Comment. *Journal of Family Therapy*, 24(2): 125–34.

Eiser, I., Dare, C., Hodes, M., Russel, G.F.M., Dodge, E. and LeGrange, D. (2000) Family therapy for adolescent anorexia nervosa: the results of a controlled comparison of two family interventions. *Journal of Child Psychology and Psychiatry*, 41: 727–36.

Fadden, G. (1998) Research update: psycho-educational family interventions. *Journal of Family Therapy*, 20: 293–309.

Goldstein, M. and Miklowitz, D. (1995) The effectiveness of psycho-educational family therapy in the treatment of schizophrenia disorders. *Journal of Family Therapy*, 17: 263–80.

Gordon, D., Arbuthnot, J., Gustafson, K. and McGreen, P. (1998) Home-based behavioral systems family therapy with disadvantaged delinquents. *American Journal of Family Therapy*, 16: 243–55.

Gustafsson, O., Kjellman, N. and Cederbald, M. (1986) Family therapy in the treatment of severe childhood asthma. *Journal of Psychosomatic Research*, 30: 369–74.

Harrington, R., Kerfoot, M., Dyer, E., McNiven, F., Gill, J., Harrington, V., Woodham, A. and Byford, S. (1998) Randomized trial of a home-based family intervention for children who have deliberately poisoned themselves. *Journal of the American Academy of Child and Adolescent Psychiatry*, 37: 512–18.

Hazelrigg, M.D., Cooper, H.M. and Borduin, C.M (1987) Evaluating the effectiveness of family therapies: an integrative review and analysis. *Psychological Bulletin*, 101: 428–42.

Hengeller, S., Birduin, C., Melton, G., Mann, B., Smith, L., Hall, J., Cone, L. and Fucci, B. (1991) The effects of multi-systemic therapy on drug use and abuse in serious juvenile offenders: a programme report from two outcome studies. *Family Dynamic Addiction Quarterly*, 1: 40–51.

Ialongo, N., Horn, W., Pascoe, J., Greenberg, G., Packard, T., Lopez, M., Wagner, A. and Puttler, L. (1993) The effects of multi-model intervention with attention-deficit hyperactive disorder children: a 9 month follow-up. *Journal of the American Academy of Child and Adolescent Psychiatry*, 32: 182–9.

Kolko, D.J., Brent, D.A., Baugher, M., Bridge, J. and Birmaher, B. (2000) Cognitive and family therapies for adolescent depression: treatment specificity, mediation, and moderation. *Journal of Consulting and Clinical Psychology*, 68: 603–14.

Lask, B. and Matthews, D. (1979) Childhood asthma: a controlled trial of family psychotherapy. *Archives of Diseases in Childhood*, 55: 116–19.

Leff, J., Vearnal, S., Brewin, C.R., Wilff, G., Alexander, B., Asen, E., Dayson, D., Jones, E., Chisholm, D. and Everitt, B. (2000) The London Depression Intervention Trial: randomised control trial of antidepressants vs couples therapy in the treatment and maintenance of people with depression living with a partner: clinical outcome and costs. *British Journal of Psychiatry*, 177: 95–100.

March, J. (1995) Cognitive behavioural psychotherapy for children and adolescents with OCD: a review and recommendations for treatment. *Journal of the American Academy of Child and Adolescent Psychiatry*, 34: 7–18.

March, J., Mulle, K. and Herbel, B. (1994) Behavioural psychotherapy for children and adolescents with OCD: an open trial of a new protocol-driven treatment package. *Journal of the American Academy of Child and Adolescent Psychiatry*, 33: 333–41.

Markus, E., Lange, A. and Pettigrew, T. (1990) Effectiveness of family therapy: a meta-analysis. *Journal of Family Therapy*, 12: 205–21.

McFarlane, W.R., Lukens, E., Link, B., Dushay, R., Deakins, S.A., Newmark, M., Dunne, E.J., Horen, B. and Toran, J. (1995) Multiple-family therapy and psychoeducation in the treatment of schizophrenia. *Archives of General Psychiatry*, 52: 679–87.

Nicol, A., Smith, J. and Kay, B. (1988) A focused casework approach to the treatment of child abuse: a controlled comparison. *Journal of Child Psychology and Psychiatry*, 29: 703–11.

Robin, A., Siegel, P. and Moye, A. (1995) Family versus individual therapy for anorexia: impact of family conflict. *International Journal of Eating Disorders*, 17: 313–22.

Sanders, M., Shepherd, R., Cleghorn, G. and Woodford, H. (1994) The treatment of recurrent abdominal pain in children: a controlled comparison of cognitive behavioural family intervention and standard paediatric care. *Journal of Consulting and Clinical Psychology*, 62: 306–14.

Serketich, E.W. and Dumas, J.E. (1996) The effectiveness of behavioural parent training to modify antisocial behaviour in children: a meta-analysis. *Behaviour Therapy*, 27: 171–86.

Shadish, W.R., Ragsdale, K., Glaser, R.R. and Montgomery, L.M. (1995) The efficacy and effectiveness of marital and family therapy: a perspective from meta-analysis. *Journal of Marital and Family Therapy*, 21: 345–60.

Silver, E., Williams, A., Worthington, F. and Philips, N. (1998) Family therapy and soiling: an audit of externalising and other approaches. *Journal of Family Therapy*, 20: 413–22.

Simpson, L. (1990) The comparative efficacy of Milan family therapy for disturbed children and their families. *Journal of Family Therapy*, 13: 267–84.

Stanton, M.D. and Shadish, W.R. (1997) Outcome, attrition, and family-couples treatment for drug abuse: a meta-analysis and review of the controlled, comparative studies. *Psychological Bulletin*, 122: 170–91.

Waldron, H.B. (1996) Adolescent substance abuse and family therapy outcome: a review of randomized trials. *Advances in Clinical Child Psychology*, 19: 199–234.

Webster-Stratton, C. and Hammond, M. (1997) Treating children with early onset conduct disorders: a comparison of child and parent training interventions. *Journal of Consulting and Clinical Psychology*, 65: 93–109.

8 Reflections and critique 2005

In this final chapter we want to pull together some of the threads that connect different approaches in systemic therapy but also to make some connections to other therapies. In addition, we want to indulge in some crystal ball gazing to consider possible developments in the twenty-first century. Reviewing the literature, we find the following statements in *The Book of Family Therapy* (Mendelsohn and Napier 1972) which, in our opinion, could just as easily have been written in 2005:

> Family therapists are a curious and distinctive breed among mental health professionals. They have broken down a number of professional taboos, especially concerning secrecy, and they practise openness, direct observation of therapy and give each other live supervision, the sharing of experiences, and they treat people as persons rather than as patients. Mavericks that they are, they are relatively unconcerned with the formal degrees [family therapists] have, they tend to practise what they preach and are relatively frank about their own family struggles, thereby decreasing the usual distance between the professional and seeker of help. Family therapists have strong convictions about the validity of their work and firmly believe they're where the action's really at.

While in 2005 colleagues would say that family therapy and systemic practice are part of the mental health establishment, there is, in our view, still a maverick element. Committing ourselves to being influenced by feedback and listening collaboratively means we are constantly and publicly demonstrating our own process of change. Another reason for systemic practice probably remaining the chosen modality for a minority of therapists is the sheer complexity and emotional demand on practitioners when talking with more than one person at a time, which makes a systemic approach simultaneously more authentic and more daunting for practitioners and clients alike.

It may, therefore, be helpful to take a bird's-eye view of what we see as the key contributions to psychotherapy of a systemic approach. The original ideas, as we have seen, came from the fields of cybernetics and systems theory. Central to both of these was the concept of feedback. If we pause to think for a moment, we realize that this concept has become as widespread as, for example, the concept of the unconscious in psychodynamic theory. The value of, for example, offering comments on people's performance has been central to education and training prior to the formal explication of the concept of feedback in the 1950s. However, the application of the concept in the area of human relations has offered some radical revisions to many of our previously cherished concepts. For example, the notion of a stable, invariant, biologically determined personality is challenged by the notion of people's actions and experiences as shaped by the processes of feedback in different social contexts and co-creation of shared meanings. Even within a family a daughter may, for example, act and experience herself as a different person when alone with her mother, caught in the middle of a conflict between her parents or playing with her siblings.

In clinical work a systemic approach moves us away from a rigid, positivistic view of people and problems, away, for example, from attempts to assess and explain, to a propositional 'as if' view where the emphasis is on understanding the context (circumstances and relationships) where the problem occurs. Since people are seen as part of their social systems and the complexity of their interactions and spirals of feedback is too great to allow simple predictions, it frees us as therapists from becoming drawn into futile searching for 'the truth'. That is not to say that we ignore 'facts', such as abuse or the economic conditions in which a family are immersed, but that we are less likely to be led into becoming set in how we see and explain difficulties. Sometimes this propositional view may be puzzling to others. One of us recently presented with his therapy team an outline to the community mental health team (CMHT) of the systemic therapy service that had been developed for families in the adult mental health services. There was considerable interest expressed in the service, especially in the way we worked together as a team. The consultant psychiatrist heading the CMHT repeatedly asked us if we ever disagreed about the best treatment for a family, what happened if we disagreed and who had the final say. We replied that, rather than attempting to reduce differences, we welcomed these and utilized them with our families. For example, the family could be invited to listen to our reflecting team discussion, or the therapist could share with the family some of the differences of opinion in our team. If the therapist had a clear view of what they wanted to do which differed from the supervision team we could employ the therapist's ideas pragmatically, as an experiment, and agree to make adjustments based on the feedback from the family.

In short, a systemic approach can liberate us from trying to 'get it right', to experimenting, observing what seems to work and letting the family tell us what is helpful. In keeping with this emphasis on the importance of feedback, a systemic approach continually challenges our ideas and even our currently fashionable interests. One family (Mr and Mrs B) gave us feedback in our final sessions with them that one of the things they had found most useful was the suggestion that the parents go out together as a couple and perhaps discuss their future and how best to help their daughter, who had been very embroiled in their conflicts. In part this was a relatively straightforward and structural suggestion reminiscent both of the first phase of systemic family therapy and the third phase, invariant prescription (Palazzoli *et al.* 1989). On the other hand the father had experienced an earlier reflecting team discussion as critical of his position – intransigent about making a commitment to repairing his relationship with his wife. This certainly was not the intention of the team in their discussion, nor the focus of what they felt they had said. However, it was what the father had received. A commitment to listening to the feedback from a family helps to avoid forming possibly mistaken assumptions about the effects of our messages to them or what they believe. Fundamentally the issue is not about getting it right but of offering ideas that family members may be able to use. George Kelly (1955) referred to therapy as enabling an elaboration of a person's belief system. Likewise, systemic therapy regards offering ideas and stimulating curiosity in families as enriching and opening the doors to changes in behaviour.

Current state of the art

As we saw in Chapter 3, contemporary approaches are much inspired by social constructionist theories. However, strands from earlier approaches coexist along with developments of interest in language, conversation and a collaborative approach to therapy. The third phase, as we have seen, puts much less emphasis on techniques and more on the process of family therapy as a collaborative conversation. However, these approaches exist, for example, alongside solution-focused therapy, which is inspired by earlier strategic approaches. Though solution-focused approaches do have some overlap with social constructionist therapies, it is also possible that they have gained considerable popularity because they claim to be relatively brief. In the context of state-funded services, such as the National Health Service in Britain, this is obviously attractive since they are less of a drain on staff time and other resources. Arguably the relative speed of family therapy in comparison to other psychotherapies is still one of its perceived strengths.

It is fair to say that many, if not most, experienced practitioners employ ideas or strands from the earlier phases in the development of systemic theory and practice. Taking heed of Jackson's (1965a) original caution to regard family concepts, such as rules, homeostasis, boundaries, and so on 'as if' rather than objective entities allows us to employ a whole range of ideas. Moreover, we should note that social constructionism is not another theory to compete with others but more a critical position or meta-theory that allows us to consider how other theories develop and are employed (Dallos and Urry 1999). Therefore we can employ earlier ideas pragmatically without becoming obsessed by whether they are true or not. As in our example above, it may be possible to continue to employ eminently useful ideas, such as strengthening the parental subsystem, if we do so in a collaborative way. For example, Mrs B commented that it had been useful that we 'told them to go out as a couple'. Mr B immediately added that, 'No, we weren't told, we were asked . . . he never told us to do anything, just made suggestions and asked the right questions . . . he's quite crafty, really, I think'.

Fifteen years ago, in the midst of phase II (late 1980s), hearing a client call a therapist 'crafty' might have generated conversations among therapists about the extent to which a therapist thus described was being manipulative or therapy itself misunderstood by one client. Today we would probably be pleased that the client felt able to offer the therapist their feedback and take it as evidence of the client's experience of the non-expert stance of the therapist. In the world of family therapy and systemic practice, 'same behaviour, different meanings' might be a slogan for clients and therapists alike.

As we survey the field in 2005, systemic practice is well established around the world. Possibly Britain has a leading position in the application of systemic ideas in health and welfare agencies as well as in private practice. Far more professionals in Britain have a family therapy qualification than there are family therapy posts. Nevertheless, in CMHTs and social service departments up and down the country, the work of systemic practitioners is noticed and sometimes acknowledged by admiring colleagues. What we hear is noticed is the capacity of systemically trained practitioners to clarify context and 'see the wood from the trees'.

It is also possible that different therapeutic approaches, psychodynamic, cognitive, behavioural, rational-emotive and systemic, are now and will be more and more in conversation with each other. This may be one of the most positive legacies of social constructionism in that it allows us to regard various approaches as different discourses or ways of explaining problems without getting caught in unhelpful debates about which is correct. Also, research into how psychotherapies work has been revealing a number of common factors, such as the importance of the therapeutic alliance, the readiness of clients to embark on therapy, and when it is most appropriate to work collaboratively as opposed to a more directive approach. This suggests some commonalities across therapies about what helps to produce change. Similarly, an exploration of what stimulates change across a wide range of contexts – political, military, industrial, educational and personal – was one of the projects attempted earlier by the MRI team at Palo Alto (Watzlawick *et al.* 1974).

In Chapter 4 we discussed as one of the ideas that keep knocking on the door the role of emotions and feelings in family life and family therapy. Throughout the history of systemic family therapy feelings and emotions have played a critical role. However, rather than seeing emotions as embedded in the residues of past experience, a systemic view has regarded feelings as shaped both by the past and current interactions. An analysis of emotions, especially in terms of the patterns of attachments connecting generations of families, is an important theme that is likely to continue to develop into the twenty-first century. As we have seen, recent studies of attachment suggest that the family members' abilities to represent their relationships with each other internally and to have internal reflections and dialogues is significantly related to their attachment experiences (Fonagy *et al.* 1994). A level of emotional security and connection appears to be necessary for children in families to be able to reflect on and creatively generate ways of seeing and solving the inevitable problems that arise. Similarly, this also suggests that a level of trust is an essential ingredient of family (and other) therapies in order for change to occur. Again this connects with the realization of the importance of the therapeutic alliance.

A related exciting area of development may be the increased interest in how each member of a family internalizes their experiences. Some of the earliest experiences children have are of the ways their parents act towards them and towards each other. The nature of these experiences shapes the internal landscape of the child. Importantly, they shape the child's abilities to empathize and develop ideas about others' minds – to become able to see things from other people's points of view. Though interest in this is not new as such, there are fascinating developments from attachment theory and observations of family conversations. A related area is work on how children learn some core abilities, such as memory, and how families collaboratively construct memories of previous events (Edwards and Middleton 1988; Crittenden 1998; McCabe 1991). As a way of understanding both family life and the processes of therapy it is vital to explore more broadly the nature of memory. For example, a frequently observed phenomenon is that one member of a family, frequently the mother, takes on the role of the narrator and others of mentor and censor. Similarly, observational studies of non-clinical families have suggested that such role-taking is a typical feature of how families collectively co-construct memories each time they engage in reminiscing of events (Hirst and Manier 1990). Such studies fit with contemporary narrative approaches with their emphasis on how the past may be variously edited and reappraised each time a family engages in recalling events and experiences (Anderson and Goolishian 1988; Penn and Frankfurt 1994).

Crystal ball gazing

In Chapter 7 we reviewed some approaches to research and evaluation in family therapy. There is a growing interest in developing research, and this has become a part of family therapy training. As we have seen, family therapy originally arose from a research base in communications and observational studies of family dynamics. In the impetus to apply ideas the research emphasis possibly receded but will continue to regain a central position. Already such research is revealing important connections between different therapies, such as the importance of the therapeutic alliance and insights into what other aspects of therapy families find helpful. Perhaps one of the important evolutions of research has been a move towards a collaborative vs expert researcher format. Instead of doing research to or on families, there is an increasing emphasis on collaborative research, which invites families to reflect and comment on a researcher's emerging findings and attempts to include family members' own accounts.

Developmental perspectives

Systemic theory and therapy have possibly shied away from attempting to produce yet more developmental models. It has been argued that these can easily lapse into becoming linear and inflexible. There have been some attempts, such as the family life cycle models, but these have received considerable criticism on the grounds that they tended to become normative and blaming, for example, in suggesting that some family environments are more maladaptive or pathological than others. However, there is a need to consider developmental processes, otherwise family therapy runs the risk of simply staying at a pragmatic level of what helps to produce change but without any notion of how problems evolve. Furthermore, without knowledge of human growth and development it is difficult for family therapy to move towards offering some ideas regarding prevention and resilience. One approach which may continue to be fruitful is the exploration of family history – the patterns of attachments and resulting narratives that families hold about the nature of their early relationships and how these serve to shape their current dynamics. An exploration with a family, for example of the patterns of attachments through three generations, can help to generate new connections and narratives about their current relationships. Systemic therapy's emphasis on current patterns of interactions may increasingly be woven in with a collaborative appraisal with families of how their patterns may be showing aspects of history repeating itself. Some of the British schools of family therapists have been particularly influential in promoting such an analysis of family dynamics in their family historical contexts (Papadopoulos and Byng-Hall 1997).

Review and summary

We have argued that it helps to distinguish between systemic family therapy as having developed through three phases and a fourth period taking us into a look at current practice in 2005. More specifically, we have suggested that it helps to differentiate the second phase – with its emphasis on the subjective and unique nature of family – and perspectives drawn from the third phase – featuring the application of social constructionist ideas where the emphasis is on commonalties of experience, for example, the common experiences of women in families and of families of ethnic minorities. At the same time we have suggested that the first phase recognized some of the connections between individual experience and culture, for example in emphasizing some of the cultural norms and values that guided families' and therapists' assumptions and expectations. Though arguably some of these ideas were at times naive or at worst oppressive, they did recognize that families did not simply exist in a subjective social vacuum, as some excesses of constructivism might suggest.

We suggest that as therapists it is necessary and possible to keep in mind the three phases of systemic practice. In the first phase, first-order perspectives draw our attention to patterns and regularities in families' lives and experiences. In extreme cases, such as abuse, it makes sense to acknowledge realities of actions and processes. The emphasis on communication as complex and multi-faceted also helps us to be more attentive to the emotional and behavioural aspects of family life.

In the second phase, a second-order view, however, cautioned us to consider the uniqueness of what such actions may mean to a particular family and to be sensitive to differences between families who superficially appear to display similar patterns and problems.

In the third phase, social constructionism in some ways turns the clock back, alerting us that family life can be predictable and rule-bound, but with the recognition that these tendencies are not simply constructed by families but shaped by the cultural context, including economic realities and the commonly held ideas or discourses about family life. These common aspects of any given culture can be seen to shape family life so that certain patterns and regularities appear; for example, despite considerable changes, common patterns of gender roles and emotional styles are still played out. In a culture where affordable childcare is not readily available, women are likely to take on the bulk of childcare and consequently become more involved with their children, with the men being more peripheral.

We have also indicated that since the first edition of this book family therapy can be seen as having moved into a fourth phase which has involved an integration of perspectives, such as psychodynamic and attachment theory and systemic theory. We have also witnessed the development and application of systemic ideas to other contexts, such as institutions and organization, and also to work with individuals and parts of family systems. We might even suggest that we have witnessed a much broader assimilation of systemic ideas – for example, we frequently now hear politicians mention 'systemic' factors when they discuss problems such as crime, violence and drug usage. Certainly this connects to the imaginative ideas of the pioneer of systemic family therapy, Gregory Bateson. He had argued that linear, reactive thinking was one of the curses of Western societies and has fuelled conflicts and wars. Let us hope he was right – that an awareness of circular patterns and a move away from linear thinking, blame and hubris in human relations may be a positive step forward not only, as we have seen, in relation to family problems but also to a wide range of human situations and conflicts.

Integrations

Along with many other practitioners, we find it helpful to start by looking for patterns in the families with whom we work, and to consider how what we are seeing is partly our own personal view or prejudice, and also how families and our own views are shaped by the wider cultural context. We argue that in the third phase we can move nearer to a neutral and compassionate view. In contrast to the earlier phases, we could either explicitly or implicitly blame families for their difficulties. Instead we are hopefully more alert to the idea that both family members and we as therapists need to assume responsibility where necessary. For example, it helps to understand that, though abuse can be comprehended in terms of regimes of privilege accepted in a culture, unless this is challenged and resisted the abuse will be perpetuated. At times one implication for therapy is to have 'political' conversations with families where we explore not only their private histories but also the history of their culture.

The ability to describe and distinguish context – the situation or circumstances in which certain relationships and problems are enacted – is probably the single most important contribution of family therapy and systemic practice to the field of psychotherapy. More than any of the other psychotherapies, family therapy enables professionals to work with relationships in a way that promotes the renegotiation of relationships and empowers clients to view themselves and those with whom they are most importantly connected as relational beings who must negotiate life transitions for better or for worse and, when it is for worse, have and can create opportunities for vital renegotiations of life transitions and relationships.

The work of a family therapist and systemic practitioner is mostly about facilitating such renegotiation and is therefore not limited to talking with families, but is useful for consultation with colleagues, for the internal and external consultant, for working with therapeutic groups, team building and in education and primary care settings.

The list of applications is long and is a tribute to the creativity of therapists and practitioners alike. It is this ability to be versatile and flexible in the application of systemic ideas which most characterizes the British scene. Our hope is that this book will be used both as a resource for people new to the field and that more experienced practitioners will see themselves and their ideas in these pages and be stimulated to continue to develop innovative practice in the field of family therapy and systemic practice.

Postscripts

Interaction focused therapy: The Don Jackson Legacy – *Wendel A. Ray*[1,2]

Abstract

Don D. Jackson was one of the most prolific pioneers of the family and brief therapy, the founder of this discipline. This pioneering work was carried out by Jackson and his colleagues around the 1950s and the 1960s, first together with G. Bateson and then at the Mental Research Institute. His works still influence most of the systemic approaches of therapy still in use till the very day: from the brief therapy model developed after the death of Jackson at M.R.I. to the strategic work of Jay Haley and Cloe Madanes, from the structural model developed by Salvador Minuchin, to the work of the Milan School and the solution-focused therapy of De Shazer. The author revisits Jackson's career, which was brought to an end at an age of 48 years by a tragic and unexpected death, recollecting his successes and his contributions in the founding of the International Theory and its application to brief and family therapy. The cybernetic model together with the basic notions regarding systems, social constructivism, the use of circular questioning and others are only a fragment of the influence generated by Jackson on the majority of the brief and family therapy models. Just like clay that holds together the foundation blocks, Jackson's contributions continue to be the cohesive element that bounds most of our present systemic approaches – these act as a testimony of the vitality, the courage and the far-sighting vision of Don D. Jackson after more than thirty years from his death.

[1] *Mental Research Institute, Palo Alto, CA.*

[2] *Marriage and Family Therapy at The University of Louisiana at Monroe.*

How did Don Jackson influence the field of family therapy? How did Watts influence the steam engine? He made it. Others have refined the steam engine into a better, more efficient machine. I'd say that is what Don did for family therapy, he established the discipline. Others have gone on to refine it.

Richard Fisch, M.D.
Founder & Director,
Brief Therapy Center, MRI

If Don D. Jackson, MD, was alive today he would be popular even though controversial. That was so when he was making his contributions. Jackson was a systems purist, and purists of any kind, at least in the soft science of family studies, are not in vogue, rather they are controversial. In this age of compromise, where integration is the buzz word of the family therapy field, and funding from pharmaceutical companies has all but extinguished talk therapies from the curriculum of psychiatric training programs, advocates of a purely relational approach are hard to come by.

But there was a time in the not too distant past that many in the behavioral sciences hung on every word Don Jackson wrote or spoke. His tragic and unanticipated death in January 1968 at the age of 48 stunned the emerging field of family therapy, and the effects of this loss continue to reverberate throughout the discipline. It is my privately held conviction that the gradual shift away from the firm grounding of family theory and therapy in system and communications theory began soon after Jackson's articulate and convincing voice fell silent.

Who was Jackson and why would brief family therapists find his work interesting today? Jackson was one of the most prolific of the early family and brief therapy pioneers. He was a therapist of genius – one of those rare people who could produce lasting changes in a family, often within only one or a few sessions. When Jackson is remembered it is for the contributions he made to family theory – family homeostasis, family rules, the marital quid pro quo, and with long time collaborators Gregory Bateson, Jay Haley, and John Weakland, the concept of the double bind.

In a career that spanned a brief 24 years Jackson's accomplishments are nothing short of astonishing. Author or co-author of more than 130 professional papers and seven books, Jackson won virtually every prestigious award in the field of psychiatry: the Freida Fromm-Reichmann award for contribution to understanding of schizophrenia, the first Edward R. Strecker award for contribution to treatment of hospitalized patients, he was named recipient of the 1967 Salmon Lecturer.

In 1958 Jackson founded the Mental Research Institute (MRI), the first institute in the world specifically for the purpose of studying interactional processes and teaching family therapy (staff writer, 1958 a&b, Jackson, 1968 a&b). The first family therapy training program funded by the US government was at the MRI. In collaboration with Jay Haley and Nathan Ackerman, Jackson founded the first family therapy journal, *Family Process*.

To educate the larger medical community about interactional theory, Jackson helped found and was an editor for a medical news journal, *Medical Opinion and Review*. In order to create a forum from which researchers in the newly emerging field of family therapy could publish their work, Jackson helped found and was the editor of *Science and Behavior Books*.

These accomplishments, as impressive as they are, only hint at the reason Jackson's contributions retain their importance – like the great pyramids of Gîza, they are the surviving artifacts, a mere framework of a once thriving vision of this fallen leader.

Who was Jackson and how did he develop such an uncommon understanding of interactional processes? Jackson received his medical training at Stanford Medical School, graduating in early 1944. After completing his residency, Jackson spent two years in the U.S. Army, specializing in neurology. Then, from August 1947 to April 1951, Jackson trained at Chestnut Lodge in Maryland, and the Washington School of Psychiatry, two of the most prestigious analytic institutes then in existence, under the tutelage of Harry Stack Sullivan. Sullivan offered a radically alternative definition of psychiatry as 'the study of processes that involve or go on between people . . . the field of interpersonal relations, under any and all circumstances in which these relations exist . . . it seems a personality can never be isolated from the complex of interpersonal relations in which the person lives and has his being' (Sullivan, 1945, pp. 4–5).

Jackson fully embraced the implications of Sullivan's Interpersonal Theory, which so profoundly influenced the direction of his career that Jackson can legitimately be characterized as being 'Sullivanian'. At the same time, after Jackson returned to Palo Alto, California to enter into private practice in April 1951, the differences between Sullivan and Jackson soon became evident. The *primary* difference between Sullivan and Jackson is that Sullivan worked with mentally ill individuals *in isolation* from their families, envisioning his brilliant Interpersonal Theory by *inferential* conception of what *past* interpersonal relations must have been like to so severely restrict patients. In contrast, Jackson extended Sullivan's theory by focusing on the actual relationship between one individual and other individuals *in the present* as *Primary Data*.

The fundamental shift in the conception of causality, from looking at past causes of behavior to placing the primary emphasis on the relationship between the symptom bearer and significant others in the present happened, in part, by accident. Palo Alto is a small, university town, and Jackson could not avoid running into the relatives of some of his patients. On one occasion, in mid 1951, one of Jackson's patients, a young psychotic female, was making solid progress. Jackson asked the young woman's mother to stay at home and allow her daughter to come to the next session alone. When the session came around, Jackson saw the mother was sitting in the lobby with her daughter. The mother's refusal to follow Jackson's suggestion irritated him. So Jackson invited the mother to join her daughter in what was one of the first family sessions ever reported. The results were interesting to Jackson and he began experimenting with family therapy:

I became interested in family therapy . . . when I went from Chestnut Lodge to Palo Alto . . . which is a small university town. I couldn't avoid the relatives; and this led to a lot of surprising and sometimes not very pleasant results. I became interested in the question of family homeostasis, which seemed most marked in the families where a schizophrenic patient was able to live at home. If he then went through psycho-therapy and benefited from it, any move on his part would usually produce all sorts of disruptions at home . . . At any rate, for practical reasons, I started seeing the patients' parents, and then eventually . . . the parents and patient together (Jackson, 1962).

Jackson was just beginning to outline a purely here and now, interactional theory and conjoint family approach to therapy when yet another fortuitous turn of events occurred that would have profound ramifications for the future field of family and brief therapy – Don Jackson met Gregory Bateson. On a bleak day in January 1954 Jackson was giving a lecture on the concept of family homeostasis at the Veterans Administration Hospital in Menlo Park, California. Gregory Bateson was in the audience and approached Jackson after his talk. Bateson felt Jackson's work related to research he was involved in with Jay Haley, John Weakland, and William Fry. As a result of this meeting Jackson soon became a member of the projects. Collaboration with Bateson, Haley, Weakland, and Fry opened new vistas for Jackson. He now had ongoing interaction with a group of thinkers equal to himself in conceptual abilities and daring[3].

[3] John Weakland (1988) described the rich body of ideas that constitute Interactional Theory as having emerged not so much from any one individual, but, rather, as the product of the *interaction between* the members of what has become known as the Palo Alto Group, primarily Gregory Bateson's research team, Jackson, Jay Haley, John Weakland, and William Fry, during the ten year long series of research projects on the nature of paradox in communication processes, and later under the leadership of Jackson at the Mental Research Institute (MRI), where such notable people as Jules Riskin, Virginia Satir, Paul Watzlawick, Richard Fisch, Janet Beavin-Bavelas, and Antonio Ferreria joined the team. A source of fertile input into the group's work were the many visiting experts, including such eminent scholars as Norbert Wiener, Alan Watts, Weldon Keys, Freida Fromm-Reichmann, Ray Birdwhistell, among many others, and especially Haley and Weakland's detailed study of Milton H. Erickson – all of whom can be considered to have contributed to the creation of Interactional Theory.

Now for a special treat. The Jackson Archives at the Mental Research Institute contain thousands of written documents, film and audio recordings. One file contains pieces of a book Jackson was working on but was never published. Following is an outline of seventeen 'principles, assumptions, and postulates,' Jackson believed central to understanding human interaction:

1. A person is always attempting to define the nature of his relationship with other people, as he interacts with them. (Related to idea of seeking or maintaining one's identity?) (Could this be viewed as a 'driving force' of this theory?)
2. (Reciprocal of #1) So long as a person is interacting, i.e., alive, he is never not seeking to define the nature of relationship; There is no 'not caring,' there is never a 'resting state'.
3. At times this tendency (to define nature of relationship) is in sharper focus than at other times. (This leaves open the question of whether the principle operates more strongly at some times compared to others).
4. The dimensions of 'nature of relationship' are exhaustively defined as 1) symmetrical and 2) complementary (offering or asking). Therefore all interaction may be seen in these terms.
5. 'Character traits', 'symptoms,' are a person's typical ways, in an interaction, of attempting to define the nature of relationship.
6. Interaction between two or more people may be seen as a system, which at any given time has some kind of central point of equilibrium. (The central point is probably inferred, i.e., conceptual, rather than factual.) The system is maintained (and perhaps operationally gotten at or defined?) by a series of governors (homeostatic mechanisms).
7. There is always a tendency towards maintaining the status quo. (Is this another 'driving force'?)
8. At the same time, there is also always present a tendency towards change in the system. (This follows, partly at least, from no. 1 and 6). Therefore, the system is never conceptually static.
9. The nature of the system (including its equilibrium point and governors) may be modified by the introduction of new parameters. (Can these be conceptualized as 'rules'?)
10. 'System' is quite abstract – it will be manifested or defined by the occurrence of repetitive sequences of specific patterns of qualifications and ways of attempting to define the nature of relationship.
11. 'Homeostatic mechanisms' also are abstractions. They will be revealed indirectly by observing repetitive patterns of qualifications, etc.
12. All messages have both a report and command aspect. (Report of the speaker's state? Command refers to attempting to define nature of relationship?) This needs further spelling out.

13. All messages are modified by either disqualifications or affirmations. (The cutoff point for meta-messages to prevent the problem of infinite regression needs to be clarified.)
14. A given message, in analysis, is arbitrarily seen in relation to the immediately previous message. A simplification such as this is necessary, in order to avoid an otherwise potentially infinitely complex task of viewing every message in relation to all previous messages. Justification of this particular cutoff point must be empirical.
15. Knowledge of the prior history of a system is not necessary for studying the current patterns of interaction. I.E., in terms of this theory, a cross-sectional approach is sufficient.
16. Particular patterns of a system (i.e. particular kinds of equilibriums) will tend to be associated with particular kinds of individual behavior (including character traits, symptoms, etc.). This assumption does not exclude 1) possible constitutional factors, or 2) the effect of an external event(s) (acts of God).
17. A statement can always be prefaced by 'I have the right to say such and such in this relationship' (Jackson, 1962, Unpublished draft).

While most of the premises in this early synthesis appeared in more refined form in later publications (Jackson, 1965 a & b, Watzlawick, Beavin-Bavelas, Jackson, 1967), the uncompromisingly interactional focus of his thinking is clear.

Jackson's approach focused singularly on family *process*:

With our proclivity for the individual view of things, it runs against the grain to see ourselves as participants in a system, the nature of which we little understand. Yet I am convinced that we can make such dire appraisals (and such undeserved praises) only by translating a highly complex composite of people and context into a term which is then inappropriately applied to an individual (Jackson, 1963, The sick, the sad, the savage, and the sane).

The extent to which Jackson's Interactional Theory and its clinical application permeate the field of family and brief therapy is a tribute both to his willingness to share ideas with others and his commitment to point the way for psychiatry, psychology, social work, and the other applied human sciences to make the discontinuous shift from monadic explanations of human behavior to a perspective which is contextual in orientation, placing *primary focus* on the relationship between individuals. Jackson described the fear of change and the illusion of stability central to many relationship conflicts as a 'tug of war' (1967), cutting through the oversimplifications and reductionistic thinking inherent in theories of human behavior which attempt to explain the individual in trivializing, artificial isolation from the context of which he or she is part.

Jackson's most enduring contribution to understanding the nature of humankind was his expansion of the definition of behavior beyond looking at the individual in vitro to the development of an awareness of behavior as a manifestation of 'relationship in the widest sense' (Nos Nex, 1967). This uncompromising appreciation of context represents a revolutionary leap, an evolutionary step potentially as significant as when 'the organism gradually ceases to respond quite "automatically" to the mood-signs of another and becomes able to recognize . . . the other individual's and its own signals are only signals' (Bateson, 1955/1972, p. 178). A discontinuous paradigmatic shift in the Kuhnian sense (Kuhn, 1970), which has changed in profound ways the order of data appropriate to understand behavior (i.e. the relation between individuals in distinct contrast to a monadic view), context, and how causality in human behavior is conceptualized (cybernetic in contrast to lineal).

Paul Watzlawick (1988) and Janet Beavin-Bavelas (1998) describe the groundbreaking book Pragmatics of Human Communication as having been the product of their effort to understand and describe Jackson's incredible theoretical and clinical abilities. After months of observing Jackson conduct interviews and asking him questions in an effort to comprehend his incredible clinical acumen, Jackson, exasperated, drafted an outline and suggested they write the book which was to become one of the cornerstones of an Interactional Theory of human behavior:

A phenomenon remains unexplainable as long as the range of observation is not wide enough to include the context in which the phenomenon occurs. Failure to realize the relationship between an event and the matrix in which it takes place, between an organism and its environment, either confronts the observer with something 'mysterious' or induces him to attribute to his object of study certain properties the object may not possess. Compared with the wide acceptance of this fact in the biological sciences, the behavioral sciences seem still to base themselves to a large extent on the monadic view of the individual and on the time-honored method of isolating variables (Watzlawick, Beavin, & Jackson, 1967, p. 21).

Extending a relational understanding of human behavior beyond the mental health sciences, and disseminating these ideas to non-professional as well as professional audiences can be seen in Jackson's collaboration with famed author and close friend William Lederer. In the first systemically oriented marital self help book, Mirages of Marriage (1968) Lederer and Jackson write:

The systems concept helps explain much of the previously mysterious behavior which results whenever two or more human beings relate to one another. We know that the family is a unit in which all individuals have an important influence – whether they like it or not and whether they know it or not. The family is an interacting communications network in which every member from the day-old baby to the seventy-year-old grand-mother influences the nature of the entire system and in turn is influenced by it. For example, if someone in the family feels ill, another member may function more effectively than he usually does. The [family as a] system tends, by nature, to keep itself in balance. An unusual action by one member invariably results in a compensating reaction by another member. If mother hates to take Sunday drives but hides this feeling from her husband, the message is nevertheless somehow broadcast throughout the family communication network, and it may be Johnny, the four-year-old, who becomes 'carsick' and ruins the Sunday drive (p. 14).

This shift of primary focus from the intrapsychic processes of the individual to the relationship between members of the individual's relational system can be seen in the work of many of the eminent clinician-theoreticians of today (Keeney, 1983, 1987; Tomm, 1987, 1988; Penn, 1983, 1986; Palazzoli et al., 1980; Cecchin, Lane, and Ray, 1993, 1994; Papp, 1983; Boscolo et al., 1987).

The pioneering work done in the 1950's and 1960's by Jackson and his colleagues, first in the Bateson projects and later at the Mental Research Institute, inform most present day systemically oriented approaches to therapy. The non-pathological, non-normative, interactional focus originated by Jackson, form the most fundamental premises underlying the Brief Therapy Model, developed after Jackson's death, at the Mental Research Institute (Watzlawick, Weakland & Fisch, 1974; Fisch, Weakland & Segal, 1982; Weakland & Ray, 1995; Ray & de Shazer, 1999), the strategic work of Jay Haley and his colleagues (Haley, 1963; 1976; 1980; Madanes, 1981 & 1984), the structural model developed by Salvador Minuchin and his colleagues (Minuchin, 1974; Minuchin & Fishman, 1982; Stanton & Todd, 1982), the work of the Milan Associates both before and after their split into two separate groups (Palazzoli et al., 1978; Palazzoli et al., 1989; Boscolo et al., 1987), the Solution Focused brief therapy approach of de Shazer and his associates at the Brief Therapy Center of Milwaukee (de Shazer, 1982, 1985), the work of Keeney and his colleagues (Keeney & Ross, 1985; Keeney & Silverstein, 1986; Keeney, 1987; Ray & Keeney, 1992), the work of Andersen (1987), and even the 'Post-Modern' narrative orientations of Anderson & Goolishian (1990), Hoffman (1993), and Michael White (1989), as well as most other systemically and contextually oriented approaches.

The cybernetic model and basic notions about systems (for example, if change occurs in one part of the system, the rest will change to accommodate that change), social constructionism, ignoring most of the received wisdom of the day, attending to pragmatics (i.e. who does what when and to whom in the present), accepting and going with the symptom, speaking the client's language, using circular questioning, prescribing behavior at one order of abstraction to address the organization of the system at another order of abstraction are but a few of the ways Jackson influenced present day work of most models of family and brief therapy in practice today. Since Jackson's death, the work of his colleagues at the MRI have continued to inform most of the family and brief oriented systemic work being done around the world today.

Therapeutic work which is directed toward changing the organization of the family, for example, by interrupting problematic coalitionary processes across generational lines, and strengthening the boundaries of various subsystems, are ways in which the structural therapy of Salvador Minuchin, both through reading Jackson (Minuchin, 1987) and a ten year affiliation with Jay Haley, has been influenced by Jackson. The coherent set of theoretical premises and techniques of clinical practice, set forth by Jackson continue to provide the solid bedrock on which the rest of the systemically oriented theoreticians and clinicians have built. The influence of Jackson continues to ripple across the work of the rest of the systemically oriented theoreticians and clinicians. The original Milan group and the subsequent work by both Palazzoli's, and Boscolo and Cecchin's groups has been strongly influenced by Jackson. Such fundamental elements of their work as circular questioning, hypothesizing, positive connotation, the use of rituals and tasks, attending to the implications of language as evidenced in the shift from using the verb tense 'to be' to 'to seem,' and attending to the importance of the referring person are all ideas originally pioneered by Jackson.

The work of MRI, Haley, Minuchin, the Milan groups, de Shazer and Berg's Solution Focused orientation have, in turn, influenced such notable clinicians and theoreticians as members of the Ackerman group including Peggy Papp, Peggy Penn, and Joel Bergman, as well as other eminent members of the field such as Karl Tomm, Steve de Shazer, Goolishian and Anderson, Tom Andersen, Lynn Hoffman, and Michael White. Even within the Behavioral Family Therapy orientation, albeit at the literal level, practitioners have explicitly adopted such fundamental concepts as the marital quid pro quo (Stewart, 1974; Jacobson & Margolin, 1979).

Why should clinicians, theoreticians, academicians, and students be interested in Jackson's work? Because Jackson's Interactional Theory permeates the fields of family and brief therapy. Like mortar that holds together the bricks, Jackson's contributions continue to be the cohesive element which binds together most present day systemic orientations – a living testimony to the vitality, courage, and far-reaching vision of Don D. Jackson more than thirty-five years after his death.

Since his death, regardless of all the rhetoric about being rooted in a systemic and contextual orientation, the field has yet to achieve the potentialities once imagined by its founders for ushering in a revolutionary shift in how human problems are conceptualized and managed. Instead of consensual validation across schools about the systemic nature of the theoretical base, there continues to be a pervasive lack of appreciation of the fundamental difference between individual theory and interactional theory. A consequence has been efforts to blend the two theories which are doomed to confuse both orientations because they focus on distinctly different orders of phenomena, with diametrically opposite implications for treatment. What has resulted is a field which remains theoretically muddled, unable to offer a genuinely alternative perspective, and fragmented into various camps, each claiming to possess a better understanding of the nature of behavior and change than the others, with no unified direction or understanding of its purposes or goals. In the presence of this fragmentation, the field has yet to produce a giant of the stature of a Freud, capable of blazing a path into the future. Had Jackson lived, one cannot help but wonder whether or not he would have attained such stature.

The shift of focus, set forth by Jackson and his colleagues, from the individual to the relationship between, and from the 'reality' of pathology to the 'construction of ecologically respectful realities,' carries implications far beyond the field of family and brief therapy. These ideas have ramifications of global proportions which influence concerns from ecology to the world political arena.

How today's issues would have been addressed by Jackson is, to some extent, unknowable. One can speculate, however, that Jackson's utter disdain for reductionistic, non self-referential thinking, in all its manifestations, would have continued. His call for appreciation of the interconnected nature of behavior and context would undoubtedly have endured. Certainly he would have continued to take to task those within the human sciences who advocate a non-contextual, individual pathology-oriented research and treatment approach to human problems in living. Unquestionably his razor sharp intellect, and skill at being persuasive, would have been aroused by the recent resurgence of a shared belief in the viability of individual diagnostics and genetic explanations of 'individual pathology.'

What difference would it make if the fields of brief and family therapy reawakened to the implications of Jackson's insights? Could these fields, thoroughly committed to a world view rooted in cybernetics, and attentive to the implications of the paradigmatic shift Jackson represented, truly lead the way for human kind to transcend the linear causal mentality so prevalent today? Perhaps. Hope still exists for such a paradigmatic transformation, as can be evidenced in the on-going work of Ray, Watzlawick, Fisch, Schlanger, Anger-Díaz, and Bobrow that continues at the MRI, in the work being done by Giorgio Nardone and team in Arezo Italy, in the continuing work by

Jay Haley, in the exploration that continues by cybernetic theoreticians such as Brad Keeney, and in the continuing exploration and application of Milton Erickson's work by Zeig, Rossi, and others. It is equally likely that the opportunity for such a transformation has passed. The effects of humankind's long standing addiction to the illusion of power and control may have, as one of Jackson's closest colleagues Gregory Bateson (1970) suggests, already corrupted the ecology beyond the point of recovery. Does the echo of Don Jackson's voice still resonant enough to make a difference?

Irreverence, curiosity and circularity: the systemic psychotherapy of Gianfranco Cecchin

John Hills[1,2]

Systemic family therapy, or systemic psychotherapy as family therapy has come to be known, is an interesting hybrid. Its origins derive from a curious confluence of psychoanalysis, humanistic practice, cybernetics, hypnosis based strategic practice from Milton Erickson and structural ideas – all directed at ways of intervening in family relationships. In turn, recent therapies such as brief, solution focused and narrative owe some of their origins to this therapeutic tradition. Like other therapies, we have our heroes, heroines and innovators. One such died recently and in the tragic circumstances of a road accident in northern Italy. Gianfranco Cecchin was 72 and was killed while travelling from his home on Lake Garda to Milan where he worked, in the early hours of 2 February 2004.

Less known outside the confines of systemic family therapy, Cecchin ranks among the leading thinkers and originators of this approach. He was born near Vicenza in 1932 and trained in psychiatry and psychoanalysis. In 1971 he joined in a collaborative alliance with three other psychoanalytically informed psychiatrists, Luigi Boscolo, Mara Silvini Palazolli and Guiliana Prata, all interested in psychotherapeutic work with families. They came to be known as the Milan group or the Milan Associates from their practice base at the Centro per lo Studio della Famiglia, Milan.

Influenced by the ideas of the British-born anthropologist, Gregory Bateson, about communication and its relationship to mental health (he helped develop the double-bind theory of schizophrenia), they evolved a way of engaging with families, of gathering and processing information in the therapeutic relationship. This method, now gener-

[1] *The Psychotherapist* issue 23, 2004.

[2] Tutor, Systemic Psychotherapy Course, Tavistock Clinic, London.

ally known as *circular questioning*, centred on the concept of circularity. If 'questioning is the piety of thinking' (according to the German philosopher Heidegger), then circular questioning is the piety of systemic therapy for the Milan Associates. Simple in its conceptualization, demanding in its effective use, it is the systemic therapy equivalent of *free association* in analytic therapy – a core principle of technique and method. To work well, like free association it requires attentive listening, space, pace and attention to the emergent material.

Circularity, as formulated by the Milan Associates, describes the multi-directional operation of feedback between the therapist (or therapy team, since this is the usual method of training practice, using a one-way screen and open reflection between team members in the presence of the family) and the family, and among the members of the family present in the session (if some members were absent they would still be 'held in mind' and feature in the feedback process of circularity).

Every psychological relationship and time domain constitutes information or 'news of difference' – the material of a session – organized, conceptualized, perceived, disclosed or simply observed by both the members of the family system and that of the therapeutic system. Therefore *mood and feeling states* (individual, dyadic, triadic and collective); *cognitive states* (problem solving, thinking, beliefs and fantasies); *behaviour states* and the different attributions of meaning and intention; *relationship states* (between the various family members, between the observers and the observed), the *what*, *how* and *when* of communication – all this was part of the mapping of connection and difference that circular questioning sought to make explicit, moving the subordinated and unreflected elements of the family's 'holding in mind', into the forefront of holding.

The process was a brilliantly conceptualized phenomenology of family intersubjectivity, an encapsulation of a psychology of interpersonal perception that R.D. Laing and others were developing. Here was a kind of therapist's Rough Guide to those interrelational entanglements of Laing's *Knots*.

For example, 'Jill thinks that Jack thinks he makes her unhappy'. The therapist, in the presence of them both, might ask Jack, 'What are the signs that make you feel Jill is unhappy?' or ask Jill, 'How are you so sure Jack believes he makes you unhappy?' or ask both, 'How do you let each other know when you are happy?' Or, to open up the exploration to Jack, 'Do you think you make other people unhappy as well as Jill?' or to Jill, 'Do you think Jack's powerlessness to make you happy extends to the way he feels towards himself?'

The process is infinite in its possibilities and seeks to map and define the projective processes that imbue relationships with their tension and interest, building a richer, clearer sense of what is real between differing perspectives.

Trainees are taught it, and once mastered it is a powerful instrument of exploration, discovery and systemic and personal insight. It needs, like all psychotherapy, to be conducted with empathy, and self-reflexivity. Our own original family is our conscious and unconscious 'default' position. The potencies of counter-transference, projective identification – to say nothing of our own gender, class, sexual orientation, cultural and world-view identifications – organize the way we process the information of circularity. Life stage location makes us more likely to identify or form alliances with different intergenerational figures (the family systemic therapist, like the ageing actor, is better equipped for some roles than for others as time passes).

To counteract this, the Milan Associates devised an integrated method in their 1980 paper 'Hypothesizing – circularity – neutrality' (Palazzoli *et al.* 1980). *Hypothesizing* identified the systemic speculations (based on a systemic psychodynamic) while *neutrality* was the stance the therapist adopted to be openly responsive to the simultaneous multi-perspectives available (and wary of his own distorting lenses of experience and unexamined assumptions about family life). Like a surfer on the waves, the therapist would ride the family's psychologically organized relational and narrative life without tumbling beneath the family's treacherous undertow of their games and transactional rules. Neutrality was the attitude of mind, hypothesizing was a study of the local currents and eddies and circular questioning the surfboard to maintain buoyancy.

This stance – if it were ever possible to maintain effectively in the face of very different information – made the therapist appear like a researcher. Cecchin modified this to *curiosity*, a respectful interest and openness to whatever it was in the family's way of seeing things that did not fit either with each other's view, their wish for or their attempt to secure change. Conventional ideas, fixed beliefs, anxieties and perceptions were to be gently challenged with puckish lightness of respectful humour and charm and the authority of irreverence. Encouragement would be given to strengths and resourcefulness. Through irreverence, curiosity and questioning the therapist behaved almost in a Socratic way. The aim was not to clarify philosophical assumptions, but to free up some of the family's aspirations towards well-being. It was a movement towards holding different perceptions of each other in mind in their shared presence.

Tributes published recently in the systemic family world caught the essence of Cecchin's very Mediterranean intelligence, gracious, generous, free-thinking, passionate while using passion through the service of intelligence rather than the emotions; a puckish ability to take many different positions. He communicated a sense, often present in southern Europeans, that well-being is connected with joyful embracing the pleasures of existence while keeping a respectful eye out for suffering that may be sudden and transformational. His life was certainly congruent with his beliefs. He was graceful and gracious. Like Carl Rogers and Irvin Yalom, the therapeutic technique and method he pioneered, in the end, could not be disembodied from the full human availability of the person.

References

Anderson, H. & Goolishian, H. (1988, October). Systemic practice with domestic violence. Paper presented at the American Association for Marriage & Family Therapy, New Orleans, La.

Andersen, T. (1987). The reflecting team: Dialogue and meta-dialogue in clinical work. Family Process, *26* (4), 415–428.

Bateson, G. (1955). A theory of play and fantasy: A report on theoretical aspects of the project for study of the role of paradoxes of abstraction in communication. In Psychiatric Research Reports (2), December, 39–51.

Bateson, G. (1970). An anthropologist views the social scene. [Cassette recording of a talk given at the Mental Research Institute, Jan., 1970]. Palo Alto, CA: The MRI.

Bateson, G. (1972). Steps to an ecology of mind. NY: Jason Aronson Inc.

Bergman, J. (1985). Fishing for barracuda: Pragmatics of brief systemic therapy. NY: Norton.

Boscolo, G., Cecchin, G., Hoffman, L., & Penn, P. (1987). Milan systemic family therapy. NY: Basic Books.

Cecchin, G., Lane, G., & Ray, W. (1993). From strategizing to non-intervention: Toward irreverence in systemic practice. Journal of Marital & Family Therapy, 19 (2), 125–136.

Cecchin, G., Lane, G., & Ray, W. (1992). Irreverence: A Strategy for Therapists' Survival. London, UK: Karnac Books (Distributed in U.S. by Brunner/Mazel).

de Shazer, S. (1982). Patterns of brief family therapy: An ecosystemic approach. NY: Guilford.

de Shazer, S. (1985). Keys to solution in brief therapy. NY: Norton.

Fisch, R., Weakland, J., & Segal, L. (1982). The tactics of change: Doing brief therapy. San Francisco, CA: Jossey-Bass.

Hoffman, L. (1986). Beyond power and control: Toward a 'second order' family systems therapy. Family Systems Medicine, *3*, 381–396.

Hoffman, L. (1989). A constructuivist position for family therapy. The Irish Journal of Psychology, *9* (1), 110–129.

Jackson, D. & Weakland, J. (1961). Conjoint family therapy: Some considerations on theory, technique and results. Psychiatry, *24* (2), 30–45.

Jackson, D. (1964). The sick, the sad, the savage, & the sane. Paper presented as the annual academic lecture to the Society of Medical Psychoanalysts & Department of Psychiatry, New York Medical College.

Jackson, D. (1962). Unpublished draft.

Jackson, D. (1963). The sick, the sad, the savage, and the sane. Unpublished manuscript.

Jackson, D. (1965a). The study of the family. Family Process.
Jackson, D. (1965b). Family rules – Marital Quid Pro Quo. Archives of Psychiatry.
Jackson, D. (1967a). The Fear of Change. Medical Opinion & Review.
Jackson, D. (1967b). Schizophrenia: The nosological nexus.
Jackson, D. (Ed.). (1968a). Foreword, Communication, Family and Marriage (Human communication, volume 1). Palo Alto, CA: Science & Behavior Books, pp. v.
Jackson, D. (Ed.). (1968b). Foreword, Therapy, Communication and Change (Human communication, volume 2). Palo Alto, CA: Science & Behavior Books, pp. v.
Jacobson, N. & Margolin, G. (1979). Marital Therapy, NY: Brunner/Mazel.
Keeney, B. (1983). Aesthetics of change. NY: The Guilford Press.
Keeney, B. & Ross, J. (1983). Learning to learn systemic therapies. Journal of Strategic & Systemic Therapies, *2* (2), 22–30.
Keeney, B. & Ross, J. (1985). Mind in therapy: constructing systemic family therapies. NY: Basic Books.
Keeney, B. & Silverstein, O. (1986). The Therapeutic voice of Olga Silverstein. NY: The Guilford Press.
Keeney. B., & Ray, W. (1996). Resource focused Therapy. In M. Hoyt, Ed., Constructive Therapies, II. NY: Guilford, pp. 334–346.
Kuhn, T. (1970). The structure of scientific revolution, 2nd edition. Chicago, IL: Chicago University Press.
Lederer, W., & Jackson, D. (1968). Mirages of Marriage, New York: W. W. Norton.
Mackler, L. (1977). Donald D. Jackson 1920–1968 Bibliography. In L. Wolberg & M. Aronson (Eds), Group Therapy An Overview (pp. v–lx). NY: Grune & Stratton.
Madanes, C. (1981). Strategic family therapy. San Francisco, CA: Jossey-Bass.
Minuchin, S. (1974). Families & family therapy. Cambridge, MA: Harvard University Press.
Minuchin, S. & Fishman, H. (1982). Family therapy techniques. Cambridge, MA: Harvard University Press.
Minuchin, S. (1987). My many voices. In J. Zeig (Ed.), The Evolution of Psychotherapy. NY: Brunner/Mazel, pp. 5–13.
Palazzoli, M., Boscolo, L., Cecchin, G., & Prata, G. (1980). The problem of the referring person. Journal of Marital & Family Therapy, *6* (1), 3–9.
Palazzoli, M., Boscolo, L., Cecchin, G., & Prata, G. (1980). Hypothesizing-circularity-neutrality: Three guidelines for the conductor of the session. Family Process, *19* (1), 3–12.
Palazzoli, M., Boscolo, L., Cecchin, G., & Prata, G. (1978). Paradox & counter paradox. NY: Jason Aronson.
Papp, P. (1983). The process of change. NY: Guilford Press.
Penn, P. (1982). Circular questioning. Family Process, *21* (1), 267–280.
Penn, P. (1985). Feed-forward: Future questions, future maps. Family Process, *24* (3), 299–310.
Ray, W., & Keeney, B. (1992). Resource Focused Therapy. London, UK: Karnac Books.
Ray, W., & de Shazer, S. (1999) Evolving Brief Therapies. Iowa City, IA: Geist & Russell.

Reusch, J. & Bateson, G. (1951). Communication: The social matrix of Psychiatry. NY: Norton.

Sullivan, H. (1945). Conceptions of Modern Psychiatry. Washington, DC: W. A. White Foundation.

Stanton, M., Todd, T., & Associates (1982). Family Therapy of Drug Abuse. NY: Guilford.

Staff writer (1958). New Family Research Institute on the Mid-Peninsula. Palo Alto Times, May 7.

Staff Writer (1958). New Institue Opens in Palo Alto. Palo Alto Times, Oct. 11.

Stewart, R. (1980). Helping Couples Change. NY: Guilford.

Tomm, K. (1987). Interventive interviewing: Part I: Strategizing as a fourth guideline for the therapist. Family Process, *26* (1), 3–14.

Tomm, K. (1987). Interventive interviewing: Part II: reflexive questioning as a means to enable self-healing. Family Process, *26* (2), 167–184.

Watzlawick, P., Beavin, J. & Jackson, D. (1967). Pragmatics of human communication: A study of interactional patterns, pathologies & paradoxes. NY: Norton.

Watzlawick, P. (1988, June). [Personal interview with Paul Watzlawick, Ph.D., senior research fellow, MRI & former colleague of Don D. Jackson]. Palo Alto, CA: Mental Research Institute.

Weakland, J., & Ray, W. (1995). Propagations: Thirty years of Influence from the Mental Research Institute, New York: Haworth.

White, M. (1989). Selected Papers. Australia: Dulwich Publications.

Topic reading lists

Adults with mental health problems

Anderson, C. and Holder, D. (1991) Women and serious mental disorders. In M. McGoldrick, C.M. Anderson and F. Walsh (eds) *Women in Families: A Framework for Family Therapy*. New York: W.W. Norton.

Bennett, D., Fox, C., Jowell, T. and Skynner, A.C.R. (1976) Towards a family approach in a psychiatric day hospital. *British Journal of Psychiatry*, 129: 73–81.

Bennum, I. (1993) Family management and psychiatric rehabilitation. In J. Carpenter and A. Treacher (eds) *Using Family Therapy in the 90s*. Oxford: Blackwell.

Birch, J. (1985) The madman theory of war: a possible application in therapy. *Journal of Family Therapy*, 7: 147–59.

Chase, J. and Holmes, J. (1990) A two year audit of a family therapy clinic in adult psychiatry. *Journal of Family Therapy*, 12: 229–42.

Department of Health (1990) The Care Programme Approach for people with a mental illness referred to specialist psychiatric services. In *Caring for People – Community Care in the Next Decade and Beyond*, Cm. 849. London: HMSO.

Dosen, A. and Day, K. (eds) (2001) *Treating Mental Illness and Behavior Disorders in Children and Adults with Mental Retardation*. Washington, DC: American Psychiatric Press.

Goldstein, M. and Miklowitz, D. (1995) The effectiveness of psycho-educational family therapy in the treatment of schizophrenic disorders. *Journal of Marital and Family Therapy*, 21(4): 361–76.

Haley, J. (1975) Why a mental health clinic should avoid family therapy. *Journal of Marriage and Family Counselling*, January, 1: 2–13.

Ingamells, D. (1993) Systemic approaches to psychosis, part 1. The systemic context. *Australian and New Zealand Journal of Family Therapy*, 14(1): 21–8.

Ingamells, D. (1993) Systemic approaches to psychosis, part II. Systemic psychotherapy. *Australian and New Zealand Journal of Family Therapy,* 14(2): 85–96.

Jones, E. (1987) Brief systemic work in psychiatric settings where a family member has been diagnosed as schizophrenic. *Journal of Family Therapy,* 9: 30–45.

Kuipers, L. and Bebbington, P. (1985) Relatives as a resource in the management of functional illness. *British Journal of Psychiatry,* 147: 465–70.

AIDS/HIV

Bor, R., Miller, R. and Goldman, E. (1993) HIV/AIDS and the family: a review of research in the first decade. *Journal of Family Therapy,* 15: 187–204.

Bor, R., du Plessis, P. and Cooper, J. (2004) The impact of disclosure of HIV on the index patient's self-defined family. *Journal of Family Therapy,* 26(2): 167–92.

Bowser, B.P.W., Stanton, D. and Coleman, S.D. (2003) Death in the family and HIV risk-taking among intravenous drug users. *Family Process,* 42(2): 291–304.

Faithful, J. (1997) HIV positive and AIDS infected women: challenges to mothering. *American Journal of Orthopsychiatry,* 67(1): 144–51.

Matriani, V.B., Prado, G., Feaster, D.J., Robinson-Batista, C. and Szapocznik, J. (2003) Relational factors and family treatment engagement among low-income, HIV-positive African American mothers. *Family Process,* 42(1): 31–45.

Miller, R., Goldman, E. and Bor, R. (1994) Application of family systems approach to working with people affected by HIV disease – two case studies. *Journal of Family Therapy,* 16: 295–312.

Rait, D.S., Ross, J.M. and Rao, S.M. (1997) Treating couples and families with HIV: a systemic approach. In M.F. O'Connor and I.D. Yalom (eds) *Treating the Psychological Consequences of HIV.* San Francisco: Jossey-Bass.

Salt, H., Bor, R. and Palmer, R. (1995) Dangerous liaisons: issues of gender and power relationships in HIV prevention and care. In C. Burck and B. Speed (eds) *Gender, Power and Relationships.* London: Routledge.

Walker, G. (1991) Sexuality in the context of HIV infection. In *In the Midst of Winter.* New York: W.W. Norton.

Assessment

Davidson, R., Quinn, W.H. and Josephson, A.M. (2001) Assessment of the family. Systemic and developmental perspectives. *Child and Adolescent Psychiatric Clinics of North America,* 10: 415–29.

See also Key Texts, Chapters 4 and 5.

Attachment

See Key Texts, Chapter 4.

Attention deficit hyperactivity disorder

Ayers, T., Sellers, T., Schneider, D., Gottschling, H. and Soucar, E. (2001) Danforth's comments on parent training research: a rejoinder. *Child and Family Behavior Therapy*, 23(2): 65–6.

Salle, H. and Forse, I. (2002) General and differential effects of behavioural and systemic family therapy in treating children with ADHD. *Zeitschrift für Klinische Psychologie, Psychiatrie und Psychotherapie*, 50(3): 281–99.

Salle, H. and Trosbach, J. (2001) Behaviour and family therapy for attention deficit hyperactivity disorder in children: differences in evaluation between experts in observable therapeutic results. *Zeitschrift für Klinische Psychologie, Psychiatrie und Psychotherapie*, 49(1): 33–48.

Velazquez, M. (2002) A program designed to improve emotion regulation in AHDD boys at risk for conduct disorder/oppositional defiant disorder. *Dissertation Abstracts International, Section B: The Sciences and Engineering*, 63(1-B): 554.

Child abuse

Asen, K.E., George, E., Piper, R. and Stevens, A. (1989) A systems approach to child abuse: management and treatment issues. *Child Abuse and Neglect*, 13: 45–57.

Summer, J. (1998) Multiple family therapy: its use in the assessment and treatment of child abuse. A pilot study. Unpublished MSc thesis, Birkbeck College and Institute of Family Therapy.

Child protection and the legal framework

Bentovim, A. (1992) *Trauma Organized Systems: Physical and Sexual Abuse in Families* (revised edition). London: H. Karnac.

Byrne, N. and McCarthy, I. (1995) Abuse, risk and protection. Fifth province approach to an adolescent sexual offences. In C. Burck and B. Speed (eds) *Gender, Power and Relationships*. London: Routledge

Crowther, C., Dare, C. and Wilson, J. (1990) 'Why should we talk to you? You'll only tell the court!' On being an informer and a family therapist. *Journal of Family Therapy*, 12: 105–22.

Dutton, C.J. (1995) Autonomy and connection: gendered thinking in a statutory agency dealing with child sexual abuse. In C. Burck and B. Speed (eds) *Gender, Power and Relationships*. London: Routledge.

Furniss, T. (1983) Mutual influence and interlocking professional family process in the treatment of child sexual abuse and incest. *Child Abuse and Neglect*, 7: 207–23.

Glaser, D. (1991) Treatment issues in child sexual abuse. *British Journal of Psychiatry*, 159: 769–82.

Nelson, T.S., Fleuridas, C. and Rosenthal, D.M. (1986) The evolution of circular questions: training family therapists. *Journal of Marital and Family Therapy*, 12(2): 113–27.

O'Brian, C. and Bruggen, P. (1985) Our personal and professional lives: learning positive innovation and circular questioning. *Family Process*, 24: 311–22.

Penn, P. (1982) Circular questioning. *Family Process*, 21(3): 267–80.

Penn, P. (1985) Feed-forward: future questions, future maps. *Family Process*, 24(3): 299–310.

Smith, G. (1993) *Systemic Approaches to Training in Child Protection*. London: Karnac Books.

Street, E. (1994) A family systems approach to child–parent separation: 'developmental closure'. *Journal of Family Therapy*, 16: 347–65.

Tomm, K. (1985) Circular interviewing: a multifaceted clinical tool. In D. Campbell and R. Draper (eds) *Applications of Systemic Family Therapy*. London: Academic Press.

Tomm, K. (1987) Interventive interviewing. Part I. Strategizing as a fourth guideline for the therapist. *Family Process*, 26: 3–13.

Tomm, K. (1987) Interventive interviewing: Part II. Reflexive questioning as a means to enable self-healing. *Family Process*, 26: 167–83.

Tomm, K. (1988) Interventive interviewing: Part III. Intending to ask lineal, circular, strategic, or reflexive questions? *Family Process*, 27: 1–15.

Circular interviewing

Brown, J. (1997) Circular questioning: an introductory guide. *Australian and New Zealand Journal of Family Therapy*, 18(2): 109–14.

Cronen, V. and Lang, P. (1994) Language and action: Wittgenstein and Dewey in the practice of therapy and consultation. *Human Systems*, 5: 5–43.

Cronen, V. and Pearce, B. (1985) Toward an explanation of how the Milan method works. In D. Campbell and R. Draper (eds) *Applications of Systemic Therapy*. London: Academic Press.

Cronen, V.E., Johnson, K.M. and Lannamann, J.W. (1982) Paradoxes, double binds, and reflexive loops: an alternative theoretical perspective. *Family Process*, 21: 91–112.

Cronen, V., Pearce, B. and Tomm, K. (1985) A dialectical view of personal change. In K.J. Gergen and K.E. Davis (eds) *The Social Construction of the Person*. New York: Springer-Verlag.

Hannah, C. (1994) The context of culture in systemic therapy: an application of CMM. *Human Systems*, 5: 69–81.

Hannah, C. and McAdam, E. (1991) Violence, part I: Reflections on our work with violence. *Human Systems*, 2: 201–16.

Lang, P., Little, M. and Cronen, V. (1990) The systemic professional: domains of action and the question of neutrality. *Human Systems*, 1: 39–55.

McAdam, E. and Hannah, C. (1991) Violence, part II: Creating the best context to work with clients who have found themselves in violent situations. *Human Systems*, 2: 212–16.

Roper-Hall, A. (1997) Working systemically with older people and their families who have 'come to grief'. In P. Sutcliffe *et al.* (eds) *Systemic Approaches to Therapeutic Work*. Basingstoke: Macmillan.

Consultation

Manojlovic, J. and Partridge, K. (2001) A framework for systemic consultation with acute ward systems. *Clinical Psychology*, 3: 27–30.

Rosenberg, B.A. (2000) The human architecture of community building: a sustained application of systemic consultation. *Dissertation Abstracts International. Section A: Humanities and Social Sciences*, 60(12): 4623.

Coordinated management of meaning

Burnham, J. and Harris, Q. (1996) Emerging ethnicity: a tale of three cultures. In K. Dwivedi and V.P. Varma (eds) *Meeting the Needs of Ethnic Minority Children*. London: Jessica Kingsley.

Divorce and mediation

Barrett, J. (1991) *To and Fro Children: A Guide to Successful Parenting after Divorce*. London: Thorsons.

Bird, R. and Cretney, S. (1996) *Divorce: the New Law – The Family Law Act*. Family Law Publishing.

Brown, F.H. (1989) The postdivorce family. In B. Carter and M. McGoldrick (eds) *The Changing Family Cycle*. Boston: Allyn & Bacon.

Burck, C. and Daniel, G. (1995) Moving on gender beliefs in divorce and stepfamily process. In C. Burck and B. Speed (eds) *Gender, Power and Relationships*. London: Routledge.

Carrère, S. and Gottman, J.M. (1999) Predicting divorce among newlyweds from the first three minutes of a marital conflict discussion. *Family Process*, 38(3).

Gately, D.W. and Schwebel, A.I. (1991) The challenge model of children's adjustment to parental divorce: explaining favorable postdivorce outcomes in children. *Journal of Family Psychology*, 5(1): 60–81.

Gorell Barnes, G. and Dowling, E. (1997) Rewriting the story: children, parents and post divorce narratives. In J. Byng-Hall and R. Papadopoulos (eds) *Multiple Voices: Narratives in Systemic Family Psychotherapy*. London: Duckworth.

Ricci, I. (1980) *Mom's Home, Dad's Home: Making Shared Custody Work*. London: Collier Macmillan.

Roberts, M. (1997) *Mediation in Family Disputes: Principles of Practice* (2nd edn). Aldershot: Arena.

Robinson, M. (1991) *Family Transformation during Divorce and Remarriage: A Systemic Approach*. London: Routledge.

Robinson, M. (1993) Comment on promoting co-operative parenting after separation. *Journal of Family Therapy*, 15: 263–71.

Robinson, M. (1993) A family systems approach to mediation during divorce. In J. Carpenter and A. Treacher (eds) *Using Family Therapy in the 90s*. Oxford: Blackwell.

Robinson, M. (1997) *Divorce as Family Transition: When Private Sorrow Becomes a Public Matter*. London: H. Karnac.

Simpson, B. (1998) *Changing Families: An Ethnographic Approach to Divorce and Separation*. Oxford: Berg.

Stern Peck, J. and Manocherian, J.R. (1989) Divorce in the changing family life cycle. In B. Carter and M. McGoldrick (eds) *The Changing Family Cycle*. Boston: Allyn & Bacon.

Street, E. (1994) *Counselling for Family Problems*. London: Sage.

Walker, J. (1988) Divorce and conciliation: a family therapy perspective. In E. Street and W. Dryden (eds) *Family Therapy in Britain*. Milton Keynes: Open University Press.

Wallerstein, J. (1989) *Second Changes*. London: Bantam.

Wallerstein, J. and Kelly, J. (1980) *Surviving the Break-Up*. London: Grant McIntyre.

Domestic violence

Almeida, R.V. and Durkin, T. (1999) The cultural context model: therapy for couples with domestic violence. *Journal of Marital and Family Therapy*, 25(3): 313–24.

Bograd, M. (1999) Strengthening domestic violence theories: intersections of race, class, sexual orientation, and gender. *Journal of Marital and Family Therapy*, 25(3): 275–89.

Goldner, V. (1999) Morality and multiplicity. *Journal of Marital and Family Therapy*, 25(3): 325–36.

Jacobsen, N.S. and Gottman, J.M. (1998) *When Men Batter Women: New Insights into Ending Abusive Relationships*. New York: Simon & Schuster.

Jasinski, J.L. and Williams, L.M. (eds) (1998) *Partner Violence: A Comprehensive Review of 20 Years of Research*. Thousand Oaks, CA: Sage.

Jory, B. and Andersen, D. (1999) Intimate justice II: Fostering mutality, reciprocity, and accommodation in therapy for psychological abuse. *Journal of Marital and Family Therapy*, 25(3): 349–63.

Vetere, A. and Cooper, J. (2001) Working systemically with family violence: risk, responsibility and collaboration. *Journal of Family Therapy*, 23: 85–101.

Vetere, A. and Cooper, J. (2003) Setting up a domestic violence service. *Child and Adolescent Mental Health*, 8: 61–7.

Eating disorders

Bruch, H. (1988) *Conversations with Anorexics*. New York: Basic Books.

Colahan, M. and Robinson, P. (2002) Multi-family groups in the treatment of young adults with eating disorders. *Journal of Family Therapy*, 24(1): 17–30.

Coyne, J.C. and Anderson, B.J. (1989) The psychosomatic family reconsidered ii: recalling a defective model and looking ahead. *Journal of Marital and Family Therapy*, 15: 139–48.

Dallos, R. (2003) Using narrative and attachment theory in systemic family therapy with eating disorders. *Clinical Child Psychology and Psychiatry*, 8(4): 521–35.

Dare, C. and Eisler, I. (1995) Family therapy. In G.I. Szmukler, C. Dare and J. Treasure (eds) *Handbook of Eating Disorders: Theory, Treatment and Research*. New York: Wiley.

Dare, C. and Eisler, I. (2000) A multi-family group day treatment programme for adolescent eating disorder. *European Eating Disorders Review*, 8: 4–18.

Dare, C., Eisler, I., Russel, G.F.M. and Szmukler, G.I. (1990) The clinical and theoretical impact of a controlled trial of family therapy in anorexia nervosa. *Journal of Marital and Family Therapy*, 16(1): 39–57.

Kearney, R. (1996) Attachment disruption in anorexia nervosa and bulimia nervosa: a review of theory and empirical research. *International Journal of Eating Disorders*, 20(2): 115–27.

Le Grange, D. *et al.* (1992) Evaluation of family treatments in adolescent anorexia nervosa. *Journal of Family Therapy*, 14: 177–92.

Minuchin, S., Rosman, B.L. and Baker, L. (1978) *Psychosomatic Families: Anorexia Nervosa in Context*. Cambridge, MA: Harvard University Press.

Palazzoli, M.S. (1974) *Self-Starvation: From the Intrapsychic to the Transpersonal Approach*. London: Chaucer.

Scholz, M. and Asen, E. (2001) Multiple family therapy with eating disordered adolescents: concepts and preliminary results. *European Eating Disorders Review*, 9: 33–53.

Stierlin, H. and Weber, G. (1986) *Unlocking The Family Door: A Systemic Approach to the Understanding of Anorexia Nervosa*. New York: Brunner/Mazel.

van Furth, E. (1991) Parental expressed emotion and eating disorder. Doctoral dissertation. Utrecht, Department of Psychiatry.

Vandereycken, W., Kog, E. and Vanderlinden, J. (eds) (1989) *The Family Approach to Eating Disorders*. New York: Springer Press.

Education and family therapy

Blow, K. (1997) Using ideas from systemic family therapy in the context of education: introducing not knowing to the world of education. *Educational and Child Psychology*, 14(3): 57–62.

Dawson, N. and McHugh, B. (2000) Family relationships, learning and teachers – keeping the connections. In C. Watkins, C. Lodge and R. Best (eds) *Tomorrow's Schools – Towards Integrity*. London: Routledge.

Doerries, D.B. and Foster, V.A. (2001) Family counselors as school consultants. *Family Journal*, 9(4): 391–7.

Fadden, G. (1998) Research update: psychoeducational family interventions. *Journal of Family Therapy*, 20(3): 293–309.

Freedman, J. and Combs, G. (2001) Facilitating a narrative culture in a school: a report and proposal. *Journal of Systemic Therapies*, 20(3): 49–59.

Kecskemeti, M. and Epston, D. (2001) Practices of teacher appreciation and the pooling of knowledges. *Journal of Systemic Therapies*, 20(3): 39–48.

Morton, G. (2002) The educational therapy contribution to a family systems approach. *Psychodynamic Practice*, 8(3): 327–41.

Ethics and systemic family therapy

Boszormenyi-Nagy, I. (1985) Commentary: transgenerational solidarity – therapy's mandate and ethics. *Family Process*, 24: 454–60.

Bray, J.H., Shepherd, J.N. and Hays, J.R. (1985) Legal and ethical issues in informed consent to psychotherapy. *American Journal of Family Therapy*, 13: 50–60.

Doherty, W. and Boss, P. (1991) Values and ethics in family therapy. In A. Gurman and D. Kniskern (eds) *The Handbook of Family Therapy, Volume II*. New York: Brunner/Mazel.

Donovan, M. (2003) Family therapy beyond postmodernism: some considerations on the ethical orientation of contemporary practice. *Journal of Family Therapy*, 25(3): 285–306.

Gilligan, C. (1982) *In a Different Voice: Psychological Theory and Women's Development*. Cambridge, MA: Harvard University Press.

Gurman, A.S. and Kniskern, D.P. (1978) Deterioration in marital and family therapy: empirical, clinical and conceptual issues. *Family Process*, 17: 3–20.

Holmes, S. (1994) A philosophic stance, ethics and therapy – an interview with Harlene Anderson. *Australian and New Zealand Journal of Family Therapy*, 155–61.

Inger, I. and Inger, J. (1994) *Creating an Ethical Position in Family Therapy*. London: H. Karnac.

Krull, M. (1987) Systemic thinking and ethics. In M. Hargens (ed.) *Systemic Studies Vol. I: A European Perspective*. Broadstairs: Borgmann.

Lakin, M. (1988) The ethical minefield of marital and family therapies. In *Ethical Issues in the Psychotherapies*. Oxford: Oxford University Press.

Raffin, C. and Prata, G. (1998) From methodological to ethical rigour. *Human Systems*, 9(3–4): 203–12.
Seedhouse, D. (1988) *Ethics: The Heart of Healthcare*. Chichester: Wiley.
Tamasese, K., Tuhaka, F. and Waldergrave, C. (2000) Address delivered at conference on Institutionalized Racism and Social Justice: Therapeutic and Organisational Strategies, Institute of Family Therapy, London (2 June).
Von Foerster, H. (1990) Ethics and second order cybernetics. Plenary Address at the Paris International Conference on Systems and Ethics, Epistemology and New Methods, July.
Waldergrave, C. (2000) Address delivered at conference on Institutionalized Racism and Social Justice: Therapeutic and Organisational Strategies, Institute of Family Therapy, London (2 June).
Walrond-Skinner, S. and Watson, D. (eds) (1987) *Ethical Issues in Family Therapy*. London: Routledge & Kegan Paul.
Wendorf, D. and Wendorf, R. (1985) A systemic view of family therapy ethics. *Family Process*, 24: 443–60.
Zygmond, M.J. and Boorhem, H. (1989) Ethical decision-making in family therapy. *Family Process*, 28: 269–80.

Exiles, refugees and asylum seekers

Chaitin, J. (2003) 'Living with' the past: coping and patterns in families of Holocaust survivors. *Family Process*, 42(2): 305–22.
Papadopoulos, R. (2001) Refugee families: issues of systemic supervision. *Journal of Family Therapy*, 23(4): 405–22.
Papadopoulos, R. and Hildebrand, J. (1997) Is home where the heart is? Narratives of oppositional discourse in refugee families. In R. Papadopoulos and J. Byng-Hall (eds) *Multiple Voices: Narrative in Systemic Family Psychotherapy*. London: Duckworth.
Pejovic, M., Jovanovic, A. and Djurdjic, S. (1997) Psychotherapy experience with patients treated for war psychotraumas. *Psychiatriki*, 8(2): 136–41.
Spoljar, V. (2000) Genograms of exile and return families in Croatia – a medical anthropological approach. *Collegium Antropologicum*, 24(2): 566–78.
Waldegrave, C. (1998) The challenges of culture to psychology and postmodern thinking. In M. McGoldrick (ed.) *Re-visioning Family Therapy: Race, Culture, and Gender in Clinical Practice*. New York: Guilford Press.
Woodcock, J. (2000) Refugee children and families: theoretical and clinical approaches. In K. Dwivedi (ed.) *Post Traumatic Stress Disorder in Children and Adolescents*. London: Whurr.
Woodcock, J. (2000) A systemic approach to trauma. *Context*, 51: 2–4.
Woodcock, J. (2001) A dozen differences to consider when working with refugee families. *Context*, 54: 24–5.
Woodcock, J. (2001) Threads from the labyrinth: therapy with survivors of war and political oppression. *Journal of Family Therapy*, 23(2): 136–54.

Family and parenting interventions

Burbach, F.R. and Standbridge, R.I. (1998) A family intervention in psychosis service integrating the systemic and family management approaches. *Journal of Family Therapy*, 20(3): 311–25.

Hendrix, H. and Hunt, H.L. (1998) *Giving the Love that Heals*. New York: Simon & Schuster.

Segal, L. (2000) *Why Feminism: Gender, Psychology, Politics*. Oxford: Polity Press.

Family life cycle

Boyd Franklin, N. (1993) Race, class and poverty. In F. Walsh (ed.) *Normal Family Processes*. New York: Guilford Press.

Carter, E. and McGoldrick, M. (eds) (1989) *The Changing Family Life Cycle* (2nd edn). Boston: Allyn & Bacon.

Coupland, N. and Nussbaum, J.F. (1993) Introduction: discourse selfhood and the lifespan. In *Discourse and Lifespan Identity*. London: Sage.

Dallos, R. (1991) Images of families and the family life cycle. In *Family Belief Systems, Therapy and Change*. Buckingham: Open University Press.

Goldner, V. (1991) Generation and gender: normative and covert hierarchies. In M. McGoldrick, C.M. Anderson and F. Walsh (eds) *Women in Families: A Framework for Family Therapy*. New York: W.W. Norton.

Haley, J. (1986) The family life cycle. In *Uncommon Therapy*. New York: W.W. Norton.

Hawley, D.R. and Dehaan, L. (1996) Toward a definition of family resilience: integrating lifespan and family perspectives. *Family Process*, 35: 283–98.

Lieberman, S. (1998) History containing systems. *Journal of Family Therapy*, 20: 195–206.

McGoldrick, M. and Gerson, R. (1989) Genograms and the family life cycle. In B. Carter and M. McGoldrick (eds) *The Changing Family Life Cycle*. Boston: Allyn & Bacon.

McGoldrick, M., Herman, M. and Carter, B. (1993) The changing family life cycle. In F. Walsh (ed.) *Normal Family Processes*. New York: Guilford Press.

Robinson, M. (1991) *Family Transformation during Divorce and Re-marriage: A Systemic Approach*. London: Routledge.

Walsh, F. (1993) Conceptualization of normal family processes. In F. Walsh (ed.) *Normal Family Processes*. New York: Guilford Press.

Walters, M., Carter, B. and Papp, P. (1988) *The Invisible Web: Gender Patterns in Family Relationships*. New York: Guilford Press.

Feminist theory and family therapy

Jones, E. (1998) A feminist systemic therapy? In I. Bruna Seu and M.C. Heenan (eds) *Feminism and Psychotherapy: Reflections on Contemporary Theories and Practices*. London: Sage.

Ussher, J.M. (2003) The ongoing silencing of women in families: an analysis and rethinking of premenstrual syndrome and therapy. *Journal of Family Therapy*, 25(4): 388–405.

Vatcher, C.A. and Bobo, M. (2001) The feminist/emotionally focused therapy practice model: an integrated approach for couple therapy. *Journal of Marital Family Therapy*, 27(1): 69–83.

Forensic psychiatry

Baker, K.A. (1999) The importance of cultural sensitivity and therapist self awareness when working with mandatory clients. *Family Process*, 38(1): 55–67.

Geelan, S. and Nickford, C. (1999) A survey of the use of family therapy in medium secure units in England and Wales. *Journal of Forensic Psychiatry*, 10(2): 317–24.

Formulation

See Key Texts, Chapter 5.

Gay and lesbian families and family therapy

Amundson, J., Stewart, K. and Valentine, L. (1993) Temptations of power certainty. *Journal of Family and Marital Therapy*, 19(2): 111–23.

Anderson, S.C. (1996) Addressing heterosexist bias in the treatment of lesbian couples with chemical dependency. In J. Laird and R.J. Green (eds) *Lesbians and Gays in Couples and Families: A Handbook for Therapists*. New York: Jossey-Bass.

Black, E.I. (1993) *Secrets in the Family and Family Therapy*. New York: W.W. Norton.

Boscolo, L. and Bertrando, P. (1996) *Systemic Therapy with Individuals*. London: Karnac Books.

Bozett, F.W. and Sussman, M.B. (1990) *Homosexuality and Family Relations*. New York: Harrington Park Press.

Carter, E.A. and McGoldrick, M. (eds) (1989) *The Changing Family Life Cycle* (2nd edn). Boston: Allyn & Bacon.

Clunis, M. and Gren, G.D. (1988) *Lesbian Couples*. Seattle: Seal Press.

Falco, K. (1991) *Psychotherapy with Lesbian Clients: Theory in Practice*. New York: Brunner/Mazel.

Gassinger, R.E. (1991) The hidden minority. Issues and challenges in working with lesbian and gay men. *Counselling Psychologist*, 19: 157–76.

Giddens, A. (1993) *The Transformation of Intimacy, Sexuality, Love and Eroticism in Modern Society*. Oxford: Polity Press.

Gonsiorek, J.C. (1982) *A Guide to Psychotherapy with Gay and Lesbian Clients*. New York: Harrington Park Press.

Green, R.J. (1996) Why ask, why tell? Teaching and learning about lesbians and gays in family therapy. *Family Process*, 35(3): 389–400.

Green, R.J., Bettinger, M. and Zacks, E. (1996) Are lesbian couples fused and male couples disengaged? In J. Laird and R.J. Green (eds) *Lesbians and Gays in Couples and Families: A Handbook for Therapists*. New York: Jossey-Bass.

Hewson, D. (1993) Heterosexual dominance in the world of therapy. *Dulwich Centre Newsletter*, 2: 14–20.

Kitzinger, C. (1987) *The Social Construction of Lesbianism*. London: Sage.

Kurdek, L.A. (1995) Lesbian and gay male close relationships. In A.R. D'Augelli and C.J. Patterson (eds) *Lesbian and Gay Identities over the Lifespan: Psychological Perspectives on Personal, Relational and Community Processes*. New York: Oxford University Press.

Laird, J. (1993) Lesbian and gay families. In F. Walsh (ed.) *Normal Family Processes* (2nd edn). New York: Guilford Press.

LaSala, M.C. (2000) Lesbians, gay men and their parents: family therapy for the coming out crisis. *Family Process*, 39: 257–66.

Long, J.K. (1996) Working with lesbians, gays and bisexuals: addressing heterosexism in supervision. *Family Process*, 35(3): 377–88.

Malley, M. and Tasker, F. (1999) Lesbians, gay men and family therapy: a contradiction in terms? *Journal of Family Therapy*, 21: 3–29.

Malley, M. and Tasker, F. (2004) Significant and other: systemic family therapists on lesbians and gay men. *Journal of Family Therapy*, 26(2): 193–212.

Markowitz, L. (1991) Gays and lesbians are out of the closet. Are therapists still in the dark? *Family Therapy Newsletter*, January/February: 27–35.

Marvin, C. and Miller, D. (2000) Lesbian couples entering the 21st century. In P. Papp (ed.) *Couples on the Fault Line: New Directions for Therapists*. New York: Guilford Press.

McCann, D. (1998) To say or not to say? Dilemmas in disclosing sexual orientation. *Context*, 40.

McWhirter, D.P. and Mattison, A.M. (1984) *The Male Couple. How Relationships Develop*. Englewood Cliffs, NJ: Prentice Hall.

Peplau, L.A. (1991) Lesbian and gay relationships. In J.C. Gonsiorek and J.D. Weinrich (eds) *Homosexuality: Research Implications for Public Policy*. Newbury Park, CA: Sage.

Pharr, S. (1988) *Homophobia. A Weapon of Sexism*. Inverness: Chardon Press.

Roth, S.A. (1988) Psychotherapy with lesbian couples: individual issues, female socialization and the social context. In M. McGoldrick, C.M. Anderson and F. Walsh (eds) *Women in Families: A Framework for Family Therapy*. New York: W.W. Norton.

Scrivner, R. and Eldridge, N.S. (1995) Lesbian and gay family psychology. In R.I.T. Mikesell, D.D. Luterman and S. McDaniel (eds) *Integrating Family Therapy: Handbook of Family Psychology and Systems Theory*. Washington, DC: American Psychological Association.

Simon, G. (1996) Working with people in relationships. In D. Davis and C. Neal (eds) *Pink Therapy: A Guide for Counsellors and Therapists Working with Lesbian, Gay and Bisexual Clients*. Buckingham: Open University Press.

Shernoff, M. (1998) Coming out in therapy: the PC way isn't always the right way. *Family Therapy Networking*, March/April: 23–4.

Slater, S. and Mencher, J. (1995) The lesbian family life cycle: a contextual approach. *American Journal of Orthopsychiatry*, 61(3): 372–82.

Stacey, K. (1993) Exploring stories of lesbian experiences in therapy: implications for therapists in a post-modern world. *Dulwich Centre Newsletter*, 2: 3–13.

Strommen, E.F. (1990) Hidden branches and growing pains: homosexuality and the family tree. In F.W. Bozett and M.B. Sussman (eds) *Homosexuality and Family Relations*. New York: Harrington Park Press.

Tasker, F.L. and Golombok, S. (1997) *Growing up in a Lesbian Family*. New York: Guilford Press.

Ussher, J. (1991) Families and couples therapy with gay and lesbian clients. Acknowledging the forgotten minority. *Journal of Family Therapy*, 13: 131–48.

Weeks, J. (1995) *Invented Moralities: Sexual Values in The Age of AIDS*. Oxford: Polity Press.

Weston, K. (1991) *Families We Choose: Lesbians, Gays, Kinship*. New York: Columbia University Press.

Gender – men

Bograd, M. (1990) Women treating men. *Family Therapy Networker*, May/June.

Erkel, T.R. (1990) The birth of a movement. *Family Therapy Networker*, May/June.

Frosh, S. (1995) Unpacking masculinity: from rationality to fragmentation. In C. Burck and B. Speed (eds) *Gender, Power and Relationships*. London: Routledge.

Keeney, B. and Bobele, M. (1989) A brief note on family violence. *Australian and New Zealand Journal of Family Therapy*, 10(2): 93–6.

McGregor, H. (1990) Conceptualising male violence against female partners. *Australian and New Zealand Journal of Family Therapy*, 11(2).

Mason, B. and Mason, E. (1990) Masculinity and family work. In R.J. Perelberg and A. Miller (eds) *Gender and Power in Families*. London: Routledge.

O'Brien, M. (1990) The place of men in a gender-sensitive therapy. In R.J. Perelberg and A. Miller (eds) *Gender and Power in Families*. London: Routledge.

O'Connor, T. (1990) A day for men. *Family Therapy Networker*, May/June.

Pittman, F. (1990) The masculine mystique. *Family Therapy Networker*, May/June.

Taffel, R. (1990) The politics of mood. *Family Therapy Networker*, September/October.

Walters, J., Tasker, F. and Bichard, S. (1990) Men in therapy. 'Too busy'? Fathers' attendance for family appointments. *Journal of Family Therapy*, 23(1): 3–20.

Waters, D. and Saunders, T.J. (1996) I gave at the office. *Family Therapy Networker*, March/April.

White, M. (1995) A conversation about accountability. In *Re-authoring Lives: Interviews and Essays*. Adelaide: Dulwich Press.

Gender – women

Barnes, G.G. (1990) 'The little woman' and the world of work. In R.J. Perelberg and A. Miller (eds) *Gender and Power in Families*. London: Routledge.

Burck, C. and Daniel, G. (1990) Feminism and strategic therapy: contradiction or complementary? In R.J. Perelberg and A. Miller (eds) *Gender and Power in Families*. London: Routledge.

Clark, M. and Kilworth, A. (1990) Why a group for women only? In R.J. Perelberg and A. Miller (eds) *Gender and Power in Families*. London: Routledge.

Conn, J. and Turner, A. (1990) Working with women in families. In R.J. Perelberg and A. Miller (eds) *Gender and Power in Families*. London: Routledge.

Ellman, B. and Taggart, M. (1993) Changing gender norms. In F. Walsh (ed.) *Normal Family Processes*. New York: Guilford Press.

Goldner, V. (1991) Feminism and systemic practice: two critical traditions in transition. *Journal of Strategic and Systemic Therapies*, 10(3–4).

Hare-Mustin, R.T. (1991) The problem of gender in family therapy theory. In M. McGoldrick, C.M. Anderson and F. Walsh (eds) *Women in Families: A Framework for Family Therapy*. New York: W.W. Norton.

Hicks, S. and Anderson, C.M. (1991) Women on their own. In M. McGoldrick, C.M. Anderson and F. Walsh (eds) *Women in Families: A Framework for Family Therapy*. New York: W.W. Norton.

Imber-Black, E. (1991) Rituals of stabilization and change in women's lives. In M. McGoldrick, C.M. Anderson and F. Walsh (eds) *Women in Families: A Framework for Family Therapy*. New York: W.W. Norton.

Jones, E. (1990) Feminism and family therapy: can mixed marriages work? In R.J. Perelberg and A. Miller (eds) *Gender and Power in Families*. London: Routledge.

Jones, E. (1995) The construction of gender in family therapy. In C. Burck and B. Speed (eds) *Gender, Power and Relationships*. London: Routledge.

Layton, M. (1989) Mother: making her real – the mother journey. *Family Therapy Networker*, September/October: 23–35.

McGoldrick, M. (1991) Sisters. In M. McGoldrick, C.M. Anderson and F. Walsh (eds) *Women in Families: A Framework for Family Therapy*. New York: W.W. Norton.

MacKinnon, L. and James, K. (1992) Raising the stakes in child-at-risk cases – eliciting and maintaining parents' motivation. *Australian and New Zealand Journal of Family Therapy*, 13(2): 59–71.

Miller, A.C. (1990) The mother–daughter relationship and the distortion of reality in childhood sexual abuse. In R.J. Perelberg and A. Miller (eds) *Gender and Power in Families*. London: Routledge.

Segal, L. (1995) Feminism and the family. In C. Burck and B. Speed (eds) *Gender, Power and Relationships*. London: Routledge.

Smith, G. (1995) Hierarchy in families where sexual abuse is an issue. In C. Burck and B. Speed (eds) *Gender, Power and Relationships*. London: Routledge.

Walsh, F. (1991) Reconsidering gender in the marital quid pro quo. In M. McGoldrick, C.M. Anderson and F. Walsh (eds) *Women in Families: A Framework for Family Therapy*. New York: W.W. Norton.

Wylie, M.S. (1989) Mother: making her real – the mothering knot. *Family Therapy Networker*, September/October: 43–51.

General practice

Stange, K.C. (2001) Integrative ways of thinking and generalist practice. *Families, Systems & Health*, 19(4): 375–6.

Zubialde, J.P. and Aspy, C.B. (2001) It is time to make a general systems paradigm reality in family and community medicine? *Families, Systems & Health*, 19(4): 345–60.

Historical overview

Broderick, C.B. and Schrader, S.S. (1991) The history of professional marriage and family therapy. In A. Gurman and D. Kniskern (eds) *The Handbook of Family Therapy, Vol. II*. London: Guilford Press.

Burck, C. (1995) Developments in family therapy in the last five years. *ACPP Review and Newsletter*, 17(5): 247–54.

Campbell, D., Draper, R. and Crutchley, E. (1991) The Milan systemic approach to family therapy. In A. Gurman and D. Kniskern (eds) *The Handbook of Family Therapy, Vol. II*. London: Guilford Press.

Doherty, W.J., McDaniel, S. and Hepworth, J. (1994) Medical family therapy: an emerging arena for family therapy. *Journal of Family Therapy*, 16: 31–46.

Goldenberg, I. and Goldenberg, H. (2000) *Family Therapy: An Overview* (5th edn). Pacific Grove, CA: Brooks/Cole.

Hoffman, L. (1985) Beyond power and control: toward a 'second order' family systems therapy. *Family Systems Medicine*, 3(4): 381–96.

Hoffman, L. (1990) Constructing realities: the art of lenses. *Family Process*, 29: 1–12.

Jenkins, H. (1990) Annotation: family therapy – developments in thinking and practice. *Journal of Child Psychology and Psychiatry*, 31: 1015–26.

Jones, C.W. and Linblad-Goldberg, M. (2002) Eco-systemic structural family therapy. In F.W. Kaslow (ed.) *Comprehensive Handbook of Psychotherapy*. New York: Wiley.

Lawson, D. and Prevatt, F. (1999) *Casebook in Family Therapy*. Belmont, CA: Brooks/Cole.

McGoldrick, M. (ed.) (1998) *Re-visioning Family Therapy*. New York: Guildford Press.

McDaniel, S.H., Lusterman, D.D. and Philpot, C.L. (eds) (2001) *Casebook for Integrating Family Therapy: An Ecosystemic Approach*. Washington, DC: American Psychological Association.

Piercy, F.P., Sprenkle, D.H. and Wetchler, J.L. (eds) (1996) *Family Therapy Soucebook* (2nd edn). New York: Guilford Press.

Tomm, K. (1984) One perspective on the Milan systemic approach: Part one: Overview of development theory and practice. *Journal of Marital and Family Therapy*, 10: 113–25.

Illness and learning disability

Altschuler, J. (1993) Gender and illness: implications for family therapy. *Journal of Family Therapy*, 15: 381–401.

Goldberg, D., Magrill, L., Hale, J., Damaskinidou, K., Paul, J. and Tham, S. (1995) Protection and loss: working with learning disabled adults and their families. *Journal of Family Therapy*, 17: 263–80.

Herz Brown, F. (1989) The impact of death and serious illness on the family life cycle. In B. Carter and M. McGoldrick (eds) *The Changing Family Cycle*. Boston: Allyn & Bacon.

Rolland, J.S. (1993) Mastering family challenges in serious illness and disability. In F. Walsh (ed.) *Normal Family Processes*. New York: Guilford Press.

Selekman, M.D. (1996) Turning out the light on a seasonal affective disorder. *Journal of Systemic Therapies*, 15(3): 40–51.

Sloman, L. and Konstantareas, M. (1990) Why families of children with biological deficits require a systems approach. *Family Process*, 29: 417–29.

Vetere, A. (1993) Using family therapy in services for people with learning disabilities. In J. Carpenter and A. Treacher (eds) *Using Family Therapy in the 90s*. Oxford: Blackwell.

Wilson, J., Fosson, A., Kanga, J. and D'Angelo, S. (1996) Homeostatic interaction: a longitudinal study of biological, psychosocial and family variables in children with cystic fibrosis. *Journal of Family Therapy*, 18: 123–39.

Marital work

Berns, S.B., Jacobsen, N.S. and Gottman, J.M. (1999) Demand/withdraw interaction patterns between different types of batterers and their spouses. *Journal of Marital and Family Therapy*, 25(3): 337–47.

Bograd, M. (1999) Battering and couples therapy: universal screening and selection of treatment modality. *Journal of Marital and Family Therapy*, 25(3): 291–312.

Carpenter, J. and Treacher, A. (1989) *Problems and Solutions in Marital and Family Therapy*. Oxford: Basil Blackwell.

Carr, A. (1991) Milan systemic therapy: a review of 10 empirical investigations. *Journal of Family Therapy*, 13: 1–57.

Clulow, C. (ed.) (1993) *Rethinking Marriage: Public and Private Perspectives*. London: Karnac Books.

Clulow, C. (ed.) (1995) *Women, Men and Marriage*. London: Sheldon Press.

Dallos, S. and Dallos, R. (1997) *Couples, Sex and Power: The Politics of Desire*. Buckingham: Open University Press.

Foreman, S. and Dallos, R. (1992) Inequalities of power and sexual problems. *Journal of Family Therapy*, 14: 349–69.

Gordon, L. (1993) *Passage to Intimacy*. New York: Simon & Schuster.

Hendrix, H. (1998) *Getting the Love You Want*. New York: Henry Holt & Co.

Jones, E. and Asen, E. (2000) *Systemic Couple Therapy and Depression*. London: Karnac.

Kaplan, H.S. (1979) *Disorders of Sexual Desire, Vol. II*. New York: Brunner/Mazel.

Lederer, W. and Jackson, D.D. (1968) *The Mirages of Marriage*. New York: W.W. Norton.

Leff, J., Vearnals, S., Brewin, C., Wolff, G., Alexander, B., Asen, E., Dayson, D., Jones, E., Chisholm, D. and Everitt, B. (2000) The London Depression Intervention Trial: an RCT of antidepressants versus couple therapy in the treatment and maintenance of depressed people with a partner: clinical outcomes and costs. *British Journal of Psychiatry*, 177: 95–100.

Lerner, H.G. (1989) *The Dance of Intimacy*. Glasgow: Pandora.

Lerner, H.G. (1990) *The Dance of Anger*. Glasgow: Pandora.

Lerner, H.G. (2001) *The Dance of Connection*. New York: Harper Collins.

Levant, R.F. and Silverstein, L.B. (2001) Integrating gender and family systems theories: the 'both/and' approach to treating a postmodern couple. In S.H. McDaniel, D.D. Lusterman and C.L. Philpot (eds) *Casebook for Integrating Family Therapy: An Ecosystemic Approach*. Washington, DC: American Psychological Association.

Paul, N.L. and Paul, B.B. (1975) *A Marital Puzzle*. New York: W.W. Norton.

Ruszczynski, S. (1992) Notes towards a psychoanalytic understanding of the couple relationship. *Psychoanalytic Psychotherapy*, 6(1): 33–48.

Ruszczynski, S. (1993) *Psychotherapy with Couples*. London: Karnac Books.

Ruszczynski, S. and Fisher, J. (1995) *Intuitiveness and Intimacy in the Couple*. London: Karnac Books.

Sager, C.J. (1976) *Marriage Contracts and Couple Therapy*. New York: Brunner/Mazel.

Tannen, D. (1990) *You Just Don't Understand*. New York: Ballantine Books.

Watzlawick, P., Beavin, J. and Jackson, D.D. (1967) *Pragmatics of Human Communication*. New York: W.W. Norton.

Willi, J. (1982) *Couples in Collusion*. New York: Jason Aronson.

Willi, J. (1984) The concept of collusion: a combined systemic–psychodynamic approach to marital therapy. *Family Process*, 23: 177–85.

Milan systemic therapy

Anderson, T. *et al.* (1985) Circular questioning and shifting relationships. *Australian and New Zealand Journal of Family Therapy*, 6(3): 145–50.

Bowman, G. and Jeffcoat, P. (1990) The application of systems ideas in a social services field-work team. *Journal of Family Therapy*, 12: 243–54.

Burbatti, G. and Formenti, L. (1988) *The Milan Approach to Family Therapy*. New York: Jason Aronson.

Burnham, J. (1986) Intervening. In *Family Therapy: An Introduction*. London: Tavistock.

Campbell, D. (1995) Family therapy and beyond: where is the Milan systemic approach today? *Child Psychology and Psychiatry Review*, 4: 76–84

Campbell, D. and Draper, R. (1985) *Applications of Systemic Family Therapy*. London: Academic Press.

Cecchin, G. (1987) Hypothesizing, circularity, and neutrality revisited: an invitation to curiosity. *Family Process*, 26(4): 405–14.

Cronen, V. and Walsh, W. (1985) Towards an explanation of how the Milan method works. An invitation to a systemic epistemology and the evolution of family systems therapy. In D. Campbell and R. Draper (eds) *Applications of Systemic Family Therapy*. London: Academic Press.

Cronen, V.E., Johnson, K.M. and Lannamann, J.W. (1982) Paradoxes, double binds, and reflexive loops: an alternative theoretical perspective. *Family Process*, 21: 91–112.

Hayward, M. (1989) The Socratic method. Unpublished paper, Child and Family Centre, Mount Gould Hospital, Plymouth.

Hoffman, L. (1981) The systemic model. In *Foundations of Family Therapy: A Conceptual Framework for Systems Change*. New York: Basic Books.

Jones, E. (1993) *Family Systems Therapy: Developments in the Milan Systemic Therapies*. Chichester: Wiley.

Jones, E. (1988) The Milan method – quo vadis? *Journal of Family Therapy*, 10: 325–38.

Mason, B. (1993) The Cardiff systemic model – a brief definition. Paper presented at the Family Institute, Cardiff.

O'Brian, C. and Bruggan, P. (1985) Our personal and professional lives: learning positive connotation and circular questioning. *Family Process*, 24: 311–22.

Palazzoli, M.S., Boscolo, L., Cecchin, G. and Prata, G. (1980) The problem of the referring person. *Journal of Marital and Family Therapy*, January: 3–9.

Palazzoli, M.S., Boscolo, L., Cecchin, G. and Prata, G. (1980) Hypothesizing – circularity – neutrality: three guidelines for the conductor of the session. *Family Process*, 19(1): 3–12.

Real, T. (1990) The therapeutic use of self in constructionist/systemic therapy. *Family Process*, 29: 255–72.

Silver, E. (1991) Should I give advice? A systemic view. *Journal of Family Therapy*, 13: 295–309.

Tomm, K. (1985) Circular interviewing: a multifaceted clinical tool. In D. Campbell and R. Draper (eds) *Applications of Systemic Family Therapy*. London: Academic Press.

Ugazio, V. (1985) Hypothesis making: the Milan approach revisited. In

D. Campbell and R. Draper (eds) *Applications of Systemic Family Therapy*. London: Academic Press.

Walsh, W. and McGraw, J. (1996) Milan model of family systems therapy. In *Essentials of Family Therapy*. Denver, CO: Love.

Multi-agency perspectives

Anderson, H. and Goolishian, H.A. (1991) Thinking about multiagency work with substance abusers and their families. *Journal of Strategic and Systemic Therapies*, 10 (Spring).

Bentovim, A. (1992) *Trauma Organized Systems: Physical and Sexual Abuse in Families* (revised edition). London: H. Karnac.

Carpenter, J. and Treacher, A. (eds) (1993) *Using Family Therapy in the 90s*. Oxford: Blackwell.

Crowther, C., Dare, C. and Wilson, J. (1990) 'Why should we talk to you? You'll only tell the court!' On being an informer and a family therapist. *Journal of Family Therapy*, 12(2): 105–22.

Dare, J., Goldberg, D. and Walinets, R. (1990) What is the question you need to answer? How consultation can prevent professional systems immobilizing families. *Journal of Family Therapy*, 12: 355–69.

Dimmock, B. and Dungworth, D. (1983) Creating manoeuvrability for family/systems therapists in social services departments. *Journal of Family Therapy*, 5: 53–69.

Dowling, E. and Osborne, E. (1994) *The Family and the School: A Joint Systems Approach to Problems with Children* (2nd edn). London: Routledge.

Fruggeri, L., Telfner, U., Castellucei, A., Marzari, M. and Matteini, M. (1991) *New Systemic Ideas from the Italian Mental Health Movement*. London: H. Karnac.

Furniss, T. (1983) Mutual influence and interlocking professional family process in the treatment of child sexual abuse and incest. *Child Abuse and Neglect*, 7: 207–23.

Gopfert, M., Webster, J. and Seeman, M. (1996) *Parental Psychiatric Disorder: Distressed Parents and Their Families*. Cambridge: Cambridge University Press.

McDaniel, S.H., Lusterman, D.D. and Philpot, C.L. (eds) *Casebook for Integrating Family Therapy: An Ecosystemic Approach*. Washington, DC: American Psychological Association.

Smith, G. (1993) *Systemic Approaches to Training in Child Protection*. London: H. Karnac.

Multiple family therapy

Asen, E. (2002) Multiple family therapy: an overview. *Journal of Family Therapy*, 24(1): 3–16.

Bishop, P., Clilverd, A., Cooklin, A. and Hunt, U. (2002). Mental health matters: a multi-family framework for mental health intervention. *Journal of Family Therapy*, 24(1): 31–45.

Narrative approaches to therapy

Adams-Westcott, J., Dafforn, T.A. and Sterne, P. (1993) Escaping victim life stories and co-constructing personal agency. In S. Gilligan and R. Price (eds) *Therapeutic Conversations*. New York: W.W. Norton.

Chang, J. and Phillips, M. (1993) Michael White and Steve de Shazer: new directions in family therapy. In S. Gilligan and R. Price (eds) *Therapeutic Conversations*. New York: W.W. Norton.

Epston, D. (1993) Internalizing discourses versus externalizing discourses. In S. Gilligan and R. Price (eds) *Therapeutic Conversations*. New York: W.W. Norton.

Epston, D. (1993) Internalized other questioning with couples: the New Zealand version. In S. Gilligan and R. Price (eds) *Therapeutic Conversations*. New York: W.W. Norton.

Epston, D., White, M. and Murray, K. (1992) A proposal for a re-authoring therapy: Rose's revisioning of her life and a commentary. In S. McNamee and K. Gergen (eds) *Therapy as Social Construction*. New York: Sage.

Foucault, M. (1975) *The Birth of the Clinic: An Archaeology of Medical Perception*. New York: Random House.

Foucault, M. (1979) *Discipline and Punish: The Birth of the Prison*. London: Peregrine Books.

Freedman, G. and Combs, J. (1996) *Narrative Therapy*. New York: W.W. Norton.

Freedman, G. and Combs, J. (1996) The narrative metaphor and social construction. In *Narrative Therapy*. New York: W.W. Norton.

Freedman, G. and Combs, J. (1996) Shifting paradigms from systems to stories. In *Narrative Therapy*. New York: W.W. Norton.

Geertz, C. (1983) *Local Knowledge: Further Essays in Interpretative Anthropology*. New York: Basic Books.

Hart, B. (1995) Re-authoring the stories we work by situating the narrative approach in the presence of the family of therapists. *Australian and New Zealand Journal of Family Therapy*, 16(4): 181–9.

Kaye, J., Wood, A. and Stinson, S. (1992) The family interaction test. A preliminary study of a method of interpreting narratives about the family. *Australian and New Zealand Journal of Family Therapy*, 13(2): 79–86.

Luepnitz, D. (1992) Nothing in common but their first names: the case of Foucault and White. *Journal of Family Therapy*, 14(3): 281–4.

Mattingly, C. (1998) *Healing Dramas and Clinical Plots: The Narrative Structure of Experience*. Cambridge: Cambridge University Press.

Minuchin, S. (1998) Where is the family in narrative family therapy? *Journal of Marital and Family Therapy*, 24: 397–403.

Munro, C. (1987) White and the cybernetic therapies: news of difference. *Australian and New Zealand Journal of Family Therapy*, 8(4): 183–92.

Papadopoulos, R.K. and Byng-Hall, J. (eds) (1997) *Multiple Voices: Narrative in Systemic Family Psychotherapy*. London: Duckworth.

Tomm, K. (1993) The courage to protest: a commentary on Michael White's work. In S. Gilligan and R. Price (eds) *Therapeutic Conversations*. New York: W.W. Norton.

Weingarten, K. (1998) The small and the ordinary: the daily practice of a postmodern narrative therapy. *Family Process*, 37: 3–15.

White, M. (1983) Anorexia nervosa: a transgenerational system perspective. *Family Process*, 22: 255–73.

White, M. (1989) *Selected Papers*. Adelaide: Dulwich Centre Publications.

White, M. (1990) *Narrative Means to Therapeutic Ends*. New York: W.W. Norton.

White, M. (1991) Deconstruction and therapy. *Dulwich Centre Newsletter*.

White, M. (1997) *Narratives of Therapists' Lives*. Adelaide: Dulwich Centre Publications.

White, M. (2000) Exploring notions of spirituality and religion. *Context*, 48 (April): 5–8.

Zimmerman, J.L. and Dickerson, V.C. (1994) Using a narrative metaphor: implications for theory and clinical practice. *Family Process*, 53: 233–45.

Other models

Androutsopoulou, A. (2001) The self-characterisation as a narrative tool: application in therapy with individuals and families. *Family Process*, 40(1): 79–94.

Box, S. (1998) Group processes in family therapy. *Journal of Family Therapy*, 20: 123–32.

Barnes, G.G. (1981) Family bits and pieces. In S. Walrond-Skinner (ed.) *Developments in Family Therapy*. London: Routledge & Kegan Paul.

Bentovim, A. (1979) Towards creating a focal hypothesis for brief focal family therapy. *Journal of Family Therapy*, 1: 125–36.

Cade, B. (1980) Strategic therapy. *Journal of Family Therapy*, 2: 89–99.

Cade, B. (1987) Brief/strategic approaches to therapy: a commentary. *Australian and New Zealand Journal of Family Therapy*, 8: 37–44.

de Shazer, S. and Kim Berg, I. (1997) 'What works?' Remarks on research aspects of solution focused brief therapy. *Journal of Family Therapy*, 19: 121–4.

Duncan, B.L. (1992) Strategic therapy, eclecticism, and the therapeutic relationship. *Journal of Marital and Family Therapy*, 18(1): 17–24.

Hayes, H. (1991) A re-introduction to family therapy: clarification of three schools. *Australian and New Zealand Journal of Family Therapy*, 12: 27–43.

Israelstam, K. (1988) Contrasting four major family therapy paradigms: implications for family therapy training. *Journal of Family Therapy*, 10: 179–96.

Jenkins, H. (1985) Orthodoxy in family therapy practice as servant or tyrant. *Journal of Family Therapy*, 7: 19–30.

Prosky, P.S. and Keith, D.V. (eds) (2003) *Family Therapy as an Alternative to Medication: An Appraisal of Pharmland*. New York: Brunner-Routledge.

Rigazio-DiGilio, S.A. (2000) Relational diagnosis: a constructive-developmental perspective on assessment and treatment. *Journal of Clinical Psychology*, 56(8): 1017–36.

Stiefel, I., Harris, P. and Rohan, J.A. (1998) Object relations family therapy: articulating the inchoate. *Australian and New Zealand Journal of Family Therapy*, 19(2): 55–62.

Pilgrim, D. (2000) The real problem for postmodernism. *Journal of Marital and Family Therapy*, 21: 585–613.
Sloper, P. (1999) Models of service support for parents of disabled children. What do we know? What do we need to know? *Child: Care, Health and Development*, 25: 85–99.

Paradigm shift

Bateson, G. (1972) *Steps to an Ecology of Mind: Mind and Nature*. New York: Jason Aronson.
Bateson, M.C. (1987) *Where Angels Fear*. New York: Macmillan.
Birtchnell, J. (2001) Relating therapy with individuals, couples and families. *Journal of Family Therapy*, 23: 63–84.
Boscolo, L., Cecchin, G., Hoffman, L. and Penn, P. (1987) Introduction. In *Milan Systemic Family Therapy: Conversations in Theory and Practice*. New York: Basic Books.
Broderick, C.B. and Schrader, S.S. (1991) The history of professional marriage and family therapy. In A. Gurman and D. Kniskern (eds) *The Handbook of Family Therapy, Vol. II*. New York: Brunner/Mazel.
Capra, F. (1988) *Uncommon Wisdom*. New York: Bantam New Age Books.
Capra, F. (1996) *The Web of Life: A New Scientific Understanding of Living Systems*. New York: Anchor Books.
Cecchin, G. (1994) *The Cybernetics of Prejudice*. London: H. Karnac.
Cecchin, G., Lane, G. and Ray, W.L. (1993) *Irreverance: A Strategy for Therapists' Survival*. London: H. Karnac.
Dallos, R. (1997) Cybernetics and family therapy. In *Interacting Stories*. London: H. Karnac.
Gustafson, J.P. (1986) *The Complex Secret of Brief Psychotherapy*. New York: W.W. Norton.
Gustafson, J.P. (1986) Bateson and the inferno. In *The Complex Secret of Brief Psychotherapy*. New York: W.W. Norton.
Guttman, H.A. (1991) Systems theory, cybernetics and epistemology. In A. Gurman and D. Kniskern (eds) *The Handbook of Family Therapy, Vol. II*. New York: Brunner/Mazel.
Hendrix, H. and Hunt, H.L. (2004) *Receiving Love*. New York: Atria Books.
Hoffman, L. (1993) *Exchanging Voices: A Collaborative Approach to Family Therapy*. London: H. Karnac.
Hoffman, L. (1994) Beyond psychology: the rise of the social therapies. Unpublished paper.
Klein, D.M. and White, J.M. (1996) *Family Theories*. London: Sage.
Marris, P. (1996) *Politics of Uncertainty*. London: Routledge.
Schön, D. (1983) *The Reflective Practitioner*. New York: Basic Books.
Walsh, W.M. and McGraw, J.A. (1996) *Essentials of Family Therapy*. Denver, CO: Love.

Personal and professional development

Bacigalupe, G. (1998) Cross-cultural systemic therapy training and consultation: a postcolonial view. *Journal of Systemic Therapies*, 17(1): 31–44.

Barnes, G.G., Down, G. and McCann, D. (2000) *Systemic Supervision: A Portable Guide for Supervision Training*. London: Jessica Kingsley.

Carnevale, F. (1999) Toward a cultural conception of self. *Journal of Psychosocial Nursing*, 37: 26–31.

Fine, M. and Turner, J. (1991) Tyranny and freedom: looking at ideas in the practice of family therapy. *Family Process*, 30: 307–20.

Flaskas, C. (1989) Thinking about the emotional interactions of therapist and family. *Australian and New Zealand Journal of Family Therapy*, 10: 1–6.

Flaskas, C. and Perlez, A. (eds) (1996) *The Therapeutic Relationship in Systemic Therapy*. London: H. Karnac.

Griffith, J. and Griffith, M. (1992) Owning one's epistemological stance in therapy. *Dulwich Centre Newsletter*, No. 1.

Haber, R. (1990) From handicap to handy capable: training systemic therapists in use of self. *Family Process*, 29: 375–84.

Hardy, K.V. and Laszloffy, T.A. (1995) The cultural genogram: key to training culturally competent family therapists. *Journal of Marital and Family Therapy*, 21(3): 227–37.

Inger, I.B. (1998) A cross-cultural consultation and training exchange. *Journal of Systemic Therapies*, 17(1): 45–61.

Jones, E. (1998) Working with the self of the therapist. *Context*, 40.

Lee, R.E., Eppler, C., Kendal, N. and Latty, C. (2001) Critical incidents in the lives of first year MFT students. *Contemporary Family Therapy: An International Journal*, 23(1): 51–61.

Odell, M. and Campbell, C.E. (1997) *The Practical Practice of Marriage and Family Therapy. Things My Training Supervisor Never Told Me*. New York: Haworth Press.

Real, T. (1990) The therapeutic use of self in constructionist/systemic therapy. *Family Process*, 29: 255–72.

Rosenbaum, R. and Dyckman, J. (1995) Integrating self and system: an empty intersection? *Family Process*, 34: 21–44.

Stratford, J. (1998) Women and men in conversation: a consideration of therapists' interruptions in therapeutic discourse. *Journal of Family Therapy*, 20: 383–95.

Weingarten, K. (1991) The discourses of intimacy: adding a social constructionist and feminist view. *Family Process*, 31: 45–59.

Race and culture

Boyd-Franklin, N. (1993) Race, class and poverty. In F. Walsh (ed.) *Normal Family Processes*. New York: Guilford Press.

Hardy, K. (1993) War of the worlds. *Networker*, July/August: 50–7.

Hardy, K.V. and Laszloffy, T.A. (1995) The cultural genogram: key to training culturally competent family therapists. *Journal of Marital and Family Therapy*, 21(3): 227–37.
Hills, J. (ed.) (1995) Ethnicity, culture, race and family therapy. *Context* special edition.
Krause, I.-B. (1995) Personhood, culture and family therapy. *Journal of Family Therapy*, 17: 363–82.
Lau, A. (1988) Family therapy and ethnic minorities. In E. Street and W. Dryden (eds) *Family Therapy in Britain*. Milton Keynes: Open University Press.
McGoldrick, M. (1989) Ethnicity and the family cycle. In B. Carter and M. McGoldrick (eds) *Changing Family Cycle*. Boston: Allyn & Bacon.
McGoldrick, M. (1993) Ethnicity, cultural diversity and normality. In F. Walsh (ed.) *Normal Family Processes*. New York: Guilford Press.
McGoldrick, M., Garcia-Preto, N., Moore Hines, P. and Lee, E. (1991) Ethnicity and women. In M. McGoldrick, C.M. Anderson and F. Walsh (eds) *Women in Families: A Framework for Family Therapy*. New York: W.W. Norton.
Moore Hines, P. (1991) The family life cycle of poor black families. In B. Carter and M. McGoldrick (eds) *The Changing Family Life Cycle*. Boston: Allyn & Bacon.
Ratna, L. and Wheeler, M. (1995) Race and gender issues in adult psychiatry. In C. Burck and B. Speed (eds) *Gender, Power and Relationships*. London: Routledge.

Reflecting processes

Andersen, T. (1987) The reflecting team: dialogue and meta-dialogue in clinical work. *Family Process*, 26: 415–28.
Andersen, T. (1991) *The Reflecting Team: Dialogues and Dialogues about the Dialogues*. New York: W.W. Norton.
Andersen, T. (1992) Reflections on reflecting within families. In S. McNamee and K. Gergen (eds) *Therapy as Social Construction*. London: Sage.
Anderson, H. (1997) *Conversation, Language and Possibilities: A Postmodern Approach to Therapy*. New York: Basic Books.
Anderson, H. (1997) A philosophical stance: therapists' position, expertise and responsibility. In *Conversation, Language and Possibilities*. New York: Basic Books.
Anderson, H. (1997) Therapy as dialogic conversation. In *Conversation, Language and Possibilities*. New York: Basic Books.
Anderson, H. and Goolishian, H. (1988) Human systems as linguistic systems: preliminary and evolving ideas about the implications for clinical theory. *Family Process*, 27: 371–93.
Friedman, S. (ed.) (1995) *The Reflecting Team in Action: Collaborative Practice in Family Therapy*. New York: Guilford Press.
Gergen, K. (1996) Therapeutic communication as relationship. Paper presented to the Dialogue and Reflection conference, Tromsø.
Hoffman, L. (1990) Constructing realities: the art of lenses. *Family Process*, 29: 1–12.

Inger, I. and Inger, J. (1994) *Creating an Ethical Position in Family Therapy*. London: H. Karnac.

James, S. *et al.* (1996) Using reflecting teams in training psychology students in system therapy. *Journal of Systemic Therapies*, 15(4): 46–58.

Lebenbaum, P. (1996) Some thoughts on social justice, therapy and that original electrical failure. Paper presented to the Dialogue and Reflection conference, Tromsø.

McNamee, S. (1996) Out of the head and into the discourse! Therapeutic practice as relational engagement. Paper presented to the Dialogue and Reflection conference, Tromsø.

Penn, P. (1996) What are the things a therapist should know? Paper presented to the Dialogue and Reflection conference, Tromsø.

Perlesz, A., Young, J., Patterson, R. and Bridge, S. (1994) The reflecting team as a reflection of second-order therapeutic ideals. *Australian and New Zealand Journal of Family Therapy*, 15: 117–27.

Pidgeon, P. (1995) The notion of identity in social constructionist therapy. *Journal of Systemic Consultation and Management*, 6: 43–52.

Shotter, J. and Katz, A.M. (1996) 'Living moments' in dialogical exchanges. Paper presented to the Dialogue and Reflection conference, Tromsø.

Sluzki, C.E. (1992) Transformations: a blueprint for narrative changes in therapy. *Family Process*, 31: 217–30.

Research

Arsen, K., Berkowitz, R., Cooklin, A. *et al.* (1991) Family therapy outcome research: a trial for families, therapists, and researchers. *Family Process*, 30: 3–20.

Carr, A. (2000) Evidence based practice in family therapy and systemic consultation II. Adult-focused problems. *Journal of Family Therapy*, 22(3): 273–95.

Cottrell, D. (2003) Family therapy for childhood depression: researching significant moments. *Journal of Family Therapy*, 25(4): 406–16.

Denzin, N.K. and Lincoln, Y.S. (1994) *The Handbook of Qualitative Research*. Thousand Oaks, CA: Sage.

Griffith, M. (1990) Can family therapy research have a human face? *Dulwich Centre Newsletter*, 2: 11–20.

Jones, E (2003) Reflections under the lens. Observations of a systemic therapist on the experience of participation and scrutiny in a research project. *Journal of Family Therapy*, 25(4): 347–56.

Kaye, J. (1990) Towards meaningful research in psychotherapy. *Dulwich Centre Newsletter*, 2: 27–38.

McNamee, S. and Fruggeril, L. (1987) Complexity of interactive change. Conference paper presented to the Speech Communication Association.

Pote, H., Stratton, P., Cottrell, D., Shapiro, D.A. and Boston, P. (2003) Systemic family therapy can be manualized: Researcy process and findings, *Journal of Family Therapy*, 25: 236–62.

Stratton, P. (1995) Systemic interviewing and attributional analysis applied to

international broadcasting. In J. Haworth (ed.) *Psychological Research: Innovative Methods and Strategies*. London: Routledge.
Stratton, P. (2003) A theory of the psychological processes of humour, and its application to explain the processes by which systemic family therapy achieves positive outcomes. In J. Henry (ed.) *Proceedings of the First European Positive Psychology Conference*. Ceicester: BPS Books.
Street, E. (1988) Family therapy training research: systems model and review. *Journal of Family Therapy*, 10: 383–402.
Street, E. (1997) Family therapy training research: an updating review. *Journal of Family Therapy*, 19: 89–111.
Vetere, A. (1988) Family therapy research. In E. Street and W. Dryden (eds) *Family Therapy in Britain*. Milton Keynes: Open University Press.

See also Key Texts, Chapter 7.

Ritual in therapy

Friedman, E.H. (1993) Systems and ceremonies: a family view of rites and passages. In E. Carter and M. McGoldrick (eds) *The Changing Family Life Cycle*. New York: Guilford Press.
Imber-Blacke, I. (1993) Idiosyncratic life cycle transitions and therapeutic rituals. In E. Carter and M. McGoldrick (eds) *The Changing Family Life Cycle*. New York: Guilford Press.
Imber-Blacke, I. (1993) Normative and therapeutic rituals in couples therapy. In E. Carter and M. McGoldrick (eds) *The Changing Family Life Cycle*. New York: Guilford Press.
Laird, J. (1988) Women and ritual in family therapy. In E. Imber-Black, J. Roberts and R. Whiting (eds) *Rituals in Families and Family Therapy*. New York: W.W. Norton.
Roberts, J., 'Alexandra' and 'Julius' (1988) Use of ritual in 'redocumenting' psychiatric history. In E. Imber-Black, J. Roberts and R. Whiting (eds) *Rituals in Families and Family Therapy*. New York: W.W. Norton.
Whiting, R. (1988) Therapeutic rituals with families with adopted members. In E. Imber-Black, J. Roberts and R. Whiting (eds) *Rituals in Families and Family Therapy*. New York: W.W. Norton.

Schizophrenia and family therapy

Berkowitz, R. (1984) Therapeutic intervention with schizophrenic patients and their families: a description of a clinical research project. *Journal of Family Therapy*, 6: 211–23.
Berkowitz, R. (1988) Family therapy in adult mental illness: schizophrenia and depression. *Journal of Family Therapy*, 10: 339–56.
Falloon, I. and Boyd, J.L. (1984) *Family Care of Schizophrenia: A Problem Solving Approach to the Treatment of Mental Illness*. New York: Guilford Press.

Falloon, I., Krekorian, H., Shanahan, J., Laporta, M. and McLees, S. (1993) A family-based approach to adult mental disorders. *Journal of Family Therapy*, 15: 147–61.

Johnstone, L. (1993) Family therapy and adult mental illness; letter to the editor. *Journal of Family Therapy*, 15: 441–5.

Jones, E. (1987) Brief systemic work in psychiatric settings where a family member has been diagnosed as schizophrenic. *Journal of Family Therapy*, 9: 3–25.

Lieberman, S. and Gopfert, M. (1983) Clarity: the management of families of the schizophrenic syndrome. *Journal of Family Therapy*, 5: 307–20.

McDonell, M.G., Short, R.A., Berry, C.M. and Dyck, D.G. (2003) Burden in schizophrenia caregivers. Impact of family psychoeducation and awareness of patient suicidality. *Family Process*, 42(1): 91–103.

McFarlane, W.R., Dixon, L., Lukens, E. and Lucksted, A. (2003) Family psychoeducation and schizophrenia: a review of the literature. *Journal of Marital Family Therapy*, 29(2): 223–45.

Sexual abuse

Bepko, C. (1989) Life cycle. In B. Carter and M. McGoldrick (eds) *The Changing Family Cycle*. Boston, MA: Allyn & Bacon.

Dutton Con, J. (1995) Gendered thinking in a statutory agency dealing with child sexual abuse. In C. Burck and B. Speed (eds) *Gender, Power and Relationships*. London: Routledge.

Durrant, M. and White, C. (eds) (1990) *Ideas for Therapy with Sexual Abuse*. Adelaide: Dulwich Centre Publications.

Essex, S. and Gumbleton, J. (1999) 'Similar but different' conversations: working with denial in cases of severe sexual abuse. *Australian and New Zealand Journal of Family Therapy*, 20: 139–48.

Gorell Barnes, G. and Henessy, S. (1995) Reclaiming a female mind from the experience of child sexual abuse. In C. Burck and B. Speed (eds) *Gender, Power and Relationships*. London: Routledge.

Hanks, H.G.L. and Stratton, P. (2002) Family therapy for physically and sexually abusing families. In K. Browne, H. Hanks, P. Stratton and C. Hamilton (eds) *Early Prediction and Prevention of Child Abuse: A Handbook*. Chichester: Wiley.

Hudson O'Hanlon, W. (1992) History becomes her story: collaborative solution oriented therapy of the after-effects of sexual abuse. In S. McNamee and K. Gergen (eds) *Therapy as Social Construction*. London: Sage.

Special contexts

Garberi Pedros, R., Compan-Poveda, E., Sanchez-Sanchez, F., Soto-Calpe, R., Regojo-Almela, M.A. and Martinez-Ros, M.T. (1996) Referral and family therapy. A systemic analysis. *Aten Primaria* 30 June, 18(2): 70–4.

Gielen, U. and Comunian, A.L. (eds) (1998) *The Family and Family Therapy in International Perspective*. Trieste: Edizioni Lint Trieste.
Pettle, S. (1998) Thinking about the future when death is inevitable: consultations in terminal care. *Clinical Child Psychology and Psychiatry*, 3(1): 131–9.

Stepfamilies

Gorell Barnes, G. and Daniels, G. (1997) Looking back and looking forward: legacies and narratives. In *Growing Up in Stepfamilies*. Oxford: Oxford University Press.
Gorell Barnes, G. and Daniels, G. (1997) Working with stepfamilies: clinical and legal contexts. In *Growing Up in Stepfamilies*. Oxford: Oxford University Press
McGoldrick, M. and Carter, B. (1989) Forming a remarried family. In M. McGoldrick and B. Carter (eds) *The Changing Family Cycle*. Boston: Allyn & Bacon.
Miller, A.C. (1990) The mother–daughter relationship and the distortion of reality in childhood sexual abuse. In R.J. Perelberg and A. Miller (eds) *Gender and Power in Families*. London: Routledge.
National Stepfamily Association (1994) *Fact File 1*, 1 (July).
National Stepfamily Association (1995) *Annual Report*. Family Puzzles.
National Stepfamily Association (1996) *Information Bulletin*, 1 (spring/summer).
O'Reilly Byrne, N. and Colgan McCarthy, I. (1995) Abuse, risk and protection. A fifth province approach to an adolescent sexual offence. In C. Burck and B. Speed (eds) *Gender, Power and Relationships*. London: Routledge.
Visher, E.B. and Visher, J.S. (1996) *Therapy with Stepfamilies*. New York: Brunner/Mazel.

Substance misuse

Bepko, C. (1989) Life cycle. In B. Carter and M. McGoldrick (eds) *The Change in Family Life Cycle*. Boston: Allyn & Bacon.
Bepko, C. (1991) Disorders of power: women and addiction in the family. In M. McGoldrick, C.M. Anderson and F. Walsh (eds) *Women in Families: A Framework for Family Therapy*. New York: W.W. Norton.
Cullen, J. and Carr, A. (1999) Codependency: an empirical study from a systemic perspective. *Contemporary Family Therapy: An International Journal*, 21(4): 505–25.
Dale, B. and Emerson, P. (1995) The importance of being connected: implications for work with women addicted to drugs. In C. Burck and B. Speed (eds) *Gender, Power and Relationships*. London: Routledge.
McDowell, T. and York, C.D. (1992) Family alcohol use: a progression model. *Journal of Strategic and Systemic Therapies*, 11(4): 19–26.

Wolin, S.J., Bennett, L.A. and Jacobs, J.S. (1988) Assessing family rituals in alcoholic families. In E. Imber-Blacke, J. Roberts and R. Whiting (eds) *Rituals in Families and Family Therapy*. New York: W.W. Norton.

Systemic work with individuals

Burck, C. and Speed, B. (eds) (1995) *Gender, Power and Relationships*. London: Routledge.

Carpenter, J. (1987) For the good of the family. In S. Walrond-Skinner and D. Watson (eds) *Ethical Issues in Family Therapy*. London: Routledge & Kegan Paul.

Jenkins, H. and Asen, K. (1992) Family therapy without the family: a framework for systemic practice. *Journal of Family Therapy*, 14(1): 1–14.

Jones, E. (1993) Working with individuals. In E. Jones (ed.) *Family Systems Therapy: Developments in the Milan-Systemic Therapies*. Chichester: Wiley.

Kerr, M.E. (1981) Family systems theory and therapy. In A. Gurman and D. Kniskern (eds) *Handbook of Family Therapy*. New York: Brunner/Mazel.

McClusky, U. (1987) In praise of feeling: theme-focused family work. In S. Walrond-Skinner and D. Watson (eds) *Ethical Issues in Family Therapy*. London: Routledge & Kegan Paul.

McClusky, U. and Bingley Miller, L. (1985) Theme focused family work: the inner emotional world of the family. *Journal of Family Therapy*, 17: 411–35.

Nichols, W.C. and Everett, C.A. (1986) *Systemic Family Therapy: An Integrative Approach*. New York: Guilford Press.

O'Hanlon, W. and Weiner-Davis, M. (1989) *In Search of Solutions: New Direction in Psychotherapy*. New York: W.W. Norton.

Street, E. and Dryden, W. (1988) *Family Therapy in Britain*. Milton Keynes: Open University Press.

Systems theory and cybernetics

Bilson, A. (1993) Applying Bateson's theory of learning to social work education. *Social Work Education*, 12(1): 46–61.

Boscolo, L., Cecchin, G., Hoffman, L. and Penn, P. (1987) From psychoanalysis to systems. In L. Boscolo, G. Cecchin, L. Hoffman and P. Penn (eds) *Milan Systemic Family Therapy*. New York: Basic Books.

Casey, D. (2002) Therapy and ecology: viewing the natural world through systemic lenses. *Australian and New Zealand Journal of Family Therapy*, 23(3): 138–44.

de Shazer, S. (1991) The concept of system. In *Putting Difference to Work*. New York: W.W. Norton.

Guttman, H.A. (1991) Systems theory, cybernetics, and epistemology. In A. Gurman and D. Kniskern (eds) *The Handbook of Family Therapy, Vol. II*. New York: Brunner/Mazel.

Jones, E. (1993) Postscript: developments in the systemic therapies. In E. Jones (ed.) *Family Systems Therapy: Developments in the Milan-Systemic Therapies*. Chichester: Wiley.

Keeney, B. (1983) A cybernetic description of family therapy. In B. Keeney (ed.) *Aesthetics of Change*. London: Guilford Press.

Keeney, B. (1983) Cybernetic epistemology. In B. Keeney (ed.) *Aesthetics of Change*. London: Guilford Press.

Pocock, D. (1999) Loose ends. *Journal of Family Therapy*, 21(2): 187–94.

Teams

Andersen, T. (1987) The reflecting team: dialogue and meta-dialogue in clinical work. *Family Process*, 26: 415–28.

Andersen, T. (1992) Reflections on reflecting with families. In S. McNamee and K. Gergen (eds) *Therapy as Social Construction*. London: Sage.

Davis, J. and Lax, W. (1991) Introduction to JSST special section: expanding the reflecting position in family therapy. *Journal of Strategic and Systemic Therapy*, 10: 1–2.

Hoger, C., Temme, M., Reiter, L. and Steiner, E. (1994) The reflecting team approach: convergent results of two exploratory studies. *Journal of Family Therapy*, 16: 427–37.

Kingston, P. and Smith, D. (1983) Preparation for live consultation and live supervision when working without a one-way screen. *Journal of Family Therapy*, 5: 219–33.

Kingston, P. and Smith, D. (1985) Live consultation without a one-way screen. *Australian and New Zealand Journal of Family Therapy*, 6(2): 71–5.

Selvini, M. and Selvini Palazzoli, M. (1991) Team consultation: an indispensable tool for the progress of knowledge: ways of fostering and promoting its creative potential. *Journal of Family Therapy*, 13: 31–52.

Smith, T.E., Yoshioka, M. and Winton, M. (1990) A qualitative understanding of reflecting teams I: Client perspectives. *Journal of Systemic Therapies*, 12(3): 28–43.

Trauma and terrorism

Andersen, T. (2002) Blinding and deafening moments, and threatening futures: in the wake of September 11, 2001. *Family Process*, 41(1): 11–14.

Boss, P.G. (2002) Ambiguous loss: working with families of the missing. *Family Process*, 41(1): 14–17.

Catherall, D.R. (2002) The power of community. *Family Process*, 41(1): 18–20.

Fraenkel, P. (2002) The helpers and the helped: viewing the mental health profession through the lens of September 11. *Family Process*, 41(1): 20–3.

Griffith, J.L. (2002) Living with threat and uncertainty. What the Kosovars tell us. *Family Process*, 41(1): 24–7.

Walsh, F. (2002) Bouncing forward: resilience in the aftermath of September 11. *Family Process,* 41(1): 34–6.

Violence

Cecchin, G., Lane, G. and Ray, W.L. (1992) Irreverence and violence. In *Irreverence: A Strategy for Therapists' Survival.* London: H. Karnac.

Dell, P. (1989) Violence and the systemic view: the problem of power. *Family Process,* 28: 1–14.

Goldner, V. (1990) Love and violence: gender paradoxes in volatile relationships. *Family Process,* 29: 343–64.

Goldner, V. (1992) Making room for both/and. *Family Therapy Networker,* March/April: 55–61.

Walker, G. and Goldner, V. (1995) The wounded prince and the women who love him. In C. Burck and B. Speed (eds) *Gender, Power and Relationship.* London: Routledge.

Working with adolescents and families

Bryce, G. (1986) Precipitating a crisis: family therapy and adolescent school refuser. *Journal of Adolescence,* 9: 199–213.

Haley, J. (1979) *Leaving Home: Therapy of Disturbed Young People.* New York: McGraw-Hill.

Kearney, J. (1986) A time for differentiation: the use of a systems approach with adolescents in community-based agencies. *Journal of Adolescence,* 9: 243–56.

Kraemer, S. (1982) Leaving home and the adolescent family therapist. *Journal of Adolescence,* 5: 51–62.

Nock, S.L. (2000) The divorce of marriage and parenthood. *Journal of Family Therapy,* 22: 245–63.

Olson, D. (2000) Circumplex model of marital and family interaction. *Journal of Family Therapy,* 22: 144–67.

Reimers, S. (1999) 'Good morning, Sir!' 'Axe handle.' Talking at cross-purposes in family therapy. *Journal of Family Therapy,* 21: 360–76.

Sandmaier, M. (1996) More than love. *Family Therapy Networker,* May/June: 21–33.

Selekman, M. and King, S. (2001) 'It's my drug': solution-oriented brief family therapy with self-harming adolescents. *Journal of Systemic Therapies,* 20(2): 99–105.

Seligman, P. (1986) A brief family intervention with an adolescent referred for drug taking. *Journal of Adolescence,* 9: 231–42.

Shulman, S., Rosenheim, E. and Knafo, D. (1999) The interface of adolescent and parent marital expectations. *American Journal of Family Therapy,* 27(3): 213–22.

Strickland-Clark, L., Campbell, D. and Dallos, R. (2000) Children's and adolescents' view on family therapy. *Journal of Family Therapy*, 22(3): 324–41.

Taffel, R. (1996) The second family. *Family Therapy Networker*, May/June: 36–45.

Tasker, F. and McCann, D. (1999) Affirming patterns of adolescent sexual identity: the challenge. *Journal of Family Therapy*, 21: 30–54.

Vetere, M. and Henley, M. (2002) The weave of object relations and family systems thinking: working therapeutically with families and couples in a community alcohol service. In I. Safvestad-Nolan and P. Nolan (eds) *Object Relations and Integrative Psychotherapy: Tradition and Innovation in Theory and Practice*. London: Whurr

Werner, W. and Ronald, J. (2001) *Developmental-Systemic Family Therapy with Adolescents*. Binghamton, NY: Haworth Press.

Wilson, P. (1987) Psychoanalytic therapy and the young adolescent. *Bulletin: Anna Freud Centre*, 10: 51–79.

Working with children

Campbell, D., Bianco, V., Dowling, E., Goldberg, H., McNab, S. and Pentecost, D. (2003) Family therapy for childhood depression: researching significant moments. *Journal of Family Therapy*, 25(4): 417–35.

Carr, A. (2000) Evidence-based practice in family therapy and systemic consultation I: Child-focused problems. *Journal of Family Therapy*, 22(1): 29–60.

Cottrell, D. and Boston, P. (2002) The effectiveness of family therapy for children and adolescents. *Journal of Child Psychology and Psychiatry*, 43: 573–86.

Freeman, J., Epston, D. and Lobovits, D. (1997) *Playful Approaches to Serious Problems: Narrative Therapy with Children and Their Families*. New York: W.W. Norton.

Lax, W. and Lussardi, D.J. (1988) The use of rituals in families with an adolescent. In E. Imber-Black, J. Robertson and R. Whiting (eds) *Rituals in Families and Family Therapy*. New York: W.W. Norton.

Nicholson, S. (1993) Troubled children, troubled marriages – whose problem is it? *Australian and New Zealand Journal of Family Therapy*, 14(2): 75–80.

O'Connor, J.J. and Horowitz, A.N. (1988) Imitative and contagious magic in the therapeutic use of rituals with children. In E. Imber-Black, J. Robertson and R. Whiting (eds) *Rituals in Families and Family Therapy*. New York: W.W. Norton.

Reimers, S. and Street, E. (1993) Using family therapy in child and adolescent services. In A. Treacher and J. Carpenter (eds) *Using Family Therapy in the 90s*. Oxford: Blackwell.

Rober, P. (1998) Reflections on ways to create a safe therapeutic culture for children in family therapy. *Family Process*, 37: 201–13.

Scholz, M., Asen, E., Gantchev, K., Schell, B. and Suss, U. (2002) A family day clinic in child psychiatry. The Dresden model – concepts and first experiences. *Psychiatrische Praxis*, 29(3): 125–9.

Schweitzer, J. and Ochs, M. (2003) Systemic family therapy in school refusal behavior. *Praxis der Kinderpsychologie und Kinderpsychiatrie*, 52(6): 440–55.

Strickland-Clark, L., Campbell, D. and Dallos, R. (2000) Children's and adolescents' views on family therapy. *Journal of Family Therapy*, 22(3): 324–41.

Taffel, R. (1991) How to talk with kids. *Family Therapy Networker*, July/August: 39–70.

Tomm, K. (1989) Externalizing the problem and internalizing personal agency. *Journal of Strategic and Systemic Therapies*, 8(1): 54–8.

Watchell, E.F. (2001) The language of becoming: helping children change how they think about themselves. *Family Process*, 40(4): 369–84.

White, M. (1984) Pseudo-encorpresis: from avalanche to victory, from vicious to virtuous cycles. *Family Systems Medicine*, 2(2): 114–24.

Wilson, J. (1998) *Child Focused Practice: A Collaborative Systemic Approach*. London: H. Karnac.

Working with individuals

Boscolo, L. and Betrando, P. (1986) *Systemic Therapy with Individuals*. London: Karnac Books.

Hendrix, H. (1992) *Keeping the Love You Find*. New York. Simon & Schuster.

Jenkins, H. (1989) Family therapy with one person: a systemic framework for treating individuals. *Psihoterapija*, 19: 61–73.

Working with older adults

Anderson, W.T. and Hargrave, T.D. (1990) Contextual family therapy and older people: building trust in the intergenerational family. *Journal of Family Therapy*, 12: 311–21.

Benbow, S., Egan, G. and Mariotte, A. (1990) Using the family life cycle with later life families. *Journal of Family Therapy*, 12: 321–41.

Richardson, C.A., Gilleard, C.J., Lieberman, S. and Peeler, R. (1994) Working with older adults and their families – a review. *Journal of Family Therapy*, 16: 225–40.

Roper-Hall, A. (1993) Developing family therapy services with older adults. In J. Carpenter and A. Treacher (eds) *Using Family Therapy in the 90s*. Oxford: Blackwell.

Walsh, F. (1989) The family in later life. In E. Carter and M. McGoldrick (eds) *The Changing Family Life Cycle*. Boston: Allyn & Bacon.

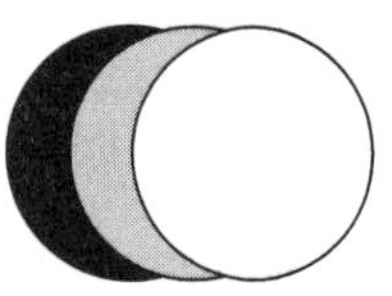

Formats for exploration

A frequent cry from therapists and trainees alike is, 'What do I say next? How can I get them to talk about X?' The formats for exploration given in this chapter represent some of the tried and tested ways we have developed in working with different, often difficult, situations. These formats are not intended to be precise blueprints or instructions to be followed; rather they are to be looked upon as signposts and markers on the territory which can provide ideas about the route for practitioners to take in different contexts, and suggestions about how to use the feedback from clients.

Format for exploration of communicational styles

The de-escalation of negative affect, not the reciprocation of positive affect (the quid pro quo hypothesis) discriminated happy from unhappy marriages in our studies.

(Gottman 1982)

The aim of this exercise is to develop skills in analysing communication and to develop a critical perspective, including an awareness of the potential subjective nature of inferences about communication.

Trainees split into two groups; one will take part in a role play in which a family is interviewed by a therapist, and the rest of the group will act as observers/supervision team, who carry out an analysis of the family's communicational styles and of the communication between therapist and family. This *external* analysis by the observers is then compared and contrasted with the *internal* (participant) observations of the participants in the role play.

Role play: Trainees offer a family scenario and people volunteer to take part in the role play. This group separates in order to enter into the family roles. A genogram summarizing the family and presenting problems is depicted.

Observers: Observers discuss: (a) the dimensions that will be employed for the communicational exercise; (b) aspects of the open-ended analysis:

1 The following dimensions are employed for the *family as a whole:*

	1	2	3	4	5	6	7	
Clear	–	–	–	–	–	–	–	Confused
Critical	–	–	–	–	–	–	–	Positive
Equal	–	–	–	–	–	–	–	Unequal
Enmeshed	–	–	–	–	–	–	–	Differentiated
Direct	–	–	–	–	–	–	–	Covert
Stable	–	–	–	–	–	–	–	Escalating
Sensitive	–	–	–	–	–	–	–	Insensitive

2 *Individual communicational styles:* relative contribution to the discussion, communicational tactics, intentions and meta-communication, attempts to clarify intentions, etc. Each observer focuses their analysis on one participant. If possible, at least one participant has more than one observer in order to be able to offer some indication of inter-rater reliability – perceived differences.

3 *Sequential analysis:* analysis of sequences of communication, especially in subgroups such as parents, mother–child, father–child, sibling subsystem. Note examples of positive and negative escalations, for example, symmetry,

mutual attacking vs praising, complementarity, one person attacking the other, validating/placating to de-escalate sequences.

4 *Language employed:* recurring phrases, metaphors, recurring words and concepts.

5 *Gender differences:* dominance, initiation, use of questions vs assertions, emotional sensitivity to each other's communications and underlying feelings and intentions, etc.

Participants: Participants also fill in the scales and consider their experience of the interaction, including categories above, while observers are carrying out the analysis.

Discussion: Observers offer their external ratings of the group as a whole on the dimensions and briefly a summary for each individual participant while participants remain in role. The feedback should not become too personally negative or attacking in any way. The participants then offer their overall ratings and impressions of the group and indicate impressions of each others' styles, intentions and tactics.

The similarities and differences between the external and internal analysis are drawn out. Implications for therapy are considered, for example family's observation of their communication on video playback, specific work with subgroups of the family to clarify communication, etc.

For notes

Format for exploring the value of the consultation process

1 In trios, each person is asked to think about a problem he or she might have in working with couples or families in his or her place of work (or in applying systemic thinking to therapeutic work with individuals).
2 Each person describes the conflicts or contradictions he or she experiences in trying to deal with this problem.
3 One person agrees to be interviewed by another and the third acts as an observer.
4 The interviewer for about 10 minutes should use circular questions to:

- identify the patterns of behaviour that have developed around the conflicts;
- formulate ideas on how this pattern maintains important relationships and beliefs in the workplace;
- explore which behaviours of the interviewee maintain this pattern.

5 After 10 minutes, the interviewer and observer talk, with the interviewee eavesdropping, and develop a hypothesis.
6 After 10 minutes, the interviewer continues asking questions to explore the hypothesis.
7 After 10 minutes, the interviewer and observer meet to decide what feedback to give to the interviewee (intervention).
8 The interviewer offers the feedback to the interviewee and invites the interviewee to give some feedback to interviewer and observer to discuss the process of the exercise and, in particular, to address the question of what difference the consultation has made to their thinking about the problem.
9 Each member of the trio is then asked to comment on their learning about consultation as a result of the exercise.

For notes

Format for exploration of balance of power in relationships

Create a simulation with a couple, one or two therapists and an observing team.

1 *Explore decision-making*:

- How are decisions made?
- Who usually makes the decisions, has the final say?
- Areas of expertise – do they have responsibilities for decisions in different areas?
- How were these specializations decided?
- Are these specializations common, gender stereotyped, etc.?
- How are differences/disagreements dealt with, resolved?

2 *Explore influence tactics*: How does each partner influence the other? What tactics are used? Examples include: threats, flattery, involving others, negotiation, crying, bribery, withdrawing, promises, reasoning.

3 *Explore power bases*: Explore what resources each partner has in order to exert influence, remembering there are:

- *objective power bases* – power that is relatively independent of the relationship: money, physical strength, education, property, technical skills, etc.; and
- *subjective power bases* – power that is tied into the relationship and exists as long as the relationship exists: attractiveness to the other, fulfilling the other's needs, reassurance, company, sexual attraction to each other, interest in the other, care of the home, care of children.

4 *Summarize for each partner*:

	Her	*Him*
Power bases		
Influence tactics		

5 *Discussion*:

- Who has more power and/or influence and why? What are the effects on the relationship?
- What are the culture, gender and gender inequalities, common problems posed for couples?
- What are the changes over the life cycle of their relationship? Was the relationship better/worse when power was more/less equal?
- How would the relationships change if the distribution were different?
- As a couple, how can they try to resist societal/cultural bases of gender inequalities?

6 *Feedback from the observing team.*

Format for exploring co-therapy issues

- Who is in charge? Is there a professional hierarchy to be acknowledged, such as consultant and social worker?
- How do you agree or disagree on what to do in a session?
- Do you share and/or respect one another's beliefs about how change occurs for clients?
- Can you disagree in the session with co-therapist?

Ground rules: Make a contract with your co-therapist.

Therapist 1 Therapist 2

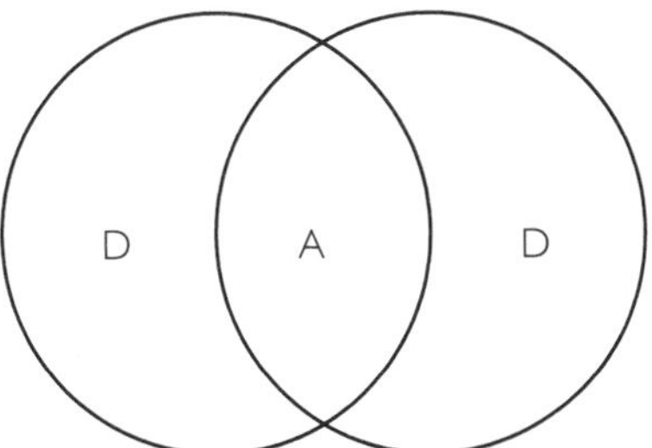

A = Area of agreement D = Area of disagreement

These areas need to be explicit at the outset of working together.
Before: Discuss and agree on strategies and themes to explore.
After: Review and plan for next time, responses to families and feedback.

Co-therapy will be uncomfortable for therapists and family if A and D are not stated.

Advantages of co-therapy:

- good for beginning therapists and students;
- therapist can operate an observer/participant model;
- good with very needy families where there is very early deprivation;
- can be good with single-parent families;
- good for demonstrating to families how to communicate clearly and openly;
- therapists support one another in challenging system, promoting ideas for change and responding to resistance in system to change.

Disadvantages of co-therapy

- more time-consuming for professionals in the long run;
- can inhibit development of individual style;
- can induce dependency.

Format for exploration of communication

The aim of this exercise is to enable a pair to become aware of how their communicational styles may be constructing unhelpful circularities or escalating sequences. The pair are asked to role-play a couple, a parent and a child, two friends, client and therapist, and be interviewed by a third person.

A typical problematic communication sequence or episode is identified. The interviewer tracks the circularity and asks the pair to enact the sequence.

- The interviewer asks A: 'What is it about the way B communicates that is difficult?'
- A demonstrates.
- The interviewer asks A: 'How does that feel? How could B could do it differently so that you felt better?'
- A demonstrates.
- The interviewer asks B: 'Could you try that?'
- B discusses, negotiates.
- A and B rerun the sequence.
- B tries new style.
- The interviewer asks A: 'Did that feel better? How? Why?'

Then go through the same sequence again, with the interviewer beginning by questioning B.

Finally, the interviewer asks both: 'Do you think you might be able to try that? What might get in the way?'

For notes

Format for exploration of the life cycle of a couple's relationship: plotting the development of the relationship

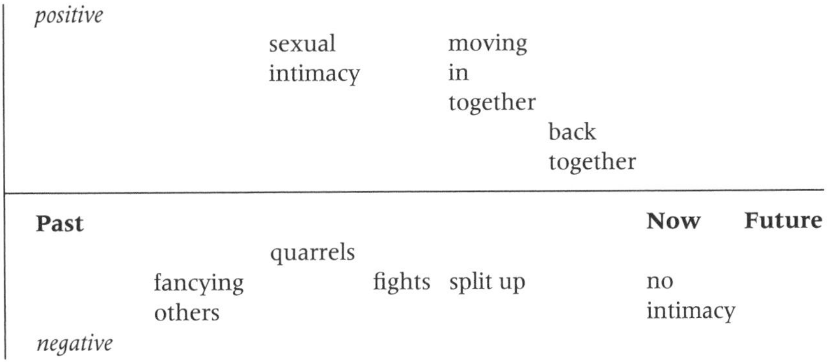

positive

sexual intimacy

moving in together

back together

Past **Now** **Future**

quarrels

fancying others

fights

split up

no intimacy

negative

Couple's relationship

- Plot what the couple regard as key positive and negative events so far in their history and stories.
- Discuss agreements and disagreements.
- Explore explanations for these events.
- Discuss initial expectations and beliefs and how these have shaped their relationship.
- What were their initial perceptions of each other?
- How might their relationship have developed differently – positively and negatively?
- What are their expectations of the future? What might stay the same, what may change?
- How do they think the history of their relationship constrains or frees up possibilities?

For notes

Format for exploring couple relationships

What brings you here today?
(Aspects of Loss and Separation)
Consequences of script

Past

Two people making one whole: individual strengths	*What was the script?* *What did parents and grandparents think of you getting together?* *How do you want to rewrite the script?*	Your dreams and hopes What needs are not being met? Disappointments What are your responses to disappointment and failure?

Present

What do you have to do to become as determined to succeed at the relationship as you are not to yield to more hurt/=[??]make yourself vulnerable again	*Rewrite the script*	What keeps you together? What stops you: (a)getting closer? (b)separating? What hurts now? Can you imagine recovering? Process of change How would you like to be able to be together?

Future

	Developing a story you like	Monitor and rebuild Develop and observe relationship Rules for feedback *Two separate people creating relationship* *Managing, accepting and enjoying difference*

For notes

Format for an exploration with disappointed clients

Often clients come to us having already been to one or many other agencies and are full of complaints, or clients return to us after one or two sessions, saying: 'Yes, but you haven't fixed Johnny/Lucy and that's what we wanted'. This format offers the practitioner ideas about what should be covered in a session and suggests questions to ask along the way.

What	*How*
Acknowledge the possibility of a fresh start in therapy. What would you like us to be able to do? What else has been tried? What do we need to talk about for this not to be a waste of your time? What do you think has been useful for this family, what has not been useful? We wanted you to fix Lucy/Johnny. We need to negotiate and/or clarify what you want from us. Let us renegotiate our contract. Identify differences. Note differences that are problems and those differences that are not.	How would you like us to listen to you? What would you like us to be able to do? What else has been tried? What do you think has been useful for this family, what has not been useful? How would you like us to listen to you? How will we know if we are listening as well or worse than . . .? What difference would you like us to make here? I want to get clear in my mind what is important to you. What do we need to talk about for this not to be a waste of your time? Let's ask Lucy/Johnny their views and what they want. May we? Are there any connections/links between what everyone is saying and what clients would like to be different? Do these ideas/wishes seem like a good basis for our work today? We have talked, in our first session, about working together on X. Is that no longer important or relevant? When we met last time we agreed to work on X. Do we need to change that now/today or agree something different for today? If *we* were able to work together on X what would change look like *or* what would *we* be able to do? *How would these changes show in relationships in your family?* Are there other changes in relationships you would like to look forward to?

Format for a couple exploring beliefs and expectations using a family tree

First plot the couple's genogram with each partner's parents, siblings and relationships. Then explore constructs/beliefs through the genogram:

- Who is most or least like each partner?
- Which relationship is most or least like the couple? In what ways?
- How have these relationships evolved and changed?
- What explanations do the couple have for the causes of these changes?
- How have other couples resolved/managed problems?
- How does the couple think their parents (or other significant relationships in the genogram) have influenced their relationship?
- What have the couple tried to incorporate or copy from their parents' (or other) relationships, or tried to avoid or reject?
- What social, cultural or historical factors may have influenced the relationships?

For notes

Format for developing observational skills

When watching a practitioner at work, consider the following questions as you observe:

1 What theory do you see the practitioner using?
2 What skills do you see the practitioner using?
3 What ideas do you have about the practitioner's use of herself/himself?
4 When the practitioner gets stuck, how does s/he deal with that?
5 What theory does s/he use when s/he gets stuck?
6 Why do you think the consultant phones through and why at that time?
7 What aspects are making you tense and why do you think this is the case?

For notes

Format for developing reflective practice

Useful questions to ask yourself when monitoring your behaviour as a practitioner:

A What are you doing (when with clients)? That is, an explanation for what you are doing in relation to how you hope what you are doing will make a difference.
B What is the feedback you are getting to A?
C How do you use the feedback?
D What are you learning from A, B and C?

For notes

Format for exploration for a first session

As we have said, formats offer guidelines for practitioners. Here the *what* column identifies areas of work for a first session or meeting, while the *how* column suggests questions for practitioners in accomplishing this piece of work.

What	*How*
1 Introduce the setting, team and how we work.	What brought you here? Who else is involved?
2 Track the history of referral (see below).	Who referred the client (attendance of referrer preferred). What other agencies are involved? What has helped/not helped in past?
3 Assessment of whether referral is appropriate. Can the team offer anything?	
4 Exploration of family members' expectations, why the family has come. Identify areas of work with the family and agree to start work *or* agree not to work.	Other family members/friends with views/ideas about the problem and for us to be helpful what would we have to do/what would have to happen between us for coming here to be useful?
5 History of problem • When did it begin? • How does it show? • For whom is it a problem?	

History of referral

Which agencies? Map network.
What is the client's significant relationship system?
What is the client's definition of the problem?
Interest clients in how we are thinking about what they are telling us.
Redefine the problem.
Contract/engagement with client.
Clarifying expectations with respect to change/realistic goals. What has it been like talking with us?
Agree on next appointment and agenda.

Format for exploration of the ending of therapy

People often ask us how to end therapy. A simple format is offered here based on the idea of a review session, which can be the last session or happen by arrangement with clients several weeks or up to six months after the last appointment. The aim of this review session is to enable clients to take positions from which they can comment on the process of therapy, their learning and change.

What	*How*
Create a context for a conversation about therapy.	Looking back, what has happened for you as a family since we began meeting? How have our meetings been as you expected and/or different?
Enable clients to review the experience of being in therapy.	What has happened to the concerns/worries that brought you to therapy? Are there any ways in which you are different together as a family since we began working together?
Enable clients to give feedback to therapist and one another.	For my own learning [therapist says] what would you like me to know about what went well and what I could have done differently in our sessions?
Clarify with clients that they feel they know how to monitor their relationships and access help when necessary.	Are you able to talk with one another about how things are between you and say if anyone feels uncomfortable? If relationships ever became very strained again or symptoms appeared, what would you want to do for one another?

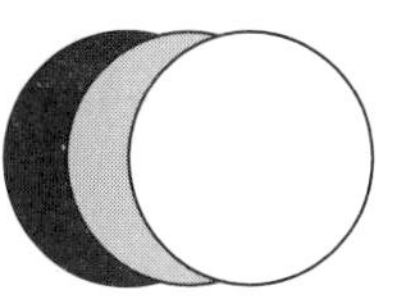

Glossary of terms

analogic: a non-verbal means of communicating, using physical movements and expressive bodily actions, including speech tone and volume variations. There is often a close equivalence between the content of what is being communicated and the choice of these means. For example, irritation might be expressed by a clipped intonation, the lips compressed without a smile.

circularity: the situation where what happens is in some way determined by some precursor event and has also had some effect on that first event, where it is not possible to determine 'which came first, the chicken or the egg'. This way of viewing the world grew out of biology and ecology. It is consistent with a *linear conception* if the latter is seen as treating just one small segment of a larger interrelated whole.

circular questioning: questions asked with the intention of revealing differences between people who are members of some system. The questioner expects that the answer will help them to refine their *working hypothesis* (see below) and so to become interested in asking a further question based on feedback from their respondent. It is this process between the questioner and the respondent, driven by feedback, which changes the respondent's perspective on their situation and stimulates new thinking.

co-construction: a form of interaction between two individuals or groups where neither prejudges the form that the output of their interaction will take, but each puts forward their respective contributions, confident that the result will be more effective than a similar effort being made by either of them alone (see also *hermeneutic*).

complementarity: a form of relationship where two people or groups, although differing in characteristics or attributes, find that they can fit together in achieving a shared goal, either by accepting reciprocity (as in a hierarchical, one-up-one-down fit), or by the periodic and accepted reversal or alteration of their relative position.

cybernetics: derived from the Greek word meaning 'to steer'. Cybernetics is the science of systems which are capable of self-direction and guidance by the ability to alter their activity on the basis of information returning feedback about the results of previous action. Cybernetics has led to the development of so-called 'intelligent' systems.

discourse: conveys the important idea (after Wittgenstein) that our concepts, the basis of our thinking, are expressed by words, which are located in language. We use these to engage *in action* with others to accomplish practical, ceremonial, and communicative activities. We can talk therefore of the *speech-act* as central to our interactions with others. This constitutes a form of life or reality in which a person can be seen as a meeting point of many discourses, for example, a *discursive* subject.

double-bind: a form of contradictory communication seen (Bateson *et al.* 1956) to be causal in the development of schizophrenia and other disturbances. The central aspects are contradictory communication in different modalities (e.g. saying 'I love you' with a tense and angry bodily posture) and an overarching injunction that the incongruity is not to be discussed and that the participants must not attempt to leave the relationship.

ecology of ideas: the collection of individuals' beliefs – usually implicit or unconscious – that, by their interconnectedness and mutual relevance, underpin a social system.

epistemology: the study of how we think and arrive at decisions, how we explain how we know what we know. A system of ideas or connected beliefs about how we view and explain the world, cf. George Kelly's (1955) notion of a 'construct system'.

equifinality: a law of system relationships which holds that the same eventual goal can be reached from differing starting points and by differing intervening processes/steps.

expressed emotion: a set of factors relating to the emotional tone in family life – critical remarks, emotional overinvolvement and general warmth or coldness. High expressed emotion – extreme criticisms, coldness and overinvolvement – in families is seen to increase the chances of relapse of members recovering from mental illness.

feedback: information about the results or consequences of a previous action returning or looping back into a system in order to regulate subsequent action. The connection can be positive feedback, which increases the initial behaviour emitted leading to escalation, or negative feedback, leading to a reduction of the divergence from some stable setting or equilibrium.

first-order cybernetics: this is the view that biological and social systems can be seen as self-regulating systems analogous to mechanical systems. It is argued that families can be objectively described in terms of how they function and maintain balance states or homeostasis.

hermeneutic: interpretative (as of texts), but used also to refer to the process by which meaning and understanding are recognized as evolving in dialogue between people.

instructive interaction: an episode between people where the intent and belief of one person is that the knowledge or beliefs that they hold can be transmitted to the other so that they will end up being able to use such knowledge or beliefs in precisely the way intended by the 'instructor'. This form of 'teaching' contrasts with experiential learning types of interaction, where the objective of one person is to facilitate the development of the other's capacity for gaining new insights.

linear thinking: the established view of causation derived from classical science that one event, A, directly causes another event, B, to occur. In relation to family life it would be a view that one member can directly cause another to do, say, think or feel something. Similarly, ideas about internal dispositions such as personality can be employed to offer linear explanations (e.g. that Jane complains at Robin because she has a 'controlling' personality).

meta-: (as in 'taking up a meta-position') taking a view of an issue from a different, usually higher, level, for example, metaphysics.

mind-maps: the internalized sense of the connectedness of experiences that an individual has built up through interactions with others that gives security in making decisions about action or in making sense of new experiences.

modernism: the belief that it is possible, by objective and 'scientific' research, to arrive at general, universally applicable explanations of 'how things work', at theories and quantifiable 'models' of phenomena that can be used to predict and control events, from the way plants grow to the way people behave (see also *universal solutions*).

modernity: the *paradigmatic* position in which reality is held to exist independent of the observer, and where objectivity in the study and description of another person, group, or phenomenon is held to be possible.

multiple realities: the perspective that results when reality is viewed as being created by social interaction, so that, in principle, 'there are as many universes as there are willing describers' (Watzlawick 1984).

negative connotation: the opposite of *positive connotation* (see below) where the explanation for a situation emphasizes a harmful or destructive effect or intent.

neutrality: a stance maintained by a therapist or professional, showing equal and non-judgemental interest in the beliefs and explanations of each family member. This reflects in constructionist thinking the awareness of *multiple realities* (see above). The stance alone can lead to a significant shift in behaviour among system members who have only been used to privileging one construction of a situation in their attempts to solve a problem.

paradigm: a widely shared way of viewing and explaining 'how things work around here' for a given community that is largely unspoken and resistant to challenge (see also *mind-maps*).

positive connotation/frame: form of *reframing* (see below) in which behaviour or situations that are experienced negatively by clients are explained in ways that suggest a positive intention for the system as a whole in the behaviours of the other people or groups associated with the problem (see also *negative connotation*).

positivism: (as in 'logical positivism') a point of view that puts forward scientific observations as the only basis for assessing 'truth', and that considers arguments not based on observable data as meaningless (see also *modernism*).

praxis: most simply translated as personal theory-in-action or the practical living out of one's central ideas, conditioned by a *hermeneutic* (see above) approach to understanding and developing this form of knowledge.

progressive hypothesizing: devised by the Milan team, this is an approach which is a microcosm of the scientific method – testing and revision of hypotheses based on experimentation and gathering of new data. It involves the formulation of an initial working hypothesis about the relationship between the symptom/s and the family dynamics. This is seen as propositional and subjected to continual review and revision.

psychodynamic: the practice of psychotherapy, based on the theories of Freud, where the benefit for the client is held to derive from the giving of 'insights' by the therapist, and the use of this insight by the client to come to different understandings of relationships, including those cases where what happens between the therapist and the client is interpreted by the therapist as repeating a pattern between the client and some significant person in their past.

punctuation: the act of choosing the point of view from which one will explain a complex set of interrelated events, as in describing to a listener the reasons for a bad relationship by starting with the actions of one of the parties.

reductionism: the belief in a method for understanding how complex systems work by breaking their operation down into small subprocesses, each of which is affected by relatively few major variables, making the measurements and prediction of outcomes more manageable.

reflexivity: where some action, statement, or question 'turns back on itself' and leads to some change in the state of the initiating system component. Used, for example, in the context of 'reflexive questions' where a professional, by asking a particular question that refers to concepts or meanings held by the client system, intends to influence the clients to reorganize their understanding of those concepts in such a way that the issue is seen in a different light.

reframing: putting forward an alternative explanation about a situation clients perceive as problematic so the situation ceases to be viewed as problematic.

Rogerian: a form of psychotherapy developed by Carl Rogers, where the chief benefit is held to derive from the therapist showing unconditional positive regard for the client, and which encourages the free expression of feelings associated with the problem incidents and relationships.

second-order cybernetics: the view that a 'system' invariably involves an act of observation. Hence there can be no objective system as such, but the system is an 'as if' construction. In family therapy the analysis moves to looking not just at the family dynamics but also the nature of the interactions between the family and the therapist.

strategic therapy: where the therapist negotiates goals with the family and then devises tasks for the family members to perform, in the process making it difficult for them to continue with what have been diagnosed as 'non-normal' behaviours. It may also help the family to achieve a transition in its evolution which had previously been blocked.

structure-determined change: derived from biology, this view proposes that the form that change takes in a system is determined by the laid-down structures of that system. In the case of human social systems, the change is linked to the prevailing beliefs and sense of context that each person has arrived at as a result of their earlier social interactions, and which are used by the individual or group as a basis for deciding on action in response to perturbations of their system.

structural therapy: where the problems experienced by a family or other system are held to be related to some deficiency in structuring their relationships (such as unclear or absent intergenerational or role boundaries). The therapist/consultant acts as a member of the system in an interaction to block or disrupt what are seen as unhelpful interactions, so that by experiencing themselves in a more 'normal' relationship with others, people behave differently, and the problem they previously experienced disappears.

symmetrical: (as in 'symmetrical relationship') where people interact with each other in similar ways, usually unconscious, that lead them to mirror each other's actions, leading to escalating interchanges in which each attempts to reassert advantage over the other or even to compete for who is most 'ill' or in need.

systemic hypothesis: the ideas that professionals draw together and which connect the behaviour of all the members of the system, recognizing their particular views of the context and providing an explanation for the presence of the symptom.

triangulation: a process in which two people who are in conflict attempt to recruit a third person on to their side against the other (e.g. parents attempting to entice a child into taking their side or a couple attempting to draw a therapist into taking sides).

universal solutions: ideas put forward that are held to provide a generally applicable answer to a frequently occurring problem, or a means of approaching a particular task which, if followed, will always lead to successful accomplishment. These ideas derive typically from a modernist and positivist epistemology.

working hypothesis: the ideas that a professional draws together from initial contacts with the problem system concerning what may lie behind the difficulties being presented. These ideas are meant to guide the consultant's initial explanation or research and to surface more information about distinctions held by members of the problem system. With this new information, the consultant revises the hypothesis or forms a new one, to continue the process until the professional/s can articulate a *systemic hypothesis* (see above).

British texts

We list here key British texts that have appeared in the three developmental phases we have identified. We mention only books published by British authors and not journal articles or journals. *The Journal of Family Therapy,* however, deserves mention as a journal that is currently rated by readers worldwide as one of the most popular. Where we have omitted to mention authors and/or publications, we acknowledge here the impossibility of being totally inclusive and ask for the forbearance of any authors we have accidentally omitted to mention.

Phase I: 1950s to mid-1970s

Balint, M. (1957) *The Doctor, His Patient, and the Illness.* London: Pitman.

Laing, R.D. and Esterson, A. (1964) *Sanity, Madness and the Family.* London: Tavistock.

Howell, J.G. (1968) *Theory and Practice of Family Psychiatry.* London: Oliver and Boyd.

Laing, R.D. (1970) *Knots.* New York: Randolph House.

Phase II: mid-1970s to mid-1980s

Skynner, R. (1976) *One Flesh: Separate Persons: Principles of Family and Marital Psychotherapy.* London: Constable.

Lieberman, S. (1978) *Transgenerational Family Therapy.* London: Croom Helm.

Waldrond-Skinner, S. (ed.) (1979) *Family and Marital Psychotherapy: A Critical Approach.* London: Routledge & Kegan Paul.

Waldrond-Skinner, S. (ed.) (1981) *Developments in Family Therapy: Theories and Applications since 1948*. London: Routledge & Kegan Paul.

Bentovim, A., Gorell-Barnes, G. and Cooklin, A. (eds) (1982) *Family Therapy. Complementary Frameworks of Theory and Practice*, Vol. 1. London: Academic Press for the Institute of Family Therapy.

Bentovim, A., Gorell-Barnes, G. and Cooklin, A. (eds) (1982) *Family Therapy. Complementary Frameworks of Theory and Practice*, Vol. 2. London: Academic Press for the Institute of Family Therapy.

Whiffen, R. and Byng-Hall, J. (eds) (1982) *Family Therapy Supervision: Recent Developments in Practice*. London: Academic Press; New York: Grune and Stratton.

Campbell, D., Reder, P., Draper, R. and Pollord, D. (1983) *Working with the Milan Method: Twenty Questions*. London: Institute of Family Therapy. (Occasional papers on family therapy No. 1.)

Treacher, A. and Carpenter, J. (eds) (1984) *Using Family Therapy: A Guide for Practitioners in Different Professional Settings*. Oxford: Basil Blackwell.

Phase III: mid-1980s to 2000

Campbell, D. and Draper, R. (eds) (1985) *Applications of Systemic Family Therapy*. London: Academic Press.

Campion, J. (1985) *The Child in Context: Family-Systems Theory in Educational Psychology*. London: Metheun.

Dowling, E. and Osborne, E. (eds) (1985) *The Family and the School: A Joint Systems Approach to Problems with Children*. London: Routledge & Kegan Paul.

Hospital for Sick Children, London (1985) *Focal Family Therapy and Related Papers 1978–1985*. London: Hospital for Sick Children.

Will, D. and Wrote, R.M. (1985) *Integrated Family Therapy. A Problem-centred Psychodynamic Approach*. London: Tavistock Publications.

Barker, P. (1986) *Basic Family Therapy* (2nd edn). London: Collins.

Kennedy, R., Heymans, A. and Tischler, L. (eds) (1987) *The Family as In-patient: Working with Families and Adolescents at the Cassel Hospital*. London: Free Association Books.

Waldrond-Skinner, S. and Watson, D. (eds) (1987) *Ethical Issues in Family Therapy*. London: Routledge & Kegan Paul.

Burnham, J.B. (1986) *Family Therapy: First Steps Towards a Systemic Approach*. London: Routledge.

Falloon, I.R.H. (ed.) (1988) *Handbook of Behavioural Family Therapy*. London: Routledge.

Street, E. and Dryden, W. (eds) (1988) *Family Therapy in Britain*. Milton Keynes: Open University Press.

Campbell, D., Draper, R. and Huffington, C. (1989) *Second Thoughts on The Theory and Practice of the Milan Approach to Family Therapy*. London: DC Associates.

Perelberg, R.J. and Miller, A.C. (eds) (1990) *Gender and Power in Families*. London: Routledge.

Robinson, M. (1991) *Family Transformation During Divorce and Remarriage. A Systemic Approach*. London: Routledge.

Draper, R., Gower, M. and Huffington, C. (1992) *Teaching Family Therapy*. London: H. Karnac.

Asen, K.E. and Tomson, P. (1992) *Family Solutions in Family Practice*. Lancaster: Quay Books.

Bentovim, A. (1992) *Trauma-Organized Systems: Physical and Sexual Abuse in Families* (revised edition). London: H. Karnac.

Bor, G. and Miller, R. (1992) *Internal Consultation in Health Care Settings*. London: H. Karnac.

Campbell, D., Draper, R. and Huffington, C. (1992) *A Systemic Approach to Consultation*. London: H. Karnac.

Campbell, D., Draper, R. and Huffington, C. (1992) *Second Thoughts on the Theory and Practice of the Milan Approach to Family Therapy*. London: H. Karnac.

Campbell, D., Draper, R. and Huffington, C. (1992) *Teaching Systemic Thinking*. London: H. Karnac.

Draper, R., Gower, M. and Huffington, C. (1992) *Teaching Family Therapy*. London: H. Karnac.

Fruggeri, L. *et al.* (1992) *New Systemic Ideas from the Italian Mental Health Movement*. London: H. Karnac.

Inger, I. and Inger, J. (1992) *Co-Constructing Therapeutic Conversations: A Consultation of Restraint*. London: H. Karnac.

Jones, E. (1992) *Working with Adult Survivors of Child Sexual Abuse*. London: H. Karnac.

Mason, B. (1992) *Handing Over Developing Consistency Across Shifts in Residential and Health Settings*. London: H. Karnac.

Hoffman, L. (1993) *Exchanging Voices: A Collaborative Approach to Family Therapy*. London: H. Karnac.

Jones, E. (1993) *Family Systems Therapy: Developments in the Milan Systemic Therapies*. Chichester: John Wiley.

Carpenter, J. and Treacher, A. (eds) (1993) *Using Family Therapy in the Nineties*. Oxford: Blackwell.

Cecchin, G., Lane, G. and Ray, W. (1993) *Irreverence: A Strategy for Therapists' Survival*. London: H. Karnac.

Keeney, B.P. and Ray, W.A. (1993) *Resource Focused Therapy*. London: H. Karnac.

Smith, G. (1993) *Systemic Approaches to Training in Child Protection*. London: H. Karnac.

Campbell, D., Coldicott, T. and Kinsella, K. (1994) *Systemic Work with Organisations: A New Model for Managers and Change Agents*. London: H. Karnac.

Cecchin, G., Lane, G. and Ray, W. (1994) *The Cybernetics of Prejudices in the Practice of Psychotherapy*. London: H. Karnac.

Huffington, C. and Brunning, H. (1994) *Internal Consultancy in the Public Sector: Case Studies*. London: H. Karnac.

Inger, I. and Inger, J. (1994) *Creating an Ethical Position in Family Therapy*. London: H. Karnac.

McCaughan, N. and Palmer, B. (1994) *Systems Thinking for Harassed Managers*. London: H. Karnac.

Reimers, S. and Treacher, A. (1994) *Introducing User-friendly Family Therapy*. London: Routledge.
Asen, E. (1995) *Family Therapy for Everyone: How to Get the Best Out of Living Together*. London: BBC Books.
Burck, C. and Daniel, G. (1995) *Gender and Family Therapy*. London: H. Karnac.
Burck, C. and Speed, B. (eds) (1995) *Gender, Power and Relationships*. London: Routledge.
Byng-Hall, J. (1995) *Rewriting Family Scripts: Improvisation and Systems Change*. London: Guilford Press.
Campbell, D. (1995) *Learning Consultation: A Systemic Framework*. London: H. Karnac.
Farmer, C. (1995) *Psychodrama and Systemic Therapy*. London: H. Karnac.
Boscolo, L. and Bertrando, P. (1996) *Systemic Therapy with Individuals*. London: H. Karnac.
Flaskas, C. and Perlesz, A. (eds) (1996) *The Therapeutic Relationship in Systemic Therapy*. London: H. Karnac.
Altschuler, J. with Dale, B. and Byng-Hall, J. (1997) *Working with Chronic Illness: A Family Approach*. Basingstoke: Macmillan Press.
Dallos, R. (1997) *Interacting Stories: Narratives, Family Beliefs and Therapy*. London: H. Karnac.
Fredman, G. (1997) *Death Talk: Conversations with Children and Families*. London: H. Karnac.
Papadopoulos, R. and Byng-Hall, J. (eds) (1997) *Multiple Voices: Narratives in Systemic Family Psychotherapy*. London: Duckworth.
Robinson, M. (1997) *Divorce as Family Transition: When Private Sorrow Becomes a Public Matter*. London: H. Karnac.
Wilson, J. (1998) *Child-focused Practice. A Collaborative Systemic Approach*. London: H. Karnac.
Hildebrand, J. (1998) *Bridging the Gap: A Training Module in Personal and Professional Development*. London: H. Karnac.
Barker, P. (1999) *Basic Family Therapy* (3rd edn). Oxford: Blackwell.

Additional British texts for second edition: 2000–2004

Byng-Hall, J. and Papadopoulos, R. (eds) (1997) *Multiple Voices: Narratives in Systemic Family Therapy*. London: Duckworth; New York: Routledge.
Carr, A. (1997) *Family Therapy and Systemic Practice*: Lanham, MD: University Press of America.
Dallos, R. (1997) *Interacting Stories: Narratives, Family Beliefs and Therapy*. London: H. Karnac.
Gorrell Barnes, G. and Daniels, G. (1997) *Working with Stepfamilies: Clinical and Legal Contexts. Growing Up in Stepfamilies*. Oxford: Oxford University Press.
Roper-Hall, A. (1997) Working systematically with older families who have 'come to grief'. In P. Sutcliffe *et al.* (eds) *Systemic Approaches to Therapeutic Work*. Basingstoke: Macmillan.

Barker, P. (1998) *Basic Family Therapy*. Oxford: Blackwell Science.

Gorrell Barnes, G. (1998) *Family Therapy in Changing Times*. London: Macmillan.

Gorrell Barnes, G., Thompson, P., Daniel, G. and Burchardt, N. (1998) *Growing Up in Step Families*. Oxford: Clarendon.

Krause, I.B. (1998) *Therapy Across Culture*. London: Sage Publications.

Wilson, J. (1998) *Child Focused Practice: A Collaborative Systemic Approach*. London: H. Karnac.

Cooklin, A. (1999) *Changing Organizations: Clinicians as Agents of Change*. London: H. Karnac.

Barnes, G.G., Down, G. and McCann, D. (2000) *Systemic Supervision: A Portable Guide for Supervision Training*. London: Jessica Kingsley.

Carr, A. (2000) *Family Therapy: Concepts, Process and Practice*. Chichester: John Wiley & Sons.

Dallos, R. and Draper, R. (2000) *An Introduction to Family Therapy*. Buckingham: Open University Press.

Dowling, E. and Gorrell Barnes, G. (2000) *Working with Children and Parents through Separation and Divorce*. London: Macmillan.

Gorrell Barnes, G., Down, G. and McCann, D. (2000) *Systemic Supervision: A Portable Guide for Supervision Training*. London: Jessica Kingsley.

Jones, E. and Asen, E. (2000) *Systemic Couple Therapy and Depression*. London: H. Karnac.

Littlejohn, S.W. and Domenici, K. (2000) *Engaging Communication in Conflict: Systemic Practice*. London: Sage.

Asen, E. (2001) *Multiple Family Therapy: The Marlborough Model and its Wider Social Implications*. London: H. Karnac.

Buchanan, A. (2001) *Families in Conflict – Perspectives of Children and Parents on the Family Court Welfare Service*. Cambridge: Polity Press.

Byng-Hall, J. and Papadopoulos, R. (eds) (2002) *Multiple Voices: Narratives in Systemic Family Therapy*. London: H. Karnac.

Campbell, D. and Mason, B. (eds) (2002) *Perspectives on Supervision*. London: H. Karnac.

Kissane, D.W. and Bloch, S. (2002) *Family-Focussed Grief Therapy: A Model of Family-Centred Care During Palliative Care and Bereavement*. Buckingham: Open University Press.

Krause, I.B. (2002) *Culture and System in Family Therapy*. London: H. Karnac.

Mason, B. and Sawyer, A. (eds) (2002) *Exploring the Unsaid: Creativity, Risks and Dilemmas in Working Cross-Culturally*. London: H. Karnac.

McCann, D. (2002) Lesbians, gay men, their families and therapy. In A. Coyle and E. Kitzinger (eds) *Lesbian and Gay Psychology: New Perspectives*. Oxford: Blackwell.

Asen, E., Young, V., Tomson, D. and Tomson, P. (2003) *Ten Minutes for the Family*. London: Routledge.

Johnsen, A. (2004) *Self in Relationships: Perspectives on Family Therapy from Developmental Psychology*. London: H. Karnac.

References

Abbey, C. and Dallos, R. (2004) The experience of the impact of divorce on sibling relationships. *Clinical Child Psychology and Psychiatry*, 4(4): 241–59.

Abu-Lughood, L. and Lutz, C.A. (1990) Introduction: emotion, discourse and the politics of everyday life. In C.A. Lutz and L. Abu-Lughood (eds) *Studies in Emotion and Social Interaction*. Cambridge: Cambridge University Press.

Ainsworth, M.D.S., Blehar, R.M.C., Waters, E. and Wall, S. (1978) *Patterns of Attachment: A Psychological Study of the Strange Situation*. Hillside, NJ: Erlbaum.

Alexander, J. and Parsons, B. (1973) Short-term behavioural interventions with delinquent families: impact on family processes and recidivism. *Journal of Abnormal Psychology*, 81: 219–50.

American Psychiatric Association (1980) *Diagnostic and Statistical Manual of Mental Disorders*, 3rd edn. Washington, DC: American Psychiatric Association.

Andersen, T. (1987) The reflecting team: dialogue and meta-dialogue in clinical work. *Family Process*, 26: 415–28.

Andersen, T. (ed.) (1990) *The Reflecting Team*. New York: W.W. Norton.

Anderson, H. (2001) Postmodern collaborative and person-centred therapies: what would Carl Rogers say? *Journal of Family Therapy*, 23(4): 339–61.

Anderson, H. and Goolishian, H.A. (1988) Human systems as linguistic systems: preliminary and evolving ideas about the implications for clinical theory. *Family Process*, 27: 371–93.

Anderson, H. and Goolishian, H. (1992) The client as expert: a not-knowing approach to therapy. In S. McNamee and K. Gergen (eds) *Therapy as Social Construction*. London: Sage.

Anderson, H., Goolishian, H.A. and Windermand, L. (1986) Problem determined systems: toward transformation in family therapy. *Journal of Strategic and Family Therapy*, 4: 1–13.

Arnow, B., Taylor, C., Agras, W. and Telch, M. (1985) Enhancing agoraphobia treatment outcome by changing couple communication. *Behaviour Therapy*, 16: 452–67.

Asen, E. (2004) Collaborating in promiscuous swamps – the systemic practitioner as context chameleon? *Journal of Family Therapy*, 26(3): 280–5.

Barclay, R., Guevremont, D., Anastopoulos, A. and Fletcher, K. (1992) A comparison of three family therapy programs for treating family conflicts in adolescents. *Journal of Consulting and Clinical Psychology*, 60: 450–62.

Barlow, D., O'Brien, G. and Last, C. (1984) Couples treatment of agoraphobia. *Behaviour Therapy*, 15: 41–58.

Barret, P., Dadds, M. and Rappee, R. (1996) Family treatment of childhood anxiety: a controlled trial. *Journal of Consulting and Clinical Psychology*, 64: 333–42.

Bateson, G. (1958) *Naven*, 2nd edn. Stanford, CA: Stanford University Press.

Bateson, G. (1972) *Steps to an Ecology of Mind: Mind and Nature*. New York: Ballantine Books.

Bateson, G. (1980) *Mind and Nature: A Necessary Unity*. London: Fontana/Collins.

Bateson, G., Jackson, D.D., Haley, J. and Weakland, J.H. (1956) Towards a theory of schizophrenia, *Behavioural Science*, 1(4): 251–64.

Baucom, D., Shoham, V., Mueser, K., Daiuto, A. and Stickle, T. (1998) Empirically supported couple and family intervention for marital distress and adult mental health problems. *Journal of Consulting and Clinical Psychology*, 66: 53–88.

Beck, A.T. (1967) *Depression: Clinical, Experiential and Theoretical Aspects*. New York: Harper & Row.

Bell, J. (1961) *Family Group Therapy*, Public Health Monograph No. 64. Washington, DC: US Government Printing Office.

Bennum, I. and Lucas, R. (1990) Using the partner in the psychosocial treatment of schizophrenia: a multiple single case design. *British Journal of Clinical Psychology*, 29: 185–92.

Berg, I.M. (1991) *Family Preservation: A Brief Therapy Workbook*. London: BT Press.

Bergin, A.E. and Garfield, S.L. (eds) (1994) *Handbook of Psychotherapy and Behaviour Change* (4th edn). New York: Wiley.

Berkowitz, R. (1987) Rating expressed emotion from initial family therapy sessions (a pilot study). *Journal of Family Therapy*, 9: 27–37.

Bion, W.R. (1961) *Experience in Groups*. New York: Basic Books.

Bion, W.R. (1970) *Attention and Interpretation*. London: Tavistock.

Black, D. and Urbanovicz, M. (1987) Family intervention with bereaved children. *Journal of Child Psychology and Psychiatry*, 28: 467–76.

Blood, R.V. and Wolfe, D.M. (1960) *Husbands and Wives: The Dynamics of Married Living*. New York: Free Press.

Blow, K. and Daniel, G. (2002) Frozen narratives? Post-divorce processes and contact disputes. *Journal of Family Therapy*, 24(1): 85–104.

Bordin, E. (1979) The generalizability of the psychoanalytic concept of the working alliance. *Psychotherapy, Theory, Research and Practice*, 16: 252–60.

Boscolo, L. and Bertrando, M. (1996) *Systemic Therapy with Individuals*. London: Karnac Books.

Bowen, M. (1971) The use of family theory in clinical practice. In J. Haley (ed.) *Changing Families: A Family Therapy Reader*. London: Grune and Stratton.

Bowlby, J. (1969) *Attachment and Loss, Vol. 1*. London: Hogarth Press.

Bowlby, J. (1973) *Attachment and Loss, Vol. 2: Separation, Anxiety and Anger*. London: Hogarth Press.

Boyle, M. (1990) *Schizophrenia: A Scientific Delusion?* London: Routledge.

Brent, D., Holder, D. and Kolko, D. (1997) A clinical psychotherapy trial for adolescent depression comparing cognitive, family and supportive treatments. *Archives of General Psychiatry*, 54: 877–85.

Brewin, C.R. (1988) *Cognitive Foundations of Clinical Psychology*. London: Lawrence Erlbaum Associates.

Brunk, M., Hengeller, S. and Whelan, J. (1987) Comparisons of multisystemic therapy and parent training in the brief treatment of child abuse and neglect. *Journal of Consulting and Clinical Psychology*, 55: 171–8.

Burbach, F. and Stanbridge, R.I. (1998) A family intervention in psychosis service integrating the systemic and family management approaches. *Journal of Family Therapy*, 20(3): 311–25.

Byng-Hall, J. (1985) The family script: a useful bridge between theory and practice. *Journal of Family Therapy*, 7: 301–7.

Byng-Hall, J. (1995) Creating a secure base: some implications of attachment theory for family therapy. *Family Process*, 34: 45–58.

Byng-Hall, J. (1998) Evolving ideas about narrative: re-editing the re-editing of family mythology. *Journal of Family Therapy*: 20(2): 133–43.

Cannon, W. (1932) *The Wisdom of the Body*. New York: W.W. Norton.

Carr, A. (2000a) Evidence-based practice in family therapy and systemic consultation. *Journal of Family Therapy*, 22(1): 29–60.

Carr, A. (2000b) Evidence-based practice in family therapy and systemic consultation II. *Journal of Family Therapy*, 22(3): 273–96.

Carter, E. and McGoldrick, M. (1980) *The Family Life Cycle: A Framework for Family Therapy*. New York: Gardner Press.

Cassidy, J. and Shaver, P.R. (eds) (1999) *Handbook of Attachment: Theory, Research and Clinical Application*. London: Guilford Press.

Cecchin, G. (1987) Hypothesising, circularity and neutrality revisited: an invitation to curiosity. *Family Process*, 26(4): 405–14.

Chamberlain, P. and Rosicky, J. (1995) The effectiveness of family therapy in the treatment of adolescents with conduct disorders and delinquency. *Journal of Marital and Family Therapy*, 21: 441–59.

Cooley, C.H. (1922) *Human Nature and the Social Order* (revised edn). New York: Scribner's.

Crittenden, P.M. (1998) Dangerous behaviour and dangerous contexts: a thirty-five year perspective on research on the developmental effects of child physical abuse. In P. Trickett (ed.) *Violence to Children* (pp. 11–38). Washington, DC: American Psychological Association.

Dadds, K., Schwartz, S. and Sanders, M. (1987) Marital discord and treatment outcome in behavioural treatment of child conduct disorders. *Journal of Consulting and Clinical Psychology*, 55: 396–403.

Dallos, R. (1991) *Family Belief Systems, Therapy and Change*. Buckingham: Open University Press.

Dallos, R. (1997) *Interacting Stories, Narratives, Family Beliefs and Therapy*. London: H. Karnac.

Dallos, R. (2004) Attachment narrative therapy: integrating ideas from narrative and attachment theory in systemic therapy with eating disorders. *Journal of Family Therapy*, 26(1): 40–66.

Dallos, S. and Dallos, R. (1997) *Couples, Sex and Power: The Politics of Desire*. Buckingham: Open University Press.

Dallos, R. and Draper, R. (2000) *An Introduction to Family Therapy: Systemic Theory and Practice*, 1st edn. Buckingham: Open University Press.

Dallos, R. and Procter, H. (1984) Family processes. In *D307 Social Psychology*. Milton Keynes: Open University.

Dallos, R. and Urry, A. (1999) Abandoning our parents and grandparents: does social construction mean the end of systemic therapy? *Journal of Family Therapy*, 21(2): 161–86.

Dallos, R., Neale, A. and Strouthos, M. (1997) Pathways to problems – the evolution of 'pathology'. *Journal of Family Therapy*, 19: 369–401.

Dare, C., Eisler, I., Russell, G.F.M. and Szmukler, G.I. (1990) The clinical and theoretical impact of a controlled trial of family therapy in anorexia nervosa. *Journal of Marital and Family Therapy*, 16(1): 39–57.

de Shazer, S. (1982) *Patterns of Brief Therapy: An Ecosystemic Approach*. New York: Guilford Press.

Dell, P.F. (1982) Beyond homeostasis: toward a concept of coherence. *Family Process*, 21: 21–41.

Doane, J. (1978) Family interaction and communication deviance in disturbed and normal families. *Family Process*, 17: 357–76.

Doane, J.A., West, K.L., Goldstein, M., Rodnick, E.H. and Jones, J.E. (1981) Parental communication deviance and affective style. *Archives of General Psychiatry*, 38: 679–85.

Doane, J.A., Falloon, I.R., Goldstein, M.J. and Mintz, J. (1985) Parental affective style and the treatment of schizophrenia. *Archives of General Psychiatry*, 42: 34–42.

Doane, J.M., Goldstein, M.J., Falloon, I.R.H. and Doane, J.A. (1984) Interactional correlates of expressed emotion in families of schizophrenics. *British Journal of Psychiatry*, 144: 482–7.

Dunn, R. and Schwebel, A. (1995) A meta-analytic review of marital therapy outcome research. *Journal of Family Psychology*, 9: 58–68.

Duvall, E. (1977) *Marriage and Family Development*. Philadelphia: Lippincott.

Edwards, D. and Middleton, D. (1988) Conversational remembering and family relations: how children learn to remember. *Journal of Social and Personal Relations*, 5: 3–25.

Eels, T.D. (1997) *Handbook of Psychotherapy Case Formulation*. New York: Guilford Press.

Eiser, I. (2002) Comment. *Journal of Family Therapy*, 24(2): 125–34.

Eiser, I., Dare, C., Hodes, M., Russel, G.F.M., Dodge, E. and LeGrange, D. (2000) Family therapy for adolescent anorexia nervosa: the results of a controlled comparison of two family interventions. *Journal of Child Psychology and Psychiatry*, 41: 727–36.

Fadden, G. (1998) Research update: psycho-educational family interventions. *Journal of Family Therapy*, 20: 293–309.

Feeney, J.A. (1999) Adult romantic attachments and couple relationship. In J. Cassidy and P.R. Shaver (eds) *Handbook of Attachment: Theory, Research and Clinical Application*. London: Guilford Press.

Ferreira, A.J. (1963) Family myths and homeostasis. *Archives of General Psychiatry*, 9: 457–63.

Flaskas, C. (2002) *Family Therapy beyond Postmodernism: Practice Challenges Theory*. Hove: Brunner-Routledge.

Fonagy, P., Steele, M., Moran, G.S. and Higgit, A.C. (1993) Measuring the ghost in the nursery: an empirical study of the relations between parents' mental representations of childhood experiences and their infants' security attachment. *Journal of the American Psychoanalytic Association*, 41: 957–89.

Fonagy, P., Steele, M., Steele, H., Higgit, A. and Target, M. (1994) The Emanuel Miller memorial lecture 1992: the theory and practice of resilience. *Journal of Child Psychiatry*, 35: 231–57.

Foreman, S. and Dallos, R. (1992) Inequalities of power and sexual problems. *Journal of Family Therapy*, 14: 349–71.

Foucault, M. (1975) *The Archeology of Knowledge*. London: Tavistock.

Foucault, M. (1979) *The History of Sexuality*, Vol. 1. London: Allen Lane.

Freeman, J., Epston, D. and Lobovits, D. (1997) *Playful Approaches to Serious Problems: Narrative Therapy with Children and Their Families*. New York: W.W. Norton.

Freud, S. (1958) Three essays on the theory of sexuality. In *The Standard Edition of the Complete Psychological Works of Sigmund Freud* (Vol. 7, pp. 124–245). London: Hogarth Press.

Frosh, S., Burck, C., Strickland-Clark, L. and Morgam, K. (1996) Engaging with change: a process study of family therapy. *Journal of Family Therapy*, 18: 141–61.

Gergen, K.J. (1985) The social constructionist movement in modern psychology. *American Psychologist*, 40: 266–75.

Glaser, B.G. and Strauss, A.L. (1967) *The Discovery of Grounded Theory*. Chicago: Aldine.

Goffman, E. (1971) *Asylums*. Harmondsworth: Penguin.

Goldner, V. (1991) Sex, power and gender: a feminist analysis of the politics of passion. *Journal of Feminist Family Therapy*, 3: 63–83.

Goldner, V., Penn, P., Sheinberg, M. and Walker, G. (1990) Love and violence: paradoxes of volatile attachments. *Family Process*, 29.

Goldstein, M. and Miklowitz, D. (1995) The effectiveness of psycho-educational family therapy in the treatment of schizophrenia disorders. *Journal of Family Therapy*, 17: 263–80.

Gordon, D., Arbuthnot, J., Gustafson, K. and McGreen, P. (1998) Home-based behavioral systems family therapy with disadvantaged delinquents. *American Journal of Family Therapy*, 16: 243–55.

Gottman, J.M. (1982) Emotional responsiveness in marital conversation. *Journal of Communication*, summer: 108–20.

Gurman, A.S. and Kniskern, D.P. (1978) Research on marital and family therapy: progress, perspectives and prospects. In S.L. Garfield and A.E. Bergin (eds) *Handbook of Psychotherapy and Behaviour Change: An Empirical Analysis*, 2nd edn. New York: John Wiley.

Gustafsson, O., Kjellman, N. and Cederbald, M. (1986) Family therapy in the treatment of severe childhood asthma. *Journal of Psychosomatic Research*, 30: 369–74.

Haley, J. (1962) Whither family therapy? *Family Process*, 1: 69–100.

Haley, J. (1963) *Strategies of Psychotherapy*. New York: Grune and Stratton.

Haley, J. (1966) Towards a theory of pathological systems. In G.N. Zuk and I. Boszormenyi-Nagy (eds) *Family Therapy and Disturbed Families*. Palo Alto, CA: Science and Behavior Books.

Haley, J. (ed.) (1971) *Changing Families: A Family Therapy Reader*. New York: Grune and Stratton.

Haley, J. (1973) *Uncommon Therapy: Psychiatric Techniques of Milton H. Erickson, M.D.* New York: W.W. Norton.

Haley, J. (1976a) *Problem Solving Therapy*. San Francisco: Jossey-Bass.

Haley, J. (1976b) Development of a theory: a history of a research project. In C.E. Sluzki and D.C. Ransom (eds) *Double Bind: The Foundation of the Communicational Approach to the Family*. New York: Grune and Stratton.

Haley, J. (1987) *Problem Solving Therapy*, 2nd edn. San Francisco: Jossey-Bass.

Hall, J. (1978) Gender effects in decoding non-verbal cues. *Psychological Bulletin*, 85: 845–75.

Hare-Mustin, R.T. (1991) Sex, lies and headaches: the problem is power. *Journal of Feminist Family Therapy*, 3: 39–61.

Harlow, H. and Harlow, M.K. (1962) Social deprivation in monkeys. *Scientific American*, 207: 136–44.

Harvey, J.H., Orbuch, T.L. and Weber, A.L. (eds) (1992) *Attributions, Accounts and Close Relationships*. London: Springer-Verlag.

Hazan, C. and Shaver, P.R. (1987) Romantic love conceptualized as an attachment process. *Journal of Personality and Social Psychology*, 52: 511–24.

Hazelrigg, M.D., Cooper, H.M. and Borduin, C.M. (1987) Evaluating the effectiveness of family therapies: an integrative review and analysis. *Psychological Bulletin*, 101: 428–42.

Hendrix, H. and Hunt, H.L. (1998) *Giving the Love that Heals*. New York: Simon & Schuster.

Hengeller, S. (1997) The development of effective drugs services for youth. In J. Egerston, D. Fox and A. Leshner (eds) *Treating Drug Abusers Effectively*. New York: Blackwell.

Hengeller, S., Birduin, C., Melton, G., Mann, B., Smith, L., Hall, J., Cone, L. and Fucci, B. (1991) The effects of multi-systemic therapy on drug use and abuse in serious juvenile offenders: a programme report from two outcome studies. *Family Dynamic Addiction Quarterly*, 1: 40–51.

Hesse-Biber, S. and Williamson, J. (1984) Resource theory and power in families: life cycle considerations. *Family Process*, 23(2): 261–70.

Hirst, W. and Manier, D. (1990) Remembering as communication: a family recounts its past. In D. Middleton and D. Edwards (eds) *Collective Remembering*. London: Sage.

Hoffman, L. (1976) Breaking the homeostatic cycle. In P. Guerin (ed.) *Family Therapy: Theory and Practice*. New York: Gardner Press.

Hoffman, L. (1993) *Exchanging Voices: A Collaborative Approach to Family Therapy*. London: H. Karnac.

Hollway, W. (1989) *Subjectivity and Method in Psychology*. London: Sage.

Homans, G. (1961) *Social Behaviour: Its Elementary Forms*. New York: Harcourt Brace Jovanovich.

Horvath, A. and Symonds, B. (1991) Relations between working alliance and outcome in psychotherapy. *Journal of Counselling Psychology*, 38: 139–49.

Ialongo, N., Horn, W., Pascoe, J., Greenberg, G., Packard, T., Lopez, M., Wagner, A. and Puttler, L. (1993) The effects of multi-model intervention with attention-deficit hyperactive disorder children: a 9 month follow-up. *Journal of the American Academy of Child and Adolescent Psychiatry*, 32: 182–9.

Jackson, D. (1957) The question of family homeostasis. *Psychiatry Quarterly Supplement*, 31: 79–99.

Jackson, D. (1965a) The study of the family. *Family Process*, 4: 1–20.

Jackson, D. (1965b) Family rules: marital quid pro quo. *Archives of General Psychiatry*, 12: 589–94.

Jackson, S.W. (1985) Acedia the sin and its relationship to sorrow and melancholia. In A. Kleinman and B. Good (eds) *Culture and Depression: Studies in the Anthropology and Cross-cultural Psychiatry of Affect and Disorder*. Berkeley: University of California Press.

Jacoby, R. (1975) *Social Amnesia: A Critique of Conformist Psychology from Adler to Jung*. Boston: Beacon Press.

James, K. and McIntyre, D. (1983) The reproduction of families: the social role of family therapy? *Journal of Marital and Family Therapy*, 9(2): 119–29.

Johnson, S. (1998) Listening to the music: emotion as a natural part of systems theory. *Journal of Systemic Therapies*, 17(2): 1–17.

Johnstone, L. (1993) Are we allowed to disagree? *Forum*, 56: 31–4.

Jones, E. and Asen, E. (2000) *Systemic Couple Therapy and Depression*. London: Karnac Books.

Kantor, D. and Lehr, W. (1975) *Inside the Family*. San Francisco: Jossey-Bass.

Keeney, B. (1983) *Aesthetics of Change*. New York: Guilford Press.

Kelly, G.A. (1955) *The Psychology of Personal Constructs*, Vols 1 and 2. New York: W.W. Norton.

Kolko, D.J., Brent, D.A., Baugher, M., Bridge, J. and Birmaher, B. (2000) Cognitive and family therapies for adolescent depression: treatment specificity, mediation, and moderation. *Journal of Consulting and Clinical Psychology*, 68: 603–14.

Korzybski, A. (1942) *Science and Sanity: An Introduction to Non-Aristotelian Systems and General Semantics*. Lancaster, PA: Science Books.

Kraemer, S. (1997) What narrative? In R.K. Papadopoulos and J. Byng-Hall (eds) *Multiple Voices*. London: Duckworth.

Kuhn, T. (1970) *The History of Scientific Revolutions*. Chicago: Chicago University Press.

Laing, R.D. (1966) *The Politics of the Family and Other Essays*. London: Tavistock.

La Rossa, R. (1986) *Becoming a Parent*. Beverly Hills, CA: Sage.

Lask, B. and Matthews, D. (1979) Childhood asthma: a controlled trial of family psychotherapy. *Archives of Diseases in Childhood*, 55: 116–19.

Larner, G. (2000) Towards a common ground in psychoanalysis and family therapy: on knowing not to know. *Journal of Family Therapy*, 22(1): 61–83.

Leff, J., Berkowitz, R., Shavit, N. *et al.* (1989) A trial of family therapy versus a relatives' group for schizophrenics. *British Journal of Psychiatry*, 154: 58–66.

Leff, J. and Vaughn, C. (1985) *Expressed Emotions in Families: Its Significance for Mental Illness*. New York: Guilford Press.

Leff, J., Vearnal, S., Brewin, C.R., Wilff, G., Alexander, B., Asen, E., Dayson, D., Jones, E., Chisholm, D. and Everitt, B. (2000) The London Depression Intervention Trial: randomized control trial of antidepressants vs couples therapy in the treatment and maintenance of people with depression living with a partner: clinical outcome and costs. *British Journal of Psychiatry*, 177: 95–100.

Leff, J., Alexander, B., Asen, E., Brewin, C.R., Dayson, D., Vearnals, S. and Wolff, G. (2003) Modes of action of family interventions in depression and schizophrenia: the same or different? *Journal of Family Therapy*, 25(4): 357–71.

Leiper, R. (2001) *Working through Setback in Psychotherapy*. London: Sage.

Lidz, T., Cornelison, A.R., Fleck, S. and Terry, D. (1957) The intrafamilial environment of schizophrenic patients: II. Marital schism and marital skew. *American Journal of Psychiatry*, 114: 241–8.

Luborsky, L. (1984) *Principles of Psychoanalytic Psychotherapy. A Manual for Supportive-Expressive Treatment*. New York: Basic Books.

Lutz, C.A. (1990) Engendered emotion: gender, power and the rhetoric of emotional control in American discourse. In C.A. Lutz and L. Abu-Lughood (eds) *Studies in Emotion and Social Interaction*. Cambridge: Cambridge University Press.

Madanes, C. (1981) *Strategic Family Therapy*. San Francisco: Jossey-Bass.

Main, K., Kaplan, N. and Cassidy, J. (1985) Security in infancy, childhood, and adulthood: a move to the level of representation. In I. Bretherton and E. Water (eds) *Monographs of the Society for Research and Child Development*, Serial No. 209.50: Nos 1–2. Chicago: University of Chicago Press.

Main, M. (ed.) (1993) *A Typology of Human Attachment Organization Assessed in Discourse, Drawings and Interviews*. New York: Cambridge University Press.

March, J. and Mulle, K. (1998) *OCD in Children and Adolescents: A Cognitive-Behavioral Treatment Manual*. New York: Guilford Press.

March, J., Mulle, K. and Herbel, B. (1994) Behavioural psychotherapy for children and adolescents with OCD: an open trial of a new protocol-driven treatment package. *Journal of the American Academy of Child and Adolescent Psychiatry*, 33: 333–41.

Markus, E., Lange, A. and Pettigrew, T. (1990) Effectiveness of family therapy: a meta-analysis. *Journal of Family Therapy*, 12: 205–21.

Marx, K. and Engels, F. (1970) *The German Ideology*, ed. C.J. Arthur. New York: International Publishers (first published 1846).

Mason, B. (1993) Towards positions of safe uncertainty. *Human Systems: The Journal of Systemic Consultation and Management*, 4: 189–200.

Maturana, H. (1978) Biology of language: the epistemology of reality. In G.A. Miler and E. Lennerberg (eds) *Psychology and Biology of Language and Thought*. New York: Academic Press.

Maturana, H. and Varela, F.J. (1980) *Autopoiesis and Cognition: The Realization of the Living*. Dordrecht: D. Reidel.

McFarlane, W.R., Lukens, E., Link, B., Dushay, R., Deakins, S.A., Newmark, M., Dunne, E.J., Horen, B. and Toran, J. (1995) Multiple-family therapy and psychoeducation in the treatment of schizophrenia. *Archives of General Psychiatry*, 52: 679–87.

McKinnon, L. and Miller, D. (1987) The new epistemology and the Milan approach: feminist and socio-political considerations. *Journal of Marital and Family Therapy*, 13: 139–55.

Mead, G.H. (1934) *Mind, Self and Society*. Chicago: University of Chicago Press.

Mendelsohn, M. and Napier, A. (1972) The book of family therapy. In A. Ferber, M. Mendelsohn and A. Napier (eds) *The Book of Family Therapy*. New York: Science House.

Miller, W. and Rollnick, S. (1991) *Motivational Interviewing: Preparing People to Change Addictive Behaviour*. New York: Guilford Press.

Minuchin, S. (1967) *Families of the Slums: An Exploration of Their Structure and Treatment*. New York: Basic Books.

Minuchin, S. (1974) *Families and Family Therapy*. Cambridge, MA: Harvard University Press.

Minuchin, S., Montalvo, B., Guerney, B.G. Jr., Rosman, B.L. and Schumer, F. (1967) *Families of the Slums: An Exploration of their Structure and Treatment.* New York: Basic Books.

Minuchin, S., Rosman, B. and Baker, L. (1978) *Psychosomatic Families: Anorexia Nervosa in Context.* Cambridge, MA: Harvard University Press.

Morawetz, A. (1984) The single-parent family: an author's reflections. *Family Process,* 23(4): 571–7.

Muncie, J., Wetherell, M., Dallos, R. and Cochrane, A. (eds) (1997) *Understanding the Family.* London: Sage.

National Institute for Clinical Excellence (2001) *The Guideline Development Process: Information for National Collaborating Centres and Guideline Development Groups.* London: NICE.

Nicol, A., Smith, J. and Kay, B. (1988) A focused casework approach to the treatment of child abuse: a controlled comparison. *Journal of Child Psychology and Psychiatry,* 29: 703–11.

Olson, D.H. (1989) Circumplex model of family systems VIII: Family assessment and intervention. In D.H. Olson, C.S. Russel and D.H. Sprenkle (eds) *Circumplex Model: Systematic Assessment and Treatment of Families.* New York: Haworth Press.

Olson, D.H., Sprenkle, D.H. and Russel, C.S. (1979) Circumplex model of marital family interaction. *Family Process,* 18: 3–28.

Olson, D.H., Russel, C.S. and Sprenkle, D.H. (eds) (1989) *Circumplex Model: Systematic Assessment and Treatment of Families.* New York: Haworth Press.

Palazzoli, M.S., Cecchin, G., Prata, G. and Boscolo, L. (1978) *Paradox and Counter Paradox: A New Model in the Therapy of the Family in Schizophrenic Transaction.* New York: Jason Aronson.

Palazzoli, M.S., Boscolo, L., Cecchin, G. and Prata, G. (1980) Hypothesizing – circularity – neutrality: three guidelines for the conductor of the session. *Family Process,* 19(1): 3–12.

Palazzoli, M.S., Cirillo, S., Selvini, M. and Sorrentino, A.M. (1989) *Family Games: General Models of Psychotic Processes in the Family.* London: H Karnac.

Papadopoulos, R. and Byng-Hall, J. (1997) *Multiple Voices: Narrative in Systemic Family Psychotherapy.* London: Duckworth.

Papp, P. (1980) The Greek chorus and other techniques of paradoxical therapy. *Family Process,* 19: 45–57.

Papp, P. and Imber-Black, E. (1996) Family themes: transmission and transformation. *Family Process,* 35: 5–20.

Pare, D.A. (1995) Of families and other cultures: the shifting paradigm of family therapy. *Family Process,* 33: 217–31.

Pearce, W.B. and Cronen, V.E. (1980) *Communication, Action and Meaning.* New York: Praeger.

Penn, P. and Frankfurt, M. (1994) Creating a participant text: writing, multiple voices, narrative multiplicity. *Family Process,* 33(3): 217–31.

Perelberg, R.J. and Miller, A. (1990) *Gender and Power in Families.* London: Tavistock Routledge.

Piaget, J. (1955) *The Child's Construction of Reality.* London: Routledge & Kegan Paul.

Pinsof, W.M. (1988) Strategies for the study of family therapy process. In L.C. Wynne (ed.) *The State of the Art in Family Therapy Research.* New York: Family Process Press.

Pinsof, W.M. and Catherall, D.R. (1986) The integrative psychotherapy alliance: family, couple and individual therapy scales. *Journal of Marital and Family Therapy*, 12: 132–51.

Pistole, M.C. (1994) Adult attachment styles: some thoughts on closeness–distance struggles. *Family Process*, 33: 147–59.

Pollner, M. and Wikler, L. (1985) The social construction of unreality. *Family Process*, 24(2): 241–59.

Popper, K.R. (1962) *Conjectures and Refutation*. New York: Basic Books.

Potter, J. and Wetherell, M. (1987) *Discourse Social Psychology: Beyond Attitudes and Behaviour*. London: Sage.

Prochaska, J. and DiClemente, C. (1992) Stages of change in the modification of problem behaviours. In M. Herson, R.M. Eisler and P.M. Miller (eds), *Progress in Behaviour*. Sycamore, IL: Sycamore Press.

Procter, H.G. (1981) Family construct psychology. In S. Walrond-Skinner (ed.) *Family Therapy and Approaches*. London: Routledge & Kegan Paul.

Procter, H.G. (1985) A construct approach to family therapy and systems intervention. In E. Button (ed.) *Personal Construct Theory and Mental Health*. Beckenham: Croom Helm.

Procter, H.G. (1996) The family construct system. In D.C. Kalekin-Fishman and B.M. Walker (eds) *The Construction of Group Realities: Culture, Society and Personal Construct Theory*. London: Krieger.

Quinn, W.H., Dotson, D. and Jordan, K. (1997) Dimensions of therapeutic alliance and their associations with outcome in family therapy. *Psychotherapy Research*, 7: 429–38.

Rachman, S.J. and Wilson, G.T. (1980) *The Effects of Psychological Therapy*. Oxford: Pergamon Press.

Ray, W.A. (2004) Interaction focused therapy: the Don Jackson legacy. *Brief Strategic & Systemic European Review*, No. 1: 36–44.

Reiss, D. (1988) Theoretical versus tactical inferences: or, how to do family research without dying of boredom. In L.C. Wynne (ed.) *The State of the Art in Family Therapy Research*. New York: Family Process Press.

Robin, A., Siegel, P. and Moye, A. (1995) Family versus individual therapy for anorexia: impact of family conflict. *International Journal of Eating Disorders*, 17: 313–22.

Robinson, M. (1993) *Family Transformation through Divorce and Remarriage: A Systemic Approach*. London: Routledge.

Rogers, A. and Pilgrim, D. (1997) The contribution of lay knowledge to the understanding and promotion of mental health. *Journal of Mental Health*, 6: 23–35.

Sanders, M., Shepherd, R., Cleghorn, G. and Woodford, H. (1994) The treatment of recurrent abdominal pain in children: a controlled comparison of cognitive behavioural family intervention and standard paediatric care. *Journal of Consulting and Clinical Psychology*, 62: 306–14.

Schachter, S. and Singer, J.E. (1962) Cognitive, social and physiological determinants of emotional state. *Psychology Review*, 69: 379–99.

Serketich, E.W. and Dumas, J.E. (1996) The effectiveness of behavioural parent training to modify antisocial behaviour in children: a meta-analysis. *Behaviour Therapy*, 27: 171–86.

Shadish, W.R., Ragsdale, K., Glaser, R.R. and Montgomery, L.M. (1995) The efficacy and effectiveness of marital and family therapy: a perspective from meta-analysis. *Journal of Marital and Family Therapy*, 21: 345–60.

Shimanoff, S. (1983) The role of gender in linguistic reference to emotive states. *Communication Quarterly*, 30: 174–9.

Silver, E., Williams, A., Worthington, F. and Philips, N. (1998) Family therapy and soiling: an audit of externalising and other approaches. *Journal of Family Therapy*, 20: 413–22.

Simon, R. (1992) *One on One: Interviews with the Shapers of Family Therapy*. New York: Guilford Press.

Simpson, L. (1990) The comparative efficacy of Milan family therapy for disturbed children and their families. *Journal of Family Therapy*, 13: 267–84.

Slade, P. (1982) Towards a functional analysis of anorexia nervosa and bulimia nervosa. *British Journal of Clinical Psychology*, 21: 167–79.

Speed, B. (2004) All aboard in the NHS: collaborating with colleagues who use different approaches. *Journal of Family Therapy*, 26(3): 260–80.

Sprenkle, D.H. and Moon, S.M. (1996) *Research Methods in Family Therapy*. London: Guildford Press.

Stanton, M.D. and Shadish, W.R. (1997) Outcome, attrition, and family-couples treatment for drug abuse: a meta-analysis and review of the controlled, comparative studies. *Psychological Bulletin*, 122: 170–91.

Stith, S.M., Rosen, K.H., McCollum, E.E., Coleman, J.U. and Herman, S.A. (1996) The voices of children: preadolescent children's experiences in family therapy. *Journal of Marital and Family Therapy*, 22: 69–86.

Urry, A. (1990) Towards a feminist practice in family therapy: premisses. In R.J. Perelberg and A. Miller (eds) *Gender and Power in Families*. London: Routledge.

Vaughn, C.E. and Leff, J.P. (1985) The influence of family and social factors on the course of psychiatric illness. *British Journal of Psychiatry*, 15: 157–65.

Vetere, A. and Dallos, R. (2003) *Working Systemically with Families: Formulation, Intervention and Evaluation*. London: Karnac.

Vetere, A. and Gale, T. (1987) *Ecological Studies of Family Life*. Chichester: John Wiley.

Vetere, A. and Henley, M. (2001) Integrating couples and family therapy into a community alcohol service: a pantheoretical approach. *Journal of Family Therapy*, 23(1): 85–102.

Vivian-Byrne, S.E. (2001) What am I doing here? Safety, certainty and expertise in a secure unit. *Journal of Family Therapy*, 23(1): 102–17.

von Bertalanffy, L. (1968) *General Systems Theory: Foundation, Development, Application*. New York: Brazillier.

von Foerster, H. and Zopf, G.W. (eds) (1962) *Principles of Self-Organization*. New York: Pergamon.

Vostanis, P., Burnham, J. and Harris, W. (1992) Changes of expressed emotion in systemic family therapy. *Journal of Family Therapy*, 14: 15–27.

Waldron, H.B. (1996) Adolescent substance abuse and family therapy outcome: a review of randomized trials. *Advances in Clinical Child Psychology*, 19: 199–234.

Walsh, F. (1996) The concept of family resilience: crisis and challenge. *Family Process*, 35: 261–81.

Watts, A.W. (1961) *Psychotherapy East and West*. Harmondsworth: Penguin.

Watzlawick, P. (1978) *The Language of Change*. New York: Basic Books.

Watzlawick, P. (1984) *The Invented Reality*. New York: W.W. Norton.
Watzlawick, P., Beavin, J. and Jackson, D.D. (1967) *Pragmatics of Human Communication*. New York: W.W. Norton.
Watzlawick, P., Weakland, J.H. and Fisch, R. (1974) *Change: Principles of Problem Formation and Problem Resolution*. New York: W.W. Norton.
Weakland, J. (1962) Family therapy as a research arena. *Family Process*, 1: 63–8.
Weakland, J. (1976) Toward a theory of schizophrenia. In C.E. Sluzki and D.D. Ransom (eds) *Double Bind: The Foundation of the Communicational Approach to the Family*. New York: Grune and Stratton.
Weakland, J., Fisch, R., Watzlawick, P. and Bodin, A.M. (1974) *Brief Therapy: Focused Problem Resolution*. New York: W.W. Norton.
Webster-Stratton, C. and Hammond, M. (1997) Treating children with early onset conduct disorders: a comparison of child and parent training interventions. *Journal of Consulting and Clinical Psychology*, 65: 93–109.
Weiner, N. (1961) *Cybernetics*. Cambridge, MA: MIT Press.
Weiner, N. (1967) *The Human Use of Human Beings: Cybernetics and Society*, 2nd edn. New York: Avon.
White, M. (1995) *Re-authoring Lives: Interviews and Essays*. Adelaide: Dulwich Centre Publications.
White, M. and Epston, D. (1990) *Narrative Means to Therapeutic Ends*. New York: W.W. Norton.
Williams, J. and Watson, G. (1988) Sexual inequality, family life and family therapy. In E. Street and W. Dryden (eds) *Family Therapy in Britain*. Milton Keynes: Open University Press.
Winnicott, D. (1971) *Therapeutic Consultations in Child Psychiatry*. London: Hogarth Press and Institute for Psychoanalysis.
Wynne, L.C. (ed.) (1988) *The State of the Art in Family Therapy Research*. New York: Family Process Press.
Wynne, L.C., Ryckoff, I., Day, J. and Hirsch, S. (1958) Pseudo-mutuality in the family relationships of schizophrenics. *Psychiatry*, 21: 205–20.
Yin, R.K. (1994) *Case Study Research*. London: Sage.
Young, J. (1990) *Cognitive Therapy for Personality Disorders: A Schema Focused Approach*. Sarasota, FL: Professional Resources Press.

Index

COUNSELLING SKILLS IN SOCIAL WORK PRACTICE
SECOND EDITION

Janet Seden

- In what ways is counselling relevant to contemporary social work?
- How do counselling skills integrate with social work roles and responsibilities?

This book examines these skills and their applicability, drawing from social work and counselling theories and methods using clear, practical examples. Skills are discussed with reference to social work knowledge and values illustrating how, when used competently, contextually and sensitively they can appropriately underpin good social work practice. Questions and activities for self development are linked to the practices discussed.

This new edition of *Counselling Skills in Social Work Practice* has been thoroughly revised to reflect the National Occupational Standards for social work which identify the importance of communication skills and a developmental understanding of people in their social contexts. The chapters are linked to the six key roles for social work practice.

This book builds on the strengths of the first edition, as well as addressing the challenges of practice in relevant legislative and policy contexts. The book includes:

- Evidence of how the competencies which underpin counselling practice are directly transferable to effective social work practice
- Practical advice on communication skills
- Examples of how to build effective working relationships; a whole chapter is now devoted to the specific skills required for working within inter-agency and multi-disciplinary teams

This book is key reading on the subject of ethical and effective social work for those teaching, studying or practising in the field.

Contents

192pp 0 335 21649 8 Paperback